THE WRIGHT STUFF:
FROM NBC TO AUTISM SPEAKS

Bob Wright
with Diane Mermigas

RosettaBooks®

New York, 2016

Library of Congress Control Number: 2015956049

Cover design by Brehanna Ramirez
Interior design by Alexia Garaventa

ISBN (hardcover): 978-0-7953-4692-7
ISBN (EPUB): 978-0-7953-4693-4
ISBN (Kindle): 978-0-7953-4806-8

www.RosettaBooks.com

To my wife of 48 years Suzanne Wright, my partner in life, business and Autism Speaks, and my daughter Katie Wright Hildebrand, the mother of Christian, who is the true founder of Autism Speaks.

In Memoriam
As an only child, I learned to accept responsibility for my actions from my father Gerald Franklin Wright, and to have empathy for all people and be passionate about my beliefs from my mother Catherine Drum Wright.

A Word from Bob

This book began as a simple personal remembrance for my immediate family and friends, but with the encouragement of longtime friends and colleagues, I soon found myself writing an insider's tale of NBC transitioning from pioneer broadcaster to global media conglomerate. And then, as our family lives were rapidly consumed by a crusade to unlock the causes and cure for autism, the development of Autism Speaks became undeniably part of my story.

But I should probably start at the beginning.

I was born Robert Charles Wright on April 23, 1943, in Hempstead, Long Island, New York.

After completing my education at Chaminade High School in Mineola, Long Island, and Holy Cross in Worcester, Massachusetts, I graduated from the University of Virginia School of Law. I went on to pass the bar exams in Virginia, New York, Massachusetts, and New Jersey. I had been with General Electric for 18 months when I left for Newark to become law secretary for Chief Justice Lawrence Whipple of the federal district court of New Jersey. I then spent 3 years in private practice before returning to GE and my 40-year career there.

I eagerly moved from law into business management during my first high-level appointments at GE Plastics (its fastest growing unit then) before becoming president and CEO of Cox Cable Communications in Atlanta. I returned to GE in 1983 as head of audio electronics and housewares and eventually became president and CEO of GE Capital in Stamford, Connecticut. All this happened before 1986, when I plunged into 2 decades as CEO of NBC and NBC Universal.

In 2007 I retired as chairman and CEO of NBC Universal and as GE vice chairman in 2008. My wife and soul mate for almost 50 years, Suzanne Wright, worked with me to cofound Autism Speaks, a global nonprofit advocacy and research group, in 2005. It was a year after our oldest grandchild, Christian, was diagnosed at age 2. I leveraged my skills, contacts, and personal wealth to improve the quality of life for autistic children and their families.

There are some striking and instructive parallels between my two overarching passions—transforming NBC into a global powerhouse and developing Autism Speaks into a proactive non-profit with a business model. I have been described as a low-key contrarian risk-taker and that has been a benefit to them both. I was the anti-mogul at NBC with a GE pedigree and an entrepreneur with a law degree. Applying the same business acumen and passion to further awareness, advocacy, and answers at Autism Speaks has created a progressive philanthropic template that is not without critics.

This book was intentionally organized into my two worlds: business and autism. Although at many moments they collided in my life, they also shaped and embellished their unique journeys. Writing this book afforded me a unique perspective on events of the past 40 years in a way that could benefit others.

Throughout my life, I have followed a few fundamental principles that I believe are essential for success in any endeavor. With those principles as filter and the voices of people I worked with for added dimension, I offer my personal story of leadership as both example and inspiration. My hope is that readers of all ages and persuasions—whether or not they have experience in business or autism—take what they can from my challenges and the lessons they impart to make the world a better place. There is much to do, many new stories to write and so much we can accomplish working together.

Editor's Note

from Diane Mermigas

My first wide-ranging interview with Bob was in late 1986. I was a national business reporter and he had just stepped out of the GE stable into the network television horserace. Quietly undeterred in his plans to revolutionize the industry, Bob's entrepreneurial drive and innovative vision were as compelling then as they are today.

In the years that followed, our regular discussions always morphed into a lively exchange of ideas. For more than 3 decades, we shared a passion and curiosity about the forces reshaping media. So, it was fitting that Bob asked me to help tell his story, which, in typical fashion, evolved from a simple personal journal into a leadership treatise.

At the same time, Bob and Suzanne's nonprofit trailblazing at Autism Speaks became an unexpected second act for their skills and contacts guided by her heart, his head. As someone familiar with special needs children, I understood their family's angst and struggle with autism.

The book's vignettes are rooted in more than 100 interviews exploring many common issues, personalities, and companies.

If *The Wright Stuff* naturally embraces the multifaceted encounters and challenges permeating Bob's professional and personal lives, it is because they are inseparable. Together they provide a powerful profile in mastering change.

TABLE OF CONTENTS

A Word from Bob   5

Editor's Note   7

PROLOGUE: The First Grandchild   11

ACT ONE. 2004: Annus Notabilis

1. The Biggest Deal of All   23

2. The Fierce Determination of a Grandmother   39

3. "OK—I'll Make It $25 Million."

   The Bernie Marcus Factor   41

4. Reflections on Success   47

ACT TWO. 1969–2012: Corporate Transformation

5. First Days   55

6. Media Baptism by Fire: Cox Cable   64

7. This Thing Called Cable   75

8. Chuck Dolan, Cablevision, and Me   88

9. The Business of CNBC   103

10. Rebuilding After a Firestorm: The *Dateline* Fiasco   115

11. Creating the Must-See TV Money Machine   133

12. Travels with Johnny Carson   150

13. The Ted Turner Factor   159

14. Olympic Gold   170

15. NBC + Microsoft = MSNBC   183

16. Dante's Inferno: The *Queen Mary 2*

    Became the *Exxon Valdez!*   201

17. Rebooting Network-Affiliate Relations   220

18. Leaving NBC and GE   234

19. Comcast Takes Over   248

20. My Roller-Coaster Ride with Jack Welch   261

21. Suzanne Wright: My Life's Partner   272

ACT THREE. 2004–Present: Nonprofit Transformation

22. 1 in 166: The Hidden Epidemic   291

23. Building from Scratch, Block by Block   300

24. Building Block #1: Global Expansion   304

25. Building Block #2: Political Muscle   310

26. Building Block #3: Grassroots Strength   320

27. Building Block #4: Business Principles   325

28. Building Block #5: Strategic Alliances   331

29. The Future for Autism Families   339

30. Vaccines and Other Controversies: A House Divided   358

31. MSSNG: From Beijing to Google   377

EPILOGUE: Christian at Fourteen   402

Appendix A: NBCU

Vintage Wright: What Next?   414

Some Deal Hits and Misses   437

Where Are They Now?   444

Appendix B: Autism

What We Learned About Autism   450

Autism Speaks 10th Anniversary Highlights   454

Acknowledgements   458

Index   465

PROLOGUE:
The First Grandchild

August 31, 2001, when our first grandchild was born, was one of the happiest days of my life.

OK. That's just about the lamest, corniest cliché in the English language. Doesn't make it any less true. From our oldest daughter, Katie, and her husband, Andreas, this beautiful little boy came into our world.

We had no way to know it at the time, of course, but soon this same beautiful child would profoundly change our lives. And in response, I would take everything I had learned about running a business in nearly 40 years and pour it all into a not-for-profit organization born from heartbreak. That labor of love, developed with my wife of 48 years, Suzanne, is Autism Speaks.

From the very beginning, Christian put a little drama into our lives. My daughter Katie had gone to her obstetrician for what she thought was a regular checkup several weeks before the baby was due, but the doctor discovered her amniotic fluid was low and decided to deliver by cesarean that same day. So with nothing but the clothes on her back, off she went to Columbia Presbyterian Hospital in New York. I imagine a young woman would want her mother with her at a time like that, but Suzanne was not in town, so poor Katie was stuck with me.

❖ **Katie Wright.** I'd always imagined my mom would be there for the birth, but she was in Nantucket and she wasn't going to be back in time. But who was in New York? My dad and my grandmother, Ruth.

I think my dad was nervous, but he kept it under control. He spent a lot of time on the phone with my mom, who was very upset she couldn't be there, and then with his assistant, trying to arrange flight information for Mom, cancel other appointments, call everybody else and tell them what's happening, do this, then this, then this. I'm sure if it was a movie, it would have been a funny scene. And it's the Friday before Labor Day, which complicated everything, but he's so on top of things, getting everyone in place, doing what he does best. And all the while, Ruth was sitting there quietly. Ruth had had four kids. And she was saying, "Don't worry. It will be fine."

And it was. Christian was the most beautiful little baby. He looked like a little angel, with beautiful pink skin and lots of blond, curly hair and big blue eyes.

By the time Mom rushed in, it was all over. She was so excited, she was just bubbling: "I got to see the baby. I got to hold the baby." And she was just so happy. ❖

❖ **Suzanne Wright**. I remember thinking, I'm looking at my first grandson and how lucky we were that my mother was there. He had a great-grandmother, he had a grandmother and a grandfather, and we were all there, to welcome this beautiful little boy. It's natural for new mothers and grandmothers to think their babies are beautiful. But everyone who saw Christian described him as a beautiful, healthy baby. Everything seemed so normal.

Katie and Andreas stayed with us at first because the baby was born 2 weeks early and their new house wasn't ready yet. But that was just so exciting because I now had him for breakfast, lunch, and dinner. I could hardly wait to hold a baby again.

Sometimes I would go in the room and just watch him. Bob did the same thing. I loved watching him holding the baby and looking at him with such delight. In those first 2 weeks babies open up their eyes, and you could see him looking around and wondering what this world was all about. I'm pretty spiritual, and it seemed like a first awakening. I had a small bottle of holy water that a friend had brought back from Fatima, and I would bless him with it. And every night when I said my prayers, I would say, God, please protect him.

I remember when my own babies were little, I would count their toes. Ten toes, everything is fine, just what it should be. But you never know what's down the road. ◈

In the first months, Christian's development matched expectations. At well-baby checkups, doctors noted that he was very animated, smiling often, had good eye contact, was learning to sit up at the appropriate time. In some respects, especially language, he was even ahead, babbling at 6 months, speaking single words at 10 months. And his social development was right on track too; he clearly loved being with his parents and grandparents. Suzanne developed a particularly close bond with the baby. Even as an infant, Christian lit up with excitement whenever he saw her; by the time he began to walk, he would run to jump into her arms the minute she came through the door.

Today, talking about Christian's first year, we all use the word "normal" often. I recall giving him a bath in the kitchen sink, with lots of tickling and giggling. Having fun on the playground, playing peekaboo with his grandmother, normal games like that.

It only gradually became clear that everything was not normal.

Before he was even a year old, Christian began to show signs of trouble. Something was always off. Either it was bouts of severe diarrhea, or high temperatures, or terrible eczema all over his body.

Right after he got the standard 1-year vaccinations, he developed a very high fever and screamed for hours. Katie was so frightened she called her husband to come home from work, and they put the baby in an ice bath to bring down the fever. When they called the doctor, they were told the reaction was completely normal.

Looking back, it seems we heard that over and over from doctors: "It's nothing to worry about; he'll be fine." I can hardly bear to think about it.

Soon after Christian's first birthday, his condition started deteriorating. He was sick a lot and would sometimes start screaming for no obvious reason. We could see he was clearly slipping backward. Suzanne was distraught. He used to rush up to her babbling "I love you, love you," but now when she came to visit he would run away, hide under the table, and begin a screaming tantrum.

❖ **Suzanne Wright.** He didn't want to play, he wouldn't let me hug him, he wouldn't let me comb his hair. I couldn't engage him at all. And then he started slapping himself and walking around on his toes. I didn't have a clue, but in my heart of hearts, I knew something was very wrong.

At first I was really angry. I couldn't imagine how this was happening. Then I went to grief. Then I really felt very sorry for myself that this is happening to our family. And then I had to stop the feeling of constant sorrowing and grief because I had to get stronger in order to really face what was about to happen. I said the same prayer over and over: God, you've got to help me with this. ❖

We had absolutely no idea what was happening or where to turn for answers. Then things got profoundly worse.

Starting when he was about 18 months old, Christian was sick all the time. He had a staph infection so severe he had to be hospitalized; he had strep throat twice, pneumonia, frequent high fevers, cellulitis in both eyes, unrelenting diarrhea, and severe rashes. His toes turned red and swollen, and he had red streaks up both legs. All this meant an endless round of doctor visits.

His behavior changed, too. He became moody and withdrawn and extremely anxious. At a time when most babies grow out of stranger anxiety, Christian was getting worse. He would cling tightly to his mother, screamed when other people touched him. During medical checkups, he cried nonstop. He had difficulty sleeping, would cry all night long. His speech patterns deteriorated; he would repeat words over and over, or he would stop talking altogether. We were rapidly losing him.

No one could explain what was happening to this child. Doctors couldn't find any physical problems and just kept saying he was fine. Katie told me at one point she felt like shouting, "You think he's fine?! You weren't in the car with me on the way home from the pediatrician's office; it's a three-mile drive and I had to pull over four times because Christian was screaming so strangely I thought he was dying."

Christian was in free fall. He couldn't recognize any of us. He couldn't communicate in any way we could understand. This was a boy who'd had a very large vocabulary only 6 months earlier. And he could run, catch, throw, do things like that. All of a sudden all of those things were gone. He couldn't respond to your questions. He couldn't offer any comments. He couldn't look you in the eye. Over a span of about 8 weeks, he lost everything. And I mean everything.

He wasn't *that* child anymore. He was gone.

———

Soon afterward, desperate for answers, Katie managed to get an appointment with a developmental pediatrician. As part of the examination, this pediatrician asked Katie a number of very specific questions. At home that evening, Katie began replaying those questions in her mind. Because she has a Masters of Education degree in counseling, Katie had in her home library a copy of the *Diagnostic and Statistical Manual of Mental Disorders (DSM-5)*, which clinicians and psychiatrists use to diagnose psychiatric illnesses. She pulled it out.

❖ **Katie Wright**. As I worked my way through the *DSM-5*, I realized that all the pediatrician's questions were about autism. I threw up. I knew she was right.

But I had to be sure. So I called her office the next day and finally got her. "Katie," she said, "you know I can't talk about this on the phone."

"If you don't talk to me, I'm going to explode."

"Yes," the doctor finally admitted, "that's what I'm talking about. Autism."

OK, I thought to myself. This is bad, but the doctors will know exactly what to do and we'll do it. We'll do everything they say and it will get better.

But first we had to get a complete diagnosis. Poor Christian went through 2 full days of tests by a whole team of specialists, including a child psychiatrist, a neurologist, a pediatric gastroenterologist, a radiologist, and several others. And all the time we were in the waiting room, me and my mom and dad, I was thinking, "They're going to be able to help us; now we'll know what it is and then we can start fixing it." And then the team came into the room. They began by explaining what they had eliminated: he doesn't have a brain tumor, he doesn't have cancer, he doesn't have any medical condition we can find. Instead, they say, he has PDD-NOS.

And my mom asked, "What on earth is that?"

"It stands for pervasive developmental disorder not otherwise specified."

"But what does it *mean?*"

"It's autism," they said.

"Well, why didn't you say autism?"

They don't want to say the A word. They don't want to say it because it scares everybody. ❖

It quickly became apparent that the team of doctors could offer little help. We all use different words to describe it, but we all remember the same thing.

They were very apologetic, but there really wasn't any plan of action that they would outline for him—except for us to seek help on our own: speech therapy, occupation therapy, behavior therapy.

As Suzanne put it, "They gave us the diagnosis and basically said good-bye and good luck."

Christian, meanwhile, was disintegrating. By the time he was 2½, he began hitting himself, banging his head against the wall, biting his shirt. He screamed all night long and drooled so constantly and so copiously that his shirt collar was always wet by noon. Doctors prescribed steroids to counteract inflammation, but they made him very aggressive toward his baby brother, 2 years younger. An adult always had to be present, otherwise Christian would bite his brother and pull his hair. And the high fevers, red rashes covering his entire body, and fierce diarrhea never stopped.

While everyone was still reeling, still scrambling to figure out the next step, we had a chance to enjoy a family vacation in Florida. It was here that we experienced what Katie still calls the worst day of her life.

❖ **Katie Wright**. It was March 2004. Andreas and I and our two boys were visiting my parents in Florida. Christian was 2½ and Mattias was still an infant. The first day we were there, Christian was hyperactive, running around in circles and knocking things off tables. But on the second morning, he was very different when he woke up—listless and unfocused and highly irritable. There was no fever, no obvious symptoms, but he just seemed very sick.

Andreas had planned to spend the day golfing with my dad, but now he wondered if he should cancel. No, we all said, go ahead; you need a break, we'll be fine. So Mom and I decided to take Christian to play on the beach, something he very much loved to do, hoping that this would snap him out of the mysterious fog.

On the way toward the beach, I suddenly noticed something very frightening. Christian's face and one side of his body had gone slack, his tongue was hanging out, he was drooling. It almost seemed like he was having a stroke, but then we figured that couldn't be right because he was still standing upright. So we decided to keep going. Christian loved the beach, and I was hoping he would snap out of it in those happy surroundings.

But he didn't. He was like a living, walking ghost. I tried snapping my fingers in front of his face but got no reaction. His tongue was hanging out of his mouth and his shirt was soaked with drool. I was holding him so tight, crying hysterically, trying not to throw up.

We went back to the house as quickly as we could and tried to feed Christian, hoping that might bring him around. It didn't help. He walked around and around in circles, drooling, not saying a word. We had no idea what to do. I called his doctors at Columbia Hospital and they told me I was overreacting. Give it a day and things will be fine, they said. Don't worry, they said.

In the late afternoon, when the men returned from golfing, Christian was still the same. Andreas kept trying to connect with him, offering his favorite toys and reading to him from a familiar storybook. But Christian would not say a word, just stared in that frozen, catatonic way. Finally Andreas sat on the couch next to Christian and sobbed. I had never seen him cry like that before, nor since.

Then my dad put his hand on my shoulder and said, "Let's go for a ride, honey." ❖

I have never felt so helpless. This precious boy, our first grandson, was disappearing before our very eyes. Katie and Andreas were falling apart, and I didn't know how to help them. But at the moment, all I could think was that we needed some fresh air.
So we climbed into the car and rode around for nearly an hour. Usually Katie would be teasing me about that car, saying convertibles are for younger men, but this time she just sat quietly and looked at the sky. She seemed almost numb. After a while we stopped and walked for a bit. I tried to find some words of comfort, but all I could think to do was say out loud what was in my heart: That I knew things seemed awful but that we would get through it. That I would always be proud that Christian was my grandson. That no matter what, Suzanne and I would always take care of him.

———————

It seems almost impossible now, when I think of it, but at almost the exact same period of time, I was engineering the most significant business deal of my entire career: the merger between NBC and Vivendi Universal, an incredibly complex arrangement that ultimately saved both companies.

And shortly after that, I first heard the name Bernie Marcus. His visit in July planted the seed that became Autism Speaks.

2004 was a year of extraordinary highs and lows.

ACT ONE. 2004:
Annus Notabilis

1
The Biggest Deal of All

NBC headquarters
30 Rockefeller Plaza
Executive office of Bob Wright, 52nd floor
New York City

There are times in your life when events change everything. They transform the way we live, work, and think. And so it was in August 2004. Just as my family was coming to grips with our grandson Christian's diagnosis of autism, I was deep in the final stages of closing what would become the biggest deal NBC had ever attempted—acquiring the entertainment businesses of the French conglomerate Vivendi Universal. The stakes were huge. It is not overdramatizing the matter to say that the network's future existence depended on a successful outcome.

At the same time, Christian's young life depended on solving the puzzle of autism, a condition that was rapidly consuming his 2-year-old development and sense of wonder and devastating his parents. There was no national organization to provide any answers to families of autistic children. We were fighting that battle alone. Over time, there was no separating the angst and labor of these parallel challenges; they became the defining forces in my life.

———————

Creating a merger with Vivendi Universal was a long, grueling process. Brandon Burgess, Robert Jaffe, and I had already been working on it for more than a year. The French conglomerate was a perfect strategic fit for the expanding NBC, which I was struggling to build, but it was not going to be easy.

Vivendi first appeared on our radar in early 2003. At the time, it was a classic story of corporate overreaching: a dysfunctional patchwork of utility and entertainment assets engineered by an ambitious, ego-driven chairman, the investment banker Jean-Marie Messier. When the crazy assortment of acquisitions began collapsing around his ears, Messier was booted out. Vivendi, with $18 billion in debt, was on the brink of bankruptcy. Now, desperate to cut their losses, they were looking for a white knight rescue and $16 billion in cash for their entertainment units. Messier's failure was our opportunity.

The challenge—like the opportunity—was unprecedented. We not only had to win over Vivendi but also NBC's corporate parent, General Electric. Once again, as often before, I found myself having to carefully maneuver between two very different cultures: GE's buttoned-down industrial framework and NBC's media mindset. That required a 2-pronged strategy that had to be executed with unbelievably delicate timing.

Vivendi owned the Universal film studio, Universal theme parks, big cable networks, and a TV production and distribution company, all of which were underperforming. We had to convince GE that NBC could improve those operations and that we would benefit from owning them. That was the key. I understood, with a deep certainty, what GE's top management did not yet grasp—that the entire television industry was being turned on its head by cable and the Internet. NBC needed scale and balance to offset the coming tsunami, and acquiring Universal was the perfect solution.

GE never would have allowed us to acquire such unpredictable businesses separately, because it considered them high risk. The corporate giant, anchored in power systems, aircraft engines, and appliances, was unnerved by fickle consumer tastes. The idea of having its finely polished Six Sigma image tied to such pop culture hits as *Meet the Fockers* and *Dawn of the Dead* was distasteful, to say the least. The ebb and flow of our primetime schedule was about all the entertainment volatility GE could bear. To me, the irrational, cyclical success of films and TV shows was a risk pattern that, once understood, could be capitalized on.

Brandon Burgess, my chief deal strategist, had been making the case for a transformative acquisition since May 2002. That kind of prewiring and staging well in advance of asking GE to provide capital for something outside of its comfort zone was imperative. You could not expect GE to respond the way you needed it to in an auction timeframe.

At the time GE was satisfied that NBC's broadcast business generated plenty of money, but we knew that would not last. Consolidation was coming, and we were not big enough. Even the French knew NBC was nearing a tipping point. The production pacts for *Friends, Frasier,* and *Law & Order* would end in 2004, and the rights would revert to the studios that produced them. At that point their robust ratings and profits would disappear into rerun syndication, a lucrative area in which NBC could not participate. That would weaken NBC's advertising income and push NBC over what Burgess called "a linear cliff." In particular, all 456 episodes of Dick Wolf's *Law & Order* franchise, which had generated

$1 billion for NBC since its 1990 premiere, would revert to its owner, Universal. All that would change if we owned Universal.

So, we had a 2-year window to replace those profitable primetime series with new programs that would generate the same kind of strong ratings and advertising revenues. Usually, that involved a scattershot process of trying new pilots and hoping the unpredictable TV fans would like some of them. That in itself was trying enough, but it was being complicated by a major shift in consumer habits toward subscription-based cable. And there was this new interactive platform called the Internet. It was the elephant in the room that no one at NBC wanted to talk about, or knew how to.

I thought NBC's best defense was to invest its resources and GE's money where consumers were going: cable channels and websites. They could provide an economic hedge to our fragile advertising base. The other networks were seeing the same trends and were responding with aggressive mergers and acquisitions. We were the only ones that didn't have a strong entertainment cable presence. Acquiring Universal, we argued, would be NBC's game changer, a bold but rational consolidation move with big global implications.

At the same time, we also had to convince the French that what we were proposing—a partnership and gradual takeover—would be better than the outright cash sale they wanted. A partnership would allow Vivendi to benefit from GE's expertise and resources in creating a new company with more value and higher returns. Operating outside the traditional auction process right from the start with this strategy was part of what Brandon Burgess called "our charm offensive."

We proposed a complex, ambitious merger between two "strategics"—two public companies with intersecting business interests but very different agendas and dynamics. We would have to manage this sprawling entertainment concern inside the GE conglomerate in a way that would help everyone feel comfortable and get their money back. That would mean integrating assets while realigning our primary cash contributor, the NBC TV Network, as we moved from a broadcast business to a subscription cable business. Our revenues would shift from 90 percent advertising at NBC and 100 percent fees at Vivendi to a 50/50 split after the merger. That was a pretty nice fit that took pressure off both companies.

But timing was everything.

A year earlier, we had looked at a possible merger with AOL Time Warner. They had lost more than $150 billion in market cap in the 2 years after the two companies merged. It would have been a steal, most likely executed as a hostile takeover. But GE's board of directors feared the wrath of shareholders if NBC were to become tangled in a media debacle. Up until that time, our boldest acquisitions were only safe bets: gaining majority ownership of the Bravo cable channel from Rainbow Media and buying Telemundo, a major Spanish-language network.

So it was not surprising that GE chairman Jeff Immelt was cautious about our plan. His initial response was to limit GE's investment to $500 million cash and the assumption of $1.9 billion in Vivendi debt. Burgess and I moved quickly to concoct a clever deal structure in which GE would make payments to Vivendi directly out of the newly merged company's income. It was an arrangement not even Immelt could resist.

Our plan called for GE to be 80 percent managing owner of NBC Universal, with an option to buy the remaining 20 percent and take NBCU public within 5 years. In the meantime, we would pay the French about $800 million annually out of the company's overall $3.5 billion earnings. Initially, GE would pay only $3.8 billion out of pocket to acquire Universal for $14.5 billion and assume $1.9 billion of Vivendi debt. At that time, NBC was valued at $22 billion with $1.6 billion in annual cash flow with all of its core news, sports and entertainment operations intact. The merged company would have a public value of at least $42 billion, putting it on par with peers like Walt Disney Co., valued at $43 billion, and Rupert Murdoch's News Corp., valued at $41 billion.

Now we were ready to start negotiating in earnest.

❖ **John Malone, president Tele-Communications Inc., founding chairman CEO Liberty Media.** You go into these situations hearing what the other side wants and knowing what you want. But the chance of engineering a creative, tax-efficient deal that is a win-win for all concerned is always slim. It's financial or structural problem solving—not something everyone enjoys or does well. It's even trickier when it is a three-way negotiation that involves a corporate parent. So, it's astounding to me that NBC Universal ever came to be! There was a severe mismatch between an industrial conglomerate that measured itself on quarterly earnings and a media company that was trying to grow and change within an industry that had completely different metrics.

The Universal deal took GE deeper into the media and entertainment business than GE chairman Jack Welch, at least, had ever intended to go. It forced GE to stop relying on the cash flow generated by NBC's broadcasting to fund GE Capital, where the money could be invested at higher returns. It shifted the company's focus and balance sheet to cable, where the earnings over time far exceed anything from NBC in its best days. I never understood why they didn't just convert the NBC TV Network into a cable network. But the fact that Bob was able to finally pull it off under Jack's successor, Jeff Immelt, was quite a miracle. And it didn't hurt that Vivendi was so needy at the time. ❖

So Brandon Burgess fired off a letter to Paris detailing NBC's merger rationale. The French responded almost immediately that they would listen. Our first formal presentation to Vivendi senior management was in the GE executive suite on the 53rd floor of 30 Rockefeller Plaza on May 28, 2003. They were upbeat and intrigued by the possibilities but restless about having to wait for their money.

We pointed out that over time, NBC's management know-how would yield greater revenue and value. NBC already was the top-rated US broadcast TV network, NBC News was the leading domestic news organization, CNBC was one of the most popular cable networks, and Telemundo was the only dedicated Spanish-language channel among its peers. The merged company's cable portfolio would stretch from USA and the Sci-Fi Channel (which was rebranded SyFy in 2009) to MSNBC and Bravo. NBC's major TV production and syndication would be matched by Universal's healthy film production and distribution and its library of more than 5,000 films and 34,000 hours of television.

Vivendi was looking for $16 billion, but in the end they went along with our plan because they could not get $14 billion from other auction bidders. Shareholders were pressuring the company to liquidate its assets and redistribute the cash so it could go forward with new cellular phone and energy businesses. So Vivendi concluded that our deal gave them a way out of the chaos and a second chance at life.

Part of our pitch to Vivendi was to point out that their cable network contracts were not being renewed and program distribution could not be guaranteed. David Zaslav explained how dangerous it was to so rapidly deplete revenues and profits, but he knew how to fix the problem.

We began hammering out more of the details in a meeting on July 8, 2003, in my executive dining room at 30 Rock. On the Vivendi side were Jean-Bernard Lévy, their chief operating officer, and his advisors, Bruce Hack and Robert DeMetz. Hack came to Vivendi from Seagram, owned by the Bronfman family. To show you how tangled up everything was, Seagram had sold its cable networks to Vivendi in 2000 and now wanted them back, because Edgar Bronfman Jr. missed being in the Hollywood limelight. DeMetz was a senior executive vice president overseeing Vivendi's divestitures. Lévy was the senior negotiator; he was incredibly sharp and serious. They were all difficult to deal with and battled us on everything. They hovered over the process like commandos ready to strike. We knew it was not going to be a pretty picture.

A week later, both companies brought their 25-person negotiating teams of lawyers, accountants, and investment bankers to New York to fashion a deal under the code name Project Vineyard. The talks began with great intensity and enthusiasm, only to become mired in details. The negotiations were excruciating for both sides. They pored over critical issues and mind-numbing particulars, looking for ways to minimize risk and taxes while maximizing return on investment. I struggled to keep control of the process. We worked hard to use GE's resources and clout as leverage while maintaining day-to-day control. There were endless, exhausting presentations to analysts, to GE and Vivendi executives, and to our own NBC personnel. It seemed that we were always trying to solve impossible problems and meet deadlines with insufficient data.

Vivendi CEO Jean-René Fourtou and I had many long, involved private meetings over lunch in my executive dining room. By late July, we were doing day-long meetings at 30 Rock, which then spilled over into working dinners. We wanted to transform Vivendi's generic auction into an exclusive discussion with us as a preferred partner for the Universal assets. For their part, the

French were comforted to some extent by GE's credibility and balance sheet. They also did not want to deal with typical media types, and that gave us an edge over other bidders.

Still, John Malone's Liberty Media, MGM billionaire Marvin Davis, Viacom, and Comcast poked their heads up for a look. Chuck Dolan's Cablevision Systems made a joint bid with Edgar Bronfman Jr., whose strained sale of the USA Network to the French made him a liability. They all dreaded plowing through the complex agreements that had been negotiated by Messier, the deposed Vivendi chairman, including a film distribution arrangement with Steven Spielberg that would take time and money to unwind.

The most irritating matter Fourtou and I had to deal with involved high-powered media mogul Barry Diller. Years earlier he had sold Messier the USA and Sci-Fi cable networks in exchange for a 5 percent ownership stake in Universal. But the cable networks' licensing agreements were about to expire and Diller had not renegotiated them, plus his original deal with Universal came with too many convoluted rights and conditions. In the end we opted to buy him out for close to $1 billion to protect our new company from any further disruption.

Incidentally, this wasn't NBC's first attempt to acquire Universal's cable assets, or our first go-round with Barry Diller. In 1999, Jack Welch and I had been meeting with Edgar Bronfman Jr. to explore the possibility of merging NBC with all of his family's media businesses, including the USA and Sci-Fi cable networks and Universal Studios. Despite his disdain for risky showbiz economics, Welch had supported the deal. The new merged company would have been headed by Barry Diller as chairman and CEO, and I would have been the chief operating officer. GE would have had a 60 percent stake and the Bronfman family 40 percent. In the end, Edgar Bronfman Sr. did not want to yield control of his media assets to anyone—not even NBC. Then, the very next year, the Bronfmans sold the cable networks to Vivendi, and so now they were back on the table.

Eventually, we were able to get our corporate agendas aligned in a way that made both Vivendi and GE comfortable, and the GE board reviewed and endorsed our strategic imperative on July 24, 2003.

❖ **Brandon Burgess, executive VP NBC Business Development and Digital Media.** This deal got done the way it did because it required the creative financing that GE could handle. But staging was critical, which is why we started planting seeds with GE management a year before we knew we would have to begin repositioning NBC. When you also throw in having to manage the French and Barry Diller, the Universal deal became one of the great juggling acts of all time. But if it hadn't been for those complexities, we probably would not have been the preferred suitor or the winning bidder. If it were plain and simple, other companies would have won the prize. As long as we weren't going to try to steal the assets outright, the deal was ours to lose. ❖

The next big issue was valuation: $5 billion for the USA cable network, $1.1 billion for the Sci-Fi cable network, $800 million for USA Studios and $3.1 billion for the Universal film studio. The negotiating teams battled over which assets would be part of the deal and which would be sold. GE was willing—but reluctant—to include Universal's $1.3 billion theme parks just to get the deal done, but they drew the line at Vivendi's struggling $2.4 billion electronic games unit. That particular issue provided one of the few light moments, and ultimately a nice touch of irony.

Burgess, who had suggested including the games company, wasn't ready to give up. He found himself staying up very late at night, playing a beta version of an online game that Vivendi's Activision unit was working on—a little something called *World of Warcraft*. The game was officially launched a few months after the merger (as the latest iteration of an existing Warcraft franchise) and instantly became a $1 billion phenomenon, completely transforming the video game sector.

By the dog days of summer, all Burgess and I had mustered was an agreement to continue negotiating. And then, in one of those amazing moments that you couldn't arrange if you tried, everything changed. And Brandon Burgess was right in the middle of it.

❖ **Brandon Burgess.** Bob Wright and I on the NBC side and Jean-Bernard Lévy on the Vivendi side had put in many hours polishing a dog-and-pony presentation for Vivendi's top brass and our banking advisors. On August 15, Vivendi expected to see second-round bids to narrow the field of suitors. Lévy and I worked late on the 13th, kept at it overnight and into the next day. Suddenly, just after four p.m. on August 14, all the lights in the room went out.

It took us a few minutes to realize that the lights were out in the entire city. We read in the *New York Times* the next day that it was the largest blackout in American history. Hundreds of people were stuck in elevators, 600 subway cars were trapped underground, all airports and most communication systems were shut down. Restaurants were frantically cooking up all their perishables, ice cream shops were giving away their goods to anybody who walked by. The sidewalks and streets were jammed with thousands of people who had decided to walk home, dodging cars that had become stranded when the traffic lights went out.

What should we do? I figured, what the heck, let's keep going. So I suggested we move over to my apartment, not too far away. I found a flashlight somewhere, and we made our way down the stairs, 52 flights. The whole city was dark and quiet. This total, eerie quiet. We got through the crowds on the sidewalk, and I led the way up 9 flights at my apartment building. Saira, who would soon become my wife, had gone out to get supplies from a neighborhood market, so we ate crackers and cheese by candlelight while we continued working.

At that moment, I knew the deal was sealed. I thought to myself, these guys wouldn't be sitting here for hours by candlelight in my living room in midtown Manhattan if they didn't intend to make it happen. By the end of that week, we celebrated the growing list of points the companies agreed on with a working lunch at 30 Rock, including foie gras Bob Wright had flown in.

A week later, on August 29, 2003, the two chief executives, GE's Jeff Immelt and Vivendi's Jean-René Fourtou, signed off on a preliminary deal. "Preliminary" meaning there was still a lot to do. We all continued working throughout that Labor Day weekend, except for me. I took time out Friday evening to get married. ❖

I knew this merger was the right thing to do. I really believed that NBC would be in real jeopardy without it. I had to keep reminding myself of that because there were many moments when my team and I were tested; too many problems that seemed insurmountable and too many impossible deadlines. Getting from the preliminary agreement in early September that simply stated our intentions to a detailed merger pact 4 months later was a real battle because it depended on a million things that had to be done. Either party could have walked away at any time—and almost did. What keeps you going under such pressure? Passion.

A fierce commitment to getting the job done. Plus, in the end, like most tough negotiations, it came down to pure economics and relationships—most importantly the one between me and Vivendi's salvation chairman, Jean-René Fourtou.

On September 28, 2003, in the midst of negotiating the final agreement, I went to Paris for several days to meet with Fourtou, just the two of us. We ended up talking about personal things like our backgrounds, our families, and interests. It created a new bond between us and completely altered our working relationship. It turned out Jean-René was not some artificial lump of bricks any more than I was. We still had the same issues, but now we had a little bit more latitude to deal with each other, and I had a more respectful view of him after that trip. To this day, I think of him with great fondness.

❖ **Jean-René Fourtou, chairman and CEO Vivendi.** I remember when Bob invited me to his home in Connecticut, and it was a very important visit because we all had very mixed feelings about these negotiations. Negotiating with GE was very difficult. My guys wanted to stop the negotiations all the time because it was very, very hard and very process oriented. You had the impression that you had a deal only to realize that you still had no deal. And, frankly, without Bob, we would never have finished. He has the personal qualities that make you want to do a deal with him. Bob was more of my world. He is not one of the California guys. ❖

I worked back channels to keep the deal alive when our own negotiating teams were in a stalemate. Twice, the French nearly pulled out of the negotiations, exasperated with the financial rigors of GE's rigid process. The complexities of the proposed international match, which made this a dealmaker's dream and played to GE's strength, also nearly killed the deal. The negotiations almost always came down to two CEOs on the phone or in a room, hammering out the last tough fine points.

May 12, 2004, the day the NBCU merger finally closed, was the happiest day of my professional life. We had managed to engineer and pull off the kind of corporate marriage that no one, including the two parties, could argue with or sabotage. We had headed off all the challenges and potential pitfalls. It just made too much sense.

We all gathered in my New York office the night before—Fourtou, Lévy, Burgess, me, and a few others—to sign final documents and celebrate with champagne. The next day there was a bicoastal press conference and analyst briefing, and later an employee rally at Universal's amphitheater in Los Angeles. At an afternoon employee town hall, I assured the troops—who had tolerated three new owners over the prior decade—that the power of GE's balance sheet would enable us to take risks and make investments that would be otherwise impossible. With this integrated company, we were going to develop, produce, and market entertainment, news, and information across all the assets and create significant new value.

And we did. Consider that 8 years later, in 2013, Bernstein Research estimated the value of NBC Universal's cable networks alone at $24 billion. Comcast CEO Steve Burke achieved $4 billion cash flow from NBCU that easily translates into $40 billion to $45 billion of market value.

NBCU's financials strengthened almost immediately, as we had predicted they would. We promised and delivered on more than $500 million in synergies (cost savings and efficiencies) in the first 18 months. Revenues doubled to $15 billion while operating profits increased more than 25 percent. The merged company's TV production arm became the third-biggest producer of television, behind only Warner Bros. and Fox.

Besides Brandon Burgess, many other team players from NBC and GE were instrumental in this success, including David

Zaslav, Jeff Zucker, Randy Falco, John Eck, Bruce Campbell, and Rick Cotton.

From the beginning, I considered the merger a means to an end, a way to create the diversified media giant I had always envisioned. Universal's cable channels changed everything for NBC, generating more than $2 billion annually, or more than twice the best revenues from NBC's broadcast network. It capped $20 billion in deals Burgess and I engineered from 2000 to 2005 to hedge NBC out of a declining broadcast business and into the exploding global cable and Internet industries.

Universal was a homerun acquisition; it was about as good as you could get in the media business. I thought this was my crowning jewel because it gave NBC Universal all of the tools to be successful over a long period of time as a very large media company, whether GE owned it or someone else. And eventually, someone else would.

❖ **Herbert Schlosser, early president NBC and mentor to Bob Wright.** When you merge with another company, it's never a slam dunk, and there never are any guarantees. But when you can do something entrepreneurial and create more than you begin with, that's more than just deal making. Bob was in a position to seize the opportunity to get NBC more heavily into cable and help transform cable into a machine for creating unique content. Today, that all is at the heart of NBCU's profits, and cable is television's content core. ❖

Wright to the Point

Looking back now, I think the one reason I was able to maintain control during these difficult negotiations was that it actually gave me a sense of relief. In our family, we were all consumed with trying to help my grandson, Christian, in a situation that was totally *out* of our control. I had never felt so helpless. The Universal talks were long and delicate and sometimes messy, but at least I felt I knew what was happening and could reasonably control it.

By the time we were realizing closure on the NBC Universal merger in the spring of 2004, my family and I were desperately searching for ways to cope with Christian's autism, which by then was dominating our lives.

2
The Fierce Determination
of a Grandmother

Columbia Presbyterian Hospital
New York City
February 18, 2004

◆ **Suzanne Wright.** The day we got the official diagnosis for Christian, I was about as angry as I've ever been. After 2 full days of testing on our little guy, this whole team of specialists comes out and they say, it's not this, it's not that, it's PDD-NOS.

I just looked at them. I mean, how dare they hide behind that lingo so?! I have to beg them to tell me what it is because they were afraid to say the word. But then finally they did. It's autism, they said, and then very casually added, "It's one in one hundred sixty-six." Bob and I just looked at each other.

At that moment, autism became my enemy. It was like a monster in the room. Every time you looked at this beautiful little boy and then you knew what he was going through, all I could think was, I have to get this away from him. How am I going to get this thing solved? Where do I go? How do I get help? And there was nowhere to go, there was no grandmother that I could talk to, there was nobody, because nobody was talking about it. I was determined to muster every effort, to get every help, to go anywhere I needed to go to get some answers.

In the process, I ended up meeting many other families struggling with autism. They were so desperate for answers, for some kind of help, and they had nowhere to go. I thought, my God, how could this be? How could nobody be taking care of these kids?

And then in July Bob told me that this fellow Bernie Marcus wanted to come to the house and talk with us. ❖

3

"OK, I'll Make It $25 Million."
The Bernie Marcus Factor

B y 2004, I had been in the corporate world for close to 40 years, most of that time at GE and NBC. While I was orchestrating NBC's biggest deal (the merger with Universal, described in Chapter 1), many of my peers were starting to plan their retirement. I just could not see that in my future. The people I really admire are the folks who use all their skills and resources to do good in a completely different area than their original profession, who believe it's important to serve their community, wherever there is a need.

Bernie Marcus is a perfect example of that.

Bernie Marcus is a plain-speaking multibillionaire and philanthropist who grew up in a New Jersey tenement, the son of Russian Jewish immigrants. Today, the former cofounding CEO of Home Depot is worth somewhere in the neighborhood of $2.7 billion and has given away more than $700 million of it, always with the special Bernie Marcus style. It's not the usual way of thinking about philanthropy. Bernie Marcus has his own way of doing things. Case in point: the Marcus Autism Center.

❖ **Bernie Marcus, founding CEO Home Depot and philanthropist.** When Arthur Blank and I started Home Depot, one of the first things we decided was that charity would be a big part of what we did. So now all our stores do some kind of community project. They decide on the project and everybody pitches in, and usually we're the only ones who know about it. That's OK with me; I don't need a lot of hoopla.

All Jews grow up with the idea of *tzedakah*; it's an absolute obligation to give generously to help others. When I was a child, a nickel was a big deal. Sometimes we got ice cream, and other times my mother said, "No, this one goes toward planting a tree in Israel."

Today, of course, we're talking more than a nickel. We give where there's a need, but I don't just throw money around. I always look at it from a business standpoint. There's got to be a reasonable bottom line: how many sick kids got help, how many libraries got built, how many new medicines were developed. Anybody who doesn't look at it that way is just nuts, in my opinion. Haven't they ever heard of return on investment? Haven't they ever heard of leveraging your funds?

I have my own brand of philanthropy. I started the Marcus Institute in Atlanta when one of our employees had a child with this terrible problem that no one understood. The stress of taking care of him was destroying that family. At the time, the world didn't know about autism. Doctors couldn't help; they couldn't even diagnose this child. They didn't know if he was in pain or not in pain. It was a nightmare for her, and so I went around the country looking at facilities that might help her. In the end, we started our own, and that was the Marcus Institute. It was for children with disabilities, because we didn't really know about autism at first. As time went on, we began to recognize what it was, and we changed the name to the Marcus Autism Center.

We were helping lots of children, one at a time, but we were losing money hand over fist. Now, when I give to a charity, my goal is to help them get so stable they can eventually stand on their own. And I was determined to apply that same standard to my own charity. But this one wasn't working that way. It seemed to me that one of our big problems was nobody really knew about autism, and if they did, they were scared of it. I thought we needed to find a way to help more people to understand autism, to take the mystery and the stigma away. We needed a major push for public awareness, and we needed somebody who really knew how to organize that kind of effort.

Then one day I got a call from Sam Nunn, the former US senator from Georgia. He told me about this fellow named Bob Wright. ❖

Bernie and I talked several times over the next months about Christian and about how frustrated we were trying to find some help for him. He knew exactly what we were going through, because his autism center had been working for about 12 years, and he'd seen so many families devastated. Then one day, our conversation took a different turn. Bernie had concluded that autism needed a global identity, and he wanted to meet face-to-face and talk about it.

"Sure," I said. "Come over to Rockefeller Center."

"No," he said, "I want to meet with both you and your wife."

Well, it's hard to say no to Bernie, so I invited him up to our home in Connecticut. That was July 2004.

We're sitting around the living room—Suzanne, me, Bernie, and Gary Goldstein, president and CEO of the Kennedy Krieger Institute in Baltimore, who had been working closely with Bernie. And Bernie starts his pitch: That autism is striking children all over the world and nobody knows what to do. The parents of these children are so exhausted by this, emotionally and financially, that they can't even think about fighting for money for research, or even to take care of these kids. They struggle every day, with no help whatsoever.

Bernie had been working so hard with his autism center, but he knew he wasn't making any real progress. Congress wasn't doing anything, medical professionals weren't doing anything, and he was extremely frustrated. He felt the biggest problem was the general lack of awareness about autism, and he had this idea that autism needed a public face, like what Jerry Lewis did for kids with muscular dystrophy. And that's when I realized: he didn't just want a public awareness effort; he wanted Suzanne and me to lead it.

❖ **Bernie Marcus.** Absolutely that was what I wanted—to convince the Wrights to become the face of a new program to promote autism to the American people. I had already been talking to Bob, and so I knew he was the right person, but that was the first time I was meeting Suzanne. All the time we were talking in their living room, she was so emotional. Whenever their grandson came up, she was crying, or she was angry, or so determined to *do* something. She was like a mama lion. I thought to myself, the passion in this woman… this is it. They are the perfect ones to do it. So I pledged to give seed money for the new organization if they would take it on, maybe $3 million or $5 million to start. ❖

❖ **Suzanne Wright.** All along I had been saying the problem was this huge lack of awareness about autism. And here was this very kind and wonderful man who was saying the same thing, and he really wanted to do something about it. He had the right idea to reach out to someone like Bob, and I think once he met me, he realized that we could do something together.

We had been so focused on Christian, but at the same time I kept thinking about all the families that were suffering, and nobody was helping them. Now, maybe we could do something. It was like God sent Bernie to me. I believe we are put on this earth for a reason, and here was a very big reason. If Bernie's willing to help us, we have to now help all these other people. ❖

Bernie can be very persuasive, but we couldn't give him an answer right away. At that point, everything we were doing was for Christian, and that seemed to consume us; I wasn't dealing with the community at large. Also, I was scheduled to leave for the Olympics in Greece the very next day. But in the end, I told him I'd think about it.

After I got back from Greece, Suzanne and I talked a lot about it. Finally I said, "You know, we could do something here. We really could. I'm willing to put myself out on a limb on this thing. I'm willing to try." But we needed more money. $5 million wasn't going to be enough. We needed $25 million.

Bernie was filled with passion to help children with autism, children to whom he had no obvious connection. But he didn't just offer us $25 million all at once. I wish it was that easy. It was never that easy. But Bernie badly wanted this to happen, so after 6 months of negotiations, he agreed to put up $5 million a year for five years. There was no one else doing what needed to be done nationally for these children and their families. So at that point, how could I refuse?

❖ **Suzanne Wright.** Bob was about 4 years away from retirement. I thought he was very, very brave to do this, because corporations don't necessarily like you to mix your personal charities with your title. But we looked at each other, and we said, ***"If not*** *us, who?"* As a matter of fact, I have that saying on my desk. This is not easy, this is hard. But if not us, who?

I often tell Bernie this was the best $25 million he's ever spent. Look at all the good he started. Bernie Marcus is my angel. That's what I call him. My Jewish angel. ❖

4
Reflections on Success

I believe that every experience in our life is there to teach us something, and over the years I've had tremendous opportunities to learn some critical lessons. Now, as I look both backward and forward, I can see that the most important learnings are all connected to three fundamental tenets, three bedrock principles that must be in place if we are to have any hope of success. And I mean success in any endeavor.

The first is your *responsibility*. Whatever it is you hope to achieve, you must decide how to go about changing your situation and moving forward, and then you must accept responsibility for the outcome. You cannot wait for good fortune to bring success, nor can you blame the gods when things go wrong. The responsibility for success or failure is yours.

The second is *control*. To get to success, it will be critical to maintain as much control as possible in order to defend, execute, and bring your ideas to fruition. Granted, this can sometimes be difficult to orchestrate in large organizations, but those who have a clear grasp of responsibility tend to find a way around roadblocks.

Finally, the most important of all—*passion*. Without it, nothing of significance ever gets done. With it, nothing is impossible.

These three tenets, upon which I have built my own career and life, work together, reinforcing and strengthening each other. They are the foundation of this book.

Much of my corporate life focused on transformative change. It is a constant need, perhaps now more than ever. Technology is forcing most of our large corporations and institutions to recognize that their usual business models no longer work and that they must change and innovate. But few have a clear sense of how to go about it.

I believe you should start by challenging all the regulations that have governed your operations to date. Rules and procedures and regimentation can be extremely confining, leaving no room for innovation or individual vision. That has to change. People—not companies—make a difference.

Some principles remain true across all enterprises.

When things are going well, management and workers should take responsibility. When things go wrong or fail, management must take full responsibility. Said another way, corporate success is shared by management and workers. Corporate failure is only management's fault!

You must freely **empower others** with responsibility to grasp initiatives and make something out of them. You need to unleash the ***entrepreneurial potential that may be hiding within your staff***. Let everyone know they must tolerate the status quo only long enough to change it. They must identify and analyze trends and opportunities. That is the best way—the only way—to capitalize on disruptive change.

You must seize opportunities for ***strategic partnerships***. Most corporations try to avoid partnerships because they can be difficult to manage. But they are extremely valuable. In my GE world especially, partnerships allowed us to minimize capital expenditures and leverage resources while gaining significant footholds in new businesses.

You must ***encourage people to stretch***. Is it possible for people to do more than they think they can? Yes! But it requires passion and commitment. You have to really believe in what you are doing and give others the freedom to experiment.

You must honor ***creativity and risk taking***. All large corporations and institutions are under constant pressure to change and innovate in response to new technology and economics challenging their business models. The people with the ideas and creativity to effect this change are often stifled by legacy and structure and need to be liberated from the status quo.

Bucking the establishment isn't generally taught in business schools, and it is never mandated from the boardroom, but it can be a crucial element of success, particularly when companies are grasping for solutions outside their comfort zones. The answers can come from people within—the ones who are willing to accept responsibility for maximizing their talents, controlling their ideas and passions, and moving beyond the expectations and limitations of the institution.

Use your power to ***empower others***; you will need them to execute your ideas. You will need a winning "to do" list:

- Build a strong team by playing to everyone's strengths.

- Require accountability, but give people the tools they need to excel.

- Energize people to do more than they think they can.

- Wholeheartedly encourage creativity.

- Clearly state a vision everyone can rally around.

- Encourage measured risk taking.

- Be willing to accept failure in order to succeed.

Change will happen. Don't fight it, capitalize on it.
- Make yourself the chief change agent; set an ambitious agenda for radical change.

- Pay attention to the market to maximize value.

- Watch for what's coming on the far-off horizon.

- Recognize opportunity—if necessary, create it—and be ready to respond.

- Understand the difference between being informed and being knowledgeable. More information doesn't make you smarter: it just adds mental clutter.

- Resist stubbornness and arrogance, in others and in yourself. No one knows everything.

- Ask questions; they're the catalyst for next-level thinking.

- Know how to challenge corporate mandates and balance them with your own agenda.

To completely ***transform an organization***, or create one from scratch, plan how you will use these strategies:
- Leverage your resources.

- Learn to manage risk so you don't get sabotaged.

- Develop strategic partnerships to save capital and move quickly.

- Consider mergers: recognize the value of a different business.

- Be ready to challenge the status quo; change the way people think and behave.

- Have a plan for constructively overcoming resistance. Start by giving everyone a seat at the table.

- Pursue contrarian solutions.

- Use and leverage technology.

- Gain support for your venture by promoting awareness of the value you are building.

- Invent a unique process; reinvent what you are and what you have.

If you are developing a **smaller, more nimble unit** within a larger organization, you will need all those transformation strategies, plus a few more:

- Don't try to grow too fast. Remember that being bigger often means losing control; small is good.

- Be ready to counter corporate leaders who are promoting personal interests and legacies.

- Prepare for resistance and denial.

- Avoid death by financials of a good idea or worthy cause; it's not always about money.

- Embrace your moral compass; be your own north star. Stay true to who you are and what you believe in.

It's a daunting thing, starting a new organization from scratch, especially when the stakes are as high as they were when we spoke with Bernie Marcus. Christian's condition was, and is, severe, and the anguish we all experienced, trying first to identify and later to manage this devastating illness, can only be fully understood by other families facing the same nightmare. Unfortunately, there are many of them. And for a long time, each family struggled alone, financially and emotionally broken. I wasn't at all sure I could help build a nonprofit organization that could offer support to these families.

But then I realized that I did in fact know about building organizations. I had just spent nearly 40 years doing exactly that. Even though the focus would be vastly different, the process was the same. And so we dived into building Autism Speaks, using my business experience and Suzanne's fierce passion and relentless energy.

One thing that especially strikes me now, more than a decade later, is how closely the accomplishments in one world reflect the same basic principles in the other. In both cases, the same 3 fundamental tenets guided all our actions: Throw all your passion into the project, strive to maintain control of the process, and accept responsibility for the outcome.

ACT TWO. 1969-2012:
Corporate Transformation

5
First Days

On my first day at General Electric, January 6, 1969, I had a revelation about working within large organizations that was to guide my professional decisions ever after. Almost 20 years later, on my first day as president of NBC, August 26, 1986, those guidelines were severely put to the test.

The GE power transformer plant in Pittsfield, Massachusetts, was huge—a massive brick and steel fortress covering 254 acres. Working there made you feel insignificant. Still, I was full of anticipation and awe the first time I passed through the big iron gates in front. But once I settled in to my work station and looked around me, I could see I was adrift in a corporate labyrinth. Everyone had their head down, going about their business. I was just a cog in a huge machine.

At the end of the day, I passed back through the huge stone walls and the large iron gates to the street. And I decided something that day. We all live and work behind institutional walls. Whether we spend our days in factories, high-rise offices, schools, the military, or even nonprofits, behind those walls, our individuality and enterprise are compromised by regimentation and ruled by the bottom line. But what I came to realize is that we must accept responsibility for our own success. If you want to maximize your talents, you have to take it upon yourself to move forward and find a way to make things happen. No one can do that for you. If the institution is not working for you, you have to accept responsibility for doing something about it, because the institution is not likely to help you achieve change. If you have ideas you want to develop, you may have to go outside an institution for the freedom and resources to do so. That's what I mean by taking responsibility.

But I also learned that two other ingredients are essential: passion and control. When you take responsibility for creating change, you need to develop ways to control your ideas, and you need to nurture the passion that will keep you going in the face of setbacks.

One of management's jobs is to figure out how to make people more productive, to identify and tap into their strengths. Then you have to empower them to think the unthinkable, do the un-doable, and run with that permission. If you are able to do that, you can achieve great things, and they can, too.

I left GE twice and returned twice. I first came out from behind GE's institutional wall in 1970 to be chief legal secretary to Judge Lawrence A. Whipple, chief judge of the US District Court of New Jersey. I left a second time in 1979 to build new cable systems as president of Cox Cable. Each time I returned to GE, I assumed a new leadership role in an area unfamiliar to me. In all of these diverse roles, I applied the same principles for success I developed in those early years at GE:

- Use your passion as a catalyst.

- Maintain control of your ideas.

- Take responsibility for your success.

By the time I took the helm at NBC in August 1986, I had been studying NBC and contemplating the future. I was already applying what I had learned the previous 6 years at Cox Cable and GE Capital. I knew NBC's financial vulnerabilities as well as GE's expectations. I already knew what had to change, and I knew it would not be easy.

People at NBC generally felt disdain for RCA, their previous owner, but when GE acquired RCA, and thus became NBC's new owner, they were outwardly fearful. They saw GE as a more formidable institutional owner with its own quirks and requirements. And they were not wrong. So NBC would still be stuck behind another institutional wall, and it was up to me to figure out how to set them free from GE and its own inhibitions. I was not put off by the wall of resistance I had to fight through as I told Crain Communications' Diane Mermigas after taking the helm, "I have experienced the same thing in other places. I wouldn't say that is alarming."

As it turned out, I was the right guy for the job. I was fully convinced that relying solely on its broadcast base made NBC very vulnerable, that we would have to embrace cable if we were to remain competitive and financially viable. Anyone who took the time to look ahead could see that cable was on the cusp of becoming mainstream, and we needed to be a part of that. In fact, NBC already was late getting into the cable and satellite business when I got there. Because of my time at Cox (see Chapter 6), I understood the cable business. It was absolutely clear that the two media modes needed each other. But getting there, against the resistance of NBC executives, GE higher-ups, and the station affiliates, nearly killed me.

Bringing NBC into the cable age involved nothing short of a complete transformation, and we had to do it inside our corporate parent, GE, sometimes flying under the radar. It meant getting the right people in the right places with the freedom and support to grow a subsidiary by making acquisitions, starting enterprises, and hiring talent that GE would rather we didn't. A great example is three executive producers I brought in from the outside—Don Ohlmeyer, Dick Ebersol, and Andy Lack. They didn't exactly fit GE's executive mold, but their unconventional sensibilities brought NBC to the next level.

We built teams of people who were committed to my vision of transforming NBC. Some of them were more ambitious than GE liked, but they all knew that I would back them to do whatever was needed to grow NBC. Our goal was to create a broadcast company much more significant for the changing times, and the challenge was doing that inside a conglomerate with a history of control and rigidity. So, my story is really about people who built tremendous value at a privately held company operated by guidelines of a larger public corporate parent.

Businesses are not like plants and animals. They don't grow by themselves. You have to give them a lot of Miracle-Gro. You cannot have people just settle in to their assigned responsibilities to maintain the status quo. You must push through resistance to change, often through difficult circumstances, to secure a better future.

❖ **Arthur Puccini, chief counsel General Electric plastics and chemical division.** When GE bought RCA in 1986, it also acquired NBC, an RCA subsidiary, as part of the package. So Bob had the unhappy task of trying to integrate the culture of NBC into GE. NBC had to be approached different from GE's other businesses because there was no tangible product, per se. You didn't manufacture anything. The entertainment business is completely different in the way it is managed, so it took a lot of adapting on GE's part.

Bob was able to integrate what he wanted and what GE need-ed with what existed, to come up with something that worked. He brought a whole new filter to that process. It was a gradual and steady move in the direction he knew they needed to go. ❖

❖ **Pier Mapes, president NBC Television Network.** One of the big problems GE inherited from RCA was a highly layered man-agement structure. Bob eliminated layers of executive vice presidents who were good guys with big salaries and opted for just one execu-tive vice president overseeing each of the primary areas. It allowed for many more voices and better productivity. NBC was lean, mean, and de-layered. When Bob Wright first walked in, we had 300 employees and 10 lawyers approving contracts. A year later, we had 200 employ-ees and 1 manager of boilerplate legal contracts. ❖

GE headquarters auditorium
New York City
August 26, 1986

The formal announcement of my appointment as president of NBC was made in a studio at GE headquarters on August 26, 1986. Afterward, two or three dozen senior NBC people joined Jack Welch and me for lunch at the Four Seasons. Jack and I had it all orchestrated. He played the white hat, and later I was going to play the black. He told everybody how happy GE was to have NBC and we were going to have a lot of fun together, and every-thing was going to be great. Everyone was laughing and cheering, and I was thinking to myself, this is not going to be so much fun. Jack said good-bye and he disappeared, and I had to go back to my new office on the 6th floor of 30 Rockefeller Center, where I met with all the senior NBC executives and gave them my perspective on what GE was going to do with NBC.

So I gave them my view that we would need to be aggressive about growing the business. We had to determine if we could stay in radio, which was a poor performer at the time, and we had a labor contract situation about to erupt that we had to deal with in new ways. We had a lot of business development planned to make the network more competitive while we were growing new businesses. And that would be tricky since the NBC network had only one source of revenue at the time, advertising, which wasn't going to be sufficient in the years to come. I leaned hard on the importance of selling programs to cable and even owning their own cable program services.

They didn't like what they heard. They wanted to say, everything is OK now. It was difficult for them to comprehend what I was talking about and why it was important to embrace cable when their broadcast business was the dominant force in media. There was no big-picture perspective. But there was an insatiable interest in what people thought was going on under GE, so my confidential internal memos detailing change routinely made it into the next day's newspapers, which complicated the process.

The other thing that I was not prepared for was the Wall Street analysts who followed GE back then. They liked and understood the GE-RCA merger, but they weren't at all interested in NBC. They were industrial analysts who didn't know anything about NBC or media. So, to mollify them, Jack made a point of telling them we were not going into the entertainment business; we were just doing a few television shows. And the TV shows would help sell the television sets and other appliances GE was making, so no one on Wall Street should be worried about it!

The problem with characterizing NBC as an industrial media company was that it made it harder for me to take risks by entering cable when, in fact, the biggest risk of all was repelling new technology. I spent much of my first year at NBC warning against complacency painfully evident in a 4-month labor strike by The National Association of Broadcast Employees and Technicians who were particularly dug in against change. NBC News and station affiliates flipped out at the notion we should launch our own cable news operation to compete with CNN.

At the same time, I was wooing the cable crowd. I knew they would be important partners in my growth plan for NBC, so at every opportunity I reminded them that if everyone was going to benefit from the coming growth in our deregulated industry, we all had to act cooperatively, not defensively. My ultimate strategy was to secure co-ownership positions in cable channels or systems or to create program services from scratch. To some within NBC, it looked like cavorting with the enemy, but it was the only recourse I had to save the network.

So from day one at NBC, I had a clear strategy and understanding of what needed to be done and a strategy for getting there. I knew where the broadcast television industry was headed and where cable had the potential to go. I had more opportunities than I ever expected because of the embryonic nature of the cable business I needed NBC to enter. I had everything but the funding and the green light, and for that I needed a more willing GE. From that point on I realized if I was going to accomplish anything I needed to at NBC, I would have to find ways to work around and within the institution. I would have to bring NBC out from behind GE's institutional walls.

Wright to the Point

Successful change at any company depends on assembling, managing, and empowering the right teams of people. Mandating change and encouraging fresh ideas frees workers from institutional shackles. It unleashes creativity and productivity. It provides a path to innovating and creating new value. But it requires courage.

Formidable challenges prevailed the day I began work at GE in 1969, when I took command of NBC in 1986, and when we launched Autism Speaks in 2005. In every case, I learned to rely on my team to take ownership of those challenges, embrace new ways of thinking, and tackle things too often reserved for research and development. There is no telling where the next great idea or effort might be lurking in an organization. Give people a way to excel and distinguish themselves, and they will take it every time.

Transitioning operations and staff into the unknown is unnerving unless you are clear on the organization's vision, guiding principles, and need for change. It can take years to guide a corporation through troubled waters—when months count. At times, you will be blown off course. That's when vision and execution matter: when your vision is being executed by people who get it and buy into it, and are skilled and properly motivated to get it done. In the end, people make the difference; people make it happen.

We faced major obstacles creating and growing Autism Speaks. We had to maximize the skills and resources of mostly volunteers, both parents and professionals. We had to build awareness about autism and an appreciation for the value of a united national organization whose energy and momentum could drive change.

The inevitable clash of corporate cultures, agendas, and personalities can derail any project not adequately grounded in a chief executive's strategy and conviction. Believing you can make a difference can be liberating. It enables you to overlook the fact that you might not have the right resources. It makes you believe that passion and determination just might be enough to propel you to doing great things, impossible things.

We so often walk into new jobs and companies bound by existing standards and expectations. We are easily paralyzed by institutional pressures to conform and compromise. We are lulled into believing that circumstances and change are beyond our control. You'd be surprised.

6
Media Baptism by Fire: Cox Cable

Every day of my 3-plus years as president of Cox Cable, I felt like a pioneer on the new media frontier. It was 1980 to 1983, and building cable systems from scratch in some of America's largest cities was my generation's industrial revolution. The nimble executive team I assembled was my secret weapon. We were lightning-fast at creating and presenting cable franchise proposals to municipalities and then dodging their political and economic landmines. We built several dozen new systems that put Cox on the cable map. There wasn't anything we couldn't do—or at least try. It was a liberating break from GE's rigid structure.

Ironically, though, those two companies had courted each other just a few months earlier, and we almost got married.

In the late 1970s, just as the country's first major cable channels were emerging, GE agreed to purchase Cox and merge its smattering of cable systems, television, and radio stations with those of Cox. The Cox organization, nearly a hundred years old at the time, had been known primarily for its newspapers but had established cable systems in a few states as early as 1962. In 1979, as the terms of the merger were being hammered out, the two companies looked around for someone to manage their TV assets. I surprised everyone at GE when I raised my hand and said, "You know, I'd like to do that!" And so I went to Atlanta in January 1980.

What would have been the biggest broadcasting merger of that time imploded over price. After an initial $400 million bid, GE held firm to its final $570 million offer while Cox increased its asking price to $637 million, reflecting escalating cable company values. Jack Welch did not want to jeopardize his upcoming appointment as GE chairman and CEO by pressing his board of directors for more money and was eager to demonstrate he wasn't going to be pushed around.

The deal was dead by April 1980, but by then I was hooked on the TV explosion. How could I resist?

Atlanta "Central Park" headquarters
Office of Garner Anthony
Chairman CEO Cox Communications
March 12, 1980

The collapse of its deal with GE was a blow to Cox. It would have allowed the company to participate in cable's growth while protecting its core print business. But chief executive Garner Anthony, who married into the family business, was now determined to grow Cox into a media conglomerate. He needed me to stay and help. I had already been in Atlanta for 6 months organizing a new cable team and operations while Suzanne and I built a new home and transferred our three children into private schools. Anthony called me into his office to have "the talk."

Anthony wanted Cox's hat in the cable ring in a big way, and he implored me to go out and win some big city cable system franchises. An improved compensation package and a healthy measure of autonomy sealed the deal for me. The fact is, I ended up staying at Cox because I really fell in love with the business. Cable was the best, most exciting business opportunity I saw on the horizon, and I had already seen a few good ones during my time with GE.

By 1981, I had 1 million cable subscribers and was delivering video signals by fiber-optic cable. Today, more than half of Cox's 6 million customers subscribe to digital cable, Internet, and digital telephone.

❖ **Bob O'Leary, VP finance Cox Cable Communications; executive VP and CEO Cox Enterprises.** The Cox family wasn't afraid to adopt new technology. They got into radio when it came along, then television, and later, cable television. And each of these technologies always was expected to eliminate the prior technology. But broadcasting and newspapers funded the costs of building cable franchises, which was capital intensive.

I'm sure Cox senior management was very nervous about the kinds of commitment that were being made in these cable franchise agreements. So Bob Wright had a lot of selling to do, bidding on markets like New Orleans and Tucson. In those days, Bob was bidding against early developers of cable like John Malone, and they were all trying to sell the banks and investors on the value of the cash flow that would support the heavy capital expenditures. Every municipality added as a caveat funding CNBC for new boulevards or libraries into granting cable franchises. It was like a three-ring circus!

Many broadcasters—including some people at Cox—didn't want to see cable succeed; they thought it would hurt their advertising sales. In those early years, cable was sort of the new teenager in town, a bit wild and unproven.

To his credit, Bob saw the value of cable looking out over 5 years. He was a gadget guy who liked to tinker with new technology. He understood the value that could be created from emerging technologies. ❖

We were in the middle of fast and furious cable franchising in the early 1980s, and it was up to me and my team to make things happen. We could cut through issues, create solutions on the spot, and make things happen very quickly. I was working with some pretty great people I knew I could rely on: Paul Waring, who had a GE background; Dr. Gary Tjaden from Bell Telephone Labs; Art Dwyer from GE plastics, who headed our marketing; Bob O'Leary, who served as my vice president of finance, and John Dyer, a young accountant who prepared our numbers (and eventually became CFO of Cox Enterprises and is now CEO). We just went out there and did it.

The Cox family wanted accountability and results, and otherwise stayed out of our way. But I had to fight for every mile of cable pipe—an infrastructure that now generates the lion's share of revenues and profits at Cox Enterprises. We spent a lot of time traveling to places like Dallas, Omaha, New Orleans, Tucson, Brooklyn, and Staten Island as well as Vancouver, Washington, and Portland, Oregon (where we braved the thick volcanic ashen air of an erupting Mount St. Helens). Cable was a complete mystery to most people, so we spent days in each location, meeting with residents and government organizations about the cable franchises we wanted to build. Each proposal required a huge amount of preparation and research. We put together thick binders of documents and charts for city councils and various state and local officials, explaining the planned system in detail, with all aspects of program services and fees.

The real trick was selling Cox on how cable would pay for itself. The answer turned out to be cash flow investing. John

Malone, the president and CEO of Tele-Communications Inc., became an ally. John is a libertarian; he does not like to pay taxes. It's against his religion. So cash flow investing was his perfect solution for using the depreciation and the interest that came along with being in the cable business to offset any taxability from future profits.

It was something that people understood from an accounting standpoint, but it was not the way stock analysts rated businesses. Analysts could provide commentary on a stock that was technically losing money; they could even recommend it. But losing money because the company was taking losses from the combined interest, amortization, and depreciation that were coming from all the construction, that was a different matter.

So John Malone educated a whole generation of analysts on how to invest in a business that looks like it's losing money when in fact it's building tremendous value, not paying any taxes, and getting maximum benefit out of interest deductions. I picked right up on it. I thought it was a marvelous way to understand the new cable business. We were able to convince investors, analysts, and business reporters that it was not a fad that would bankrupt the Cox family. Even now that cable is a profitable, stable business, cash flow remains an important measurement.

In many franchising contests, we competed with Warner Amex Satellite Company, which was jointly owned by Warner Communications and American Express. The rivalry between our companies came to a head during our presentations to the city council in Omaha, Nebraska. The folks at Warner had become unglued at how quickly Cox developed its own interactive service to compete with their QUBE. As we were going tit for tat on whose service was the better option, an exasperated Gus Hauser, the Warner Amex CEO, finally blurted out, "You're copying me!" I was quick to fire back. "No, we're just doing the same thing!"

We were both dug in, knowing what was at stake: having a direct line to homes that could be endlessly exploited as cable services advanced. They were very exciting times on the cutting edge of industry growth.

I eventually won the right to build cable systems in Omaha, Portland, New Orleans, Staten Island, Norfolk, and Tucson, but lost Dallas to Warner. For a time, San Diego was our core and the largest cable system in the United States with 100,000 subscribers, even though it only had 35 channels, because we could showcase everything we knew that cable would become.

One of our most aggressive franchise efforts was in New Orleans. Cox already had a foothold position in Jefferson Parish, but we wanted to connect the entire area, which was frequently ravaged by extreme weather. Many residents were lower income, and there was concern about whether enough people were willing to pay for cable services. Cox was 1 of 10 applicants bidding to build the city's first cable system. It was a formidable market to bid on and build because New Orleans has its own peculiar way of doing business. Its historical district required cables to be laid underground, beneath vintage cobblestones—in water.

And then there was the matter of New Orleans politics.

When there were just two of us left, we made the case for an $8 basic cable rate, which city officials quickly shot down to $4. I was trying to explain the need for an annual 6 percent rate increase when Marty Feldman, my very sharp local counsel, leaned over and whispered in my ear, "No way." During a break, he said, "Come with me." I followed him down the hall to a payphone, and Marty asked me to call his office. I just looked at him, perplexed. "Go ahead," Marty said, "just call my office."

As I began sifting through my pockets for a coin, I spotted the notice on the face of the phone: Deposit 5 cents. "How long has that been in effect?!" I asked. "Twenty years," Marty said, laughing. "New Orleans has never allowed the phone company to increase its rates. So good-bye dreams of 6 percent annual increases! The rates are very low and they stay low." Feldman went on to become a federal judge in New Orleans, and I went on to enjoy many fine meals in the French Quarter while agonizing through the process of building a cable system on a peninsula below sea level—relying on pay and expanded basic cable services for profits.

❖ **Art Dwyer, executive VP marketing Cox Cable, worked with Bob Wright for more than 2 decades at GE, Cox Cable, and NBC.** There are three types of chief executives. Five to eight percent are what you would call undertakers who should *not* be where they are. The great majority of CEOs—as much as 85 percent—are caretakers. They do a very good job of watching the business inch along. The remaining ones, less than 10 percent, are innovators. They bring the knowledge they have gained and a commitment to innovate to drive a business forward in new directions. That was Bob at Cox and of course later at NBC. ❖

Just as important as gains in technology were the strides we made in programming. Cable program options were exploding, and I wanted to get Cox in a good position, although it was not always easy to know what ventures would ultimately be successful. It was the early days of ESPN and MTV. Warner Communications CEO Steve Ross was dabbling with Atari. I had my first dealings with Chuck Dolan at Cablevision, who wanted us to partner in a bid for Paramount and its rich TV and film content.

But given the newness of cable and its untested economics, Cox management wasn't always game.

An example: In 1981, Cox passed on the opportunity to acquire a 20 percent equity stake in a very new ESPN. I had negotiated a deal with ABC president Fred Pierce and his right-hand man in cable, Herb Granath, to acquire half of the 40 percent interest Getty Oil was unloading in ESPN, but Cox ultimately decided it was too risky.

To be fair, at that time even ABC Sports chief Roone Arledge underestimated the potential of ESPN and cable sports, and it seemed we would be on our own developing it. I think that was what really killed the deal with Cox. By 1984, ABC assumed 80 percent ownership of ESPN and Hearst ended up with the 20 percent stake Cox could have had. Today, ESPN generates huge profits for Disney/ABC.

Another example involved the visionary maverick Ted Turner. Many of the largest media companies realized in the early 1980s the stakes were too high to go it alone in an intensely competitive market. It was especially true for Turner, who both excelled and failed because of his unbridled autonomy. Cox's offices were right down the street from where Turner was building his new headquarters. He would call me to come over to the construction site to look at the blueprints; what he really wanted was to talk about how our companies could join forces.

We were close to a deal in the spring of 1982; Cox would acquire 49 percent of his entire company and half of CNN. The night before I was going to present our proposal to the Cox board, Ted called me. "So how do you think things will go?" he asked. "I'm just not sure this is going to work, Ted," I confessed. "You would have to join the Cox board, and it's a very small board with a lot of conservative family members." Ted was getting the message. "I don't think they are going to like me. I think they are going to hate me!"

By the next morning, I had made a decision: I would tell the board that we should not acquire a half interest in Turner Broadcasting System or in CNN. There was a collective sigh of relief from the board. "We didn't want to say no to Ted, but we couldn't say yes either!" I remember one of the directors saying. Agreeing to Ted's 51 percent controlling ownership and helping to shoulder CNN's mounting rollout losses was too much—on top of which, Ted just scared the daylights out of everybody! Unfortunately Cox Broadcasting opted to align instead with Satellite News Television, a fledgling cable news service owned by ABC Westinghouse, where Bill Schwartz, head of Cox Broadcasting, had friends. I continued to work with Ted and Cox Cable was one of his biggest customers.

❖ **Art Dwyer.** Even after winning many of the cable franchises we pursued, Bob knew it would not be enough to just build the systems. He knew that programming would be the differentiator, no matter the delivery system. So he tried to position Cox to own stakes in what he thought would become major program sources, like 20 percent of ESPN and 49 percent of CNN. It turned out he was right. Can you imagine what those would be worth today? But back then, we were the new kids on the block. Cox was a traditional newspaper company in a very tight-knit, closed industry. Bob and the cable team he put together were looked upon as the rah-rah guys from GE who didn't know our ass from our elbow. But when we started winning battles for systems and programming and viewers and ad dollars, all of that changed. ❖

Learning how to define and cater to niche program audiences on cable became a science. We had to learn what people really liked and didn't like. We had to learn the hard way. We couldn't just do surveys. We had to actually put programs on the systems to find out what would sell. Fortunately, it was less expensive to produce back then, so we could experiment. We learned a lot in those early days of cable based on plain old customer reaction. If there was an outrage, the program was yanked off. If there was an outpouring of support, we ordered more. It was that simple.

All in all, I'd say we accomplished a great deal in a very short time. But eventually Cox's initial push into new cable markets started winding down.

And then one day Jack Welch called, asking me to come back to GE.

❖ **Art Dwyer.** The Cox family wasn't exactly in love with the cable business. That's why they were going to sell to GE in 1979. The company's second love was broadcasting. One of the reasons Bob didn't stay at Cox after securing so many cable franchises was that too many of the executives in charge were old-line newspaper and broadcast people with one finger on the brake and another finger on the bottom line. They were not about to do anything to disrupt Cox's 46 straight quarters of earnings growth. But that's precisely when a company should take some educated risks to assure future growth. ❖

Wright to the Point

Sometimes change is easier to institute and sell to others when there is no choice. It is part of the natural flow and order of things. While there will be plenty of resistance, there is no sense arguing about it because it will happen. What often is debated is *how* it will occur. Cable was that way for broadcasters and even for those inside its own embryonic ranks. The mainstream acceptance of cable shook traditional media economics and creativity to its core. It was the first genuine media disruptor, and I wrestled with its impact and prospects at Cox just as cable was emerging in the marketplace.

Being empowered by the Cox family to pioneer that new path made all the difference, made everything possible. That enabling force from management can make a difference between success and failure, growth and stagnation, innovation or status quo. The *how* became allowing others—including me—to find the way to make things happen as we invented one business and reinvented another. Change is more palatable when you have some minimal degree of control over shaping the new rules of play.

I learned so much at Cox. That's where I really honed my skills at giving people responsibility and empowering them to embrace new ideas and make them concrete. Those 3½ years of my life were a big testing ground for broad ideas that reached beyond media. That was when I fully understood the power of passion and control. People like to think that only independent entrepreneurs can create things. And they think that institutions have a corner on success, but that's not really true. Everything great begins within you. And all the good that comes from it must be its own reward.

Among the many lessons I learned at Cox was the value of empowering others to execute the vision and ideas you believe in passionately. It allowed me to build a risk-taking team that catered to everyone's strengths—just as I did several decades later, constructing the nonprofit Autism Speaks from the ground up. At both Cox and Autism Speaks, we did not inherit a road map, so we made up the guidebook as we went.

7
This Thing Called Cable

IRTS Newsmaker Luncheon
New York City
October 27, 1987

When I think back on it now, it could have been a disaster.

My luncheon address to a gathering of the International Radio and Television Society a year after I became president of NBC was particularly well-timed. Since practically my first day on the job, I had been determined to transform NBC into a cable player. It was an unpopular position, to say the least, and this speech was my first opportunity to publicly explain my thinking.

I was absolutely convinced we needed to be doing something different. We could not ignore the facts: viewership was slipping and so were ad revenues. Dramatic changes in competition and technology, especially cable, demanded new business models. My top priority was engaging NBC in a multiscreen, multidistributor future—a future that was rapidly becoming the present. But to the people in the room that day, cable was a dirty word. For me to push us in that direction seemed like heresy to them. They could have erupted at any moment, but they didn't.

The idea of igniting a revolution should have been better received at the time. New owners from outside the media world were taking control of the traditional broadcast networks, and they each brought a strict bottom line mentality. It was a perfect time to pursue new initiatives. Even if I had to drag them along, kicking and screaming.

My plan, I explained, was to leverage NBC's news, sports, and entertainment resources in a way that cable operators and subscribers would pay to support a second revenue stream. I told the restless crowd that our focus would be to expand our audience—not necessarily cut our own costs, as so many automatically assumed. "If our primary concern was immediate return on investment, engaging entertainment simply would never happen, and we would be overlooking the most important factor in the equation—the viewer."

And then I appealed to television's universal link. "All of us here today, representing many different kinds of players in the electronic marketplace, are in this together... we share a need to focus on and promote the positives of our business." Then I hit them with a full dose of my reality. "I've been involved in television as a cable television operator, group broadcaster, and network executive, so the old barriers and taboos don't seem quite so important to me. I see nothing wrong with broadcast television selling programs to cable television. Yes, cable is the competition, but it is also a market for programming and a source of income. The goal we could work toward is putting more quality, substance, and diversity into our end product." The time was ripe for change: alliances, partnerships, and restructuring our own businesses. "With a little enterprise and cooperation, we can save this marriage!" You could hear the gasps across the room.

These were radical notions for 1987. But we were on the cusp of a digital information and entertainment explosion. Even though it would be 12 years before Apple introduced the iPod and more than 2 decades before it launched the iPad, it was clear that speedy, ubiquitous connections and limitless storage capacity would re-shape our lives. So, I kept hammering away at one simple truth: the better the programs, the more they would be viewed in many new places. The biggest risk was not doing what we did best: pro-ducing outstanding content for every type of screen. Viewers' love affair with television was expanding, not shrinking, if we were willing to look at ourselves differently.

❖ **Tom Wheeler, president National Cable Television Assn. and Cellular Telecommunications & Internet Assn.** Bob was a heretic among broadcasters in that he believed in the future of cable. In the mid to late 70s and early 80s, most broadcasters were determined to strangle cable in the crib. They were exerting all kinds of political influence and being quite effective in exercising their political power. And it resulted in a situation where there were federal rules that limited what cable could offer. So the cable sales-man ends up saying, "Hello, I'd like to charge you a certain number of dollars a month, and drill a hole in your wall, so that occasionally you can get some different programming."

This was a holy war waged in many directions—not only against broadcasters, but also against telephone companies. Telephone companies didn't want another wire into the home, and so they also tried to deny the right to put cables on the poles. There was an ebb and flow of victories and losses on all sides that shaped the laws governing cable.

Bob and I were both young men at the time, and the cable business was a young business being created by relatively young go-getters who had a blank slate and could define the future any way they wanted. It was a little like the Internet. That's what made it so exciting! Bob knew the systems that would cost so much to build would need programming, and that the tie-up with broadcasters would be a natural, since they were the largest source of television content at that time. But this was everyone's first trip to the rodeo, so there were some rough rides for a lot of years. ❖

❖ **David Zaslav, president NBC Cable Distribution, executive VP NBC Cable.** Bob was the first broadcaster who saw that the future meant diversifying content for all platforms, and that was really his theme for more than 20 years. It sure wasn't easy. Everyone at NBC was against him. Cable was viewed like the kids' table for a long time. Broadcast was riding very high and everyone was asking, "What the hell are we doing in the cable business?!" It took years to change NBC's broadcast culture. Then he had to convince GE that they should be investing in cable—not a simple matter, either. He really pushed GE to get into the business, and he had to hire an entirely different team to pursue it. Tom Rogers, me, and a whole team. ❖

❖ **Tom Rogers, first president NBC Cable and Business Development, executive VP NBC and chief strategist.** Bob asked me to see if I could get him through those early initiatives and end up with something meaningful. We went out negotiating with the whole cable industry with the threat that we would pull the plug on our network signal if we did not have a deal. And with the new retransmission consent rules at the time, we could do it. We were in a formidable position to get this thing done, and we went through the whole industry in a relatively short period of time. ❖

Those original cable operators were all high flyers coming into their own. Many of them were becoming wealthy because of what they owned. They were different businesspeople with a different style that came into the cable business from many places. Some sold equipment and some were just entrepreneurs. But all of them were eccentric pioneers, so the press label "cable cowboys" fit. A lot of them tended to be from the west and mountain areas, where cable developed out of necessity. And they spent many years laboring hard to get the industry growing. It was a damn hard business, and they were fighting the broadcasters every step of the way. It was a silly war. Decades later, the Internet circumvented everyone in the flash of an eye. Broadcasters *and* cable were humbled by new, over-the-top technology that overrode them both.

Cable operators needed the financial ability to build their systems, which meant both a lending and an operating environment. They also needed programming in order to attract customers and increase revenues. The cable operators knew that relying on the three main broadcast networks would only go so far, and that new and better programming would require partnerships.

The difference between having programming and not having programming in the early days turned out to be the satellite. In 1976, HBO went up on satellite along with TBS and shortly after, Tribune superstation WGN. And that's when USA and many cable networks came along. That's when some broadcasters like NBC and ABC stepped forward, wondering if this wasn't an opportunity to make money reusing their program libraries. That began a phase of experimentation that carried over onto the Internet and continues today.

❖ **Herbert Granath, VP early cable program development ABC and ESPN.** When ABC ended up with 80 percent of ESPN, Leonard Goldenson, the chairman of ABC, said to me, "You know the affiliates are going to have a fit about this!" And he was right. So we thought we could soften the blow by starting out with something that presented absolutely no threat to them, and that was performing arts like full-length ballets and opera and musical performance. That programming was really cheap because nobody else in the States was doing it except for something occasional on PBS and BBC. It was really painful when Leonard told me that I was the one who was going to have to go up in front of the affiliate annual meeting and tell them we were getting into the cable programming business. Of course I got boos and hisses. Seeing the arts channel calmed everybody down. And we were the darlings of the critics. They said, "Well, this is what television was meant to be," except that nobody was watching, and therefore we had no revenues and had no income.

We struggled. We got through Arts and Entertainment, and then we started Lifetime, which was in those days called Daytime. It was an attempt to offer programming to women, other than the soaps and the game shows. When that didn't do well, we partnered again with Viacom to create Lifetime.

So now we've got two losing propositions. And it was just wonderful. I didn't have to be a genius to figure that out. So a few of us talked with John Malone, who at the time was head of TCI, about reverse cable fees in 1981. That was probably the most important decision in the history of television. John bought into that. And once he did, then the rest became easy, because all of the other cable operators fell into line. They all needed programming.

There were two problems with that. Number one, I would get hissed and booed when I got into an elevator with some of my former network friends. And number two, every time I'd walk into a cable system to try to get carriage, it was like raining rocks. I didn't know where to duck.

A couple of guys in the cable business, Ralph Roberts of Comcast and Chuck Dolan of Cablevision Systems, said to their friends in cable, "Why don't you give these guys a chance? They're willing to come in and spend some money and maybe give us some decent programming." ABC Sports was known then as the home of the Olympics, and we had Monday Night Football, and NCAA football. We would invite the sponsors and distributors to the games and tournaments. Announcers like Howard Cosell, Frank Gifford, or Don Meredith would drop by. And that really worked. Once the distributors were on your side, the parent company would embrace it.

Once I got into it, I really became convinced that this thing was going to work one day. All I wanted was to make that one day come. We were losing money on A&E, losing money on Lifetime, and we were losing big-time money on ESPN, because we had to buy sports rights in order to make ourselves relevant to the cable business. And we just didn't have much income. But by 1983, ESPN broke even with $42 million in revenues on virtually all advertising sales.

Then came must-carry, which was another radical idea at the time. On the cable side the argument was, well, we're being forced to carry this thing. And not only the major stations, but I believe the deal was that any signal that had any penetration whatsoever in the market was a must-carry, and so it took up a lot of space on the cable band. One of the reasons that ESPN is so profitable today is because they get a very large payment from cable operators for a subscriber base attracted by expensive live programming rights. What we did instead in some cases was rather than charging fees, we got cable operators to agree to carry several new cable networks we launched, like ESPN2 and the History and Biography Channels.

To appease the affiliates, we just told them straight: since we're making diminishing returns from the broadcasting business, partly because of the inroads cable was making, we needed to generate new revenues from cable. It was the only way to keep the company financially healthy. It was a painful internal battle for a long time that Bob Wright knew only too well. He helped forge the way.

But you know the biggest challenge was getting ABC, a public company, into a business which was pretty much unknown and that would lose us a lot of money for a while. I had a board of directors that I had to convince that it was worth the gamble. There are always yin and yang things going on here, and the trick is to have more yins or more yangs to stay ahead of the game. There are people in the position of making decisions who are really smart and dedicated. There are others who are riding the tide, and it may wash them over the edge. But being able to work with people who are the intelligent risk takers, as opposed to the cowboys, is the key to be able to discern when a new idea is feasible or not. ❖

One big hurdle for NBC, of course, was the financial picture. GE during the Welch period was very focused on earnings per share. EPS means you have to have accounting earnings, which startup businesses won't have. You have losses so you will have some reduction in EPS. GE didn't appreciate any business that wasn't making money. That is a positive thing for shareholders on one level, but on another level it means you are staying in a lot of businesses that are just marginally profitable, have a huge capital base, and may not have much of a future. So the story of cable television in its early days was never about EPS; it would have created tremendous losses. Financing cable was primarily done through limited partnerships where people would invest, and instead of getting cash back, they would get losses back that they could deduct, and then use it against profits from other businesses. That's what John Malone was all about. Nearly every new cable acquisition or partnership required the blessing and strategic involvement of the Yale-bred engineer-turned-cable czar. Brian Roberts has done a good job over the years of explaining tremendous losses and tremendous profits. But they still have a tendency to be measured by EPS. In cable we used to focus on a 10-year life, and the losses would run right through year 5.

Another never-ending challenge was the constant rollout of new technology. It changed everything about the economics, competitive dynamics, and business relationships, and eventually completely redefined the consumer experience. At first, it was cable; 2 decades later it was the Internet; now it's the virtual streaming connection of everything about our lives. I knew then and all through NBC's growth that it was important to track the development of new technology to integrate and seize it before we were seized by it. Even today, you don't have to jump into everything at every minute, but you have to be well-informed enough so as not to be arguing with yourself about why you are not there. The error should be on being there. Even if your new technology gamble doesn't pay off, you will benefit from the experience and knowledge gained. If you sit back on the sidelines for too long, your entry will be late and you could miss unique opportunities. You have to try.

❖ **John Malone.** Equity partnership became a staple of the way we did business. In some cases, we had opportunities to do many deals with people who had financial distress and who didn't want to sell their companies. A great example of that was Ted Turner, who had gotten himself into financial trouble with his MGM acquisition. Even though he was over leveraged, we were able to put together financing and invest ourselves to help Ted stay independent.

I was the reason NBC never got into that club. I thought that the relationship with Ted was unique. He really had demonstrated a love and relationship with the cable industry, and we trusted him. And if you were to bring in other players who had other motives, you would not be as comfortable. So we made this really a cable club investment in Ted's bailout and creation of a new board comprised of the biggest cable operators.

To have a successful partnership then or now, you have to understand what the other side's motives are in order to make those deals work. You have to roll around in your mind what you might do that's good for yourself and good for them, and fit all the intricate pieces together. The late (Liberty president) Peter Barton used to say that my mind worked like a Rubik's Cube figuring out the deal details.

It's financial or structural problem solving or an engineering problem, and it's what I do. The goal has always been to build good, scale, efficient, sustainable businesses and give them to your shareholders tax efficiently. If I had kept intact all the stakes and assets that TCI and, eventually, Liberty came to control through partnerships, it would have become a very large and a very unmanageable collection. So, we carefully used the pieces to build more value for everyone concerned. That takes time and know-how and being able to respond to the right opportunity when it is presented. That's exactly what Bob Wright did at NBC inside of GE. ❖

❖ **Herbert Schlosser.** Bob came to NBC not really knowing the company well, but he fully understood the need to take it to the next level. The business acumen he brought to the network from GE and his training as a lawyer proved invaluable as NBC and the entire media industry went through tremendous churn over more than 20 years. In 1986, cable program services were not yet fully developed, so it was all about developing guidelines and regulations that would stand the test of time involving new technology no one knew enough about. The only cable property he inherited at NBC was something I put in place. Herb Granath at ABC and Gannett were my partners in a service called The Arts.

NBC and the Rockefeller Group invested in something called The Entertainment Channel. Neither of these services was really working. So after about 6 months of negotiations, we put the two together, and that became Arts & Entertainment, owned by three partners: NBC, ABC, and Hearst.

And Bob went on to create so much more, most importantly the deal with Microsoft, which gave NBC the MSNBC channel—an entity that could bridge broadcasting and the Internet *through* cable.

When you merge with another company, it's never a slam dunk. Opportunities get lost in the shuffle, and that was more often true than not of media mergers. When NBC merged with Universal, there were no guarantees. At the time, cable was largely a distribution system for rerunning content from elsewhere. NBC seized on the opportunity to play a role in providing new content. Broadcasting was working at the time. The numbers were good. When Cap Cities bought ABC, they didn't know then that ESPN would turn out to be their most valuable asset. ESPN today is worth more than the ABC Television network, all their stations, and their studios. The same is true for NBCU; the cable networks represent the most value. So it wasn't just GE getting used to the idea, although it could see cable growing in importance and starting to chip away at the broadcast audience share. It was about people like Bob pulling the right business and legal and strategic levers, and lining up the partnerships and acquisitions to better position NBC. Having an effective game plan is one thing; having just the right mix of skills to execute it is quite another. ❖

So in spite of the misgivings of just about everyone involved, we went into cable and made a success of it. It's one chapter—a big chapter—in the unique 30-year story of GE's relationship with NBC. ABC was sold to Disney in 1994, CBS was chopped up and it is a different animal. NBC is the only one that still kept everything together—news, sports, cable, all that stuff, for that whole period of time.

Wright to the Point

Almost 2 decades later, I did it all over again—moved NBC into more cable, movies, theme parks, and the Internet. More on that later. For now, the point I want to make is that the strategies in both cases were much the same.

You start with having clarity about your business priorities: what you want or need to accomplish and why. At GE, we established our strategic objectives every year in a rigorous process we called the S-1. We would have an honest dialogue with GE's senior management about where we saw ourselves going and how we expected to get there. Imagine GE's surprise when we told them we planned on taking the major broadcaster they just bought into cable! And it wasn't that simple or that quick. But going through this process is your main defense against the danger of all successful businesses: being right for so long that you end up being wrong.

As the media landscape evolved from broadcast to cable to the Internet, we went through the same process of assessing, setting goals, and planning ways to achieve them. We developed a business model that enabled us to better compete in a changing media world. We developed strategies that reduced our exposure to volatility. Then we developed services by adding new assets and platforms to replicate what had proved successful for us before. The process was the same whether it was cable or the Internet. It was that simple and that complex.

Behind it all is a willingness to be honest with yourself, your employees, and your shareholders about the future prospects for your businesses and the marketplace in general against the back-drop of changing technology and economics. Such honesty is not easy, but it is accurate. You can't argue with it and you can't deny it. It's what took NBC from a broadcast network to a diversified media company. It takes you from where you are to where you need to be, regardless of the obstacles or characters or issues you encounter along the way.

Our ultimate success in cable and everything else we did well depended on three things: knowing our brands and who we were; encouraging risk taking and thinking outside the box without boundaries; and valuing creativity.

The mid-1980s was a frothy period during which GE and NBC became concerned that NBC was getting too much exposure to cable. Well, we were—because I wanted it that way! They were always concerned about the telephone companies becoming a big competitor and worried about satellite. It was a lesson in how you should be more fixed on where you know you need to go than getting wrapped up in all the things you think may be a problem. Risk is not always where and what you think it is.

The story of NBC is the story of anticipating change and being prepared for it. Alongside our business development strat-egy, something else was consistently at work: a commitment to innovation—because it is the only effective response to inevi-table change.

8

Chuck Dolan, Cablevision, and Me

LaGuardia Airport lounge
New York City
July 1983

❖ **Chuck Dolan, founding chairman Cablevision Systems.** I remember being thrilled to have NBC as a partner. It was the same feeling I had the first time I came to New York. I was 16 years old when I got off the train at Grand Central from my home in Cleveland, and the first thing I did was walk up Park Avenue to 51st Street and turned left to Rockefeller Center and NBC. To my mind, that was the center of New York. And that's where I landed up in business with Bob Wright. ❖

Chuck Dolan is not like anyone else in the cable industry. He is a tough negotiator but a gentleman's gentleman, plain and simple. He was the rogue spark that made even impossible ideas seem possible. The concern was never whether his ideas were brilliant or worthwhile, but how best to finance them. He would worry about that, too, a little, but never enough. And that made NBC and the deep-pocketed GE a perfect partner for him.

But that came later. In 1983, I almost went to work for him.

During my time at Cox Cable, Chuck and I often met up at cable industry meetings. We learned that we both had ties to Long Island (I was raised there, his company was based there), and we had the same deep affinity for content and programming. We quickly became friends. So when we returned from an annual cable conference late one summer afternoon in 1983, it just seemed natural to retire to a lounge at LaGuardia Airport after we landed rather than rush back to our offices, for what turned out to be a very candid conversation.

Several weeks earlier, Dolan had made me an offer—to join his family business, Cablevision Systems, as its operating CEO. In the airport lounge, away from the hustle of the workplace, we talked about it for a couple of hours over coffee and sandwiches. Our discussion was easygoing and without tension, but in the end, we couldn't make it work. I wanted more equity and autonomy than Dolan offered. So, with regret and undiminished mutual admiration, we agreed to disagree and separately went on about our business.

Our personal and professional relationship was never jeopardized. Instead, a few years later we forged a long-term partnership that was far more productive than me working for him would have been.

It happened this way. In September 1988, just 2 years into my NBC presidency, Chuck and I resumed discussions, this time about crafting an alliance between our companies that would allow us—a broadcaster and a cable operator—to pursue program opportunities neither might have otherwise done alone. We named it Rainbow Programming Services, owned 50/50 by Cablevision and NBC. It gave NBC half interest in dozens of regional sports channels and the national entertainment channels American Movie Classics (AMC) and Bravo. And it gave Cablevision a badly needed financial cushion. Although it was the eight-largest cable operator in the US, Cablevision was losing $23 million annually. Dolan knew that sharing the cost of creating and managing cable channels, and tapping NBC's know-how, would assure new revenues. With $410 million in annual operating earnings, NBC was the most profitable TV network and ready to assume risk in diversifying its cable content.

For our part, we knew that a partnership with Cablevision would give us a bridge to other cable operators with many program services we would never have attempted on our own. All in all, a perfect win-win partnership. I had a dry-run 6 years earlier at Cox when I led it into a programming partnership with Dolan's Cablevision, which was the forerunner to Rainbow Media. Chuck had offered to bring in Cox, Comcast and Tele-Communications Inc. as investors in his early collection of eclectic entertainment services at the time: Bravo, The Kung Fu Channel and The Playboy Channel. Pitching the deal to the conservative Cox family dominated board of directors was surreal! Anna Cox was a proper former US ambassador to France who enthusiastically embraced the idea of supporting televised arts on Bravo. Garner Anthony, my boss, was the open-minded but cautious husband of Barbara Cox, the chain-smoking matriarch. The room went dead silent when I mentioned Playboy until Barbara sealed the deal with a rousing, "Sounds kinda neat! That's a hell of an idea!"

That frequently was the response I got from anyone I pitched Cablevision ideas to over the years. It was everything I could do to keep up with Chuck and his unconventional notions, many of which we actually executed. I knew better than to take him lightly. Seven years after launching his first cable system, Chuck sold it to Time Warner along with Home Box Office, which he had created. That's how Time Inc. came by HBO and the valuable Manhattan cable franchise. Time Warner left Dolan the cable franchises on Long Island, which were thought to have almost no value. Chuck created Cablevision on those Long Island systems, and soon it was on its way to becoming a $1 billion cable operator. So whenever Chuck called or came by my office, I made time and listened intently. I knew another adventure was under way.

The truth is Chuck always knew there would be a way to make things financially whole, even though the process would not be pretty. He was willing to take that risk in order to move the needle. That's the kind of partner you want when you are trying to blaze new frontiers and challenge conventions.

And I'd do it again.

❖ **David Zaslav.** Bob always used his relationships to build NBC into a major cable program player, and his most important relationship was with Chuck Dolan. There was a constant ebb and flow of ideas between them, then a rigorous discussion about the channel we wanted to launch or the program direction we wanted to go, and then we would get in there and fight it out with the other team. But ultimately the strong personal relationship and respect between Bob and Chuck prevailed, and things would get done. These guys genuinely liked each other. It was like magic.

Cable was very unstable in the 1980s. It wasn't clear that programming for cable was going to be a good business. So Chuck and Bob used each other and their companies as a hedge and got twice as far together as either could alone. Back then, Chuck was limited by the size of his company as one of the smaller primary cable operators. So more times than not, NBC/GE would provide the funding and Dolan would open doors, which allowed us to take a lot more swings together.

We lost a lot of money on cable for a lot of years, and not a day went by that Jack Welch didn't ask about it. Bob's mantra was, "I know we're losing money, but we need to be here, and eventually I believe this will be a business worth betting on." And he was right. ❖

❖ **Josh Sapan, chief executive officer Rainbow Media Holdings, now AMC Networks.** When Bob agreed to make NBC a Rainbow Media partner in 1989, it was considered a daring and even foolhardy move. Cable programming was a big financial risk, so it required an explorer's mentality to try new things, knowing you might fail. Bob made a similar call 2 decades later with NBC's purchase of Universal Studios. And it also succeeded against all odds.

Chuck was the rugged individualist and tough negotiator to Bob's disciplined strategist. Bob's participation was largely one of construction: assembling the pieces and approaches that helped shape the modern cable business. You only need to look at NBC Universal's cable assets today. They contribute the lion's share of the company's overall profit, and every one of them had their roots in a vision that started with Bob. NBC's cable-ization was Bob's doing. ❖

Not everything was always hunky-dory with Chuck. We had an especially rough time over FNN. The 1991 recession prompted a pullback in advertiser spending; all media companies suffered a loss of revenues and earnings, Dolan's heavily leveraged Cablevision Systems in particular.

Failure for some is opportunity for others, and I saw this as a chance to continue our cable buildout. So we began pursuing the bankrupt Financial News Network. To me it seemed an ideal way to fortify CNBC, which was struggling to gain subscribers and advertisers. GE balked, so I turned to Cablevision, our CNBC partner, to share the risk. When Chuck began to get cold feet, I knew our alliance could be in trouble.

Cablevision was notorious for financially overextending itself; at the time, it was $1 billion in debt. It was rough for Chuck. Cablevision's losses continued to mount on the sports channels, and CNBC continued to spew red ink. Dolan told me he wanted to get out of CNBC and be reimbursed for his original $34 million investment. I told him since Cablevision was voluntarily withdrawing from our CNBC joint venture, NBC and GE were not obliged to make it whole, but he would get a large tax loss. Cablevision potentially faced serious covenant issues on some of its loans from GE Capital. So I told Chuck he could walk away from CNBC, and NBC/GE would continue the buildout.

It was a difficult discussion that rocked the core of our friendship. Chuck was stunned and disappointed. In the end, Cablevision forfeited its stake in CNBC. So NBC assumed full control of CNBC and paid $155 million for FNN, the integration of which changed the course of business. But the tension and hurt feelings from that break rippled through the partnership for years. Unfortunately when Dolan withdrew, NBC/GE had to assume 100 percent of CNBC's losses.

❖ **Tom Rogers.** You have to understand their symbiotic relationship to realize why their partnership worked in good times and bad. Chuck saw Bob as someone who was strategically smart and understood industry dynamics. Bob considered Chuck someone who appreciated the creative potential for cable programming and a willingness to try new things. They were both very tough negotiators skilled at dealing with cable's very tough crowd. Bob is extraordinarily good at seeing all sides of a controversial or difficult issue. When he and Chuck stood together on something, it was hard for anyone to resist. That's principally how they got so much done.

The respect Bob and Chuck had for each other far exceeded any friction that existed between them or their companies. On an operating basis, it was difficult to get the companies to work well together, which is why Cablevision and NBC eventually went their own way.

The low point of their partnership was when we were going after FNN to strengthen CNBC in its early years and Dolan wanted to bail on us. Cablevision was always highly leveraged and a lot of companies were struggling at the time because of the weak economy and slow cable uptake. Bob essentially told Chuck that if he didn't want to go along he could just hand over his 50 percent interest in CNBC and go home.

Marc Lustgarten, Cablevision's then chief negotiator and a principal architect of the company's growth strategy for 2 decades, was outraged. He told me that Chuck felt it was the most heavy-handed move he had ever seen in the business—and he had been involved in a lot of heavy-handed moves! After that, Cablevision began taking a harder line on many of the things we wanted to do with them, and generally became less flexible. But the partnership didn't stop functioning, and Bob and Chuck never stopped talking.

The high point of the NBC-Cablevision partnership was more personal: a Radio City Music Hall benefit Bob and Chuck organized for Marc, who died from pancreatic cancer on August 30, 1999. Marc was more than counselor; he was the heart and soul of Cablevision's thought process as it morphed from a small cable operator into a broad entertainment and sports colossus. There was comfort and hope for all of us in celebrating Marc's life and raising funds for pancreatic cancer treatment and cure. Marc would have liked the star-studded October 4 black-tie event that marked the reopening of Radio City Music Hall just a month after his death. ❖

Cablevision was the most influential driver of NBC's entry into cable. And NBC was the wind in Cablevision's sails as it struggled to gain greater footing in an industry of giants. We learned how to leverage Cablevision's position to try new things, and we sometimes got a little ahead of ourselves. In fact, there were at least two instances when our partnership failed in projects that could have had tremendous financial payoff. The cutting edge usually comes with a price.

The first was the Olympics Triplecast, our trial pay-per-view offering during NBC's telecast of the 1992 Barcelona summer games. We were taking a free-wheeling approach to showcasing the less-watched live Olympics events in ways that even ESPN did not imagine. It was universally opposed by broadcasters, cable operators, advertisers, GE—and viewers. We lost a lot of money—$100 million total. After an initial meeting with Chuck, Jack Welch was convinced the financially troubled Cablevision would not keep its promise to underwrite half of the losses. No one was more surprised than Jack when I handed him a check from Chuck for $50 million several months after the Olympics. Chuck later told me he upheld his end of the bargain because he believed that we had given the Triplecast our best effort and that other cable operators fell short on their marketing and support of the service.

We applied everything we learned from that experience to produce more profitable Olympics pay cable efforts in subsequent years, which consumers and advertisers eventually embraced. In the end, we gained more than we lost, although it was painful for us at the time.

Our second major failing was SkyCable, an alternative satellite-to-home service brainstormed by NBC, Cablevision,

General Motors' Hughes Electronics and Rupert Murdoch's News Corp. We got as far as the February 1990 press conference at New York's posh St. Regis Hotel, announcing the unusual $1.3 billion venture, before it promptly began to fray.

If SkyCable had succeeded, it eventually would have morphed into something called DirecTV. So for a $40 million investment, NBC would have had a considerable ownership stake of DirecTV's $40 billion business—a jackpot return. If we had been able to put all the pieces together, SkyCable would have been an important strategic and economic undertaking that would surely have changed the balance of media power.

❖ **Tom Rogers.** To execute on his cable plans, Bob built a separate army that was really successful and practical and aggressive—and Chuck Dolan was a general in command. There was a value to the Cablevision deal beyond the properties that we invested in. It gave us chess pieces to play the game, to not only participate broadly in the cable industry but to make other deals. The partnership overall gave us access to the cable club. This was especially true after the failure of the SkyCable venture, after which our relationship with the cable guys dramatically improved. They saw NBC, primarily a broadcast company, was willing to take a hit for them. They saw we were substantially invested in their industry with stakes in AMC and Bravo, A&E, and the History Channel and regional sports channels, in addition to creating our own from scratch like CNBC and MSNBC.

NBC ended up with a greater ownership, economic investment, and governance in many more cable channels than almost any other media company at one time. So as an anchor of the cable industry, they couldn't deny us. When Comcast assumed ownership control of NBCU in 2011, 85 percent of the operating cash flow was generated by what was arguably one of the healthiest, most competitive cable businesses in America, yet the company's overall self-esteem was low because its broadcast was in a slump. The people at NBC didn't feel like they were winners because the NBC TV Network wasn't winning. It's strange how that dynamic still prevails after all this time. ❖

30 Rockefeller Plaza
Bob Wright's office, 52nd floor
New York City
June 12, 2002

No matter what endeavors we pursued that succeeded or failed, Chuck and I remained bound by our Rainbow partnership. More than a decade later, it had expanded to include regional sports networks co-owned with cable kingpins John Malone and Rupert Murdoch, in addition to American Movie Classics, Bravo, and our own local sports and news channels. We had succeeded well enough that by 1996, Rainbow Programming accounted for 1/3 of Cablevision's estimated $2.5 billion acquisition value. By 2000, Rainbow was 26 percent (or about $1.5 billion) of NBC's $13 billion in newly created assets. Rainbow and Dolan had become so important to our company's economics, I good-naturedly referred to Chuck as "the thirteenth apostle of NBC."

So it was bittersweet, but not completely unexpected, when after 13 years, we cashed out of the Rainbow partnership in 2002, taking all of Bravo with us. It became our first major entertainment cable network. NBC unloaded its 25 percent stake in Rainbow by paying Cablevision about $400 million in GE stock and $250 million in cash for the remaining 80 percent of Bravo it didn't own. That allowed GE to maximize its return for relatively little investment. It was a choice arrangement unique to good partnerships.

Our formal business relationship ended in 2002, but our personal relationship flourished with regular telephone calls and lunches, and serving on the board of AMC Networks, which was built on Rainbow.

❖ **Brandon Burgess.** NBC's complete acquisition of Bravo in October 2002 was all about what I call harvesting the golden years. Bravo was incubated in the early 1990s and was a core element of Rainbow. We had wrestled for some time with the possibility of acquiring the channel by itself or along with other Rainbow assets. That's when we decided to buy out Cablevision and take full control of Bravo as our first major entertainment cable channel, which was a big deal at the time. It was a very attractive, seamless deal that got us into the cable entertainment business for the first time as a wholly owned operator. NBC's stake in Rainbow was worth $1 billion and the purchase price of Bravo was $1.25 billion. We owed Cablevision the increment of a quarter billion dollars, which we ended up paying for by buying $250 million in Cablevision stock and then giving that back to Cablevision in a tax-free exchange.

And the rest is history. Bravo's value tripled and its household distribution increased from the high 70s to somewhere in the mid-90s.

It was a different way of creating value than our 50/50 venture with Microsoft to create MSNBC, which NBC also eventually took over. Both were examples of transactional harvesting of NBC's investment portfolio. It took more than a decade for Bravo and MSNBC to be accepted as full assets. They helped GE get its head around the fact that we were getting competent in what we were doing in cable. After that, it was all about transforming NBC into a much bigger, diversified media company with the Universal merger. ❖

Chuck and I remained career-long friends and business partners, bobbing in and out of various programming ventures that swung from huge successes to painful failures. But they always managed to push the envelope. No one else could have pulled it off. Our daring enterprises became the glue that cemented our business and personal relationship for the next 2 decades and advanced both our industries. And I'm proud to say that our personal friendship remains undiminished.

Atlanta, Georgia
May 22, 2011

Our 2011 Autism Speaks walk at the International Plaza in Atlanta was very well attended. Suzanne and I were there to participate as usual and to speak to the crowd. Then, the night before the walk, I get a call from Chuck Dolan. He has a home down in Wellington, because some of his children are active in big-time horses, and that's the polo capital of the US. Chuck leaves me a voice message that he and his wife, Helen, want to go on the autism walk with us the next day. He wants to know where to go and when to be there.

So I call back with the particulars, warning him not to drive to the walk because there will be thousands of people there. It's easier to hire a car and have the driver drop you off at the starting point.

Now, you have to understand something about Chuck. He's in his 80s, and he refuses to have anybody drive him around Florida. Well, the next day we have the morning walk, and there is no sign of Chuck. I have people out looking for him. He doesn't carry a cell phone with him, so there is no way to contact him. Then, out of the blue, Suzanne and I see Chuck and Helen walking around in the crowd, taking it all in. Chuck's got a fancy single-lens reflex camera with him, and he's taking pictures of everything going on around him. When we finally meet up, he says, "Gee, I'm sorry we're late." And then Helen explains: Chuck got a speeding ticket!

"I can't believe I got a speeding ticket," Chuck splutters. "I was doing sixty in a forty-mile-per-hour zone. I was coming down Southern Boulevard, which is a six-lane road, and it's Sunday morning and it's *empty*. It's like the German Autobahn. People were going eighty on that road and I got stopped for going sixty!" The car he drives is a 1980s Jaguar convertible. It's not a great car. It's not a reliable car. It's not a car that an 80-something guy should be speeding around in. He's a billionaire and this car has not been restored, but he loves it. I doubt that even agreeing in September 2015 to sell his family's Cablevision Systems to French telecommunications giant Altice for $17.7 billion will change Chuck's buying habits. He remains a scrappy pioneer and a simple man with a good deal.

The thing about Chuck is he's always engaging; he is a very creative guy. He's as interested as ever in programs and ways that people can connect with material. And he has that inherent curiosity about how to do these things. The idea of connecting people and information, that's what Chuck loves to talk about. That's his whole life.

Wright to the Point

The right partnership is a powerful thing. It is a companionship of compatible resources and intersecting interests that can raise you to new heights, professionally and personally. I have been fortunate enough in my life to know three such partnerships— with Chuck Dolan; for a while with Jack Welch; and for many years with my wife, Suzanne Wright.

There are two fundamental reasons why you form a partnership. One is necessity. Maybe you don't have the ability, money, time, or effort to pursue a business endeavor yourself. Maybe there are certain resources or capabilities you don't have that the other party has, or vice versa. The second reason is that you can accomplish what you want to do more quickly and economically with an ally. Sometimes you have the cake mix and another party has the frosting. And sometimes the best strategic alliance —or "coopetition"—is with a competitor.

You have to believe that your partner can contribute enough of the right resources so that the venture becomes successful, and when it does, you can't feel bad about having a partner. You would be surprised how many people in business worry about the problems of success. They worry about whether the other guy has too much, or more than they do. A lot of that goes through people's heads in corporations all the time. They don't want to share the success with anybody.

Large companies generally like to think they know enough about something that they can do it by themselves. Sometimes that works and sometimes it doesn't. Sometimes, by the time they get it done, it's too late. Or they don't want to give up control. So they avoid partnerships if at all possible because they can be difficult to manage. They would rather just buy the assets they need, which can create other problems.

Look across the business landscape, in good times and bad, and you generally don't see a lot of partnerships or joint ventures—and there is a reason for that. They can be tricky to negotiate and execute, and there are never any guarantees they will be successful. But strategic alliances with others can be an absolute necessity to growing a company that is lodged inside a corporation that does not want to invest in your future vision. That's what I faced at NBC. Partnerships with companies like Cablevision and Microsoft were an end run around GE's aversion to taking risks and investing in emerging businesses such as cable and the Internet, where it was imperative for NBC to gain traction.

The only way I could advance my cable agenda was to identify companies that needed what we had and that had what we needed, and then negotiate a win-win arrangement to build something more together. It sounds simple. It wasn't.

And it has not been any easier trying to build Autism Speaks from scratch. We have woven together every kind of partnership we know how—from regional parent groups and legislators to Google—to secure the funding and resources we need. I'm convinced the nonprofit world needs to learn to do partnership better.

Through it all, my most successful and cherished partnership has been the one with my wife, Suzanne. For nearly 50 years, she has been the heart and soul of what we were able to accomplish at NBC as well as at Autism Speaks. To this day, we complement and support each other beautifully to get the job done.

Partnerships have been the cement that has held my life together.

9
The Business of CNBC

Office of John Malone
CEO of Tele-Communications, Inc.
Englewood, Colorado
September 7, 1988

John Malone was arguably the most powerful man in cable. His company, Tele-Communications Inc., was the nation's largest cable operator. He had an electrical engineering degree from Yale and a PhD in operations research from Johns Hopkins. But he built his reputation and fortune leveraging his strategic investments and acquisitions, which made him and TCI core to every major cable deal and issue for decades. It fittingly earned Malone the nickname Darth Vader.

Establishing, supporting, or eliminating players from the cable business made him a Vito Corleone-like figure. He would give as long as he could get something he wanted of lasting value in return. So when I was developing a strategy to move a reluctant NBC into cable, I knew just where to turn.

In September 1988 I traveled to Malone's mile-high headquarters in Englewood, Colorado, to personally appeal to his better angels to help NBC get in the cable news business. I knew he would at the very least look at any startup, acquisition, or rescue, knowing his move would set the market price for cable properties. It was an eerie experience sitting across from Malone in his office, which was noticeably devoid of television screens and other technological distractions. You could almost watch the intricate thought processes as he considered putting his money, clout, and resources to work.

By the end of that meeting, the two of us had crafted the concept for a business channel as a way for NBC to enter 24-hour cable news. Malone promised his support as long as we did not directly compete with CNN, took the struggling Tempo Television channel off his hands, and gave TCI's cable systems favorable carriage terms. Malone's handshake guaranteed TCI's broad, paid distribution of the new channel as long as it was backed by NBC News. The consummate deal maker sold us Tempo and leased a satellite transponder as a platform for the new Consumer News and Business Channel when it launched April 17, 1989. Half of CNBC's initial 10 million homes were from Tempo. And that's how NBC gained entry to the exclusive cable club.

NBC was just another chess opponent for Malone, but he had all the moves. He brilliantly leveraged what he had for more, and I left satisfied to have CNBC part of the scheme.

❖ **David Zaslav.** In order to launch CNBC, the cable guys had to let us in *their* business.

At that time, no cable channel was making money, not even CNN, and it wasn't clear that business news would do any better. But John wanted to tap the resources of NBC News to draw cable subscribers. So with a handshake agreement from John, Bob left to literally go door-to-door to the other major cable operators seeking similar support for CNBC. The new channel launched in April 1989 as the Consumer News and Business Channel. And just like that, John Malone got us in the door and into the cable news business.

When NBC finally had a cable channel of its own, CNBC, they set up in New Jersey where no one wanted to go, Bob was the only person who visited there regularly. If they had tried to make it more a part of NBC News, it would have killed it. The power and politics of NBC looked down on it. Cable was viewed as the kids' table for a long time; a place where NBC lost more than the cost of two primetime series pilots. But Bob just nurtured CNBC and stayed the course. ❖

❖ **Tom Rogers.** CNBC was a fresh voice in news that just happened to be loosely linked to NBC News, which had no distinctive presence of its own on cable. It became NBC's and the broadcast industry's first test with cable operators, network TV affiliates, and our own news division. No one trusted a broadcaster to get into cable and have any good come of it. And it became a real test of wills. It wasn't enough to demonstrate your honorable intentions. You had to be able to outsmart anyone who wanted to sabotage your efforts, including GE. Bob turned out to be our secret weapon with both. ❖

Two years later, as CNBC was still straining for acceptance inside and outside NBC, we had what I believed was a golden opportunity to fortify CNBC's resources and profits quickly and cost effectively. The long-struggling Financial News Network had filed for bankruptcy, and Tom Rogers and I negotiated a deal to acquire the troubled company. CNBC had only 18 million subscribers and mounting losses its second year. Incorporating FNN would double its subscriber base and put it on the fast track to profitability. I knew that 40 million homes were the key to success.

Then Jack Welch vetoed the deal. His argument was that it was too risky and that GE, as a rule, did not buy broken assets. But I knew NBC couldn't afford to lose the fight for FNN, and so I asked for a meeting to try to change Jack's mind.

The office of General Electric chairman CEO Jack Welch Fairfield, Connecticut
May 6, 1991

A bankruptcy court judge was about to decide FNN's fate. So, that day in Jack's office, Rogers held on like a bulldog. "Come on, Jack!" he pleaded. "This is a rare opportunity that will make all the difference. If we didn't think so, we would not have been camped out in your office the past two days!" I joined the discussion by speakerphone from New York. "This is what it takes to gain a more powerful foothold in the cable business, and it's only going to get tougher and more necessary in the future," I reminded Jack.

Welch, who insisted that each of GE's diverse businesses lead their respective fields, bellowed, "Is this a real business? Can we win it?" GE's board of directors was already uneasy about CNBC's startup losses and NBC's unpredictable entertainment economics. The unwritten rule at GE—if you bid on something, make damn sure you don't lose!—meant GE would have to increase its bid for FNN.

Jack turned to GE vice chairman Larry Bossidy, who was seated on the other side of his sprawling wooden desk. "What do you think about it?" Welch asked. "I just don't see how it makes any sense!" Bossidy responded. Glancing back over his shoulder, Welch could see Rogers was visibly stricken with disappointment. "Look, Tom. Do you really believe this?" And when Tom vehemently agreed, Welch said the magic words: "I'll reverse my decision and support the proposal if you can provide tangible evidence that John Malone will support the deal and not screw us."

"Done!" Rogers shouted. And before Welch had time to change his mind again, even before I signed off by phone from New York, Rogers was out of Welch's office to go buy himself a bankrupt cable service.

Having worked with him to hammer out new cable regulation on Capitol Hill, Rogers knew how to tap Malone's deep-seated influence and intellect. TCI was one of the major cable system operators that controlled Turner Broadcasting System, which was attempting to block NBC's acquisition of FNN on the grounds that it would be anticompetitive to its Cable News Network. In fact, Ted Turner appealed to his board of directors to back his own FNN bid. It was a vote that Malone, as a lead investor, could sway in CNBC's favor.

Rogers was betting Malone would protect his equity stake in CNBC. And he was right. Malone had every incentive to continue supporting CNBC, which was gaining a formidable, loyal viewer base and advertiser support during and after a historic stock market crash. Any disruption in the continuous stock ticker across the bottom of CNBC's screen, which was new to television in general, would solicit calls from viewers angry about not seeing their only real-time market check in the days before widespread Internet and streaming video. It turned out that business news *was* a real business.

❖ **Tom Rogers.** I remember telephoning John Malone in May 1991 to remind him that his equity interest in our business channel was being compromised by his support for Ted Turner's pursuit of FNN. To Malone's credit, Turner did not get approval from his board of controlling cable operators to aggressively bid on the faltering Financial News Network. That left NBC to make a virtually uncontested bid for FNN in bankruptcy court. Malone told Turner and other TBS board members that a run at FNN was not worth the risk of creating new monopoly concerns in Washington. Malone reasserted his pledge to provide CNBC exclusive placement on his TCI cable systems. But we kept him in check, vowing to significantly raise license fees for other NBC Network programming if TCI ever supported a competing business channel. That was the hand we played. John Malone taught us everything we knew. ❖

With solid backing from Malone, and Turner out of the way, I immediately turned to negotiate an FNN deal in bankruptcy court. GE paid $154.3 million for FNN on May 21, 1991—or $60 million more than Jack Welch intended for us to spend! CNBC hired only about 1/5 of the company's 300 employees while doubling its subscriber base to 40 million homes. Sue Herera, Bill Griffeth, Ron Insana and Joe Kernen were among the FNN anchors who became longtime contributors to CNBC.

The FNN deal provided momentum for NBC to establish CNBC's cable value while amortizing the news division's expenses even though everything about the operations was painfully kept at arm's length. CNBC became a training ground for on-air talent and less costly nonunion operations headquartered in Fort Lee, New Jersey, across the Hudson River from NBC News's Manhattan hub. Unlike broadcast television, it generated a new source of subscription and advertising revenues even as an unprofitable startup. But it wasn't until the mid-1990s, and the launch of CNBC Asia and CNBC Europe, that Jack Welch and the GE board began to appreciate its worth.

❖ **Roger Ogden, managing director NBC Europe.** Today, iPads and smartphones facilitate our ability to search for and find slivers of information. It has become second nature for us to find exactly what we are looking for. But back then, CNBC's real-time use of technology to cover business and the financial world had an impact. CNBC made the markets more democratic. It gave everyone—individual investors and senior company executives alike—the same information at the same time. It made everything about business more transparent and accountable. It created a generation of financial pundits and made names of Wall Street chief executives and their companies part of the mainstream. The new technology made it possible to push CNBC into international markets. There was no road map, so we created our own. ◈

Forging CNBC was a brutal effort. There was resistance and skepticism from everyone I had to deal with: NBC executives and TV station affiliates, advertisers, the NBC News division, and, of course, the top executives and board of directors at GE.

In the process, we demystified business news. CNBC began building segments and shows around personalities that included FNN carryovers and newcomers like David Faber. Taking their cues from ABC's fledgling ESPN, the producers created a sense of drama and urgency with countdowns and statistics and post commentary to major announcements by the Federal Reserve or big companies. It became a data-driven business, and the stock ticker across the bottom of the screen was the center.

Once we figured out that great data attracted audience and advertising revenues, we were off and running. The audience shifted from retirees to any-age educated investors. But if all we were doing was showcasing data and business news, then we would be too much like Bloomberg, so the news personalities we brought in distinguished us from the pack. It was our way of decommoditizing the business. The growth of the Internet devalued the novelty of our running stock ticker and other data, which was suddenly available to everyone everywhere on every kind of device. That's when viewers began listening to our business news anchors and expert contributors as equals. We had excellent presidents and chief executive officers of CNBC, including Al Barber, Roger Ailes, Bill Bolster, and Mark Hoffman.

And every pioneering step we took in cable further transformed broadcast television.

❖ **Tom Rogers.** It wasn't clear then—and it's still not—that major media companies have the ability to achieve productive integration between multiple parts of their business. CNBC, for a lot of reasons including its cost structure, was very much set up to be totally separate from NBC News. It was located across the river in New Jersey with nonunion employees and minimal direct involvement so as not to upset the news division status quo. As broadcast and cable got more comfortable with each other over time, branding and interaction increased. But the place where you really saw this take hold years later was on MSNBC. We had to take a low-key strategic approach to both cable news channels to make it look like we weren't even breathing the same air as CNN. ❖

❖ **Pier Mapes.** Even before CNBC's official launch, we faced huge dissatisfaction from our affiliates wary of cable. It came to a head at the affiliate convention in June 1988. Angry station general managers confronted me and Bob, demanding continuing cash compensation and program exclusivity—historical practices that were no longer economically feasible or justified with intensifying competition from cable and the Internet.

CNBC became the first battleground where many of these issues intersected. Even though some alignment between NBC and CNBC made strategic and economic sense, affiliates viewed it as the destruction of their way of life.

It got very, very tense during a closed-door session at the convention. Station owners stood up to read Old Testament passages from the Bible about truth and honesty. Bob and I just sat there listening to it all and catching the spears. When Bob finally spoke, he was strong and steady without raising his voice. He explained that CNBC was just good business and that cable was the future. We stood firm on our plans for CNBC, and the standoff made Bob even more resolved to keep the new cable channel separate from NBC News.

It was the opening battle of an affiliate-network war that raged for years. It eventually evolved into more of a mutual partnership that was redefined by changing technology, economics, and rules. The interaction and connection between the NBC TV network, CNBC, and other NBC channels are now commonplace. It's just that the years in between weren't pretty because of other major changes in network-affiliate relations that created a lot of paranoia and anxiety.

But when it came to CNBC, there were no easy trade-offs or ways to pacify their fears. All we could do is to promise there would be no encroachment on NBC News services and that the revenues generated by such cable networks eventually would offset broadcast revenue declines to keep NBC in business. It took the better part of a decade for them to see it for themselves. ❖

Ultimately, the issue became how to break through the mistrust with our own NBC insiders and affiliates while we were trying to establish an agenda for change. It was a difficult challenge because it was so unexpected. Broadcasters owned the world at that point, without teammates. No one expected cable to grow as fast and as strong as it did. When station owners realized that cable could get out of hand and that their own network was entering the fray, fears escalated about the money at stake. So their issue was protection. Broadcasters took a defensive posture with cable and satellite television, and some of their positions weren't very logical, even in the face of undeniable ratings and audience statistics.

None of this was helped by their skepticism about me, a GE executive who had spent some time as the head of a major cable company. That got in the way of them seeing that the clock was running a lot faster than they thought and that the competitive landscape was quickly changing, whether or not they liked it or agreed with it.

By the time NBC's cable portfolio included MSNBC, seven regional sports networks, and CNBC in 1997, the estimated value of the company's overall cable holdings was about $2.5 billion. But it still would be years before broadcast network affiliates began to recognize that if NBC wasn't in the cable business to win, a competitor would be.

❖ **Dick Ebersol, president NBC Sports.** Bob really believed that cable would be the future. He single-mindedly masterminded the whole way into CNBC and then found the right people to run it. The world was dazzled when they did that, because no one saw it coming. ❖

Wright to the Point

I made a decision when I came back to GE in 1983 after 3 years at Cox that I was going to pace myself, and I was going to pay a lot of attention to GE cultural issues. I was not going to let them get ahead of me, so that I wouldn't get caught off guard. I also decided that I was going to enjoy what I was doing. Whenever something I was working on wasn't enjoyable, I'd try to focus on the aspects that were enjoyable to me. It's a little like arguing with yourself. If you get tied down in the negative stuff, it will really break your back. If you ever got into any of that too deeply, you couldn't get out. You should keep yourself from being dragged down. It happened all day, every day.

Union-related matters—particularly during the development of CNBC, and later, MSNBC—were a perfect example of the kind of black hole I'm talking about. Ed Scanlon, who had formerly been the head of human relations for RCA, really enjoyed the union stuff and was very good at it, so I stayed out of a lot of it. I fully accepted responsibility for what we were going to have to do with the unions, but I also delegated it to people I was comfortable working with and trusting. Ed was an über negotiator—some called him a contract consigliere to me and Jack Welch who could stand up to any marquee talent or even 150 angry striking members from the National Association of Broadcast Engineers and Technicians storming Ed's office to protest labor negotiations.

If they had gone sour—and it didn't—I would have accepted that. It would have been my fault.

I also learned to rely on my family as an insulating factor so that I could separate from everything about the business. So that I could stay true to my roots and my principles. No matter how big you think you are, you should never forget where you came from. Because of the nature of what I did at NBC, I really could never completely separate the business because it permeated every aspect of life. But I never brought home the business problems that filled my day. The problems were fleeting; family would always be there. For a long time at NBC, I commuted back and forth from New York to Fairfield, Connecticut, so I had 3 hours in a car every day. That was a great decompression time for me. I would leave very early, at about 6 a.m., so I could get through the newspapers, read reports, and look over my agenda. I would get my thoughts clear so that when I got out of the car, I was ready to go.

That hour and a half of prep time in the morning made all the difference. The reason it is important has everything to do with leadership. Juggling so many balls, and trying to transform and grow businesses, requires motivating and monitoring teams of people to do the heavy lifting. If you don't have a clear sight of what needs to be done, they won't, either. And when you are constantly moving from one big issue or project to another and dozens of meetings in a day, it's easy to find yourself tangled up in the details instead of leading with a big-picture view of things.

Everything we accomplished at NBC was the result of teams of people working together by pulling and stretching in the same direction. Trying to make sure everyone is up to speed and focused on the same goals may sound mundane, but it is mandatory for making progress. The guy with the staff has to remind everyone where they're going and what they are doing when they get there.

10

Rebuilding After a Firestorm: The *Dateline* Fiasco

Dateline: *Waiting to Explode*
New York City
November 17, 1992

The scariest damn thing that happened at NBC, at least on my watch, came out of the news division, of all places. And it became a catalyst for jumpstarting all of NBC—news, entertainment, and sports.

It involved a rogue report on *Dateline*, NBC's weekly primetime news magazine, called "Waiting to Explode." (In retrospect, we can see the deep irony in the name.) It should have been a routine investigative report. Instead, it was designed—and manipulated—to generate ratings and attention by relying on high drama. Unfortunately, as it turned out, that drama was manufactured. Faked. It compromised NBC News's integrity and standards in ways that were unthinkable to many people, including me.

The story examined General Motors trucks whose fuel tanks exploded when rear-ended. Intriguing premise—if it were only true. The producer, Robert Read, decided to make it more convincing by staging a rear-end collision involving a Chevy pickup that exploded into a fireball. It was rigged with an incendiary device, which was not disclosed to viewers. That's the kind of thing that makes your heart sink. It defies everything a news organization stands for and works hard to achieve over time.

This is the risk you run when you empower people to take the lead and do what they think is right. They can make a wrong call for the wrong reason. I still believe it's a risk worth taking, even though this particular instance nearly devastated us.

The investigative journalism that was supposed to foster ratings and pride became a black eye. Worse still, the ratings stunt nearly destroyed the news division's credibility. News divisions were always considered the broadcast networks' jewels. Once that chain of credibility is compromised, it can never be fully regained.

NBC News took a pounding from General Motors, which immediately launched an investigation of its own. GM executives openly challenged the report's findings in a parade of press conferences, interviews, and articles. That generated angry telephone calls and correspondence from viewers who felt betrayed, and a lot of unhappy affiliates. Advertisers began yanking their commercials from *Dateline*. GM pulled tens of millions of dollars in advertising from *all* NBC News programs.

But it wasn't until February 11, 1993, that we took extraordinary damage-control measures. At the end of that night's *Dateline*, anchors Jane Pauley and Stone Phillips read a 3½-minute apology to head off GM's defamation lawsuit. The statement, carefully crafted by NBC's legal and news departments, called the crash footage "inappropriate" and conceded that "unscientific demonstrations had no place in hard-news stories at NBC." NBC agreed to pay a $2 million out-of-court settlement that included GM's legal fees and the cost of its internal investigation. Three of *Dateline*'s top producers associated with the report, including the executive producer, were dismissed. NBC News president Michael Gartner, who was unwilling to back off of his original written response to GM that he "did not believe that any statements made in the November 17 broadcast were either false or misleading," resigned. Prior to this incident, Gartner had achieved so much for NBC News. NBC's own internal investigation concluded that the report was the result of "bad judgment" and not intentional misinformation.

After the settlement was announced, I finally felt free to publicly comment, calling any such journalistic and administrative failures "indefensible." By the time of the annual affiliate convention in Orlando that May, I apologized for the embarrassment and then promised to move on with the rebirth of the network.

The *Dateline* fiasco was the kind of self-inflicted wound and moral misstep that every chief executive dreads. And it was especially ill timed.

1992 was the worst year in my NBC tenure. Our aging slate of primetime series had fallen to third in the ratings as we tried to chase almost exclusively after younger viewers primarily owned by ABC. After having dominated the primetime ratings for 6 seasons, generating more than $500 million operating profits at the peak, we had just posted a huge loss—more than $60 million. We all were demoralized by how fast and hard NBC could fall.

The *Dateline* embarrassment came at a time when we were vulnerable on all programming fronts and on our revenue and cost line. But it sparked a complete overhaul of NBC's programming—not just news, but also sports and general entertainment. Much of our later successes, especially in cable, can be traced directly to our triage efforts, even though at the time we couldn't all see that far into the future.

The way I saw it, we didn't just need time to regroup; we needed time to reinvent. *Dateline* was just the catalyst for change.

So by 1993, I decided to turn over operations to the content makers in the trenches. NBC was first and foremost a content company, and we had to do that best or we couldn't do anything else. We were going to clean house and rebuild.

❖ **Pier Mapes.** To appreciate Bob's response to our predicament, you had to understand what was going on in television at the time. Rupert Murdoch and the Fox network had a tremendous impact on NBC and NBC News. Once the fledgling fourth network won the televised rights to football and a real foothold by 1994, Rupert started raiding the networks' affiliates. Fox was hurting us all in the primetime ratings and our advertising sales. Before that, HBO and ESPN were taking some audience, but not a lot of money. Fox was the first major competitor the three networks had before cable exploded with an alphabet soup of channels like TBS and TNT and USA. That is the assault we were under in the 1990s. ❖

I made the bold call to hire three outside veteran program producers to bring their creativity to the executive suite, which normally was the domain of accountants and business-school types in three-piece suits. None of the three had experience overseeing a key network division, but they were all absolutely brilliant at creating outstanding content, and that's what we needed. Dick Ebersol was already president of NBC Sports, Don Ohlmeyer became president of NBC Entertainment, West Coast, and Andy Lack was named president of NBC News.

While the news division's problems were more publicized, all three key program hubs were troubled and in need of a new approach. All three of these guys were best known as free-spirited creators of successful content. I knew they would operate very differently from GE's typical executives. They were not administrators; they were inventors. That was a huge jolt to NBC's and GE's already rattled sensibilities. But I needed for them to take some chances, push the envelope, and mix things up. I gave each of them a month to devise an initial game plan to begin rebuilding our ratings and reputation. We needed to take swift action, set things right, and move on.

❖ **David Zaslav.** The *Dateline* incident was the scariest moment in NBC's history in my 20 years there because it was a breakdown of what NBC News and NBC were at its core. It put everything on the line. The idea that the news division would have faked something cut to the very essence of what we stood for at our best. Just when this happened, we were struggling to develop new hit series in primetime. It was a very difficult moment for us as a company.

I was at the meeting of NBC News and other network personnel in Studio 8H on April 12, 1993, when Bob made the announcement that changed the course of the company. He said that Andy Lack, Dick Ebersol, and Don Ohlmeyer—all three of whom were producers and not front-office executives—were going to run the company with him. They were reporting to him and running their divisions with plenty of autonomy.

That accomplished two important things: it got creative people running the company and helped Bob to convince GE and Jack Welch to get the hell out of there. We clearly were not going to win with a bunch of GE people running the show, based on the lows we had reached. But that was the positive legacy of it, and it was all uphill from there. Bob and those three—Lack, Ebersol, and Ohlmeyer—did a great job rebuilding and repairing the company after that. ❖

Dick Ebersol, Andy Lack, and Don Ohlmeyer had a lot in common. They were all producers of live events seen by large audiences, and they really loved what they did. They were inventive, forceful people with big egos and strong personalities. They were workhorses hungry to demonstrate they could accomplish more. I knew that the same qualities that made them ill-suited for GE's corporate offices would make NBC a success.

Ohlmeyer wasn't a scripted series producer, but he was a natural showman who knew how to create programs that millions of people watched. He began his career at ABC Sports as a protégé to the legendary Roone Arledge and had been a successful executive producer of NBC Sports events. Learning at the foot of the master how to negotiate and produce sports had prepared him for just about anything. Don looked at everything with a broader scope—and a brazen outspokenness. He had a real flair for unusual marketing and promotions, and he got involved in all aspects of sales, marketing, and station relations.

Andy Lack had impeccable credentials as a producer of acclaimed programs at CBS News. He had created the primetime news series *West 57th Street*, which offered a terrific real-time production style that was new to TV then. But like everything else in CBS primetime, the series lived in the shadow of the industry standard-bearer, *60 Minutes*, where Lack also produced special reports that garnered him scores of Emmy, DuPont, Peabody, and other awards. I brought him to NBC, on a recommendation from *Nightly News* anchorman Tom Brokaw, to defuse the *Dateline* mess and breathe new life into our news shows.

Of all the three division heads, Andy probably walked into the trickiest situation. News always has been sacred ground to the broadcast networks, a loss leader where they were hesitant to make any dramatic change. Andy had some very good ideas and a more realistic sense of the new financial realities.

Incidentally, Lack was brought back to NBC in 2014 after leading Bloomberg News. His mandate: once again restore the news division's reputation and ratings after *Nightly News* anchor Brian Williams was removed for fabricating information about his reporting experiences.

Dick Ebersol originally came to NBC in 1974, when he hired and then collaborated with Lorne Michaels to create *Saturday Night Live* and successfully launched his own *Friday Night Videos*, doing what he loved best—producing. He later moved to ABC Sports, where, like Ohlmeyer, he perfected his craft working for Roone Arledge. Then in 1989 I lured him back to head NBC Sports. I wanted him to apply the dramatic production and storytelling techniques he had learned from Arledge. He instinctively knew how to showcase and mine the human interactions that made for good television. And of course Lorne Michaels was as valuable in his own right, and even more enduring.

With *Saturday Night Live*, Lorne Michaels did something no one else has ever done: running a very difficult, very successful show on network television for more than 40 years. Guided by his genius, material has been created from scratch every week, 23 episodes a season, for 40 years. He has been the show's executive producer from the beginning, which is extremely unusual in such a fluid business. Lorne hasn't changed in all the years I have known him.

❖ **Lorne Michaels, creator and executive producer** *Saturday Night Live.* When Bob came to NBC Hollywood dismissed him as a lame cliché; a light bulb guy who didn't know anything about our world. We'd come up through different paths, but after getting to know him I found Bob to be an incredibly smart man who was very respectful of what we did on the creative side. He was an intellectual peer who always kept an open mind. No matter what came up, he always had your back. He understood our job was to sneak through their power, but it had to be funny and have some intelligence behind it, and that's very important; for creativity to flourish you have to feel protected. When you have that level of power and commitment and intelligence behind you, you can do amazing things. And you will take chances, and we did.

There was a wonderful moment with Bob and all of our *SNL* cast and writers meeting one weekend at the Mohonk Mountain House, which we did at the start of every new season. Bob came up with his oldest daughter Katie, and he talked about NBC as young, urban, and professional, which is where he wanted to go. Everybody came away from it with a clearly articulated vision of where he wants us to go that we never had before. No one had ever taken the time.

The show was in its 12th year developing a new cast which takes time, so *Saturday Night Dead* was the dominant headline. A lot of NBC's west coast entertainment executives were ready to cut the show. When asked, Warren Littlefield bluntly said it was up for grabs. Then Bob did an interview with the *New York Post*, and he came to my defense saying SNL and Lorne Michaels were here for as long as they want to be, and that was a direct knock-out blow to the west coast. He protected me and for that I will be forever grateful.

When we did something on the edge on our live show, we'd talk about it before and after, and he'd generally listen and support—even though I'm sure things like Sinead O'Connor tearing up the picture of the Pope couldn't have made Bob happy. You could just feel all the air go out of the room after that. I was doing this show that me and my friends in our 30s just wanted to watch. We pushed the boundaries because we had to give people something to stay home for on Saturday nights. ❖

Lorne was at NBC when I arrived there in 1986. He had worked as a writer on *Rowan and Martin's Laugh-In* in Los Angeles for several years before moving to New York City to begin *Saturday Night Live* in 1975. He created television's "informator" show—a cross between theater and satire, news commentary and improvisation. He has discovered and nurtured the talents of countless performers, including many who went on to be marquee names: stars like the Belushi brothers, Bill Murray, Chevy Chase, and Steve Martin. Every entertainment chief before and during my time as head of NBC was concerned that the cost to produce *SNL* and what we were paying Michaels was about three times what they thought it should be!

Don Ohlmeyer, who was a producer and head of West Coast Entertainment, protested the loudest, and he and Lorne had a very bumpy relationship. It might have partly been the biting political commentary of *SNL* players like Norman Macdonald that Don personally didn't like, or the significant property rights to the show amassed by Lorne over the course of his negotiations. I was under a lot of pressure then defending *SNL* to advertisers as big as AT&T and conservative right-wing groups like American Family, which had mastered the art of boycotting through mass mail-in campaigns. It was mostly edgy comments and recurring characters like the chain-smoking Vatican rock critic Father Guido Sarducci that sent the show's opponents over the top.

Lorne invited me to attend a summer hiatus retreat for the cast and crew he hosted one year in Mohonk in the lower Catskills, about 90 miles outside of New York City. I brought my oldest child, Katie, an avid fan and new college graduate. Once the writers and cast spent the day with me, they realized I appreciated and enjoyed the creative process and would continue to be a valuable front-office advocate. I honed respect and kinship with Lorne and his crew. Lorne and I would frequently take time to discuss controversial sketches and moves. I think he and the show lasted as long as they have because of the way Lorne handled the controversy.

He wasn't aggressive and kept his talent out of fights. There was never any screaming or name-calling. I was very comfortable with creative people, and I enjoyed being with them. They didn't have artificial limits, and they taught me that you never know how good it can be until you try something. You don't often see that outside the creative industry in a place like GE.

❖ **Warren Jenson.** In the early 1990s when Bob was building out his management team, we went through some really tough stuff. There was the battle between David Letterman and Jay Leno to succeed Johnny Carson as host of *The Tonight Show*. There was the whole *Dateline* debacle. Nighttime ratings weren't doing all that great at the time. And it seems to me, we were mostly coming up a day late and a dollar short. Every time we had a meeting about an idea we were going to pursue, the next day we would read in the trade papers about Rupert Murdoch having just done it. There was such furious, deal-a-day activity back then that it seemed someone was always a step ahead of you. One of the things Bob did was make the necessary changes midstream in 1992 so that we got through some of those tough events, and we got all of the right pieces in place. Our finance team could rip apart, analyze, and structure a transaction with the best of the best on Wall Street. Bob clearly had the support of GE. So we were able to go from reading about change to creating change and, I would argue, leading change on many fronts.

Andy Lack began to bring a different cachet to NBC News and tried to do something a little more avant-garde with *The Today Show*. Don Ohlmeyer coming to run entertainment was as big a deal as Dick Ebersol running sports. The two men were friends who shared a similar ABC Sports pedigree. People inside of NBC were shocked that the competition was being tapped to set things right. The shakeup was necessary to jumpstart the creative process, especially in primetime. Bob characterized the trio of new division heads as one-stop shopping for the creative community and a powerful front line that would restore NBC's overall leadership. And that's exactly what happened. ❖

Now I had three of my key coaches as producers; four, counting Lorne. Once everyone was on board, I urged them to reach beyond the old ways to reestablish NBC's leadership. There is no substitute for creative energy in any organization. It unleashes the best, most astonishing ideas. It gives people permission to think outside institutional parameters. That's exactly what NBC needed, and that's what we got with these three free-thinking executive producers. Even through waves of GE-ordered cost-cutting, I ran interference with GE to protect their efforts.

Lack, Ebersol, and Ohlmeyer cultivated teams of executives savvy and daring enough to test, but not violate, GE's rigid guidelines. We all knew it wasn't enough just to fix problems and reset the dials the traditional way. Our initial forays into cable already were taking us far afield of NBC's original structure and put us onto fertile ground for thinking about and doing things differently. Successful radical change was more important than a quick fix, and it depended on the ideas and courage of others.

This all unfolded against the backdrop of a media business whose fundamental economics were dramatically changing, and we were determined to change with it—or better yet, ahead of it. When you are at a company like NBC, one that has been successful but is in the throes of great change and has been acquired by an industrial conglomerate, you have two choices. You can either play your hand or you can just sit on your hand.

❖ **Don Ohlmeyer, president NBC West Coast Entertainment.** NBC approached me in the late 1980s a couple of times to run sports and news, but I didn't think news was fixable at the time. Then Bob Wright came to me in 1992 about taking over the whole West Coast Entertainment operations. My initial reaction was, why would I want to do that? But it was an interesting challenge to take a television network from third to first place in a declining business of network television with cable exploding everywhere.

The only reason I took the job was to win. I didn't care about all the heat I would get into doing what I thought was right. I didn't care what other people thought. I only cared about what came across the tube and what the audience wanted. Everybody hates change, but they don't argue when the numbers go up. ❖

I won support at NBC by demonstrating the value of bold change: Dick Ebersol and Randy Falco negotiated multiple Olympics commitments. Don Ohlmeyer and Warren Littlefield created bold series concepts and unusual marketing. Andy Lack recast *The To-day Show* completely with a curbside studio in Rockefeller Center showcasing NBC News's revitalized talent and newscasts.

After Brandon Tartikoff left in 1991 for a broader role at Paramount, Ohlmeyer and Littlefield swiftly moved to cultivate hits such as *Seinfeld, Friends, ER, Frasier, Will & Grace*, and even *Late Night with Conan O'Brien*. In the fall of 1993, the needle moved! We saw the turnaround begin with *Seinfeld* and *Frasier* on Thursday night and the official launch of Must-See TV—a phrase coined by our marketing executives John Miller and Vince Manze to launch NBC's rebranding in primetime.

❖ **Lorne Michaels**. Bob was always just honest. It turned out to be the best way to handle the Carson/Leno or Letterman transition on the *Tonight Show*. The people in the East (I was one of them) lined up behind Letterman. Mike Ovitz had his own agenda creating another buyer for late night hosts.

Afterwards, there was a lot of acrimony within the network. Dick was also on the side of Letterman at the time. And we sort of dodged this. And Carson, who Bob had a relationship with, I think stayed neutral or at least didn't talk to Bob about it. Carson later said he thought David Letterman was the heir apparent. When the decision finally came down, Letterman immediately went to CBS and Bob called me on a Tuesday night—our long writing night for SNL every week—to say the next morning he would announce a new late-night show following *Tonight* and that I would be executive producer. Bob said, "You'll figure it out, and I know it will be okay." That's when I suggested having Conan O'Brien audition from the ranks of writers we had used. And even though it was very wobbly in the beginning, Bob remained incredibly supportive. ❖

We invested well over $40 million annually in development for several years that didn't produce a single new hit. By 1995, there were signs the gamble was paying off, even in NBC's news division, where change was so often compromised by long-standing practice and privilege.

With Don's leadership, we developed new hit series and ruthlessly negotiated to keep our own hit shows (most notably *ER*) out of the clutches of the competition. We tapped Don's ability to pull strings, force change, and launch new ideas while tolerating his brash, disruptive style. There was no disputing his game-changing brilliance, or his penchant for self-destruction.

When Ohlmeyer and Littlefield finally struck gold, they beat the competition by record margins and laid a foundation for NBC to generate record annual profits—more than $500 million. By 1997–98, *ER* was number one in the primetime ratings, *Seinfeld* was number two, *Suddenly Susan* was number three, *Friends* was number four, and so on. We had 8 of the top

10 shows in primetime that year. Bang, bang! We owned the business at that point.

NBC became the only profitable national television network during Ohlmeyer's 6-year term. But Don, an Emmy Award–winning producer of sports and live entertainment, was eager to return to the production fold. So I was not surprised when he decided to leave at the end of his contract in 1999. He had fulfilled the mission and done a brilliant job of restoring NBC's primetime and late-night mojo.

At the same time the entertainment division was succeeding, NBC News restored its integrity and profitability while extending its brand to cable on CNBC. We expanded our reach with CNBC Asia and CNBC Europe and started new ventures like MSNBC and Court TV. The progressive changes Lack made to *Nightly News, Dateline,* and *The Today Show* were best remembered for the street-side studio at Rockefeller Center and delving deeper into timely topics.

NBC Sports became the first network to secure the four major league franchises at one time in football, baseball, basketball, and the Olympics, which we began bidding for in multiple-year packages. The Olympics franchise became a signature of NBC Sports and a vehicle for elevating the entire network. By then, the NBC Television Network was earning more than $1 billion a year and was able to support our cable and sports initiatives.

All of this growth occurred with the strict cost controls demanded by GE, including trimming the workforce from 8,000 employees to fewer than 5,000 and saving the company nearly $120 million in overhead. Ultimately, the goal was to convince GE that NBC was a growth business, not just a recovering business.

My vision for NBC was decidedly different from the agendas of so-called media moguls like Rupert Murdoch or Sumner Redstone. I wasn't empire building, I was trailblazing. It was not unlike what was happening at Disney at the time, where Michael Eisner and Bob Iger worked brilliantly together to take their company to impressive heights. When he got his chance to lead Disney, Iger was phenomenally successful. And CBS's Les Moonves was a close second.

All three of the senior creative executives did as well as they did because they had their own areas to manage with one mandate: improve the product and make it the best, most inventive that you can so the ratings and revenues will follow. But as gifted as they were, all were driven by huge egos and personal agendas that got the better of them from time to time.

By 1999, the chinks in the armor started showing. Andy Lack put on a full lobbying effort with Jack Welch, hoping to move into my position. And for a short time he succeeded. Just before Jack departed as GE chairman, he upended me in June 2001 by naming Lack to the new post of NBC president and chief operating officer. The following year, I quietly went to the GE board, of which I was vice chair, with concerns about why that arrangement wasn't working. By January 2003, Lack abruptly left NBC to become president and chief executive of Sony Music, to the surprise of many, and I resumed control.

Don Ohlmeyer left NBC at the end of his contract term and returned to ABC as executive producer of *Monday Night Football*, and eventually he took up painting and teaching television communications at Pepperdine University. Dick Ebersol's penchant for negotiating sports rights and Olympics deals on his own ran afoul of NBC's new owners at Comcast, and they parted company in 2011. Dick remains a trusted senior advisor to the International Olympics Committee.

❖ **Andy Lack, president NBC News and executive VP NBC.** Bob laid the framework for us to take NBC's greatest weakness and turn it into its greatest strength, and to take risks just at the moment that everyone expected NBC News to play it safe. Bob decided NBC was going to produce its way out of trouble.

So when I got there in 1993, there was an overwhelming appeal for new ideas—ideas we could chase with assurances not to worry if they didn't work. Bob and Jack wanted us to be creative, take risks, and they would decide if there was too much of a risk. They essentially said, "Just lay out your thinking behind the wish list. We'll fund it; we'll support it if we believe in it. If you can persuade us, we're off to the races together!"

Our mandate was to produce our way out of where NBC was. We set out to find the right people and back their ideas, and give confidence and responsibility to people for executing those ideas, knowing that some would work and others wouldn't. In our case, we got really lucky because they all succeeded.

I don't think any of the three of us were looking for management jobs at the time Bob convinced us to come to work at NBC. We had mostly avoided them for all the obvious reasons; being tangled in administrative stuff was not fulfilling. Bob had a new idea and a new design for how he wanted to run NBC. That evolved into Dick Ebersol having the most successful Olympics run of broadcast over a decade. It resulted in Ohlmeyer putting together an entertainment schedule that created Must-See TV. And it put into place for me the opportunity to give NBC the biggest strength in weekday primetime news of any of the three network news divisions as well as create a new event that changed morning television. What Bob and I did, by fixing *Dateline* first and then by reinventing *The Today Show* and creating a new studio outside in the plaza, was to set a new agenda for the entire news division. It gave us an opportunity to create an event every morning.

With that single move, the street-level studio for *Today*, we gained the trust of affiliates, and they gave us better clearances for all of our news shows. So by 1997, every NBC News show dominated the ratings. It was the most exhilarating project you can imagine. ❖

Wright to the Point

Most of the time, people just settle into their assigned work responsibilities. In that steady state, you'd be lucky if a business could actually maintain itself without going down. But that is not what will get you to greatness. For that, you need to do more than just maintain.

The formula is easy to describe, if not always to realize: Build a strong team, playing to everyone's strengths. Require accountability. Give people the tools they need to excel. Energize people to accomplish more than they think they can. Unlock individual potential to yield greater creativity and soaring productivity. Wholeheartedly encourage creativity and risk taking. Clearly state a vision everyone can rally around, putting the organization before self. And be willing to accept some failure in order to succeed.

When I put the three creative producers in place to manage NBC's leading businesses and craft its future, it was more than damage control. It was a solid, purposeful step on the path to transformation. That was the whole idea behind bringing Andy, Dick, and Don into the fray. They were able to get people out from behind the corporate wall to think and do things differently.

But news was not like entertainment or sports. It was and still is to some degree a sacred commodity whose integrity must be protected and defended. The loss of that integrity can be fatal. So what we did in saving NBC News from itself, protecting and growing its legacy, was hugely important to everything that came afterward.

Throwing money at a creative problem wasn't the answer for NBC in the early 1990s, but hiring and enabling great talent was. One of your jobs as CEO is to find ways to allow your best people to be more productive. So many people have such great ideas that never come to fruition inside of a big company, either because they are squashed or because they have to serve the corporate parent's greater needs. Sometimes your job is to just set them free.

One of the more unconventional ways I did this was issuing an April 23, 2001 memo to NBC's senior management and affiliated station executives. I asked for their recommendations on how best to compete in a program universe in which HBO's *Sopranos* garnered ratings and rewards because of the violence, language, and nudity—none of which were allowed on network television.

People are not perfect. You have to accept imperfection in order to strive for perfection. It's kind of a contrary thought, but that's what you have to do. If you are looking for perfection along the way, a lot of people are going to drop out. Creativity—which is essential to innovation, entrepreneurship, collaboration, and problem solving—is an imperfect process. But it will take a company to the next level.

11

Creating the Must-See
TV Money Machine

The office of General Electric Chairman CEO Jack Welch
52ⁿᵈ floor 30 Rockefeller Plaza
New York City
August 28, 1986

I'm not sure what Brandon Tartikoff was expecting when he was
summoned to Jack Welch's new office that day in 1986. After all, he
now had a new boss. GE, with Welch at the helm, had just closed
on its acquisition of RCA, which included the NBC network subsidiary. Up to that point, GE's main connection to the television industry was manufacturing TV sets, but Jack knew enough to know
GE needed Tartikoff to be part of the package.

Brandon Tartikoff was NBC's golden boy. When he succeeded Fred Silverman as network entertainment president in 1981, he
was the youngest person ever to hold that position. He jumped in
feet first, energizing NBC's limp primetime schedule one series at
a time, starting with *Miami Vice, Golden Girls,* and *Hill Street Blues.*
Then he rebranded the Thursday-night lineup into Must-See TV,
anchored by *The Cosby Show* and *Family Ties,* and by spring 1986,

NBC finished number one in the ratings for the first time in its history. Welch knew strong ratings would translate into hundreds of millions of dollars from NBC to GE coffers. He was determined to keep the golden boy committed to the peacock network even though Tartikoff worked without a contract. He was not only the creative inspiration behind NBC's newfound success, but a critical link to maintaining loyalty and support from the troops leery of "a GE suit" taking charge.

Standing at the doorway of Welch's Rockefeller Center office that day, Brandon looked like every mother's son—an affable, unassuming, lanky Yale grad known for his love affair with television. Welch bounded from his desk, hand outstretched, and bellowed, "Hello, Brandon; great job on the season win! That's what we want to see!" Brandon flashed his familiar boyish grin, shook Jack's hand, and looked over in my direction. We traded hellos and I gave him a look that said, "Don't worry; this is not going to be painful."

"Listen, Brandon, we appreciate what you are doing with NBC," Jack said, "and we want to know we can count on you going forward just as much as you can count on us." He handed an envelope to the young genius. Inside was a check for $1 million— a no-strings bonus to assure Brandon's continued contributions during my first year as his new NBC boss. Brandon didn't even flinch; his voice was steady and even. "It's been very gratifying to do this the way Grant and I had planned a few years ago: to be best and then to be first. Don't worry, Jack. I'm in."

It didn't surprise me that Brandon would acknowledge the powerful influence of Grant Tinker this way. They had made quite a team. Brandon was the 30-something wunderkind to Tinker's 60-something seasoned producer. As NBC president, Tinker had stabilized a free-falling NBC. In 5 years, he had managed to transform the third-place network, barely mustering $48 million in pretax operating, into a ratings leader generating more than $150 million in annual pretax profit. Through it all, he restored calm and dignity to NBC's chaotic entertainment division. Grant Tinker was a star who promoted an atmosphere of confidence and patience.

Now that he was stepping down as president, Tinker worked hard behind the scenes to convince RCA that the next president should come from within. But GE was adamant about being in control, and Jack had already decided I was going to take the reins at NBC. Brandon, for his part, wanted more recognition for his contributions to NBC's turnaround. So he welcomed me as the new kid on the block, someone who would respect his programming expertise.

Still, I knew I was stepping into a quagmire. No one gave me credit for the television savvy I had picked up at Cox Cable. To make things worse, there was long-standing animosity between NBC and RCA. NBC felt it had been abused and neglected by a corporate parent with industrial interests and no creative sensibilities. They expected GE to be just the same, if not more so.

By late June 1987, all this was compounded by the striking National Association of Broadcast Employees and Technicians paralyzing our television production and program schedule. In my first public comments sharing the dais with Grant Tinker and Fred Silverman, my two predecessors, at an industry lunch amid state senate and gubernatorial elections, I tried making the best of it with what I hoped was a little humor:

"Unlike a lot of people who will be making speeches in California over the next couple of months, I am not running for anything—but that hasn't always been the case. In my first year in this job I was definitely running for something. Namely—for cover! With the NABET strike, downsizing, and my memo on forming a Political Action Committee, I felt like checking into St. Elsewhere for an image transplant."

I set out from day one to immerse myself in NBC's business

and creative culture. I quickly learned that TV program development is an inexact science. There is no sure path to a hit series that could be worth hundreds of millions in advertising revenues and syndicated license fees. But some people have a knack for knowing a winning script when they read it or spotting a performer with star potential in an audition. Observing Brandon's knack for both was one of the few pleasures of my first year at NBC. He was comfortable enough in his own skin to be a respectful listener in program meetings and still deliver a blunt assessment. His candid, fluid rapport with series producers allowed him to be both encouraging and critical as he skillfully traversed their Hollywood egos and eccentricities.

Some of our best times together were visiting the sets of NBC's hit shows like *Cheers*, *Family Ties*, or *The Cosby Show*. Whenever we stopped by, it was clear that the performers and everyone behind the scenes adored Brandon. Because he respected their craft, he won their loyalty. They might well have pushed me aside as an outsider when I first arrived at NBC, but Brandon Tartikoff was my link. Brandon was a very good promoter of our shows, and all the producers knew it. So I made it a point to listen and learn.

While he was with us, Brandon brainstormed many different shows. Some flopped, others were wildly popular. His mind was always fixed on series concepts. One night when he was up tending to his infant daughter, Brandon caught Bill Cosby on *The Tonight Show* doing a hilarious stand-up routine about family life. The next day he approached the comedian about creating and starring in a domestic sitcom that became *The Cosby Show*. He conceived of an MTV-style cop show that eventually became *Miami Vice*.

During his time at NBC, Brandon demonstrated nothing less than genius. Working closely with Warren Littlefield, marketing chief John Miller, and his marketing co-creator, Vince Manze, he developed the concept of Must-See TV. Together they created an aura of change that was exactly what we needed. Independent producer Stephen J. Cannell attributed NBC's success to Brandon's "fine creative instincts" and willingness to take chances. Even after he cultivated the cornerstones of NBC's revival—*The Cosby Show, Cheers, The A-Team, Golden Girls,* and *LA Law*—Brandon was preoccupied with creating a new batch of series hits. He was like a traffic cop, masterfully managing teams of people, identifying promising scripts, producing series pilots, and shepherding new and aging shows.

And when things didn't go well, he was quick to take responsibility and set a new course. As NBC's primetime lead and series unraveled, his post-season assessment April 17, 1990 (courtesy of USC's Tartikoff Collection), was focused on positioning for the fall. "What we need is to put the blinders on, focus on the development, and stop reading the [trade] papers. These people are not our friends and have been rooting for our demise for the last 4 years. They're going to be disappointed once again. Keep the faith," Brandon wrote me.

Brandon and I would sit down at the end of every calendar year to assess the past year and plan for the future. He chose to work without a contract; he stayed because he wanted to, not because he had to. He was always worried about every show produced on his watch, and that tires a person out even if they are successful.

By 1991, Brandon was tormented by circling Hollywood agents who tried everything to lure him from NBC to run a studio. Eventually, he did just that. He went to Paramount at the urging of Creative Artists Agency's Michael Ovitz, who kept reminding Brandon he had maxed out on television experiences. In a letter of parting thoughts he wrote me June 26, 1991, on

Paramount letterhead, Brandon was critical of scheduling moves made by his second-in-command, Warren Littlefield. "You can see help and vision is needed," Tartikoff wrote. "It hurts me to see NBC get beaten by itself."

So Brandon left NBC for Paramount in 1991. That same year he was involved in a horrible car accident with his young daughter, Calla, near the family's summer home in Lake Tahoe. Suzanne and I spent about a week with his wife, Lilly Tartikoff, and both their families, keeping vigil at Washoe Medical Center in Reno, Nevada, where Calla was in serious condition and Brandon was recuperating from a broken rib and pelvis. Their parents were charming, substantive people. Lilly's parents were Holocaust survivors, and Brandon's parents were among the 61 passengers who survived the deadliest-ever collision of fully fueled Pan American and KLM jets on a foggy Canary Islands runway on March 27, 1977. Lilly was a wonderful wife to Brandon. She was his counselor and helper and a major part of the civility of Brandon's own success. We have remained close to Lilly and her family over the years.

❖ **Brandon Tartikoff, from his 1992 memoir *The Last Great Ride*.** Success is a matter of how smoothly and how wisely you adjust to the shock of the new.

It had been a little over a year since I left the catbird seat at a television network for a new job at Paramount. I knew the television business was changing. But I never realized just how fundamental those changes would be or how fast the future was rushing toward us.

During a meeting in Wright's hotel suite during the National Association of Television Program Executives in Houston in March 1990, I told him that I thought the time had come for me to leave. I had done this job for 12 years, and every year was like a dog year—each year feels like 7. My original inner circle had moved on, and I was starting to feel like Peter Pan. Every fall I greeted a new batch of eager young faces at the staff meeting, all expecting me to take them to Never-Never Land. Maybe it was time for me to grow up.

I had finally come to a crossroads, about to leave NBC, a place I'd both grown up in and helped grow.

Bob's a savvy guy. He had doubtless sensed my restlessness before the conversation and couldn't have been more gracious. Inevitably our talk drifted to my future plans. I had been seriously considering a venture into independent production. I wanted to follow through on some of my own ideas as a producer instead of trying to persuade others to execute them. And I had several series commitments at NBC which gave me some advantage and security in the risky development of shows. I told him I planned to leave in 6 months, by June. Bob asked me for an extra year to effect a more orderly transition. How could I say no to a person who let me operate with total creative autonomy for 5 years? ❖

About a year after the accident, Brandon left Paramount to spend more time with 8-year-old Calla during her long recuperation from the serious brain injury she sustained in the crash. His return to television included producing the short-lived late-night talk show *Last Call* and *The Steve Banks Show* for public television. He briefly served as chairman of New World Entertainment and co-chaired AOL's Entertainment Asylum, the first-ever interactive broadcast studio. But he continued to frequently pen me letters offering valuable friendly advice about programs, producers, and other NBC executives. Like in October 1992 when he encouraged me to launch a weekday-afternoon version of *Today* to liven up NBC's sagging daytime ratings (I wish I had!) or explaining in early October 1992 why he encouraged actor Tim Robbins's guest hosting of NBC's *Saturday Night Live* but had nothing to do with what became his controversial live monologue at the opening of the late-night show.

Brandon was only 48 when he died August 27, 1997, from Hodgkin's lymphoma.

Brandon Tartikoff and I shared a common core. We both were natives from the South Shore of Long Island, New York, making our way to Hollywood by different paths. Brandon's father worked in the garment district. My father was a heating and cooling contractor, and my mother an elementary school teacher. Our parents were old-school. Brandon, who was 6 years my junior, was the youngest network entertainment president ever when he accepted the job in 1981 at age 32. I was the youngest president/CEO of NBC when I was appointed in 1986 at age 43.

During his time at NBC, Brandon cultivated the urban-adult, slice-of-life comedies and dramas that defined NBC's revitalized brand. He godfathered the Must-See TV Thursday lineup long before the marketing slogan was officially launched in fall 1993. It's not an exaggeration to say that Brandon Tartikoff completely revitalized NBC's primetime schedule, providing a solid springboard for a complete reinvention of the network. I know he would have been a leading force for transformation of our entire industry, had he lived long enough.

❖ **Herbert Schlosser.** In broadcasting, when the ratings are good, the meetings are short.

Primetime is not the profit center now that it used to be for anyone. But NBC was focused on primetime because it finally became the top-rated network, and Grant Tinker, a handsome gentleman and skilled program producer with great taste, made it happen. So Bob had a tough act to follow. Bob took his lumps at the beginning, but GE backed him, and then he began to make the structural changes necessary to create entire new businesses like cable. ❖

Warren Littlefield, who was Brandon's deputy during the development of the greatest hit shows of that time, assumed management of Must-See TV and other program development as NBC's entertainment chief. Although he developed many new cutting-edge hits, Warren was judged very harshly in the shadow of Brandon's success and never won the individual recognition he thought he'd earned. Almost as soon as Warren took over, Brandon's popular program lineup began winding down right in the midst of the worst advertising recession since World War II. There was a lot of pressure at the time to just get rid of everyone who rode out the early 1990s recession, to clear the decks and start all over.

Warren eventually shared the job with and reported to Don Ohlmeyer. It was an awkward pairing from the start, but necessary, and somehow NBC got healthy quickly. Don brought a whole different energy and life to the place. He was a very big contributor with his larger-than-life presence, saying, "We can do this!" But some of the programs that got us healthy were continuations of earlier hits, like *Frasier*, which was a spin-off from *Cheers*. It was Warren who developed and got that on the air. He also developed *ER* and *Friends* under Ohlmeyer's 6-year leadership.

We had stellar successes. *Seinfeld* lasted 6 years at a full 27 episodes per season, *ER* ran for 10 years; so did *Friends*. They were among the last of the great adult comedies and dramas before reality TV set in and changed American primetime sensibilities yet again.

And after those shows became enormously successful, Warren was constantly under the gun from people saying "What have you done for us lately?" He and Ohlmeyer put 25 shows on the air, for 10 or 12 episodes each, and they all failed. That's a lot of shows. The first episode of every comedy cost about $1 million, and the first episode of every drama was about $3 million. You're talking about hundreds of millions of dollars by the time you are finished with this whole thing. We spent $40 million or $50 million every year on program development, for 5 or 6 years, that didn't produce a hit. Suddenly the words of CBS founder William Paley, often quoted by Brandon Tartikoff, were coming back to me: "No show that's a hit costs too much and no show that's a failure can be cheap enough."

The relative few hit shows were so strong they sustained us during this process, so we didn't resort to producing the suddenly popular reality shows until we had to. They were just coming on when Jeff Zucker became involved in entertainment programming. And they became a substitute for our inability to create sustainable drama and comedy shows. We were not always able to get the right shows on the air at the right time. The problem couldn't be solved with money, because a good program and a bad program often cost exactly the same. There are no guarantees about what will resonate with viewers.

Must-See TV had long legs. It lasted less than a decade but heavily contributed to making NBC a money machine for GE for twice as long, or about 17 years. In that time period, we just had a few bad years, and that was mostly due to the recession of 1991–93 and a poor programming cycle that came at a time when we were taking heavy losses on our first organically grown cable channel, CNBC.

In 1993, just as Must-See TV was taking hold, the rules that prohibited broadcast networks from sharing in syndication profits were abolished. Before that, the inequities were dramatic. For instance, NBC spent $2 million per episode to produce *ER*, but once the show moved to aftermarket syndication, Warner Bros., which owned the show, was entitled to all the sales revenue—$10 million per episode. The change in that law, known in the industry as fin-syn, shorthand for financial interest and syndication, was a watershed event. It set off an explosion of primetime economics. NBC and the other TV networks suddenly had a new steady revenue stream.

The financial interest and syndication rule battles impacted every one of NBC's program negotiation and creative relationships. *Miami Vice* was a good example. That show, starring Don Johnson and Philip Michael Thomas and produced by Universal, was a hit from its very first episode in 1984. It was a very good contemporary show that just knocked you out with its fast cars and sex appeal, fashionable clothes, and music rolled up in a way that was acceptable to network censors at that time. It was the most expensive show we had on the air then. So when its ratings began to decline in the fourth season, I saw it as an opportunity to propose a renewal in which NBC and Universal would share the future risks and rewards.

Universal would not hear of it. Sid Sheinberg, the studio's president and chief operating officer, was among the Hollywood heavyweights who did not want to share their wealth with the broadcast TV networks. He wanted NBC to continue underwriting all production costs, including the usual deficits.

"We've got this problem," I told Sheinberg over the phone.

"I don't have a problem," the onetime Texas lawyer fired back. "*You* have a problem!"

"Well, if we decide not to renew the show, then you have a problem."

"Then I will just take the show to another TV network!" Sheinberg threatened.

I reminded him that even the most wildly popular series can get lost in the shuffle when moved to another network, especially when its ratings begin to fall. It's not a pretty picture. I proposed evenly splitting the show's production deficit and ownership, an idea Sheinberg flatly rejected. Then I offered to pick up the entire deficit in exchange for complete ownership of the series, including previously aired episodes. That would have preserved a huge syndicated interest for Universal while sparing the studio any future deficit.

"No!" he shouted. "I don't want to see you network guys owning any shows! I am a studio and I should never be selling you any of my rights! I'd rather have the show go off the air!"

And that's exactly what happened. When Sheinberg abruptly yanked *Miami Vice* off the air as a result of that conversation, I knew the system was broken and it needed to be fixed. But I was pretty much out on a limb alone in the early 1990s, fighting Hollywood and Washington for those rights. My counterparts at CBS and ABC did not feel as compelled, and the Fox network was still new and too young to care.

Our work with legislators in Washington, where I spent a tremendous amount of time, finally broke that counterproductive cycle. It took more than a decade to change the regulations and longer than that to alter Hollywood's mindset. It seemed with the renewal of every Must-See TV hit series, a new battle had to be forged.

Taking control of content development under financial interest and syndication deregulation (fin-syn) allowed us to have a vibrant NBC productions organization. It allowed us to devote resources and talent to producing shows instead of just underwriting other people's ideas. The tenor of our negotiations and relationships with talent changed as a result because we finally could keep the cost of production in check. Overall, the return on investment in the shows we produced was multiplied many times. We had no idea just how critical this would be 3 decades later in an age of streaming media and exploiting content libraries for billions of dollars annually in a multiscreen universe. Our fin-syn efforts look brilliant today since the broadcast TV networks would be buried relying only on linear advertising. They'd be dead!

The problem with hit shows is that they eventually end, and you have to begin again from scratch with no guarantees you can achieve another spark. We owned the business in 1995 when *Seinfeld* was number one and anchoring our primetime ratings. By 1997, the tables were turned and we were desperate to re-new *Seinfeld*. I personally negotiated with Michael Ovitz to keep *Seinfeld* on the air. He controlled that show because of his position as Jerry's agent and was a forceful personality; he also received a cut from the show. But we knew Jerry's interest was waning.

The final negotiation with Jerry took place at my Trump Towers apartment in New York City with Jack Welch, me, Jerry, and his manager, George Shapiro. We all knew each other well and rather quickly settled on one more season of the show. Jerry was to be paid $67 million for one season under his personal ser-vices contract. (NBC paid separately for the show, about $3 mil-lion per episode because of an expensive supporting cast. So we were spending nearly $200 million on that one series.)

Then Jerry started to hesitate. He had demonstrated he could succeed at the daunting task of being series producer, writer, and star without help from his longtime writing partner, Larry David, who had left 2 years earlier. It's fair to say Jerry found it very dif-ficult. He wanted it to be the funniest show ever written. He was concerned about slipping ratings; he wanted to go out on top. So it was like being in jail. It wasn't fun anymore—but it couldn't have been more lucrative.

Jack Welch was flabbergasted by Jerry's hesitation. Why would anybody turn down $67 million for a year's work regardless of the ratings performance?! That 2-hour meeting broke without a signed contract. We all agreed to give Jerry some breathing room. Later that night, Jerry telephoned me. "Bob, I don't want to do it. We really should stop here. I just don't feel comfortable doing it." I asked him to take a day and speak with his team. But he called back the next day, firmly declining the offer. That was the end of it. It was a matter of professional pride for Jerry; it was never just about the money. That NBC's Must-See TV hinged on his show was our good fortune and, in the end, our problem.

The irony is that the show has earned over $500 million in secondary rights since it went off the air. *Seinfeld* is the best-managed and most successful off-air show of all time.

Donald Trump represented a completely different kind of negotiator and on-air talent.

Donald Trump and *The Apprentice* debuted on NBC in January 2004 in the waning days of Must-See TV. The series ran for 6 seasons and spawned *The Celebrity Apprentice*. But Trump, whom I had known from earlier real estate development dealings, kept on running right through the 2016 presidential race. When I ran GE Capital, Trump tried to convince GE to move its newly acquired RCA and NBC from Rockefeller Center into a Television City he proposed to build on land he bought for $40 million out of bankruptcy from the Pennsylvania Railroad. He came over to my GE Capital office in Greenwich to make the pitch, and our discussions went on for some time while I got other bids, which I used to negotiate a better deal for GE at 30 Rock.

As head of NBC, I got into business with him as half owner of his Miss Universe pageant and eventually *The Apprentice*, which suited him perfectly. I made him executive producer of Miss Universe because he was complaining about the judges and production, and he knew how to make it work for television. I remember Trump telling me, "You know me—the two things I really love in life are women and food!" He brought order to all of the shows he was part of. As ratings for *The Apprentice* rose, so did Trump's fees. The great negotiator claims to have made more than $213 million over 14 seasons from *The Apprentice* and related branded products, many of which bore his likeness.

By 2015, Trump was skillfully capitalizing on his TV-honed brand as a leading Republican presidential candidate. Suzanne and I were all too familiar with his cocky, abrasive style as longtime friends with Donald and his wife, Melania.

The rest of the world was taking a deep dive into his character. Trump is always looking for action and not afraid to negotiate with anyone—even members of Congress. He is extremely win-oriented; that is his whole being, and he's very good at sharpening and using the tools he has available. These would be very useful leadership attributes at this point in our country's history. I think people underestimate Trump's ability and cunning. He has brought to the forefront important matters like immigration and jobs in a way that can no longer be ignored. So he will bring sharp focus on the issues he can exploit, and influence others to take positions and action. It doesn't mean if he got elected he would be able to get any of it done. But he would be a fierce advocate. He would take no prisoners. His allegiance to party would be secondary to his allegiance to his own ideas and agenda. Running for office has given him political credibility. Trump will be a national political figure for many years to come.

Wright to the Point

The fine art of negotiation determines how successful your business can be, whether it is a public corporation or a nonprofit. It is your ability to persuade others to follow a strategy, to embrace a vision, to do what needs to be done. That was an especially tricky task when it came to NBC programming because of the unpredictable nature of personalities and circumstances. There was so much over which you had no control. The best you could do was to empower others to do your bidding, challenge conventions at every turn, and keep a handle on all the moving parts. Rule changes and new technology continuously reset boundaries and expectations. But the process remains the same: leverage what you know, yield to what you don't know, and ardently pursue what you want. The deregulation of the broadcast networks' financial interest in the ongoing revenues of series they underwrote leveled the playing field for us as program producers and distributors. That equalizing act altered all of television program dynamics and economics.

So, too, with the change in state laws governing insurance claims for autistic patients, who previously had struggled for any kind of coverage or recognition. The grueling grassroots crusades we waged to win insurance reform in more than 40 states were not unlike the individual victories NBC scored with program producers, particularly in the 1990s, when the TV network system was in flux. Every new negotiation brought with it the opportunity to push the envelope a little more. You can't push people in new directions without expecting pushback on the way to exciting results. If you accept the responsibility to be a powerful force for good and for necessary change, and to create something of value that didn't exist before, then the conflict and chaos are just temporary means to a more satisfying end.

That's the way I ventured into NBC's TV program culture and challenges in 1986, and into autism's troubled, disconnected landscape in 2004 (more on that in Act 3). The difference was that at NBC I had Brandon Tartikoff as a knowledgeable, innovative navigator. Suzanne and I, along with our early supporters, were on our own fashioning Autism Speaks, with only my instincts and principles that had served me so well in the business world. As it turned out, fighting to broaden insurance coverage for autism wasn't so different from changing regulations in advertising-supported television. They were necessary reforms for progress. Once goals and strategies were set and cloaked in a marketing campaign that everyone could understand—whether it was Must-See TV at NBC or raising awareness at Autism Speaks— we focused tirelessly on the risk-taking. Nothing could have been achieved without it.

12

Travels with Johnny Carson

I met Johnny Carson through NBC Entertainment chief Brandon Tartikoff when I arrived at NBC in 1986. Johnny was a man of enormous talents and a huge star, but he was also unfailingly kind, unassuming, and approachable. We hit it off right away, and over the next 15 or 16 years we had a great deal of fun together in some exotic locations. After he retired in 1992, Johnny and his wife, Alex, were always heading off to some fascinating part of the world, and Suzanne and I would frequently find ourselves lucky enough to be invited to join them. Together we traveled to Russia, Africa, Alaska, Catalina Island, England, the San Juan Islands, and Vancouver.

Johnny was no ordinary tourist. He worked hard to learn about the places we were going. He had an extraordinary gift for languages and a great deal of self-discipline. In preparation for our trip to Russia, he taught himself Russian. Before we traveled to Africa, he learned Swahili. Not many people know this, but during World War II when he was in the navy, he was assigned to a code-breaking team, a position that required great skill with numbers and memory and abstract thinking—not what you might expect from one of the greatest comedy entertainers of all time.

Russia, USSR
July 1990

In late June 1990, Johnny Carson and I planned our first trip to Russia. We both had always wanted to go, and we were especially intrigued by the political and social upheaval unfolding at the time. The dramatic transformation of the USSR grabbed our attention, and we wanted to see it firsthand. Johnny was very interested in Russian history and culture, and he even took the extreme step of learning to speak Russian.

Suzanne and I flew into Frankfurt and then to St. Petersburg to meet Johnny and his wife, Alex. We were greeted by a young man who introduced himself as a chaperone. He explained we had to listen to him and follow him. And we did, even though we knew he would have to report on us at the end of every day.

In St. Petersburg we were all eager to visit the Hermitage, the beautiful old museum. We were shocked to see, as we walked down the corridors, stacks of paintings leaning up against the wall and sculptures scattered on the floor, covered by sheets. Our guide explained these pieces had been moved from storage warehouses around Leningrad because of concern about security, given all of the change the country was going through. The fear was that the people inside those warehouses would take some of the artwork for themselves or sell it.

We learned from news stories in 2006 that more than 200 art objects, from jewel-encrusted icons and paintings to jewelry and silver chalices, were stolen. Eventually it was revealed that a handful of underpaid curators and at least one university professor had sold some of the museum pieces to antiquities dealers and pawnshops. I remembered what it felt like, the four of us wading through some of these treasures, haphazardly strewn around the rooms—shocking and surreal.

In Moscow, we went to our NBC News Bureau, which was very much in the news at the time. Jim Maceda, one of NBC's best-known news correspondents, was the bureau chief. While he was taking us around, he explained the political and social climate in Russia at the time.

On our last day in Moscow, we asked if we could go to a working-class Russian restaurant where tourists were not allowed. We ended up in a family-owned business catering to a lot of workmen and shirtsleeve types. Johnny began trying out his Russian, ordering things, and soon a lot of strange food showed up. Suzanne, Alex, and I just looked at each other. Meanwhile Johnny had turned around to the table next to us where seven or eight men were huddled around large platters of dark meat and very dark gravy—what we used to call mystery meat in college, meaning no one knew what animal it came from.

Suddenly Johnny got up, moved over beside the next table, and said something in Russian. Our tourist guide was frowning. I had my fingers crossed that this wasn't going to turn into a bad situation. And then the others pulled up a chair so Johnny could join them at the table, and pretty soon Johnny Carson was telling jokes to the Russian working men who were eating these big plates of mystery meat! And the Russian workers were laughing in just the right places, so they clearly got the punchlines.

Other people in the restaurant started looking over at that table, where an American was hosting a kind of informal comedy club. Every other joke they would toast Johnny with another shot of vodka, and by the time we got out of there, we had had more mystery meat and vodka than we care to remember. That was one of the first trips we took together, and even though it lasted only a few days, it was marvelous.

Africa, the Serengeti plain
February 1994

Although I was not keen about going on an African safari, I was willing to go along with Johnny. I figured if I could go toe-to-toe with Madison Avenue every spring in upfront sales, then a few wild animals on the open plain wouldn't scare me.

A safari chief met us in Tanzania, complete with equipment and a team of men, and took us out to the Serengeti plain, which turns out to be the world's largest racetrack, stretching through several countries. We were going out to view the great annual migration. If you get on the right spot in the track, you can witness a great movement of nature far from civilization.

In preparation for this trip, Alex Carson had called to tell us there were severe luggage restrictions. I have traveled all my life, and I take these things with a grain of salt, but I could see Alex was taking the rules literally, and she sent us information about what we should take. We had to pack everything into two small nylon bags, called a C1 and a B1. The B1 bag was the bigger of the two, but it was still pretty small; the C1 was about the size of a briefcase. So I picked up a couple of these bags from a Rockefeller Center store and brought them home to Suzanne, who gave me some stern sideways looks as if to say, "Forget it. I'm not taking my clothes in those bags!" Well, she was always trouble anyway.

So we ended up packing those bags and a lot of other bags, too. We met up with the Carsons in the Amsterdam airport, and sure enough, there were Johnny and Alex with just their two small bags. Together we flew on to Tanzania, where we were met by our guide from the safari company. All of us hopped into the truck for the first leg of the trip, the Carsons with their minimalist luggage and us with our big pile. The guide looked at me and I looked at him, and he said, "Oh well," and threw it all on the truck. And so we were off, with Johnny looking longingly at his two little bags.

That first truck took us to a breakdown area where there were a few more trucks and a bunch of guys and a lot of stuff. Next thing we knew we were on a single-engine plane, flying to an airstrip where we met up with more trucks and still more stuff. One big truck was loaded up with camping gear and another with food and supplies, and we ourselves got into a big Land Rover. We drove for hours to our camp for the first night, a remarkable spot right on the relative edge of the Serengeti plain. Suzanne and I had a tent, the Carsons had a tent, and the guys running the safari had a tent. It was like being on the 50-yard line of a football game, and in the daylight, we were thrilled to see what was going by.

Our first morning in the Serengeti, we could see elephants in the distance, and the guide said we could get closer, so we started driving into a wooded area with a narrow pathway. We could hear in the distance what we thought was thunder, but it turned out to be the elephants coming from behind us. We asked the guide, "What do we do?" And he said, "Nothing, we just stop." Even though we were in a big four-door Land Rover, the elephants were coming right next to us. The vehicle was high off the ground and they were still quite a bit higher than we were, and they were moving swiftly and banging into the Rover a little bit. There were at least 40 or 50 of them in an area of trees, and we were occupying the little trail they wanted to be on.

We wanted to go to a riverbed in the middle of the Serengeti where it is very flat, like West Texas. The guide told us that hippopotamuses hang out in the bottom of the riverbed. So Johnny and I decided to explore on foot, with the Rover creeping along behind us. We saw a big animal rising out of the riverbed covered with mud, and we both thought, "Well he can't be very fast." Then suddenly, he started up toward us, picking up speed. Johnny and I looked at each other in surprise, thinking we had better get back in the Rover, which by then was well behind us.

We were 20 yards from the Rover and the hippo was about 50 yards away, closing in on us. He came right up to the vehicle and banged it with his head. The guide told us that was just a warning; he could have knocked over the car and we would not have been able to do anything except to shoot him. Which you're not allowed to do unless it's a life-threatening situation.

That evening, as we all sat around the campfires recovering from our close encounter with the hippo, Johnny got up and joined the workers at their campfire. And sure enough, he soon had them laughing, speaking fluidly in the Swahili he mastered during the prior 6 months. It was like that Moscow restaurant all over again. The safari workers didn't know Johnny Carson from the man in the moon, but they were listening to him and laughing, and soon they started telling their own jokes. This went on for well over an hour, with Johnny doing what he loved best.

Our last day in Africa was in Nairobi. We had no personal security as we entered the airport departure terminal. We were standing in line to check in when a military truck pulled up to the doors. Out jumped 20 or so heavily armed paramilitary "troops" shouting and screaming at all of us to empty our pockets, and give them our money and passports. Johnny, Alex, Suzanne and I put everything we had in our hands into our pockets and pretended not to understand. Just as the bandits got to us, police arrived shouting over a spray of gunfire. The bandits fled and we boarded the plane and left as fast as we could. We all were wrecks with our passports and wallets intact!

Juneau, Alaska
July 1995

By the end of 1994, Johnny asked me and Suzanne to take a trip to Alaska with him and Alex the next summer. So in July 1995, we met up in Juneau.

The next day we decided to charter a plane to a nearby glacier. We flew right up to the mountain in a small, single-engine prop plane, and then landed on the glacier where the ice and snow were packed hard enough for landing. Our small plane was dwarfed by this glacier. In fact, there is nothing smaller than a small plane in Alaska. Everything in the state is so big: beautiful mountains and rock ledges.

When we were in Alaska, we took a day trip into a long fiord with a glacier at the end. We went several miles without seeing anyone. Just as we got to the glacier, we were standing on the boat's bow taking pictures when a horn blew and a large riverboat-type cruise boat came into sight. There were a few guys on the deck waving to us. Johnny waved back and more guys appeared waving. Suddenly the whole upper deck of the boat was filled with waving men. Johnny was waving like crazy as the captain came out and told us that this was a gay cruise he had seen before! Johnny glanced back at Suzanne and me and quipped, "Well they certainly must like the show!"

The next day we made our way by boat to Sable Island. John Jacob Astor had a fur-trading post here, on this small island that faces both the protected passage and the raw Pacific Ocean. When we arrived we decided we had a taste for king crab. One of the locals told us there was a man nearby who sold them. Now, when they say "not too far away" in Alaska, you have to be careful about what that means—it could be a day's journey. We were directed to an old cannery that had once employed Chinese immigrants but was owned now by someone in the lower 48. So we decided to head there, even though the captain confessed he didn't know where he was going.

We wound up in a beautiful little harbor that was the site of the cannery. Back in the day, all the fish products would come in and be sorted, cleaned, chopped up, put into cans, and shipped out. Today you can still see the remains of the dilapidated wooden structures that were housing for the Chinese workers.

We were greeted by a very large fellow named Mark who welcomed us and said yes, he had king crab for sale. But first he insisted on showing us around and introducing us to his wife. So we tied up our boat and followed him to his really tiny house, where we met his wife, Mary, who was roughly the same size as her husband. She proudly showed us all the many dolls she makes by hand at their kitchen table with authentic Eskimo and other native costumes made out of leather. "Very nice," we said, "but we're really here for the crab." Silence.

Finally Mark spoke up. "I catch king crab and I keep them in a big container out in the water. But I am not allowed to sell crabs at retail. I'm only allowed to sell them at wholesale to people who have wholesale licenses." John and I looked at each other. Then Mark continued. "But... if you were to buy some dolls, I could *give* you some crabs."

Meanwhile, my friend Johnny Carson was staring at the dolls, trying to calculate the value of a king crab in dolls. But we were determined, so we told Mark that sounded terrific, and we started grabbing dolls. When we had a handful, Mark looked over at us with an expression on his face that clearly said, "That is not a lot of crab." Several armfuls of dolls later, we were making our way back down to the dock to get the crab when Mark paused by a small shack. His parents were inside, he said, visiting from Bakersfield, California. His parents loved Johnny, he said; could we take a moment to meet them?

So Johnny and I looked at each other and shrugged, as if to say, "Well, we're here and we have the dolls and we're on our way to get the king crab, and there are two people living in that shack from Bakersfield?!"

All the windows were shut and all the shades were drawn in this shack and it had to be a hundred degrees inside as Mark introduced us to the two older people. "Mom, I want you to meet Johnny Carson." And without a blink, she looked up from her knitting, looked right at Johnny, and said, "You know, I never liked Johnny Carson." John looked at her, smiled, and said, "Nice meeting you, too, ma'am." So we just backed out the door, Mark apologizing profusely. And now we *really* wanted those crabs.

Eventually Mark pulled out of the water a cage bound by heavy chains that must have weighed 250 pounds, and took out a giant crab probably 6 feet across. We just looked at him; we weren't exactly prepared with crab-carrying equipment. "Oh don't worry," Mark said. "I'm going to kill them for you; you won't have to take them alive." Then, he stomped on that sucker with his size-13 shoe and tore it apart with his bare hands—no gloves, no equipment.

It turned out to be probably the best king crab I ever tasted in my entire life.

13

The Ted Turner Factor

The Ritz-Carlton, Buckhead
Atlanta, Georgia
January 13, 1995

The luxury suite at the Ritz-Carlton, Buckhead in Atlanta where Jack Welch and Ted Turner met to size each other up turned out not to be big enough for the both of them.

Jack and I had traveled by corporate jet from New York that morning to meet the free-spirited Turner on his home turf. My team and I had negotiated a deal for NBC to purchase Turner Broadcasting System for $23 a share. It was structured as a reverse merger that would have made TBS a publicly traded company under the new name Turner NBC, controlled by GE. Turner would remain on the new company's board as an advisory vice chairman. It was a fair offer that would give Turner scale, if not the independence or control he craved. After years of false starts with Turner, this was my best shot to bring our companies together.

The only thing left was determining whether Welch, GE's acerbic chairman CEO, and Turner, cable's most enigmatic entrepreneur, could coexist and avoid getting in each other's way. It took less than an hour for them to demonstrate that was impossible.

Everyone, including Jack—and maybe even Ted—had difficulty visualizing how an impetuous guy like Ted would fit into the GE culture. Top-ranked executives at GE and NBC were used to seeing their work as an extended part of their social structure and family life. Playing weekend golf and dining or meeting Saturday mornings around the kitchen table in my Connecticut home for an informal work session was all part of the GE/NBC protocol. Was that Ted's way? We were about to find out.

During the flight to Atlanta that morning, Warren Jenson, NBC's chief financial officer, reviewed a letter of agreement he had prepared for Jack to sign. The last line just above Jack's "all the best" sign-off and bold signature read, "Looking forward to working with you for many years to come." Jenson had added it as a friendly gesture, something he routinely did for Jack.

"I'm not saying that!" Jack bellowed. He had just spent half the plane ride doubled over in laughter with me and Jenson as they tried imagining how Turner could fit inside GE's buttoned-up corporate ethos. It was an uneasy precursor for the Ritz-Carlton exchange to come. Removing that line from the letter wasn't an easy task for Jenson in those days before digital correspondence. All he had available was a small bottle of Wite-Out in his briefcase and a copy machine at the Ritz to reconstruct the letter.

As it turned out, all the fuss was for naught.

I was the only person in the room to witness the surreal encounter. These two enterprising, outspoken empire builders had stark stylistic differences and a strong dislike for each other. Welch had set disciplined expectations for executive behavior and financial performance inside his sprawling global conglomerate with such textbook metrics as Six Sigma. Turner had revolutionized television by executing his vision for 24-hour cable news at CNN and mainstream entertainment at TBS. But his unpredictable, free-spirited nature often got him into trouble with even his closest, most forgiving constituents. Ted had been sharing his grandiose NBC takeover plans with me for years.

Jack was very interested in an NBC-Turner merger, but he didn't want to bring Ted Turner anywhere near the GE board. It was still early in Jack's GE chairmanship, and he didn't want to deal with disruptive influences. And Ted, known for outrageous statements, could certainly be disruptive. Welch decided that day he would not negotiate with Turner about an appointment to the GE board or a higher position in the organization if he asked for it. In fact, Welch wasn't going to give an inch on anything the relentless Turner requested.

For his part, Ted had already decided he would push for more money and a vice chairmanship that would assure him a prominent place on the GE board. He had worked hard to boost TBS's value to $30 a share and wanted a golden parachute. Welch wouldn't hear of it. The minute Ted opened his mouth, Jack immediately cut him off. And that annoyed Ted. And that's when the trouble began.

Turner insisted he deserved extraordinary consideration given the entrepreneurial firepower he was bringing to GE's rigid corporate ranks. His ideas, contacts, and name brand were as valuable as the hard assets NBC was buying. "I've earned it," Turner demanded, looking Welch straight in the eye and leaning far across the cocktail table separating them.

"We can't do that! We're just not set up for that!" Welch snapped. What Jack was *really* saying was that Turner was a loose cannon. He inevitably would say something outrageous that would anger shareholders and investors. Welch and the GE board were already uncomfortable with the corporation's exposure to the erratic, high-profile media world of fickle patrons and roller-coaster revenues. That uncertainty would be exacerbated by expanding NBC's portfolio to include Turner's cable networks and recently purchased MGM studio, and Turner's own element of surprise.

As the tension mounted, Ted began barking like a dog. It was his very Turner-like way of demonstrating that he could, when pushed, be subservient to Welch and GE's conservative board. It took even the extroverted Welch by surprise. Ted wanted a platform to speak from and not have to worry about managing a company anymore. But he wanted to speak on any subject at any place and any time. And that wasn't what GE was prepared to give him.

Finally, an exasperated Welch and a ramped-up Turner gruffly shook hands and bolted for the door, leaving me and my team to pick up the pieces. The outcome might have been different that day had Welch at least given the appearance of courting Turner. But he didn't even try. So we lost that one.

❖ **Warren Jenson.** All Ted wanted was for Jack to embrace him and make him feel welcome into the GE family. But the meeting was not about charming Ted. We could have collectively romanced Turner a lot better than we did. Too much of it depended on Ted having to prove that he was GE-worthy. If we had really figured out a way to make him feel welcome, we could have done the deal. If it wasn't for that very tense encounter between Welch and Turner, NBC would own Turner Broadcasting System today.

The Turner people always thought they were buying us and we thought we were buying them, and no one just wanted to say outright what was going on because nobody wanted the dialog abruptly cut off. I think Bob and Ted knew how much sense it made to bring NBC and Turner together. I don't know why we didn't circle back with Bob about it to continue to work the deal after that failed meeting between Jack and Ted. The combination would have been pretty powerful. It probably would have made a huge difference in both companies and both men's lives. Ted would have been better off with NBC than how he turned out with Time Warner.

Bob could have consolidated NBC's power sooner, although he still could have done the Universal deal later. ❖

A week later at a Los Angeles press conference, Turner very public-ly announced that merger talks between our companies had been "terminated very amicably." The talks died, he said, because GE refused to relinquish control of the broadcast network. GE imme-diately fired off a clarifying statement that it had always planned to retain 51 percent control of a merged NBC-Turner, which it estimated would have been worth about $6 billion.

In a sea of media consolidation that was creating competitors with more clout and resources, I wasn't willing to close the door on eventually achieving some Turner alliance. With $2.4 billion in debt and $427 million in annual cash flow, Turner's hand would soon be forced, and I wanted NBC to be the one to take advantage of it. But Ted and Jack always got in the way.

❖ **Ted Turner, founding chairman CEO Turner Broadcasting System and creator CNN.** I felt Welch's pro-posal was inadequate, and I was surprised he didn't know more about our company. I really like Jack, but I was disappointed that he didn't do his homework, and he really didn't make much of an effort to get me. Welch was running a big conglomerate, but he didn't understand media and he had no appreciation for what we had created globally with CNN. They decided to come after me in a serious way because I kept coming after NBC. But I wasn't about to compromise my company or who I am.

All the television networks now are part of other companies. Not a single one stands alone. At one point, I had a handshake deal to buy every one of the broadcast networks, including NBC. I either could not arrange the financing or got vetoed by the cable operators—usually Time Warner—who had a majority interest in my company. I couldn't get permission. They told me that I had enough networks, that I had enough leverage.

If I had acquired NBC, I would have merged CNN and NBC News, and my Goodwill Games and the Olympics. I would have doubled them and marketed the daylights out of them. We could have combined resources, saved a lot of money, and made a lot of money. We could have redefined the economics of television, and nobody would have been able to come close to outbidding us for the right to the Olympic Games telecasts. There is no point in sitting around and dreaming about what could have been. It was great while it lasted, and I hope we did some good. I think we did. ❖

I wasn't ready to give up completely. So a month later, on February 14, 1995, we all met up again, this time in GE's executive conference room at Rockefeller Center. Ted, Jack, and I were joined by Tele-Communications chairman CEO John Malone, a savvy, soft-spoken PhD engineer, who was arguably the most powerful man in cable. We were there to discuss NBC's proposed minority investment in Turner Broadcasting. Any such alternative alliance required the blessing of TCI and Time Warner, among the dominant cable system operators who had a collective 37 percent veto control of Turner's company. We knew we had a problem with Time Warner's veto and first option on the sale of Turner's company. Time Warner and TCI were afraid to let us into the tent because it would interfere with their own agendas. So we were denied the opportunity to become a TBS minority owner.

Malone wanted to squeeze a premium out of Time Warner in exchange for TCI's stake in Turner. Time Warner Chairman CEO Gerald Levin wanted to acquire all of Turner Broadcasting because of the strategic fit of assets. Levin and Malone simply did not want Turner to become a more powerful cable player by aligning with NBC. The meeting did not go well.

On October 10, 1996, Time Warner made Turner Broadcasting a private subsidiary by converting Turner's shares in a $7.5 billion merger that combined Warner Bros. film studio, Time Warner Cable, HBO, New Line Cinema, Hanna-Barbera, and Turner Broadcasting System entertainment networks. Turner became vice chairman overseeing his TBS assets. (In 2001, Time Warner famously merged with AOL, and Turner helplessly watched while his personal wealth plummeted by $8 billion and his AOL Time Warner stake dwindled to barely 4 percent in 2 years. He resigned from the company in January 2003, when AOL Time Warner reported the single-largest annual loss in corporate history—$99 billion.)

In late 1999, Turner tried turning the tables by convincing Time Warner to make a run for NBC, and unabashedly declared his intentions publicly at the Western Cable Show. At the time, Jack Welch was vehemently denying that he had offered to sell NBC to Time Warner for $25 billion. All through the 1990s, Welch was rumored to be exploring the network's sale to interested parties. Ted was always a willing buyer. But this turned into another dead end.

❖ **Ted Turner.** The combination with NBC would have made us stronger, quicker than we were with Time Warner. At the dawn of multichannel television, it was all about who got the most networks the quickest would win. I couldn't do that alone. My biggest regret was selling control of CNN. Any of the deals I could have done with NBC to merge our two news organizations would have been my best, most lucrative option. Jerry Levin vetoed our proposal to acquire NBC. I had a handshake deal subject to board approval, and Gerry had control of the Time Warner board. It was the closest we came. ❖

I knew that contemplating a merger with Ted Turner back in the day when he fully lived up to his reputation as "the mouth from the south" was not for the faint of heart. Everyone in the media world wanted his assets, the most sought after of which was CNN. But no one wanted Ted to be part of an acquisition package. His extroverted, bigger-than-life manner was the main impediment to getting anything done. It's also what attracted people to him: the creative, spontaneous, electrifying force. It was an innovative spark and catalyst to a fledgling cable industry. Few media peers appreciated his genius more, or were deterred less by his brazen, unpredictable nature than I was. In fact, my first effort to buy a 25 percent stake in Turner Broadcasting System for $400 million came just a year after my arrival at NBC.

Ted is an irrepressible guy who defies gravity and wins hands-down for his absolute drive and ability to get things done against all odds. I learned a lot in those early days by just watching him fall down, get back up, walk on water, and walk on air. There was no one else like him—anywhere.

Ted eventually brought himself down through his love of programming when he bought MGM. He wanted that library of film and programming to create cable channels. Ted's ultimate problem was losing control of his company. We could never cut a deal with him because each time, for various reasons, we lacked the ability to make things happen without clearance from some higher authority. We also both ultimately wanted to be in control of the single entity we created, and that wouldn't work.

In the end, the only thing we had was the longest-running unconsummated courtship in media history.

❖ **Pier Mapes.** There is no question that Ted Turner and Bob Wright were great visionaries who changed the whole paradigm over several decades despite their contrasting styles and backgrounds. Ted Turner was a formidable force in the early days of cable when suddenly everything exploded into alphabet soup—TNT, TBS, CNN, USA, ESPN. Ted deserves a lot of credit for all of this. But because he was like a bull in a china shop, it was easy for others to blow him off or write him off. That's something I don't think Bob Wright ever did. He understood Ted's drive and vision, because deep down, it was the same as his. Bob was just a lot more understated and low-key, which prevented him from getting the recognition he deserved. Two cable pioneers, underestimated for different reasons, which is maybe why they were always willing to sit down and talk about what could be, even when the television business was at its most chaotic. ❖

❖ **Ted Turner.** When I was a teenager, someone asked me what I wanted to do with my life; what did I want to accomplish? After I thought about it, I said I'd like to set an all-time record for personal achievement by one person in one lifetime. It's about how much good you do. I'm working on that.

Today, I reserve my time and thought processes for things that I still have some influence over. My greatest concerns are nuclear weapons, global climate change, overfishing the oceans, poverty, and terrorism, and ridding the world of childhood diseases. You use everything you have always used to make it happen: teamwork, enthusiasm, hard work, good mental powers, using your intelligence, coming up with good ideas first. Trying to save the world with the United Nations probably turned out to be a more worthwhile endeavor than creating a media empire with NBC. ❖

Wright to the Point

We were all about challenging conventions back in the 1970s when television was a black-and-white, three-network proposition. Back then, it was akin to making mischief because the status quo was so entrenched. Today it's all about disruption, and change has become the norm. But none of us ever has all the control we need to do what we want—not even Ted Turner in his prime. When I look back on our long-running friendship, I can see now we were bonded by the ongoing hope that our companies could advance the cause of 24-hour cable news together.

That never happened in large part because of our different styles and approaches to pursuing that goal. Ted was brazen to a fault, never thinking before speaking publicly what he knew would shock and jolt others into action. I preferred to be more subtle, even flying under the radar of my GE bosses, who were simultaneously repelled by and attracted to a media business they had trouble wrapping their industrial conglomerate arms around.

Ted might have been able to achieve all of his fondest hopes, including owning a major broadcast network, if he had been more diplomatic. But he always was true to himself first. He was destined to have more passion than control, which is never a good formula for achieving your objectives. On the other hand, without Ted's original brand of entrepreneurism, the media world would not have caught fire the way it did. His free spirit was a catalyst for change at a time when broadcasters, advertisers, and program producers, and even cable pioneers, were easily lulled into stagnation. If you ask, both of us would no doubt say without hesitation that one of our biggest regrets was never being able to pull off a deal that made us partners.

What I learned from my dealings with Ted Turner I put to work in my building of Autism Speaks. That was an even more elusive and passionate endeavor than I had known in my media career because it involved people's real-life destiny—autistic children and their families, and Christian and my family in particular. And I suddenly understood what it felt like to have your soul on fire.

14
Olympic Gold

On a steamy summer afternoon on July 29, 1995, NBC Network president Randy Falco and NBC Sports president Dick Ebersol boarded a General Electric Gulfstream IV corporate jet at Westchester County Airport near GE's Fairfield, Connecticut, headquarters. Destination: a hastily arranged meeting in Sweden with the president of the International Olympic Committee, Don Juan Antonio Samaranch.

Just a few hours earlier, Randy and Dick had been in my office at NBC's 30 Rockefeller Center in New York, making a bold pitch by telephone to Jack Welch, who was recuperating from surgery at his home on Nantucket. They made a passionate plea for NBC to bid on the US broadcast rights to two consecutive Olympic Games—the 2000 games in Sydney, Australia, and the 2002 games in Salt Lake City, Utah—instead of the single deal usually awarded 5 years in advance. The move would throw competing bidders off guard and likely win the IOC's hearty support. It would be the first time any broadcast network was simultaneously awarded rights to 2 Olympics telecasts. The sticking point was the cost. To snare the rights to both, GE might have to spend $1.3 billion.

"What's the risk?" Jack asked.

"It's pretty steep," Ebersol answered. The odds were stacked against NBC, he explained, even though it had just won rights to the 1996 summer games in Atlanta. Rival broadcast networks were aggressively lobbying for the games. A losing bid would push back the timeframe NBC could participate in another Olympics telecast, or set off a bidding war that could make the cost prohibitive.

"Well, if that's all, then let's go for it!" Jack bellowed.

That conversation launched what eventually became GE's unprecedented rights commitment to televise seven consecutive Olympics Games from 2000 to 2012. But it didn't start out that way.

Ebersol, NBC's youngest sports chief, had learned quickly that he would never get anything if he didn't ask. Just a few days before that July meeting in my office, he and Falco had secured Samaranch's approval for an unprecedented joint bid with ABC for the 2000 summer games in Sydney. Both networks were eager to keep broadcast rights out of the clutches of Australian-born Rupert Murdoch and his fledging Fox network. But I was cool to the notion. My sense was that NBC and ABC would likely compete more than cooperate for ratings, viewers, and advertisers. So we backed out of the handshake deal with ABC. No sooner was that decision made than Falco suggested we save face with the IOC by presenting a bold solo bid for double rights—something that had never been done.

❖ **Dick Ebersol.** Acquiring sports rights was probably the most difficult thing I ever had to do for NBC. The rights to events like the Olympics were so highly sought after by all the networks that you had to be more cunning and creative than usual.

My first Olympics negotiation, in 1993, was for the rights to the summer games in Atlanta. Everyone assumed NBC would lag far behind ABC. But Bob and Jack Welch and Randy Falco and I pulled off the deal for $55 million in a 1-day auction. It doesn't sound like a lot of money now, but it bought us self-confidence and a place at the Olympic table.

Fast-forward 2 years to late July 1995. I was at a party in Atlanta celebrating NBC's upcoming Olympics coverage there. Behind the scenes, the IOC and other interested parties had just verbally agreed to terms for the first-ever joint bid by two broadcast networks—NBC and ABC—for the 2000 Olympics in Sydney, Australia. Randy and I, and ABC president Dennis Swanson, had been working on the deal for weeks. Then my assistant broke into the party conversation at about 9 p.m. with a telephone message from Bob Wright. Bob was the only person *not* buying the deal. He wanted me and Randy to return to New York to meet with him early the next morning. So Randy and I flew back to New York on a chartered plane, had a quick sleepover in my Manhattan apartment, and then stumbled into Bob's office just after dawn.

Bob felt sure that the joint deal wasn't going to work. We would be competing with each other, splitting the audience and the advertiser spending. So he asked us to pull out of the deal with ABC and make a lone bid. I objected to that, because both of our networks had given their word to each other and I felt we couldn't back out.

After a long pause, Randy Falco suggested the solution might be bidding for the rights to *two* consecutive Olympic Games instead of just one. I paused a second and said, "I'm OK with that." Bob just grinned. So over the next hour and a half, Randy and I and one of my sports sales guys went in another room to analyze what kind of money we would need to have to win and produce the next two Olympics. Ninety minutes later, we were back in Bob's office. The Sydney Olympics of 2000 and the 2002 Olympics just awarded to Salt Lake City would likely cost us between $1.2 billion and $1.3 billion—which was a prodigious amount of money, even for a global conglomerate like General Electric. ❖

Wrestling the Olympic Games rights away from ABC was no small feat. Fortunately for us, Ebersol had trained at the foot of the master, ABC Sports president and Olympics executive producer Roone Arledge. Roone's technological wizardry revolutionized live sports and news events with slow-motion, instant replay, and cameras planted on the scene. Snatching the Olympics out from under Arledge and ABC would be a personal victory for Ebersol and an irresistible prospect for Jack and me.

Ebersol told us that he knew IOC president Samaranch was on a business trip to Gothenburg, Sweden. He suggested that he and Falco seize the moment by flying there immediately to lay out NBC's radical concept. After a brief pause, Ebersol asked Jack, "Could we borrow the jet?" Like a good corporate parent, Jack sent them winging with an Irish blessing. Several hours later, Ebersol and Falco were settling into the luxury beds aboard the GE corporate jet to sleep through the 8-hour flight to Sweden.

Ebersol had befriended the patriarchal Samaranch during previous negotiations. The IOC chief enthusiastically responded to NBC's proposal. "Move quickly," he told them. "You need to get the support of Dick Pound, the IOC's chief representative for the Americas, who lives in Montreal." After lurking in elevators and offices to avoid being seen publicly with Samaranch and tipping off the press hounds, Ebersol and Falco flew to Canada for a 2-hour meeting with Pound. Many of the details were hammered out there. "We didn't dare return home without the deal we went out there for," Falco later recalled. "I'm no fool!"

We kept the wraps on the deal until August 7, when NBC rocked the media and sports worlds by announcing it had acquired the rights to the 2000 Sydney *and* the 2002 Salt Lake City Olympic Games for $1.3 billion.

Then things got *really* interesting.

Later the same day, an ecstatic Samaranch telephoned Ebersol to say that he loved the deal so much that he wanted to do another just like it for subsequent games. "Really?!" a stunned Ebersol responded. Samarach suggested the three of them discuss a new round of consecutive rights when Ebersol and Falco returned to Sweden to sign the formal contract. So Ebersol telephoned my office, just as Jack and I were wrapping up a meeting, to relay the message. "Are you crazy?!" Jack screeched over the telephone speaker. And after a 30-second pause, Jack and I uniformly chimed, "Go for it!"

So Jack gave us the go-ahead to work with Samaranch on a second rights package that cost GE $2.3 billion for three more Olympic Games—Athens in 2004, Torino, Italy, in 2006, and Beijing in 2008. In 2008, NBC negotiated a third Olympics package for $2.2 billion for rights to two more consecutive games— the 2010 winter Olympics in Vancouver, Canada, and the 2012 Summer Olympics in London, England.

In the end, Falco and Ebersol negotiated a $6 billion licensing deal for an unprecedented seven consecutive Olympics Games telecasts stretching from 2000 to 2012. The IOC relationships Ebersol had nurtured since becoming president of NBC Sports in 1989 were paying off. And Randy Falco, a longtime veteran of NBC network operations, instinctively knew what NBC was capable of doing and what it needed to do. Together, they brought home a historic deal.

By 1996, NBC Sports was the undisputed king of television sports. We simultaneously held TV rights to more big sporting events than any other media company—spanning the Olympics, baseball, football, basketball, major American golf tournaments, and the Wimbledon tennis classic. We continuously evaluated how best to use these platforms to promote NBC's regularly scheduled series, competitively position our local TV station affiliates, and boost our prestige on Wall Street.

❖ **Dick Ebersol.** The IOC was blown away by the advanced production qualities and storytelling we brought to the games. We were focused on telling the athletes' stories of survival and overcoming obstacles. There was a special sense of something unique and very personal about the Olympics, which were about much more than winning medals. The games reflected who we were as people and nations, and what we might become.

The Olympics' ripple effect was amazing. The Atlanta summer Olympics propelled NBC's *Tonight Show* into a permanent lock in late-night and Tom Brokaw's *Nightly News* into dominance among network news shows just as *The Today Show* was regaining its footing. ❖

The cost efficiencies we achieved over multiple Olympics productions—from Sydney in 2000 to the London Olympics in 2012—were significant enough to assure profits. NBC amortized its Olympics costs across its expanding portfolio of cable channels, which eventually included CNBC, MSNBC, Bravo, USA, and SyFy. We signed advertisers to higher-priced, longer-term marketing agreements over successive Olympic Games and our multimedia platforms. NBC primetime entertainment series ratings improved with promotions and lead-in audiences from the Olympic Games. NBC's Olympics franchise was pure gold for GE.

❖ **Randy Falco, president NBC Television Network.** We asked our affiliates to help subsidize our five-Olympics package over 10 years, starting with the 2000 games in Sydney. It was an unheard of practice at the time that was considered borderline heresy! We actually got the station affiliates to agree to collectively pay more than $50 million a year.

As part of the agreement, we did what I thought was a very clever commercial inventory swap. We traded advertising airtime with the affiliates in parts of our program schedule that would be more valuable to them for local sales, such as leading in and out of their local newscasts and promotional cut-ins. We kept more of the commercial units to use in primetime, *The Today Show* and *The Tonight Show*—shows that the networks could price at a premium. At one point, such arrangements were collectively worth $400 million to $500 million over 10 years, representing revenues to help offset the multibillion price tag for successive Olympic Games. When live sporting events spilled over into affiliated stations' local newscasts, NBC quickly released more commercial units for them to sell to smooth over ruffled feathers. Affiliates hated when that happened, and it was our job to make it a win-win for all concerned. But that wasn't always possible.

The great thing about the Olympics, unlike any other sports events, is that we owned the US rights for years and could experiment with them at a time that digital technology was booming. In 2000, we had no idea what kind of advertising revenues would be generated from the sale of commercial airtime on television and on the Internet. We just understood things were changing, and that was as scary as it was liberating. ❖

More than a decade of Olympic Games commitments also represented a huge technological gamble for everyone involved since no one was sure about digital advances and how they would impact costs. Randy Falco and I insisted the contracts include provisions for video rights use on whatever digital devices and technology existed at the time of the Olympics Games telecasts. "We are shooting in the dark, trying to figure out what kind of interactive technology will materialize years out. We don't want to leave any money on the table," Falco told me. In 1995, most people in the world did not own a personal computer, but we knew that would change. Mainstream mobility, smartphones, and streaming from the cloud were the stuff of science fiction. NBC only began streaming Olympics events online in 2008.

In short, the Olympics made NBC a showcase for developing technology, the world's most popular live sports event, and what many say was the original reality TV.

❖ **Dick Ebersol.** With great credit to Randy and Bob, they had to figure out how best to provide for changes in technology—that went from cable to the Internet to streaming—years before they occurred. They had to contract for TV rights to encompass technology that hadn't even been invented yet. They wrote a contract that made it absolutely clear that whatever technology existed in the future, NBC would own the Olympics video rights in our part of the world no matter what transpired. Spending $3.5 billion on five Olympics telecasts over 100 days couldn't have happened anywhere else in the media world. It was all about the faith Bob and Jack Welch had in our ability to pull these things off successfully and to make money, which all but one of those Olympics did. ❖

One big reason we were able to pull off the Olympics rights coup was because we appreciated and valued cable better than our broadcast network peers in those early days. Our secret sauce was actively investing in and mining cable. ABC had as much information and insight about cable as we did. ABC also had a very promising cable property, ESPN, which even in its infancy could have been leveraged more effectively in ABC's Olympics bids. But like everyone else in network television at the time, ABC remained focused on broadcasting. All NBC had at that time was a fledgling business news service in CNBC, the promise of MSNBC, stakes in A&E, and a highly vocal bet on cable as the future of television because of its dual advertising and subscription revenue streams.

We knew we could skillfully use the Olympics to showcase our combined cable-broadcast strategy. That was our edge.

❖ **David Zaslav.** NBC's Olympics story is really all about the growth of cable. Growing NBC's cable channel holdings and investments, often through the complex dealings of industry chiefs like John Malone, was one thing. But NBC had rare control over its own cable destiny with its exclusive Olympics rights. It was our ticket to play in the cable sandbox by our own rules. We quickly learned to leverage it to our advantage, getting support from cable operators, TV stations, and advertisers. We could set our own price and terms. We could appeal directly to US television viewers in ways not possible with other kinds of programing. So the Olympics made NBC a commanding cable player in its own right. ❖

But our Olympics success was as much about me empowering the right members of my executive team as it was having the right strategy to execute.

Randy Falco, the president of the NBC network at the time, was the henchman for most of our early Olympics efforts and a huge reason for our success. It wasn't just the savvy he brought to the negotiations. It was his enthusiasm and tireless commitment. Here's an example: As facilities director for the Barcelona Olympics, Randy's job was to pull together all the production aspects on the ground, which involved hundreds of people, most of them part-timers. He worked himself to exhaustion and fractured his leg. The only way he could get around was by wheelchair, which was very challenging given the logistics. A young and strong sports executive, Jim Bell, offered to carry around his boss (Falco was 6'4" and 240 pounds) on his shoulder like a sack of potatoes.

David Zaslav played an absolutely critical role. The only reason we could branch out into cable with our televised Olympic rights the way we did is because we had the support of cable operators. And the only reason we had *that* was because David Zaslav did a hell of a job convincing even the biggest operators it was in their best interest to support our efforts.

Dick Ebersol's attention to details is what endeared him to Samaranch and others at the IOC. During the weeks of nonstop Olympics coverage, he slept, showered, and essentially lived in his makeshift office. Dick knew the key to successful Olympics coverage went beyond production values and technology to storytelling—an art he learned from the legendary Roone Arledge. Ebersol told me he wanted to capture the real-life drama of tragedy and triumph, and of the human condition, through the eyes of competing athletes from all over the world. He considered the Olympics the last refuge of family viewing: mom, dad, and the kids gathered around the video campfire for a suspenseful and inspiring display of athletics and spirit.

And Dick delivered on that promise with every Olympics telecast. Little wonder that we swiftly renewed Ebersol's contract in 1996 for 8 more years through 2004. It was the longest-running contract ever awarded an employee of NBC or GE. But I suspect what mattered more to him was the pride and prestige that NBC's Olympics won him among his industry peers.

One evening in late December 1995, when NBC and the IOC had finalized—but not yet announced—the second consecutive Olympic Games deal, Ebersol was in the back of an Italian restaurant in Midtown Manhattan being interviewed by a reporter over dinner. He was surprised to look up and see his old boss, Roone Arledge, seated across the room, having dinner with his wife. Arledge sent over a bottle of wine with a note saying how proud he was that Ebersol had made the ground-breaking Sydney and Salt Lake City deal for 2000 and 2002. Ebersol smiled and waved a high sign to Roone, surely thinking, "Just wait until he hears about the three additional Olympics we just stole out from underneath ABC for 2004, 2006, and 2008!"

These three talented men, and all the rest of the team, made NBC synonymous with the Olympics. It was an astonishing achievement in an astonishingly short period of time.

But the full Olympics story isn't all rosy. There was the little matter of the Triplecast.

No one ever talks about the great faux pas in television history without mentioning the 1992 Summer Olympics Triplecast. It was our most victorious disaster. And I would do it again.

Triplecast was a pay-per-view offering of three cable channels of specialized Olympics events that would never make it onto the network's limited airtime. It was a partnership with Chuck Dolan's Cablevision Systems, a prominent cable operator in the east (for more on that story see Chapter 8). In the end, the experiment cost both of us $50 million in losses and a media black eye.

What was never fully appreciated is just how much we learned and applied from the gutsy experience. It catapulted us into the eventually lucrative pay cable arena before anyone in the industry knew what it would be. It was years ahead of its time. Because of rapidly evolving interactivity over the next decade, every Olympics package that followed on our own cable networks put money into our pocket. But that was hardly evident at the time.

The ultimate irony is that today, NBC's Olympics franchise (good through 2020) represents the single best opportunity for Comcast to use its dominant cable systems to create an exclusive on-demand platform for the most obscure events, which viewers, advertisers, and other cable operators now routinely support.

It was just a matter of time.

Wright to the Point

The road less traveled that NBC took to snare US Olympics video rights for more than 2 decades was the result of thinking outside the box. It was part of a concerted effort by my executive team to find radically different ways to go about the routine. I gave them permission—and even orders—to take a contrarian approach to problem solving and boosting earnings. They learned that having money to invest is less important than having ideas to act on. It was my job and responsibility to enable inventive thinking and then pave the way for General Electric, Jack Welch, and the board of directors to financially support our proposals. That made it safe to try something new, whether it materialized as an improvement or a failure.

It's always interesting to see how others respond to your innovations. Others often long to do the same but don't have the courage or resources to try. In this case, the International Olympics Committee was thrilled to have a major media company fully committed to televising multiple Olympic Games years out. It allowed them to proceed more confidently with their plans and to pursue other changes that benefitted the games overall. It demonstrated that enterprise is a welcome, productive catalyst for change. Since change is inevitable, it's better to guide and own it.

The cable operators also reaped rewards of our long-term Olympics franchise. We had the technology resources to handle the extended coverage and created new options as needed, which translated into better television all around. The local affiliates also learned that they had to adapt, even to reinvent themselves. That's the path to improved economics; done right, it's a win-win for all involved.

Change will happen anyway. It's the only thing anyone can count on. So you might as well embrace and guide it. Our approach to televising Olympic events has been a textbook study in why that is good business everywhere. My development of Autism Speaks has demonstrated that this lesson is just as hard-learned and critical in the world of philanthropy, where we're dug in for the same fight.

15

NBC + Microsoft = MSNBC

S ometimes strange bedfellows just remain strange bedfellows. NBC's 1996 partnership with Microsoft was a marriage of convenience. Because our two companies anchored oppo- site ends of the media spectrum, it could well have been doomed from the start. But we kept at it, slogging through our clashing agendas and leadership styles to forge the MSNBC cable channel and website—a game changer for both of us.

It just didn't feel good at the time.

NBC News urgently wanted to develop around-the-clock cable news capability to compete with CNN, but the cost and risk were substantial; we needed a high-tech player with credibility and deep pockets. Bill Gates wanted to ride NBC News's coattails to a mainstream Internet presence. With a joint venture, the costs and risks would be shared.

The idea was to create MSNBC out of our second struggling cable channel, America's Talking, and its 23 million cable sub- scribers. We already had CNBC, our homegrown business and financial news cable channel, but we planned to take MSNBC in a different direction. That made MSNBC appear less like a frontal assault on CNN and a threat to cable operators, whose support we needed to carry the new service.

Creating MSNBC with Microsoft was an example of taking an organization where it *needed* to go even as GE, the NBC station affiliates, and my own NBC executives were fighting the proposition. NBC News was number one in the ratings under the astute leadership of News Chief Andy Lack. CNN was unchallenged on the cable news front. GE supported cable news and entertainment as long as someone else paid for it. There were a lot of people on both sides of the aisle who said, "Bob, we wouldn't mind if you just dropped that!"

The 800-pound gorilla in the equation was Microsoft. It was the dominant force in computing software but still defining its role on the Internet. But times were changing. Gates believed the Internet would quickly become a universal source of news and information and that mainstream media would assure his involvement. Earlier he had tried to negotiate a partnership with CNN but failed. Aligning with NBC News would give Microsoft a competitive edge even though the enterprise was insignificant to its earnings.

So in the summer of 1995, NBC Cable president Tom Rogers leveraged his past dealings with Microsoft to jumpstart discussions about a joint venture that would create MSNBC TV and MSNBC. com. Microsoft didn't understand the TV programming business. Neither one of us knew what to expect with the Internet, which was still uncharted territory, and neither one of us was completely comfortable with the other's business dynamics. Considering all that, it's not surprising the negotiations were very difficult.

We ended up structuring the deal in a way that was far more advantageous to us early on. And in a nice bit of irony, a critical tipping point came in the midst of a major news story.

Million Man March
Washington, DC
October 16, 1995

The makeshift studio overlooking the throngs gathered at the National Mall for the historic Million Man March on October 16, 1995, gave NBC News anchorman Tom Brokaw a special vantage point to report on the day's highly charged activities. The day-long event on the grounds of the US Capitol generated a deafening ebb and flow of sermons, speeches, and chants from scores of civil rights activists and African American community leaders. Controversy over crowd estimates and the controlling presence of the Nation of Islam and its leader, Louis Farrakhan, heightened the drama.

In the midst of it all, Brokaw stepped away for a phone conference. On the other end, at NBC's New York headquarters, Tom Rogers, NBC News president Andy Lack, and I sat anxiously in the executive conference room with Bill Gates. We were trying to craft the MSNBC deal, and things were not going well. We had decided to bring in Brokaw.

Brokaw knew the negotiations had reached a critical point. So, surrounded by swarms of camera crews and producers, the consummate newsman used the extraordinary circumstances to his advantage. "Look, Bill," Brokaw began. "I'm going to go on the air tonight at six-thirty and we'll be lucky to have six minutes of time devoted to this. If we were in business together, Microsoft could have our coverage on its website and NBC could have it on cable news. We could be running with this all day long and straight through the night, and build an audience across a much wider platform."

Gates got that. Although he professed to watch little television, he envisioned a rapidly emerging digital world in which the Internet would become the primary source of video, superseding cable in a mere 20 years. Listening to Brokaw, a wide-eyed Gates kept nodding his head.

Meanwhile, Andy Lack had prepared a video retrospective of NBC News footage reaching back to 1947. It was a vivid reminder of the digital value of NBC's rich video archives. At the same time, a live NBC News feed of the impassioned images and sounds from Washington played on conference room monitors. Together they created a dynamic display of NBC News's legacy and credibility: the video history side by side with breaking news. Everyone in the room could see the potential. Consumers would be able to access breaking news and information whenever they wanted, on cable and on the Internet. By the end of the meeting, Gates was hooked. He signed off on the joint venture. It turned out to be the easiest moment in an otherwise mercurial process.

❖ **Tom Rogers.** Early in the heady negotiations with Microsoft, Bob pulled me aside. "This one's just you and me, Tom. Can you go out there and get this thing done?" For me, this was a new fight on familiar territory. It wasn't just a matter of winning over Gates and Microsoft so they would bankroll our newest cable channel. We needed enough cable systems carrying MSNBC to assure its commercial success.

Today, the MSNBC franchise is worth billions of dollars and it makes so much sense. Back then, we were defying convention. ❖

Microsoft wanted pure news credentials for MSNBC, which meant choosing Andy Lack over Roger Ailes. So in the summer of 1995, in order to keep Microsoft from going to Turner or Comcast to enter cable news, we agreed to convert our America's Talking channel to MSNBC and have NBC News president Andy Lack oversee it. We didn't know anything about the Internet, but we knew we would get there one way or the other, and most likely faster working with Microsoft.

Andy Lack was just the serious news force we needed. Before coming to NBC, he had spent 17 years at CBS News, and he understood TV news from the inside out. We worked well together the 9 years he led the news division. Andy made news a profit center, and I knew he would make MSNBC a profitable venture—and he did. Roger Ailes was unhappy about being passed over, and on his way out the door to Fox. He openly cast doubt on plans for our unconventional Microsoft-financed news channel, and the ability of skilled executives without programming experience to make it successful. He criticized me, Jack and Andy for taking *America's Talking* away from him and instead giving him overview of CNBC, our fledgling business channel. It didn't take much to stir up the waters, for many at NBC were already skeptical about what we were trying to accomplish. Tom Brokaw and others tried to calm concerns and hold protests at bay.

❖ **Tom Brokaw, anchorman *NBC Nightly News*.** I personally reached out to Gates, big-city NBC affiliates, and my NBC News brethren in support of the new MSNBC venture. MSNBC allowed NBC to reenter cable news with a successful, functional website from the get-go. That was a huge plus. NBC's leap from analog to digital was painfully convoluted. We accepted digital news was going to be an increasingly important element on the Internet, but we didn't grasp how to mine our own resources to get there. ❖

When we went into partnership with Microsoft, we really believed they wanted to turn the whole world digital. And we believed that could help our news business. So we were willing to take the risk, knowing that Microsoft would be a tough partner. Our news division was not set up to produce digital content. Someone had to pay for that, and we knew it would not be GE.

After a series of intense meetings in New York and at Microsoft headquarters in Redmond, Washington, through the summer and fall of 1995, Gates agreed to pay $220 million for a 50 percent stake in America's Talking. Microsoft also contributed $200 million to build a new studio headquarters in Secaucus, New Jersey, and to create MSNBC.com, which it would manage. The additional licensing fees Microsoft paid for online access and use of NBC News content offset NBC's $250 million matching contribution to the cause. NBC's mounting startup losses were also shouldered by Microsoft.

Some people, looking back, say we outwitted Bill Gates. I rather think Bill knew exactly what he was doing but didn't like funding all the early startup costs. He often appeared uncomfortable with the arrangement that his team negotiated on his behalf, and he became more visibly distraught with every check he wrote. It was also obvious that he was discouraged by the slow pace of consumer adoption.

Gates underestimated the effort the MSNBC website would need to draw millions of people quickly. He misunderstood a lot of things about the Internet. He was thinking too fast about moving forward. He wanted everything to be done tomorrow. We were focused on building MSNBC cable and web, and Microsoft did not manage their end of it very well. Gates got what he wanted, and then he didn't know how to use it, and that was the real problem.

When things didn't turn out as planned, Gates began losing interest. His uneasiness became so profound that he was trying to wiggle out of the MSNBC deal just hours before it was announced to the press on December 14, 1995. In the early morning hours, Rogers, Welch, and I straggled into the office of NBC tech czar Mike Sherlock at NBC headquarters at 30 Rockefeller Center. We were joined by Greg Maffei, Microsoft's chief financial officer, and Peter Neupert, vice president of strategic relationships for Microsoft's interactive media division. The five of us huddled over a speakerphone on the desk. Gates's troubled, disembodied voice was on the other end from Asia, where he was on business.

We didn't yet have a signed agreement, just a handshake in principle, and we scrambled to button down the details. The elaborate press conference almost came off without a hitch. Randy Falco, who was head of the NBC TV network, coordinated the live satellite feeds from Germany, China, and the US—which was quite an effort in 1995. Jack and I anchored the event in NBC's famed Studio 8H. A big screen behind us displayed the boyish-looking Gates live via satellite from Hong Kong and *Nightly News* anchorman Tom Brokaw from Ramstein, Germany, where he was reporting on the political unrest in Bosnia. I proclaimed the Microsoft partnership and creation of MSNBC would "redefine the way people get their information" by providing consumers "a continuum of news." I think I managed to hide all the behind-the-scenes angst.

Gates didn't like some aspects of the deal, but he was not about to give it up. He just wanted better terms. He didn't care about people and microphones and cameras. He just wanted ownership of all the NBC News material: historical to date and going forward. And that's probably what hurt him in the end, because he didn't get involved in how they were doing all of this online. Gates assigned his Microsoft people to do it, but it wasn't a priority in Redmond.

Two weeks later, on Christmas Eve, I maintained a telephone vigil from our home in Aspen, Colorado, trying to nail down the final partnership terms with a still-reluctant Gates. I was camped out at a desk in our living room surrounded by family and friends gathered there for the holiday. I was on the phone for a long time, trying to keep the negotiations alive and wondering to myself, "Does Bill Gates know what day it is?!" He seemed totally oblivious to the fact that it was Christmas.

Despite an army of negotiators, it came down to me reconciling what we needed and what they wanted. Although the deal was finalized in late December 1995, tensions between Microsoft and NBC continued unabated through MSNBC's ceremonious launch July 15, 1996, and the periodic partnership reviews that followed. Gates sat through most of those meetings, barely uttering a word.

❖ **Warren Jenson.** We basically figured out how to work within GE's rigid system to create a risky new business involving locations outside of New York City and nonunion help. Ultimately, we were inventing a new culture with new economics. But we couldn't mandate the pace of digital and Internet adoption—by consumers or by our own affiliates and cable system operators—to satisfy Microsoft's expectations. So our partnership remained strained and never really thrived. Still, as dysfunctional as it was, it did improve NBC's ability to compete with CNN, enhance our news dominance, and strengthen our presence across many different media platforms. That took 15 years. ❖

The friction with Microsoft was eclipsed by the ire from NBC TV stations and cable system operators. No one wanted to buy into these new ways or products. Our affiliates felt entitled to exclusive use of all NBC content even though they were severely limited by available broadcast airtime. They saw our cable news shows as direct competition for viewers and advertising dollars, so they challenged our right to use our "regular" NBC material on MSNBC and CNBC.

The first major showdown took place in Phoenix during a cocktail reception at the annual affiliates meeting on May 24, 1996. Our 250 affiliates were very vocal about their fears: that NBC would move its programming and advertising to cable, destroying their 75-year partnership. I argued that cable presented us with a new reality, and that our partnership with stations could only be preserved by sacrificing exclusivity.

To counter their resistance, I drew on a set of secret weapons: my team. I asked NBC Network president Randy Falco to be peacemaker and referee. Randy took responsibility for the network and getting the stations on board. David Zaslav accepted responsibility for cable and DirecTV satellite. Randy and David nurtured relationships with all of the individual broadcast and cable companies, no two of which could be treated the same. Cyril Vetter, a highly creative songwriter, lawyer, entrepreneur, and Louisiana station owner, headed our affiliate board. He understood and accepted the marketplace's changing dynamics.

◈ **Cyril Vetter, affiliate board chairman NBC and owner WVLA-TV in Baton Rouge, Louisiana.** The hand-to-hand combat that evening began with apoplectic station executives booing Wright and Tom Rogers, who was the spear-catcher in the deal. Affiliates considered Tom an enemy to their cause, and they labeled Wright's moves pure heresy. Randy stepped in to defend his boss, only to be shouted down by the angry crowd. Then, without so much as raising his voice, Bob explained why it was time to change or die. Consumers—not stations—would determine NBC's economic fate. ◈

I did some of the best visionary work of my entire career with the NBC television stations, and I still flunked. I just couldn't get our stations to buy into cable or the Internet on anything but the most superficial level until after MSNBC forced the issue. It would be another decade before stations fully accepted the coexistence of NBC content on cable television and online. NBC maintained a Chinese wall between its broadcast network and cable news organizations. It gave the semblance to affiliates and NBC News rank and file of retaining "first rights" to the *Nightly News, Today Show,* and *Dateline* even as Microsoft and Gates were claiming it as their own.

At the same time, cable operators were also fighting us. They insisted they were not obliged to offer viewers MSNBC as a replacement for *America's Talking* in 22 million homes. David Zaslav, the number two in charge of NBC Cable at the time, was entrusted with the job of getting cable affiliates to approve. Somehow he managed to get them to buy in to the MSNBC proposition, and that meant negotiating with each of the companies that he had a personal relationship with. So we dreamed up these things and David went around the country making them happen. Randy accomplished the same on the broadcast side by having very close relationships with each of the affiliate owners. And they sometimes had to be very clever about it.

MSNBC officially launched on July 15, 1996, but it wasn't carried by a full contingent of cable systems across the country. The stand-off with cable operators came to a head a month later in an August 23, 1996, meeting with Jerry Levin, chairman CEO of Time Warner at the company's Rockefeller Center headquarters. Time Warner was on the verge of taking control of CNN through its pending acquisition of Turner Broadcasting System and didn't want to pay us to carry MSNBC.

I reminded Levin that he didn't have a choice because of the retransmission consent law, which was my trump card. Instead of collecting a cash payment from cable operators for our broadcast network signal, NBC demanded carriage of its new CNBC and MSNBC cable channels. After Time Warner capitulated, other cable operators fell in line. A year later we had to pay Time Warner a $1 million fee to retain cable carriage of CNBC and MSNBC in New York City. I was told we had to match or exceed Murdoch's offer to get carriage for Fox News there. The Fox News fight was just beginning!

❖ **John Malone.** NBC seized a unique opportunity when it created MSNBC and required cable operators to carry it if they wanted to continue accessing the NBC TV network. If the government had not instituted the new retransmission consent rules at that time, the destiny of cable programming would have been completely different. That swing in market power allowed broadcasters to essentially take over and dominate cable networks and programming, beginning with MSNBC. So some of it was by design and some of it was just good timing—the way so many important developments happened back then. ❖

Bill Gates estate
Medina, Washington
November 20, 1997

Gates was still fuming when Rogers, Lack, Welch, and I visited his mansion in Medina, Washington, on November 20, 1997, for dinner and a quarterly business review. The $120 million estate was a curious interplay of traditional media and emerging digital technology that didn't always work that well together—making it a striking metaphor for our companies' strained partnership. Gates and his family lived in the upper levels, with corporate meeting rooms and a 200-seat banquet hall on the ground floor. Monitors and control panels in every room synchronized visitors' preferences for room temperature, information, and entertainment.

Gates was uncharacteristically outgoing that evening as he ushered us into his elaborate home theater, where he quickly became flustered trying to retrieve one of the thousand-plus films stored there in his personal computer. It turned out the technology was only as good as the user—even if the user was Bill Gates!

❖ **Tom Rogers.** There was Bill Gates, pounding on the computer keyboard, unable to show the kings of media his spectacular setup. You can be the richest guy in the world and still not be able to get your toys to work when you want to.

At the next morning's partnership review, Microsoft conceded it was being forced to temper its expectations about how quickly Internet business models would develop 16 months into the MSNBC venture. Gates was more agitated over the widening gulf between his financial commitment to MSNBC and the prognosis for mass digital adoption. He suddenly saw a great imbalance in the deal we struck. We had seriously out-negotiated him.

Microsoft was making escalated payments on NBC's new cable assets Gates could care less about. It was shouldering the financial risk of MSNBC in exchange for licensing news video rights that eventually would have real value in the digital world on smartphones and tablets that didn't even exist at the time. ❖

Microsoft headquarters
Redmond, Washington
November 21, 1997

❖ **Tom Rogers.** The next day, in an executive conference room at Microsoft headquarters, Gates glared across the table at me and squirmed uncomfortably next to Jack Welch. The friction between them was fueled by a just-published *Financial Times* story ranking the world's top CEOs. Welch topped the list; Gates was second.

Watching this interaction that morning, I was suddenly struck by the irony of this quirky alliance. Each man thought they had the better piece of the MSNBC deal. Gates cared less about TV and only about controlling NBC News on the web for a hundred years and a couple hundred million dollars. Welch believed he had tricked Gates into building a cable news channel for NBC and considered the Internet a waste of time and money. Each of them accomplished what they wanted, but neither could see the value of the synergies created. They were so wrapped up in their own agendas, they failed to recognize they were creating something big that would develop over time into something even bigger. ❖

❖ **Andy Lack.** MSNBC really got on the map from 1996 to 2000 with all the drama of the Clinton years. That dispelled any doubt a 24/7 news channel would dramatically change the way NBC News would move forward in the 21st century.

But what most people don't know is that it took years of cajoling the news division into submission. For the longest time, our own people felt it was too early in the digital game for that type of consumer behavior to develop and that the cable audience wasn't ready for it. The Internet audience wouldn't come to cable. They were two separate businesses sharing some common content but couldn't yet be tied together under one umbrella. ❖

The elephant in the room during our MSNBC journey was Rupert Murdoch's Fox News, which swept onto the scene in October 1996 and disrupted the status quo. I thought it was clever and bold, making right-wing talk core to its news operations. That was largely the handiwork of Roger Ailes, who had left NBC to command a larger power base at Fox, where he began promising objective news and then delivered everything but.

We were middle-of-the-road on *America's Talking*, careful to keep it an arm's length from the news operation just because it was emotionally based programming by design. The concept was giving everyday people a platform for telling their heroic stories, large and small.

Just as we began converting America's Talking into MSNBC, Fox jumped in with a highly unconventional news model and cash payments to cable operators for news carriage, which caught everyone off guard. And that's what forced MSNBC to develop an on-air attitude that eventually settled into politically left-of-center programming. Cable operators were happy to pay for it because it helped them to neutralize the airwaves.

❖ **Tom Rogers**. MSNBC was developed and launched in July 1996 to take advantage of new laws assuring TV networks and stations that cable operators would have to pay for the retransmission of any of their program signals. Most everyone involved in news viewed cable as part of the problem rather than a solution. Fortunately, Andy Lack, the new president of NBC News, was open to solving the division's problems and advancing its cause on multiple fronts, even if it meant extending its resources to cable.

We couldn't just come forward with a new cable news channel of our own because the major cable operators, who had an ownership interest in Turner and CNN, would resist that. But nobody had a good news talk channel or a vibrant left-of-center platform. It's something we could do relatively cheaply. If we wrote the program description broadly enough, we could morph it into a news talk channel agreed to and paid for by the cable industry, using those fees as our quid pro quo for retransmission consent.

Of course, Fox had the same notion, which put our companies in a race to secure guaranteed cable subscribers. Fox was more willing than GE and NBC to pay cable operators for an audience. An initial $11 per subscriber was an ironic reversal of the retransmission fees we fought so hard for and were counting on to help fund MSNBC and CNBC. Fox claimed it was fair incentive to cable operators with limited channel capacity in those pre-digital days. The 20 million cable subscribers we inherited from NBC's America's Talking were transferred to MSNBC; NBC News got Microsoft as a new partner, and David Zaslav worked tirelessly to secure new license agreements. Even Jack Welch and Bob were making personal appeals by telephone to cable system operators.

So it was a showdown in 1996 as broadcast network news moved into position on cable, and it played out primarily between NBC and Fox. Despite its news strength, ABC abandoned attempts at cable news after spending nearly half a billion over 5 years. CBS News was never in the game. After owning cable news for more than a decade, CNN was fighting to defend its turf. ❖

The MSNBC experience gave us confidence we could productively use the Internet. It gave the news division self-assurance about what they could do with digital even before they were comfortable with it. Microsoft's half-billion–dollar investment thrust NBC into the Internet age ahead of its network peers. Today, MSNBC and NBCU's other cable networks anchor the company's profits and valuation.

But the lack of strategic clarity between cable TV and the Internet back then eventually took its toll. In 2007, MSNBC.com and MSNBC cable were decoupled. NBC bought out Microsoft's 50 percent interest in MSNBC for a mere $120 million in 2007 and then acquired Microsoft's half interest in MSNBC.com in 2012 for $300 million.

If we had created MSNBC 5 years later, the original approach of holistically tying together the Internet and cable would have resonated with more people at NBC and other traditional media companies. While MSNBC demonstrated NBC was capable of pioneering the next media frontier, it couldn't shepherd the audience.

❖ **Tom Rogers.** The MSNBC experience was the first test of a major media company's ability to integrate its vast and varied business resources across emerging platforms—against all odds. It wasn't just about the sea change in cable and television news, or the turf wars between a network's news division and local station affiliates. MSNBC became ground zero for breaking the corporate mold and playing by new rules in the new cable and Internet arenas. What we didn't count on was politically charged news competition from Fox or Microsoft's inept management of MSNBC.com.

The traditional news reporters and producers Microsoft first hired to develop content for MSNBC.com didn't understand or accept the potential value of real-time online news and information. The concept of MSNBC TV and MSNBC.com working in tandem to provide continuous coverage did not gain traction until they became a showcase for NBC News coverage of the September 11, 2001, terrorist attacks.

The tipping point for MSNBC came December 2, 2004, when Brian Williams crossed over from the White House beat to anchor a nightly newscast called *The Site* on MSNBC and another regular program on CNBC, even as he was being groomed to succeed Tom Brokaw as the network's premiere anchorman on the *NBC Nightly News*. The move triggered favorable response within NBC and throughout the TV news industry. ❖

❖ **David Zaslav.** We couldn't mandate audience convergence, which took its own course. The new culture we were creating eventually took the place of the old culture, which crumbled under the weight of changing consumer behavior, technology, and economics.

We all learned during our time at GE and NBC how to look past the horizon for the change that's coming and have the courage to act on it. There are companies that can't deal with change and have no tolerance for failure. And there are some companies—like NBC back then—that built a business strategy around both, and paid the price for years until the gamble paid off. ❖

Wright to the Point

It wasn't enough to create just another cable news channel with MSNBC in 1996. An enterprising use of the Internet to create and leverage scale made all the difference. NBC was the first traditional broadcast network to partner with Silicon Valley on a major Internet venture. That it was Microsoft made it all the more courageous and risky. That took time and lots of effort, but it never fully fused as a combined interactive force. Only now, years later, is the convergence of television and the Internet starting to take hold.

Not all industries have achieved that kind of unity. Even though the Internet is fully entrenched in everyday life today, it is still something of an enigma to many people in all kinds of business. Sadly, not all of us have developed a big-picture approach to using it in our work. Too few people in any organization connect the dots or take things to the next level on their own. And that's why progress can be so slow. We must take full advantage of the huge array of digital tools and resources we have available. It's the difference between being informed and being knowledgeable, and then putting that knowledge to work. A lot of people spend a lot of time on the Internet. They're packing themselves with information, but they are not necessarily more knowledgeable, because they don't know how to use it. Collecting data doesn't make you smarter.

If you really believe in a project, you will find ways to get it done even if it means the complex fusion of existing and new resources, old and new thinking, support and opposition. That process takes on a life of its own when it involves bigger-than-life characters like Bill Gates and Roger Ailes, or an overwhelming enigma like autism. Both Microsoft and NBC were taking a chance by moving outside their comfort zones. But that is often the only way to achieve the extraordinary.

16
Dante's Inferno: The *Queen Mary 2* Became the *Exxon Valdez!*

For more than a decade we morphed NBC into a $45 billion business. Over that same period from 1996 to 2009, General Electric created and *lost* $530 billion to catastrophes, industry blowups, and unfortunate timing in investments and core businesses. During that period, GE's stock price soared from $7 a share to nearly $60 a share in Jack Welch's best days before crashing back to $7 a share in 2009 and then settling into the mid-$20s. It was one of the greatest cycles of value creation and destruction of all time.

In the end, three almost simultaneous disasters—a housing and financial crisis in 2007–2008, an energy and insurance bust, and the 9/11 terrorist attacks—drove GE to lose nearly twice as much as the value wiped out by AOL Time Warner's ill-fated merger, which was thought to be the priciest faux pas in US mergers and acquisitions.

Then, to make matters worse, GE forfeited more than $10 billion of the value we created when it undersold NBC Universal to Comcast in 2011. GE was already reeling from huge losses in reinsurance, power generation orders, airline travel, and mortgage-backed securities. So, fearing digital media would become just another imploding investment and needing cash to restore GE Capital, the company decided to make a quick exit. The timing was dreadful. Comcast paid $30.5 billion over 2 years—about $15 billion less than NBC Universal's street value in 2006!

These complex dynamics were rarely considered in their entirety and easily missed by Wall Street and the press. But understanding what was going on at General Electric during NBC's transformational decade (1996–2006) helps explain some of the menacing twists and turns we encountered. Looking back now, it seems very much like the agonizing Inferno voyage that thirteenth-century Italian poet Dante Alighieri graphically described in *The Divine Comedy*.

Only this was a financial hell of GE's own making.

That's not what you'd expect from a conservative conglomerate consumed by process and methodology. And yet GE played some heavy investment roulette, most of it through GE Capital financial services with the goal of making greater returns outside its more predictable core industrial assets.

GE Capital grew so large it quickly contributed half of GE's earnings, some of which were used to fuel its investment engine. So when some of those investments crashed, they dragged down GE's overall worth. Jack Welch was applauded for these bold bets—before some collapsed when he retired and turned into a nightmare for his successor, Jeff Immelt.

You could say Jeff Immelt was doomed from the start. His first official day as the new announced president CEO was September 11, 2001, even though he had been president for 9 months. GE's jet engine business had been at an all-time high in orders when the 9/11 tragedies brought all commercial aviation to a grinding halt.

Power generation and jet engine orders, and consumer air travel were way off for 2 years. That's the kind of black swan that can't be anticipated, but it just killed us. GE stock traded as low as $22 a share. There was no plan B.

But the airline losses weren't the only problem. GE's stock price hit a record high of $59.88 per share September 8, 2000, after public utilities were deregulated. When Enron created a supply and demand energy bubble, GE followed it down the rabbit hole, which turned out, instead, to be a sinkhole. Enron and its top executives were taken down in the 2001 scandal, while GE lost billions of dollars on canceled orders, despite the valiant efforts of John Rice, Bob Nardelli's successor as head of power generation. The combined fallout from that scandal and the effects of 9/11 put too much pressure on GE's financial services and exposed a huge weakness in GE's reinsurance program. Anchored by Employers Reinsurance Corp. (ERC), that was the next business to self-destruct in a blaze of controversy and losses.

Immelt spent every day from 2002 to 2006 trying to get GE out of the insurance and reinsurance businesses, which turned out to be more volatile, capital intensive, and slow growing than anticipated. In 2005, GE finally spun off $2.8 billion of its insurance assets into the publicly traded Genworth Financial and made a separate $6.8 billion sale to Swiss Reinsurance Co. in 2006. GE, arguably, should never have been in the international reinsurance business.

GE barely had time to catch its breath before the US housing market deflated, vaporizing the value of its mortgage-backed securities. The timing could not have been worse. By 2008 and 2009, GE's financial services arm was racking up $32 billion in losses.

We should have been more skeptical of the housing boom and of the Internet mortgage business GE Capital invested in. For instance, in 2004, GE bought California subprime lender WMC Mortgage Corp. for $500 million—and eventually lost more than twice that. GE became so enamored of the online mortgage industry in California and in Texas in 2007 that it failed to see there was some real sloppiness going on at companies it funded. It was borderline fraud. When we started looking deeper, we realized many of the people getting mortgage loans online were unemployed and unable to make their payments.

When the real estate market crashed, GE was holding $50 billion in paper profits that went up in smoke. We were too slow liquidating our commercial real estate positions while the federal government demanded that wholesale banks like GE Capital reduce their risk and holdings.

On top of all that, GE shot itself in the foot with the decades-long multibillion-dollar dredging of New York's Hudson River to clean up 1.3 million pounds of polychlorinated biphenyls (PCBs) and other toxins that had been flowing from two GE plants for 3 decades, until banned in 1977. We thought adequate reserves were on the books years earlier. Not so.

When the dam finally burst, GE was confronted by too many major gushes that compromised its structural and financial integrity. NBC's media investments were among the bright spots. We were betting on a cable and digital future, staying out of GE's sights while we made it happen. Soon we had $30 billion in cable network value that dwarfed its broadcast TV properties.

Originally GE thought it was getting a stable subsidiary in NBC that would generate reliable cash flow to reinvest in GE Capital's new ventures. And for a long time, that was true. But there were a lot of things going on in media involving new technology that were about to challenge the broadcast business. When GE paid $6 billion for RCA in 1986, NBC's market value was about $2 billion. By the time cable giant Comcast bought it 25 years later, it was worth about $40 billion, with most of that rooted in cable television. That's the awfulness of it. I can't let the $30 billion Comcast paid for NBCU be the defining number for me. We were worth as much as $45 billion and generating $4 billion in pretax earnings just 2 years after the NBC and Universal merger closed in May 2004. ***That's the number.***

Here's the bottom line: while GE's fortunes fell, NBC's fortunes rose—but we were reduced to a footnote on the conglomerate's ledger as a core subsidiary buried under all of GE's bad business news.

❖ **Steve Burke, president Comcast Cable, then chairman CEO NBC Universal, 2009–present.** The most striking thing about NBC the last 10 years under GE ownership was the huge amount of value that was created through strategic acquisitions. Virtually all of the assets acquired when Comcast bought NBC Universal in 2009 were added during that last decade. The value of what we really bought was created outside of the NBC TV networks and stations. In fact, it would be difficult even now to calculate the value of those original core businesses if NBC had not undergone that transformation.

But it would be a very small fraction and we might not have been interested in purchasing NBC at all if that's all that was there. The NBC we bought had 100 percent of its earnings come from the cable channels, which is remarkable considering that CNBC has only been around 25 years and MSNBC half that time. The big bang was the NBC Universal deal in 2004, not just because NBC gained control of a film studio and theme parks, but it brought the powerhouse cable channels USA and Sci-Fi. That was the real master stroke by Bob in the amount of value that was added and the way the deal was structured. ❖

The ultimate irony was that GE's freefall coincided with the strongest programming NBC ever had in news, sports, and entertainment. We were able to double down on the financials. It was NBC's turn to look brilliant after maneuvering through a minefield of poor ratings and press in the early 1990s. Today, NBC Universal is generating $4 billion-plus in free cash flow for Comcast, which is what our peak was years ago.

———————

The real story here for me is *how* people built that much value at NBCU—a high-profile, privately held media company—inside a large, controlling public conglomerate with rigid guidelines, a very different agenda, and complicated internal politics. Our goal was to create something much more significant for the times, even though GE did not always make it easy.

I compare it to swimming across the English Channel. You are almost halfway across and you're exhausted. Now, do you go forward or backward? That situation happens in business all the time. You argue about whether you are halfway across or doubling down on a bad investment. If you are only a third of the way across, and you are tired, you might go back. If you are 65 percent of the way across, some people will still argue to go back, but you have a stronger case to try to finish.

GE was afraid of digital TV. GE found itself halfway across the channel and decided it was going to cut its losses and go back before it could realize a full return on its media investments. We had to expand, and when we did it became a different business, not something GE could understand or wanted to be in.

During 2009/2010 all media was in the tank. Ad sales were in a bad cycle and investing was greatly curtailed. It was a perfect time for private equity and hedge funds to get in just as established companies were tied up in knots and selling assets at bargain prices.

That's how Comcast picked up NBCU at a modest price with a structure that initially kept it off of its own books while repositioning NBCU in a digital world. GE decided to sell NBCU to Comcast by giving up 51 percent majority control (less than 2 years later, it sold the remaining 49 percent). Comcast assumed debt, which restricted the income, but it knew what to do with NBC's treasure trove of content. So GE said, "Let's take a ride on this thing with Comcast before we take it off our books; maybe we can get something more out of it." GE reported NBCU as a discontinued business nobody cared about, just to get it done and get out.

That is the same indifference that prevailed when the top forty leaders of GE's executive council were clueless about the promise of portable digital technology and summarily **dismissed an opportunity to buy into Apple** in 1996. At that time, the late Steve Jobs had been absent for 10 years from the company he'd founded, having been ousted by his own board. He would return by early 1997 to lead Apple through historic growth and changes in technology. Michael Spindler, Apple's then CEO, attended one of our corporate executive council's regular meetings to propose that GE make a strategic investment in his company. At the time Apple stock was trading around $20 a share and its $30 billion market cap was a fraction of GE's $400 billion. Spindler was in trouble and almost tearful with sweat rolling off his face. Nearly everyone thought Apple would curl up and die. But that's precisely when you want to buy into a company with promise—when it's down. We would have looked brilliant! Apple's market cap topped at $775 billion in February 2015; GE topped out at nearly a $600 billion market cap in September 2000. GE had already struggled with robotics and didn't have any stomach for personal digital electronics.

❖ **Brandon Burgess.** The businesses we acquired from 2000 to 2005 transformed NBC into a completely different thriving company anchored in cable television, movie studios, and theme parks. These were businesses GE swore it would never get into even though the payoff was huge. The merged NBC Universal generated three times the earnings as the old NBC. NBC's legacy broadcast-based earnings had already been slashed in half to about $1 billion by 2000, ebbing and flowing with the fortunes of the NBC TV network and stations.

Cable and early digital media were center stage. We advanced our hand in those areas, acquiring Universal for $12 billion paid out over 5 years, Telemundo for $2.7 billion, Bravo for $1.2 billion, and even the new San Francisco–area affiliate KNTV for $230 million. The synergistic fit of these acquisitions with NBC's assets and the creative structure of the deals resulted in $30 billion in new shareholder value. Everything went up: revenues, profits, return on investment, stock price, and market cap. We created a well-timed strategic and operational hedge around a US broadcast business under pressure. Just as NBC's core broadcast earnings were falling to near zero, the annual earnings of the newly created NBC Universal reached $3.6 billion, including the 20 percent ownership of Vivendi. Although GE was the primary beneficiary, NBC no longer was a company it was comfortable with or understood.

When GE handed off all of that $30 billion intrinsic value to Comcast in 2011, it no longer viewed NBC as a critical cash flow source for its outside financial investments, which had radically altered. For a while in the 1980s and 1990s, GE reinvested the cash flow from NBC's broadcast TV network and stations in GE Capital ventures and new businesses that yielded 15 to 20 percent return on capital compared to the single-digit returns in media. GE always provided the semblance of stability and gave us the funds for growth acquisitions—Universal being the most important.

If we had not transformed NBC's asset portfolio when we did, the way we did, the company would be in a very different situation today and most likely would not have been acquired by Comcast. It would have become dead weight for GE. ❖

GE responded to external threats and challenges to its businesses the way a lot of big companies do. They think they can avoid being impacted by some major global issue, which is not the case at all. That has more to do with arrogance than with negligence. We didn't do anything wrong, but when the rules started to change, GE thought it could get by with the only approach it knew. But it became less adept at anticipating or being able to offset those troubles because of the number of high-risk bets it was making and so many factors out of its control. GE did not move quickly to revise its operating dynamics and sensibilities, even when it ventured far outside of its core businesses. It continued to behave like an industrial production giant in its heyday, even as the world economy was moving in a different direction.

All of this was compounded by Jack Welch's two missions: to secure a high stock price and market cap for GE and to protect his legacy. GE Capital's far-reaching investment portfolio was one way he sought to achieve both. Making a failed bid for rival Honeywell in his last extended year before exiting GE was another. Worse yet, we sat on billions of no-growth or low-growth assets that severely constrained our return on investment (ROI) and return on equity (ROE). Getting that off the books was a P&L (profit and loss) discussion that got postponed forever.

It became a case price/earnings ratio woulda, shoulda, coulda.

When the stock P/E (price-earnings ratio) exceeded 25 and ran to a P/E of 40 between 1997 and 2000, GE should have used its stock for acquisitions while writing off dead, weak, or low-yielding assets. At a P/E of 30, we should have been examining why the P/E was so high and whether there were serious bubble issues emerging. We should have paid more attention to major regulatory changes between 2002 and 2004. Sarbanes-Oxley screamed for transparency. Write-offs were suddenly expected and tolerated by analysts. We should have refreshed our board of directors regularly before and after the energy and housing bubbles. We should have done a deep dive on GE capital asset risk and returns between 1996 and 2002.

Put another way, when we were rising up from 1995 to 2000 it was like waiting to board **the Queen Mary 2.** GE and many other public companies saw valuations go higher as all boats rose with the tide. Most corporate CEOS looked like managers of the century for a while. By 2001, we actually discovered we were on **the Exxon Valdez**! It turns out we were sailing around the world in a 1,100-foot tanker bleeding oil all over the place. We were sailing an entirely different ship until as late as 2009, and it was literally like voyaging through hell with no life jackets. It was like Dante's Inferno, and it was just awful!

Directors are there to protect shareholders' interests and bear responsibility when there are adverse impacts on shareholder value. Directors must pay attention to significant increases in shareholder value as measured by the P/E ratios. A P/E ratio over 25 for a large established company needs careful examination. When a P/E exceeds 30, directors should be discussing the reasons why the P/E is so high and whether there are serious bubble issues with the stock.

The GE board of directors—and I was one of them—should have provided a backstop to senior management on all of this. And for a lot of complicated reasons, that didn't happen. Anyone sitting on the GE board of directors, as I did through the end of the 1990s until 2008, had to assume responsibility for the unraveling of some businesses and GE's plunging market cap. The board should have been more vigilant about investments in reinsurance, mortgage-backed securities, and other areas new to our portfolio even before they started going south. We should have dumped or written off assets that weren't producing income and were hurting ROI.

Instead, we moved from crisis to crisis, with no inclination to examine the big picture and consider whether the problems were in fact bigger and deeper than they appeared. The drill was to put the fire out, insulate the rest of GE's businesses, and move on with only limited acknowledgment of what went wrong. An earlier course correction could have saved GE a lot of money and grief.

Overall, from 1996 to January 2009, GE created and lost $530 billion in value, in part because the board of directors and senior management failed to accept responsibility for reining in and reversing failing or threatened investments. We underestimated the lingering impact of the 9/11 terrorist attacks and GE's overall vulnerability. Nobody would have thought it was possible for GE's market value to fall from a high of $600 billion to as low as $70 billion at one point—the greatest loss of market capital in business history.

GE tanked when it lost control. The primary reason for inaction by the GE board and senior management was an unwillingness to recognize losses and promptly deal with them. We did everything possible to avoid taking losses when a business was not doing well, and just kept plugging away at it. We would change managers or marketing campaigns. It was all about absorbing the pain of not doing well for as long as they could before taking a write-off.

The fact is the GE board was seduced by GE Capital's financial promise of making money in areas that were free of the costs, accountability, and long-range goals that encumbered our other operations. GE directors were so hungry for GE Capital's earnings, they didn't want to take 10 percent of those earnings off the table to buy hedges to businesses that could have lapses.

The same thing happened with NBC. GE wanted NBC's cash flow, but it didn't necessarily want to reinvest in the company to build replacement businesses that would generate new cash flow. When we grew the broadcasting network into cable, it was like pulling teeth. American businesses right now spend most of their time planning one or two quarters. They don't have the time or energy to map out how they would like to see their businesses 10 years from now in the context of bigger changes. Many of the matters that became controversial for GE were handled the old-fashioned way at the outset and then wrestled with in the era of Sarbanes-Oxley, which required more public accountability and transparency.

For instance, we never had any serious discussion with the GE board at any meeting I attended about **alternative ownership for NBC or about opportunities to deal with private equity.** That was thinking too far down the road. That was a lost opportunity to generate value for shareholders. So many of the board deliberations about GE's relatively new business investments were more a review of the numbers than a debate about the macro industry threats to these businesses.

This is a chronic problem in business. Chief executives need strong board members when the stock is on the way up and strong board members when it's on the way down—and they should not be the same people. In both cases you should have board members who are not burdened by the past and are focused on the present to grow the stock and mitigate significant losses.

It is the responsibility of the board to protect shareholders' interest as well as the integrity of employees' rights. It is a very broad agenda.

When you are an established company and your stock hits a P/E ratio over 30, you're likely headed into a bubble. That is a time to celebrate; have a party, sell some stock along with executives, employees, and board members and start preparing for the end of the bubble. That's when the CEO should be moving board members out who have been a strong part of the bubble and moving new board members in who can deal with the downside. This generally doesn't happen or get enough attention.

There is no natural churn on boards, which should occur about every 7 to 8 years, aligning with the average length of time of the CEO. That would have been helpful if we at GE had encouraged longtime board members to follow Welch out the door and replace them with new board members better prepared for the enormous downside that followed. It would have created a natural check and balance. One of the reasons hedge funds and private equity exist is that established corporations love to buy at the top and sell at the bottom. Hedge funds and private equity do just the opposite!

❖ **Ann McLaughlin Korologos, former chairman Rand board and Aspen Institute; US Secretary of Labor 1987– 1989, director on numerous boards including GM and Microsoft.** Before we were fellow directors on the Rand Corporation board, Bob Wright and I were friends bound by tumultuous events in corporate governance. I had served most of my adult life on corporate boards of all shapes and sizes. I was on the General Motors board of directors in the 1990s when it wrestled with the aftermath of NBC's *Dateline* report that threw the carmaker's integrity and product quality into question. So when I watched from afar as one crisis after another rocked GE, I understood what my friend was going through.

What caught my attention most was when Jack Welch got into trouble pressing for exorbitant retirement benefits, like his unlimited use of the GE corporate jet for life. Even at that point in his legendary career, I thought that was wrong. I don't know how it passed the red face test. Shame on boards who allow that kind of CEO-itis to run rampant. Some boards confuse what is illegal and what is just plain wrong. Jack Welch broke no laws by asking, but seriously considering some of the excesses he wanted was wrong.

That's why it's so important for boards to have a "Rules of the Road" governing the behavior and expectations of its members—yes, even CEOs—so there is no question how they should conduct themselves. You can have tremendous talent and tremendous wisdom on a board. But without firm expectations and mandates governing boards, individual members cannot focus on matters at hand and make a difference.

I'm not sure GE ever valued its board that way. You have to look at a board the way you should look at a company. It's about people first and foremost, and inspiring them with leadership to meet challenges. ❖

The Poinsett Club
Greenville, South Carolina
October 29, 2000

There is no doubt Jack Welch's stranglehold on the GE board of directors and his distraction with selecting his successor played a part in shaping GE's and NBC's changing strategies and fortunes at the beginning of a new millennium. And Jeff Immelt and GE struggled with the consequences many years after Jack left.

That all came to a head one Sunday night in the historical, stately, colonial trappings of one of America's first private clubs. It was supposed to be relaxed cocktails and dinner at the Poinsett Club that would transition GE board members from their annual Augusta National Golf Outing late that week to the serious business of a special board meeting Monday to vote on who would be GE's new chairman CEO. But the social event turned tense as Jack turned the post-dinner talk into a makeshift discussion about succession. His goal was to address head-on the schism that had suddenly developed among board members about whether Jim McNerney or Jeff Immelt (Jack's personal favorite) should lead. Jack wanted everyone on the same page before the next day's critical succession vote.

Eighteen months earlier, Jack had created a horse race for CEO with three of GE's top business division leaders: Jim McNerney (aircraft engines), Jeff Immelt (medical systems) and Bob Nardelli (power systems). He said he would carefully evaluate all of them and then make a recommendation to the board. Prior to Greenville, I met with Jack and asked where he stood. He said Immelt was his choice and asked if I would support that call. I said yes because Jack had enormous contact with all three and was a good evaluator.

Although Welch had been playing his cards close to the vest, I was surprised because I had thought that he had orchestrated the succession plan he wanted and that the board vote was just a formality. Deciding to have the October 30 board meeting at the Greenville manufacturing plant of GE's robust power generation business appeared to be a cordial nod to Bob Nardelli, the third and least likely CEO candidate.

Everyone was already rattled by Jack Welch's abrupt decision to remain GE's chairman CEO for another year rather than stepping down at age 65 in September 2000. The merits of his unilateral decision will long be debated. In hindsight, Jack staying on longer really wasn't a good idea. He kept pushing out the dates for his retirement partly because it was what he wanted to do, partly because he was wrestling with succession, and partly, I suspect, to allow him time for one last deal. I believe he recognized that GE needed a big acquisition to maintain its share price, and unfortunately he chose Honeywell as his best solution. So he tried selling the board on the notion that they couldn't operate without him. That's some of the spin that happened with succession planning, so that it became more emotionally charged and complicated than it should have been.

I was named vice chairman of GE at age 57 in late 2000 with the understanding that I would not succeed Jack as GE chairman. It was a kind of consolation prize for me that eventually carried with it more liabilities than perks, and a huge diversion from the aggressive growth moves I continued to make as NBC chairman CEO. I was expected to be a devil's advocate and, sometimes, the voice of reason in the candidate assessments and selection of his successor. It ultimately cost me my career-long friendship with Welch, especially when it came to his divorce and his controversial GE exit package. (More on that in Chapter 20.)

As it turned out, I played a key role in shifting board sentiment in Jeff Immelt's favor that night before the succession vote. Jack seemed to be uncommonly nervous during dinner. Without any chitchat, he began an informal discussion about succession. There was certain uneasiness in the room. Jack unexpectedly turned to me and asked me to discuss my choice for a new chairman and my rationale. Suddenly I was being thrust into the role of kingmaker with no time to think. I said I thought all three candidates had terrific talents but in the end it really was a choice between McNerney and Immelt. While in my opinion both were extremely qualified, I recommended that Immelt be appointed. Jack gave a sigh of relief. My comments seemed to cut short any debate on the matter. Jack may have preferred Immelt because he was the youngest candidate and therefore could have a long run at GE, like Jack's 20 years. Jack liked the medical business that Immelt oversaw and felt he possessed the solid mind and skills to handle GE's diverse business interests.

Even the next day, there was tension and hesitation in the room as different directors took the floor to speak on the behalf of one of the three CEO candidates. And then Jack spoke, as if to get everyone on his team. I may have been the honest broker and the deciding vote in the matter—I just don't know. I recognized that Immelt was Jack's candidate, and part of my role was to be supportive. So when Jack asked me to second Immelt's nomination, I did. But no one was bending my arm.

The special board meeting ended with the selection of Immelt. Jack made a point of speaking to the two other CEO candidates. There was an excitement about what was going to take place over the next 3 or 4 days. I wonder now how Jeff feels, given the misfortunes that have defined his tenure. Although most were not of his making, Immelt—like all chief executives—can be judged not so much by what happened on his watch as by his response to it.

In hindsight, I think McNerney probably would have made a better chief executive for GE. After overseeing GE's powerful aircraft engine business, he went on to distinguish himself the most of the three CEO candidates as chairman CEO of 3M and later of Boeing. But he would have wrestled with the same issues as Immelt. The big difference is that Immelt was too beholden to Jack. Jack was always protecting and advancing his own legacy, even after he left the company, and he did that through Jeff. Immelt was somewhat naïve and grateful for the CEO appointment. Long after Jack had left, Immelt kept enhancing Jack's reputation, which was not a positive thing to do. He was given a whole year to figure this out, and he didn't.

Wright to the Point

My intricate involvement in shaping GE's post-Welch fate seems a little peculiar in hindsight. I had often moved against the grain at GE, advancing NBC's contrarian agenda. NBC was a star performer in the second half of the 1990s into the 2000s and was at the peak of its success when GE was having a terrible time. That dramatic contrast in value created and destroyed at NBC and GE is the surprising financial story here.

GE had a long-term plan for NBC, as it did for all of its businesses, but its board of directors never bought into it. NBC Universal grew enormous quickly but was not that attractive to or completely understood by the board, regardless of the lasting value we created.

The rules and expectations, the hierarchy and business sensibilities at NBC and GE were just too different to ever be reconciled. There was an irreparable break between value as NBC defined it and as GE demanded it. The risks we took yielded the kind of financial rewards GE wanted. But by then, GE was shell-shocked by its own string of failed investments and huge losses, and NBCU became a casualty. Its sale proceeds were needed to meet rigorous new banking capital requirements. It took GE until 2015 to figure out it was not suited to financial services with a plan to dismantle GE Capital and return to being 90 percent industrial dependent.

By October 2015, GE finally rose above the long-standing $25 a share price where it stagnated for so long. It is a different company, shedding businesses and returning to an industrial focus. Immelt is restructuring and dismantling GE Capital, where so much of the value creation and destruction occurred. The sale of about $120 billion in financial assets will unwind a big part of the Welch legacy. The stock did not get much of a bump on the initial news because the market was not happy with some of GE's prior investments and skeptical how it might invest the proceeds from the divestitures. There's the lingering memory of some of the largest losses and gains in stock market history.

It took activist investor Nelson Peltz and his Trian Partners' unexpected $2.5 billion stake in GE in October 2015 to immediately validate GE's plans and boost the company's stock price 10 percent. There is a growing sense GE will emerge from all of this a super-strong multinational industrial steered by digital technology that is more attractive to investors. Every dollar per share increase translates into $10 billion in additional market cap which is good for employees, shareholders and investors. Peltz's 1 percent position coupled with Immelt's efforts promise near-term upside and renewed recognition of GE as a fabulous industrial company with very strong management and wonderful employees worldwide.

17
Rebooting Network-Affiliate Relations

W hen I took over as president of NBC in September 1986, I didn't just inherit a well-known TV network. I also inherited some 200 TV stations in the NBC family, all with wildly different agendas and personalities.

NBC, like the other networks, remained dependent on negotiated partnerships with individual stations or groups of stations owned by a single company. Those over-the-air broadcasters commanded their own call letters (WXYZ-TV) and local domains where they were handsomely paid to be the exclusive outlets for NBC programs. Their local newscasts and afternoon syndicated shows especially benefited from the lead-in and lead-out audiences of popular network programs. For many, network cash compensation constituted as much as 1/3 of their annual income.

Originally, affiliate relationships were ruled by the law of simpler times. Only one station in any one city would be allowed to carry the programming of that network, the stations would have to carry *all* their network's programs, and—most significant—would be paid by the networks for that privilege.

Although no one wanted to admit it, the partnership begged for an overhaul—one I was determined to make. It was clear to me from the start, with cable television rapidly competing for viewers and advertising dollars, that this long-established practice was no longer justified. But transforming network-affiliate relations became a lot like trying to redirect the *Titanic*. It was necessary to avoid disaster but near impossible because of quickly shifting economics and defiant clinging to old ways.

While in a broader sense the competitive rules and economics of our industry were changing, the dynamics between the network and the affiliates remained stubbornly static. A constant tug-of-war centered on their uninterrupted carriage (or "clearance") of our national news, entertainment, and sports as well as splitting the airtime to sell national and local TV advertising.

As absurd as it seems today, NBC, CBS, and ABC paid their affiliates to televise original programs the stations could not otherwise afford. But compensation didn't deter some of our stations from abbreviating or completely preempting scheduled network shows in favor of their own local news and sports.

Anyone paying attention could see that the growth of cable was about to turn broadcasting on its head. But most TV station owners considered subscription-based cable and satellite TV services the enemy, believing they siphoned away viewers and advertisers and diluted their program ratings. Unlike "free" TV broadcasters, cable operators had two core revenue sources to support their coaxial pipeline to homes: advertising and subscription fees.

So the last thing our affiliates wanted to hear from me was how developing our own cable channels would strengthen NBC's chances of survival in a multichannel world. They fought us tooth and nail over the creation of CNBC and MSNBC (more details in Chapters 9 and 15). And they fought even more fiercely over another change: today the affiliates no longer receive compensation from the network for carrying the programs. The tables have been completely turned; now it's the affiliates who pay the networks.

But getting there was not easy.

The television station business was booming in the 1980s and the early 1990s. In a flourishing economy, owning a TV station or major broadcast network was like having a license to print money. There was no direct video competition; newspapers, radio, and billboards were completely different media animals. Cable television was just getting started. That monopoly cultivated an elitist attitude among some local station owners. They were emboldened by a sense of entitlement that was fostered for decades by the broadcast TV networks as their programming and promotions lifeline to American homes.

But by the late 1990s traditional media was shaken by consumers' willingness to pay monthly subscriptions to cable systems owned by the likes of Time Warner, Comcast, and Tele-Communications Inc. for specialized channels providing news, movies, and children's, nature, and sports programs. As cable began destabilizing broadcast TV, we had no choice but to reduce and eventually eliminate affiliates' cash compensation.

And then we made things worse by "tampering," as they saw it, with two of our golden franchises: network news (by establishing two cable news shows) and Olympics telecasts (by airing some events on cable).

The final straw for the stations came in 2000, when we brazenly switched our long-standing affiliation from San Francisco's KRON-TV to a small San Jose station. KNTV's willingness to richly pay NBC—rather than be paid—to carry its network programs was a watershed event. It was the first case of reverse compensation and a bold catalyst for reinventing the partnership between NBC and its affiliates.

Office of NBC CEO Bob Wright
NBC Headquarters, Rockefeller Center
New York City
February 8, 2000

Vincent Young, the CEO of Young Broadcasting, was still beaming about having outbid NBC in a record $823 million purchase of San Francisco's KRON-TV, the top-ranked station in the fifth-largest TV market. But during a brief exchange he clearly became irked. In a stark reversal of traditional network-affiliate relations, Randy Falco and I told Young Broadcasting executives that NBC would cease paying KRON $7.5 million in annual cash compensation to televise its network schedule. In fact, the tables would be turned. If he wanted to maintain the affiliation, Young would have to pay NBC $10 million every year to offset increased program costs. KRON would be rebranded NBC4, reduce 3/4 of its voluntary preemption of NBC's core primetime series (airing nightly 7 to 10 p.m.), and give the network access to its new digital data capabilities.

Young flatly rejected our take-it-or-leave-it proposition.

The very next day he tried calling our bluff, defiantly announcing that he would sever the station's 52-year ties to NBC and become an independent broadcaster. That meant hits like *ER, Friends, The Today Show, The Tonight Show,* and *NBC Nightly News* would need a new San Francisco home when KRON's NBC pact expired in the beginning of 2002.

Two days later on February 10, 2000, we shocked Young and the entire broadcasting world with plans to move NBC's affiliation to KNTV at the end of KRON's contract term. The groundbreaking arrangement called for Granite Broadcasting, the station owner, to pay NBC an average $37 million annually for the right to air its entertainment, news, and sports programs. KNTV was thus the first network affiliate to pay for programming. It was a scathing checkmate that set all network-affiliate relations in a tailspin of irreversible change.

And then the double whammy.

On December 17, 2001, ahead of the proposed affiliation switch, NBC agreed to buy KNTV from Granite Broadcasting for $230 million—a mere fraction of what Young paid for KRON. So KNTV joined the thirteen other stations already owned and operated by NBC's Television Stations Division. Then we went a step further than our network rivals by acquiring the Spanish-language network Telemundo in 2002. That created the nation's first group "duopoly," the ability to own and program two TV stations in the same market. The deregulated arrangement afforded savings to stations who could now share marketing, news-gathering, and programming expenses.

A quirky byproduct of the KNTV deal inadvertently created an advantage for cable. Beginning in 2002, nearly 400,000 viewers in the extended San Francisco–Oakland–San Jose market were unable to access NBC programs on either KNTV's over-the-air broadcast channel or on AT&T's cable channel because both regular signals were too weak to accommodate the mountainous and coastal terrain. The affiliation switch threw a meaningful fraction of the area's 2.4 million TV households into the dark, forcing them to cable—into what many broadcasters considered the enemy camp—if they wanted to continue viewing NBC.

❖ **Randy Falco.** When we called Young's bluff by switching the NBC affiliation to KNTV, KRON was forced to transform into an independent station, relying on local news and syndicated entertainment. Within 3 years, KRON's cash flow declined precipitously and its value plummeted to about $200 million. It was a dramatic demonstration of the enormous value of a network affiliation.

That triggered a windfall of affiliation negotiations in NBC's favor. Suddenly I was inundated by TV station owners calling to renew long-term affiliation deals even though we were reducing and eventually eliminating compensation and expecting their financial support for programming in return. In less than a decade, the $350 million in total affiliate compensation NBC had paid every year was wiped off the books while the network received new revenues from stations to help pay for expensive sports licenses fees and other big events. No major network had ever reversed compensation practices on its established affiliates. No one believed we could do it! ❖

❖ **Brandon Burgess.** When we switched from KRON to KNTV, I believe that was the largest reverse compensation deal for any one station in the country, and I think maybe it still is.

Other broadcasters warned NBC it was a big mistake that could create a financial disaster. The numbers tell a different story. Several years into it, KNTV was generating more than $50 million in annual cash flow. So, on a payback basis, KNTV turned out to be a very attractive acquisition. That was the beginning of NBC transforming its station portfolio and establishing more of a mutual business partnership with its station affiliates. The eventual mandatory payment of fees to broadcasters by cable operators for the retransmission of their signals was the final step in that evolution.

At a time when no one really wanted to rock the boat too much, we chose strategic change. Over time, that proved a very good move. ❖

Affiliate reform wasn't about a single event and it didn't just take hours or days or weeks; it took years—actually the better part of a decade. Probably the biggest, bloodiest battle was over cable.

While we remained dedicated to broadcasting, I knew our developing cable interests would sustain and grow the NBC TV network. Many of the affiliates understood what I was saying and why, but they still didn't like it. They feared cable would take some of the luster off of their core broadcast television business. In fact, they didn't like anything we did to expand NBC's cable presence.

I think it probably came to a head when we made CNBC a second platform for televising many of the Olympic events that didn't make it onto the network. Every 2 years after that, we added more of our cable channels to the mix until Olympic events were also televised on MSNBC, Bravo, and USA. Eventually, stations came to realize that the additional advertising and subscription revenues generated by our Olympic cable telecasts helped to offset our overall production costs and enhance our profitability from the games.

Cyril Vetter was one of the affiliate station executives who helped me fight that good fight. He was the chairman of the affiliate committee that addressed public relations, and he and Bill Bolster worked relentlessly to explain our situation. Cyril understood and accepted the economic realities we all faced. He was also one of the biggest beneficiaries of our aggressive stance because he only owned one station in a marketplace that was changing faster than he could afford to catch up with it. For a brief time before he sold, he was a stand-alone broadcaster who helped some of his bigger industry peers take a leap of faith into cable. Playing ostrich, he said, was not an option. It sounds like a no-brainer now, but back then it was blasphemous.

❖ **Cyril Vetter.** Bob's push for cable caused a lot of grousing. People were afraid cable would take away revenues that were dwindling anyway. There were a few of us who got what Bob was talking about, and some curmudgeon owners and managers who just didn't want to hear it under any circumstances. They would object to everything whether it made sense or not. They were afraid of change that inevitably was for the better.

Financial interest and syndication rule reform was a perfect example. Bob said, "Look, this is crazy that we can't own or profit from the programs that we finance. We put up millions of dollars for every show and we can't have an ownership interest in it after it leaves the network to go into syndication. It's nuts!" And, you know, even the curmudgeons in the affiliate group got their brains around that. And we had a very successful initiative. We had an affiliate convention in Washington, DC. Station managers and owners and operators really lobbied their own congressmen and the Federal Communications Commission for a rule change we eventually won. That was a nice shot in the arm for the broadcast network business, which was always being forecast to be on death's door. Those rumors are always out there, you know.

Another example of where the network and stations joined forces and made a difference was in pressing for retransmission fees. It seemed to me that allowing cable operators to take our TV signals, which were really their most valuable inroad into the home, and then package and sell it without compensating us didn't make any sense, either. It was high heresy at the time, but that's when I proposed that if cable operators carry us, they would have to pay us for our signals. It seemed like a fair choice.

The retransmission fees that are now routinely negotiated by stations and networks were intended to achieve the same equity. We're making it possible for cable operators to compete and make a living, which is fine because it benefits the American television viewing public. But they ought to at least pay us something for it because they are using our most valuable product to get their nose under the tent to generate a dual revenue stream—from advertising and viewer subscriptions—that broadcast stations don't have but should have! ❖

By the time most affiliates resigned themselves to being in the cable business, they still could not agree on what that should look like. By then, 7 broadcast networks, 280 cable channels, 4 million websites and more than 70 percent of Americans paying for video on cable or satellite were creating enormous pressures on free broadcasters. At first, our affiliate complained when we aired a 30-second CNBC report on the stock market at the end of our *Nightly News* or adopted a version of the NBC peacock in the CNBC and MSNBC logos. They considered it an infringement.

I think it was our extended news coverage of the 9/11 events on cable, particularly MSNBC, that showed everyone that our plan for the profitable coexistence of broadcast and cable could actually work. It only took 14 years from the start of our reform efforts.

❖ **Cyril Vetter.** Whether it was NBC wanting to rebroadcast *Late Night with Conan O'Brien* or *The Today Show* or secondary Olympic events on its CNBC cable business channel or on MSNBC, affiliates always wanted some meaningful period of exclusivity—like a 7-day window—that would assure them first dibs on prize content. But NBC could no longer promise exclusivity to its stations, because it needed the flexibility to televise its content wherever and however it made the most economic sense—even if it was on cable. Deregulation allowed NBC and the other broadcast networks to morph into major content players servicing all media. The biggest challenge then was maximizing revenues from a myriad of new consumer connections—which was basic and pay cable at first; then VHS and DVDs; and eventually over-the-top streaming video. After its merger with Universal, its content expanded beyond NBC network programs to include the studio's movies and TV shows.

It was clear that TV stations were going to see their viewers and advertising dollars disperse over a more expansive TV landscape of hundreds of cable channels. Advertisers were overwhelmed with understanding and reaching fragmented audiences. So I figured, why not stand in unison with NBC; I was pretty sure it would be our best ticket out of an increasingly bleak situation. The pot of money wasn't getting any bigger; it was kind of a zero-sum game growing by 5 percent to 7 percent a year, being spread to 200 or 300 outlets instead of just three broadcast TV networks.

Ultimately, you just can't fight the marketplace. Consumers are going to determine the winners and the losers no matter what you do. Whether it's business or politics or social change. So I was among the handful of affiliates at the time willing to be contrarian, which put me at odds even with other station owners. ❖

❖ **Randy Falco.** We sent NBC affiliates sideways with the suggestion—made in the heat of battle—that we might just move the NBC TV network to cable as a last resort if they didn't arm us to win in a cable-driven TV world. That's when things got wild!

During my first year as the network president in 1993, Bob made a comment in the press right before we hosted an affiliate convention in New York. He said something about if we could not adequately monetize our content or make equitable deals with affiliates in local markets, then NBC would take its network programming to cable if it had to. That sent the affiliates into convulsions.

So, at the convention, the usual private session with station executives, closed to the press and outsiders, quickly turned into a riot. They started the session with a 10-minute film about the importance of localism and what the stations did best as community touchstones. We politely sat through the video, which was obviously trying to get our goat about how we didn't understand or respect the station business, which they felt was compromised by our decision to televise some NBC programs on cable. At the end of the presentation, Alan Frank, who was the affiliate board president at the time, asked Bob for his comments.

Bob replied, very calmly, that a film like that was a slight to the thousands of people we employed at the television stations owned by NBC in the biggest cities, including New York, Chicago, and Los Angeles. At the time, NBC-owned TV stations were about a $5 billion asset. So the notion that only affiliates appreciated the value of local television was insulting. It turned an already contentious situation even worse.

It took us several years, but eventually the affiliates understood that we were not just going to decouple or abandon the relationship. We always tried to be very straightforward and honest with them. We tried to join forces in figuring out new ways we could work together. To survive and thrive in a new media marketplace, it was as much a matter of being creative as it was learning to trust each other. ❖

Another battle I fought hard for—but lost—was creating an Internet stronghold for our affiliated TV stations. In 1998, which was early in the process, I visited our stations to pitch how we could work together to develop Internet sites. I considered the Internet a critical extension of what the network and the TV stations did, supported by some owners' newspaper and publishing operations. It was a new platform to build an audience and generate revenues. It could have been an amazing exchange of content and views, but it was definitely ahead of its time. It required us to understand and learn to use new technology to our advantage. As with cable, the affiliates were leery about what they considered a threat to their status quo.

I tried to convince the affiliates how easy it would be to adapt their television product to the Internet. "This isn't as hard as you think it is," my memo began. "You're going to sell advertising on a web page that displays your news reports and video and best new ideas." I suggested that they hire a bunch of college students to randomly guide consumers and advertisers through the website, and ask them what they think. On-air telecasts could solicit online viewer response to polls and news stories that they could go to for information. They could check in to see what other viewers were saying about news events or their favorite restaurants. Local businesses that could not afford to buy airtime could advertise online. The possibilities were endless. NBC could work with stations to build an Internet platform where access and economics would create an entirely new ecosystem that would enhance—not replace—television.

I thought that if the head of NBC said it, they might be more responsive to these ideas. But I was wrong. The local stations just wouldn't budge. In 1999, at NBC's annual affiliate meeting, I gave another pitch to stations—this time with slides—about creating different online "channels." They could be for anything: real estate, cars, dining and shopping, the arts. These web pages would showcase stories and facts, chats and advertisements; even consumer posts about items for sale or services, something like Craigslist. It didn't seem complicated to me, but because it was new, station response was generally measured and uptake even slower. Some stations gave it a try but went about it the hard way. The biggest problem affiliates had with it was really understanding that the Internet could be their friend—not their enemy.

There is a valuable lesson in all this. Whatever standard you live by and whatever things you do, you will be shocked at how well you can do things in a different manner if you are open to change. You don't have to let your environment dictate your creativity.

The news organizations—any news organizations—will be the first to tell you that their resources have been cut to the bone. But there comes a point when, if you have a task to do, and you figure it will cost X to do it, and all of a sudden you don't have X, the first thing you do is try to make it work with what you do have—maybe a different way than you had planned. And maybe you land up doing something entirely different.

The idea of seeing technology as your friend rather than as your enemy is a big part of this discussion. It's human nature to run from change, but you can't. There are always better ways to do things, and if you embrace them, you thrive; if you don't, someone else will—and they'll mow you over.

Wright to the Point

Our response to developing technology determines our fate, whether we are companies or people. Technology forced change in the early days of cable and then sculpted change in an Internet era. For our NBC TV station affiliates, cable technology and the interactive options it represented were a force for change that bred as much fear as opportunity. For every kind of company in business and every nonprofit organization, technology provides tools that help us to do our jobs better. We are all believers now, past the initial learning curve. But our creative embrace of the possibilities in those early, uncertain days can make or break us.

I always figured it was better to creatively harness change than to be flattened by it.

All of the principles upon which I have based my business and nonprofit careers came into play in our transformation of the network-affiliate relationship: passion, control, responsibility, empowering others, making the most of your resources through partnerships. Whether it was programming or advertising, whether it was cable or broadcast or the Internet, whether it was affiliate relations or government relations, it took a strong, capable, determined team to put those principles to work. That's not what most people are comfortable with, but it is what's required for commanding and using change for the better.

The KRON-KNTV situation took about 2 years to unfold. If you're looking for a point in network-affiliate relations when everybody accepted what their new role was, that was probably it. And that was an extremely difficult project, incredibly well handled.

We face similar challenges with Autism Speaks, but success is less clear. Eleven years after its inception, we have accomplished a great deal toward developing awareness and resources and advocacy on behalf of children with autism and their families, but, sadly, we're no closer to finding causes and cures.

Autism Speaks no longer can wait for the scientific or medical or academic communities or government to close the gap between what we know and what we need to do. Funding and advocacy are critical but they are not enough. So we have entered a new phase of putting advanced technology to work for our cause in new ways through powerful partnerships. The best example of that at the time of this writing is the genome sequencing project in which Google is using its algorithms and data-crunching expertise to collect, analyze, and organize thousands of individual profiles. The hope is that ultimately this will allow us to identify specific autisms, diagnoses, treatments, and causes on autism's expansive spectrum.

18
Leaving NBC and GE

Chanticleer Restaurant
9 New Street, Siasconset, Nantucket, Massachusetts
August 3, 2006

On a breezy summer day in 2006, David Rubenstein and I met for lunch in the outside garden at Chanticleer, a legendary French restaurant near our homes on Nantucket Island. Rubenstein, founder of the Carlyle Group, a Washington, DC, leveraged buyout firm, was a skilled deal maker, and he was psyched about acquiring the recently merged NBC Universal.

It was a window of opportunity I had imagined for much of my NBC tenure. I gave Rubenstein GE's official position—that NBCU was not for sale—and then quickly added that I thought there was merit in a conversation about his interest. I told him GE valued NBCU at $45 billion; he didn't even flinch. By the time our discussion ended 90 minutes later, we had a pretty decent understanding of the scale of a potential deal.

It should have been easy. There was minimal risk to the private equity buyout Rubenstein and I proposed. At that point, money was cheap, interest rates were falling, and banks were flooded with cash. Every bank wanted to be private equity's partner. There was plenty of interest to do something. But nothing happened. The deal was quickly blocked by GE's new CEO, Jeff Immelt, who insisted that NBCU was not for sale. At the time NBCU had $13 billion in annual revenue, or less than 10 percent of GE's global $375 billion income.

I suppose I shouldn't have been surprised by Immelt's veto. He may have been speaking for the board. By 2006, GE was still recovering from the financial backlash of the prior 6 years of investments in insurance and from the electronic power bubble. GE, which had already waded deeper into media and entertainment than it had ever intended to go with the NBC Universal merger, decided to respond to the downturn by remarketing its core industrial businesses and more or less ignoring NBC.

When it became clear that GE had reverted to status quo, I knew it was time for me to go. So by late 2006, after 21 years at NBC and 40 years at General Electric, I agreed to retire as NBCU chairman CEO in 2007 and as GE vice chairman the following year.

If the Carlyle deal had been consummated, private equity would have had a high-profile entertainment position, I would have fulfilled my long-held desire to independently manage NBCU, and GE would have received a handsome return on its investment. It would have been a win-win for all concerned.

❖ **Brandon Burgess.** We never talked about it, but I think deep down Bob always was hoping that there would be a day when we could all separate from GE. As a publicly traded company, we could create our own stock currency to use to acquire more assets, rather than be acquired by others. That certainly would have been financially lucrative for NBC employees. A lot of people have egg on their face because of the value that was never realized when a private equity spin-off of NBCU never happened. ❖

As the business environment deteriorated and as GE's stock and some of its businesses declined, Immelt became more obliging to the GE board. At the same time, some board members took exception to my increasing involvement with Autism Speaks and were after me to retire as I approached age 65. Eventually, there was almost no clear growth path for NBCU on which I and the GE board could agree. I believed then, as I do now, that Immelt was too influenced by Jack Welch at the beginning of his chairmanship and too beholden to the GE board later on—to his and GE's detriment.

By the time I retired from GE in 2008, the corporation was vexed with housing mortgage shortfalls and capital shortfalls at GE Capital amid a chaotic stock market and unraveling economy. A year later the GE board, at Immelt's request, decided to unload NBC Universal, selling into the downside of a terrible advertising market and recession. GE knew the valuation would be considerably less than what it had been just a few years earlier if we had worked with Rubenstein to spin off NBCU as a stand-alone company. By then much of the value my team and I had worked so long and hard to build was lost.

❖ **Randy Falco.** One of the biggest mistakes Jack Welch made in his business career was not making Bob the chairman of General Electric when he left. It would be in a lot better shape than it is now. Bob would have better maneuvered the tremendous changes GE faced with 9/11 and the financial crisis, the housing bust, and the explosion of the Internet, digital technology, and mobile. After years of fighting everyone who resisted change—including GE—Bob finally started getting recognition for making the deals and having the vision that put NBCU ahead of the game. But Jack's jealousy over that may have clouded his judgment about his own succession. And GE was the big loser. ❖

GE never announced a new business leader until the day the news went public. All preparation was semisecret. The existing leader could have a say but not the final decision. In my case, Jeff Zucker, Randy Falco, and David Zaslav were the key candidates. Immelt was more comfortable with Jeff than with Randy or David. As time went on, all three had plenty of exposure to Immelt. Jeff was quick to speak, Randy was more thoughtful, and David was strong but clearly associated himself with our cable business and didn't want to move around. By mid-2006, Jeff was campaigning and Randy was dropping from Immelt's list. I made it my business to be realistic with Randy and David that their ambitions would not be achieved and they should leave, but I would help them get the best possible separation packages.

And I needed to protect my own interests. In a succinct single-page letter to Jeff Immelt dated November 27, 2006, I outlined options for the executive restructuring he wanted while protecting my full compensation through October 2008. It seemed a good time: that would be my 40th year with GE; I would be 65. It was not meant to be. In the end, the best I could negotiate was to remain chairman of NBC Universal's board of directors until May 2007 while Jeff Zucker assumed daily management as president and CEO. I continued as GE vice chairman until 2008.

Looking back now, the leadership transition that was discreetly under way in December 2006 seems a surrealistic blur. It also was a time of ironic meetings and developments that, in hindsight, seem to bring my professional life full circle. I was hammering out new content agreements with Comcast COO Steve Burke and owner CEO Brian Roberts, who would acquire NBCU just a few years later. Days earlier Suzanne and I had a "catch-up" dinner at the Four Seasons' Pool Room with Helen and Chuck Dolan. Chuck, founder and CEO of Cablevision

Systems, had been my personal friend and NBC business partner since cable's early days. Earlier that same week I met with Tom Lee and top executives of his private equity firm, Thomas H. Lee Partners. I joined them as a senior advisor while I transitioned away from NBCU and GE. My schedule was increasingly peppered with Autism Speaks–related meetings as we worked to build it into a national advocacy force. I was putting into place the steppingstones to a new phase in my life even as I privately lamented having to give up NBCU. By the time I matter-of-factly handed over my CEO title and duties to Jeff Zucker on February 6, 2007, I was resigned to the abrupt end of my 21-year tenure at NBCU.

NBCU's leadership change was as traumatic for my executive team as it was for me. Randy Falco, my longtime trusted right-hand man at NBC, was Jeff Zucker's counterpart as CEO of the NBC Television Network Group. Randy felt he had worked hard to earn the opportunity to succeed me as NBCU chief executive, and he was upset when he didn't get it. Randy's farewell dinner at Mr. Chow on East 57th Street on December 4, 2006, was a melancholy affair. He had been a huge contributor to the value we created at NBC. He and David Zaslav, president of NBC Universal Cable, and other senior members of my team who were pivotal in NBC's growth felt that, in the end, they were not properly rewarded with promotions to higher, more challenging positions—which they found elsewhere. Randy Falco left NBCU to become chief executive at AOL, which was preparing itself to spin out of Time Warner, and later CEO of Univision, the major Spanish-language broadcaster he managed to industry prominence. Zaslav, who brilliantly managed our cable business affairs, also left to become the incredibly successful CEO of Discovery Communications.

❖ **Brandon Burgess.** About that same time, Bob was putting on a pretty hard press trying to acquire DreamWorks movie studio. GE stopped that deal cold because it was drawing the line on its media investments. When Immelt pulled the rug out from underneath Bob on that one and quickly followed up with the Jeff Zucker change, then the NBCU buyout just became a lost opportunity.

It was a timing issue. The executive team that had worked so well together, maintained a constructive interface with GE, and always had Bob's back was disbanding. The folks that really understood the business were beginning to either be annoyed or leave. If they couldn't rise to their highest and best opportunity after all they had done to make this happen, they didn't want to hang around.

As it was, very little was done to assure the succession or appropriate placement of any of Bob's team. David Zaslav was sort of lost, and a lot of us were just left hanging, and then the execution of what was left there just didn't work. There was a core group of people around Bob who probably deserve a lot more credit than they ever received for making this whole thing happen for many years.

If the business team that did the NBCU deal had stayed together, there would have been a very different outcome for the company. There is a strong possibility we would have partnered with private equity to spin off NBCU and take it public. But it's always easier to say these things from the sidelines. Nothing is ever that simple. ❖

That DreamWorks acquisition Brandon mentioned would have been a golden situation for us in many respects. The film company, originally founded in 1994 by legendary producers Steven Spielberg, Jeffrey Katzenberg, and David Geffen, was a natural extension of our merger with Universal, which had a long-standing relationship with Spielberg and a long-term film distribution agreement with DreamWorks. I personally negotiated the buyout with David Geffen in the first part of 2006, in what we both thought was a very fair agreement.

But GE's board was uneasy with the ebb and flow of Hollywood economics, and Immelt procrastinated for 1 year, stringing all of us along. When the board finally signed off on the acquisition in December, it was too late. Just hours earlier, DreamWorks had accepted a slightly better $1.6 billion offer from Viacom. Putting me and my executive team in a precarious state on a deal we had already hammered out was an embarrassing demonstration of our lack of control. We felt we had lost out to GE's notorious bean counters.

The DreamWorks ordeal set the stage for my retirement from NBC in 2007 and from GE in 2008. It was an anticlimactic, bittersweet end to my 21 years at NBC and 40-year career at GE. So, I shifted my energy, resources, and passion to the nonprofit world and the development of Autism Speaks, where I was free to do my best work again.

❖ **John Eck, senior VP and chief quality officer NBCU, and CFO NBC International and Business Development.** I think Immelt approached markets as a marketer and a sales guy and thought that we needed to either sell or double down and fill niches that we weren't in. And that's what the Universal deal gave him. But then, I believe that in his view the world changed. In order to compete long-term, NBC needed to double down and try to find another consolidating acquisition. DreamWorks could have been that. But GE didn't necessarily have the cash to do that kind of transaction. So GE decided to sell control of NBC and take that cash and redeploy it where they truly had a competitive advantage, in spinning wheels, turbines, aircraft engines, those kinds of things. ❖

Bob Wright
Exit memorandum to NBCU employees
February 6, 2007

On September 1, 1986, I walked through the doors of 30 Rockefeller Center as the new president and CEO of NBC. Today, nearly 21 years later, I am writing to let you know that the time has come for me to hand over the reins. As of today, Jeff Zucker is the president and CEO of NBC Universal. I will remain vice chairman of GE and, until May 1, the chairman of the NBC Universal board of directors. A press release will be distributed shortly, but I wanted to take a moment to speak directly to you.

Most of all, I want to thank you for your support and dedication. NBC was the nation's first broadcast network, and Universal is Hollywood's longest-operating movie studio. USA Network was the first broad-based network on cable television, and Bravo, which I was involved with at birth, was close behind as a groundbreaking arts and entertainment network. We have an unparalleled legacy that extends back to the first days of our industries. I take great pride in the fact that today, nearly a century later, we continue to excel in our unchanging mission to develop, produce, and market the best entertainment, news, and information to a global audience.

Twenty-one years ago, NBC was primarily a broadcast network. Today, we are a much larger broadcaster, station owner, and so much more: a leader in cable and satellite entertainment with USA, Sci-Fi, Bravo; in news with Today, Nightly News, Meet the Press, Dateline, *and* MSNBC; *in financial information with CNBC globally. We are a significant TV production operation, the home of the Olympic Games, a leader in Hispanic broadcasting and in station ownership, and an increasingly powerful presence internationally, and with MSNBC.com and iVillage in digital media. With the addition of Universal Studios, we are now also a world-renowned film studio, film distribution operation, home entertainment business, and theme parks operator and developer. Through all this change, NBC and its peacock logo have remained a symbol worldwide for excellence in television programming.*

So you can understand why I am so proud of this company and what we have accomplished over the years. And why it is with such mixed emotions that I now end my 2 decades at the helm. But the time is right. We have good momentum, a deep bench of experienced leaders, and a skilled executive in Jeff, who knows this company inside and out and has the right mix of business knowledge, programming savvy, and marketing creativity to lead NBC Universal into a bright new era.

It has been a great privilege to lead this company. My wife, Suzanne—who has been an unfailing source of strength to me and a tireless supporter of this company—and I are blessed to have had such a long and rewarding relationship with all of you. I leave NBCU in strong, capable hands. And I leave it, and you, with pride in what we have accomplished together and confidence that the next chapter of the NBC Universal story will be the most exciting yet.

Bob

To my most senior leadership team, I added this brief e-mail note.

I just want to say to my closest associates how much I've enjoyed working with all of you. We've accomplished a lot together and had fun along the way. Now this is Jeff's ship to steer, and he'll do a terrific job. That said, I'm not disappearing completely. Although Jeff [Zucker] now has overall responsibility for the company, I am keeping my role as GE vice chairman of the board and executive officer, and also as NBC Universal board chairman for the next few months. Working together, this will be a very smooth transition.

Bob

❖ **Bernie Marcus**. In the end, I think that GE treated Bob very badly. When you let a guy like Bob Wright go the way Immelt

did, you don't really understand the intrinsic value people like
that bring to the entire organization. Bob struggled with leaving
NBCU and GE, and I think deciding to develop and work on
Autism Speaks renewed him, and helped him to redirect his passion and abilities. It helped him to understand that there are things
more important than corporate life. It saved him when he was trying to save autistic children and their families. What he's doing is
not a small thing. He's one of the heroes in America today. So out
of bad can come good. ❖

While I was increasingly minimalized at NBCU, I was inspired
by my growing involvement in Autism Speaks. Unfortunately,
it created another level of antagonism with Immelt and the GE
board that continued until I stepped down as GE vice chairman
in 2008. They were not used to one of their leading executives
maintaining a high profile in such an emotionally charged nonprofit endeavor. I was very careful about how I divided my time
and efforts between NBCU/GE and Autism Speaks. This was
the focus of my terse letter to Bill Conaty, GE senior vice president of Corporate Human Services. The fact that I signed it with
my full legal name (something I rarely do) was an indication of
my disappointment with GE's response and pressure. I had spent
much of my career beseeching others to "just call me Bob."

January 23, 2007
Dear Bill:

Following up on our discussions—

*Post the announcement of my stepping down as CEO of NBCU
prior to my retirement, in addition to GE assignments that I may accept,
as part of my work, I will continue to be active in charitable, educational,
and service organizations. I may also join the boards of or be advisor to*

businesses, and engage in business activities that do not compete with GE in a meaningful way.

Sincerely,

Robert C. Wright

The irony was that, by default, GE positively shaped us and our autism cause. Andy Shih, who led Autism Speaks' international science projects, put it succinctly: "The Wrights bring rigorous business processes to the advocacy world. While other executives (such as Bill Gates and Ted Turner) have been effective philanthropists, the Wrights brought a laser focus on the stakeholders and return on investment in autism advocacy."

❖ **Marianne Gambelli, president NBC Universal Broadcast Sales.** It was tough watching all of this from the trenches. You felt like you were watching a really bad movie or a dysfunctional family operate, even though NBC was doing well. It all started to implode under the weight of the merger with Universal. NBC was not familiar with many of Universal's businesses, such as the studio, theme parks, and even cable. Jeff Immelt was still new to running GE, so there was a lot of the stress on the organization.

I think that nobody understood the complexity of combining these different businesses, and I think that everybody on the broadcast side thought they understood the cable side, and they didn't. So they cut a lot of people and costs, and the GE culture took over and everything got more complicated than anyone expected because GE didn't understand the media and entertainment business. We spent those first couple of years trying to bring the businesses together, and we were trying to take all these new assets to market together. We charted a new course. Everybody takes credit for it now, but back then the entire organization was battling us on it. ❖

❖ **Art Dwyer.** If Bob had been a younger man at the time, I think he might've put the deal together with private equity and bought NBC Universal himself. Bob could have still been at NBC. I've never worked for anybody who was more loyal, and I think the same can be said for the people who worked for Bob. I don't know what was behind his retirement. It was very evident that Jeff Immelt thought NBC would lose key players if he didn't move to put a new regime in place, but I don't think he had the key players he thought they had. The guys that were really important, frankly, didn't want the job, but they would've stuck with Wright.

Bob is such a modest guy that he won't really eagerly talk about his own disappointments or reservations, or how he dealt with some of what came down, especially towards the end of his tenure. I think Jack Welch may have been envious of the accolades Bob was getting for making successful deals and having a progressive vision for NBC. And that clouded Jack's judgment about his own succession. When you think of Bob's sensibilities and big-picture orientation, his ability to put so many pieces together for a solution to a complex situation, his training as a lawyer and his genuine interest in learning and exploring new things—these are qualities that would have made GE great. ❖

Wright to the Point

Things often happen for a reason, even though at the time we question the timing and circumstances. What we expect to happen sometimes doesn't, and we're disappointed—even devastated. And later, something else happens instead that is more meaningful and right. You just couldn't see it coming. So you have to go through the difficult emotions.

That's what happened at the end of my time at NBCU and GE. You expect someone to acknowledge the difference you made and what you helped accomplish. Whether they do or not, you still head out the door wondering what hit you, where the years went, and how what you did will stand up to the test of time. It happens even to the biggest executives; maybe especially the CEOs who are in charge for so long, only to come to the realization that companies and organizations go on. They go on differently, but they go on.

I wasn't sure what life held for me after NBC and GE. Autism Speaks was created out of a need and quickly consumed us. It's turned out to be a lot more work than either I or Suzanne expected. And that's left me little time to sit and wonder what NBCU would be today if we had succeeded with those last few deals—with private equity and DreamWorks.

When organizations change or die there isn't much anyone can say about it. People either embrace the change or leave the cause. That's when you realize it is all about the doing while you are there—while you can still make a difference with your vision and passion. There's no looking back, only forward.

We have the advantage of telling a story that has a beginning and an end that match up with public events. This is a 30-year media adventure for GE that has an end. And I'm the one that had control of the staff and sheep during most of that time. That is the uniqueness of it. I shepherded the flock and a company, and nurtured and executed on a vision for a longer time than anyone in my position in media. But I didn't make things happen—the people I gathered around me did, so this is their story. This is their achievement. There's even credit there for GE, even though it felt like they were working against us most of the time.

Everything has its place in this story. GE's merger of its broadcast and cable holdings with Cox fell through back in 1980, but it gave me my media education. My time heading GE Capital taught me a lot about negotiating and structuring deals that I could not have otherwise appreciated, even with my legal background. GE's acquisition of RCA landed me at NBC. And from then on I was hooked—hooked on what a broadcaster could become in the evolving age of cable, and then hooked on what a broadcast-cable company could become in the Internet era with digital interactivity.

The highlight of all my time at NBC was the Universal acquisition. I don't think GE or NBC ever completely appreciated what it brought us. When NBCU became such a big part of GE, they became overwhelmed with the financials. When you become overwhelmed with the financials of something, you have to be careful, because it can overshadow the passion and vision that make companies great—that make life remarkable.

19
Comcast Takes Over

Lunch meeting between Bob Wright and Steve Burke
21 Club
21 W. 52nd Street, New York City
April 6, 2010

Having a heartfelt talk with your successor before he takes command of an enterprise like NBC Universal is a little like staring at yourself in the mirror: all at once you know where you have been and where you are, but you're still not sure where you are going.

Steve Burke had always been a friendly face in a sea of cable operators, so I was particularly pleased when, several years after I had left NBC, he asked to get together. In all our interactions with Comcast, I found him to be a quick learner and smooth negotiator, so much so that the company's founding Roberts family relied on him to manage its flourishing cable systems and program holdings. Now that Comcast was taking command of NBCU, Steve had a daunting job description: transform the country's leading cable operator into a full-fledged media conglomerate against the backdrop of changing technology. Like me, Steve had to do that working inside of a larger entity over which he had no control.

There was historical precedence for a major cable distributor owning global film and television content. Time Warner had done it for years. It was now imperative, given consumers' unconstrained ability to pull in content from many different sources. By the time Comcast acquired a 51 percent controlling stake in NBC Universal on January 28, 2011, we had grown the company's value 15 times beyond the broadcast network GE bought in 1986. The cable networks that GE never wanted us to build or buy were collectively valued at $23.7 billion; the NBC broadcast network and owned TV stations were worth $3.6 billion, according to Bernstein Research. Our Universal acquisition added $5.6 billion in theme parks GE didn't know what to do with and a $790 million film studio and library whose business GE didn't understand. At one point, NBCU's market value topped $45 billion, which included its many investments and minority interests.

Steve appreciated that transformation more than most industry executives because of his own pedigree. Television was in his blood. His father, the late Dan Burke, was half of the widely respected team of (Tom) Murphy and Burke that built Capital Cities from a family broadcaster into a media powerhouse when they shocked the industry by acquiring ABC for $3.5 billion in 1985. Like his father, who presided for years as CapCities/ABC CEO, Steve was content to be the quintessential deputy and trusted advisor who put family first and good business second. In 1998, Comcast lured Steve from Walt Disney, where he had developed its international holdings and helped integrate Disney and CapCities/ABC after their $19 billion merger in 1995. The Harvard Business School graduate moved his wife, Gretchen, and their five children to the company's Philadelphia headquarters to work closely with CEO Brian Roberts and his father, Comcast founding chairman Ralph Roberts. Like me,

Steve was so convinced about the promise of cable that he opted for Comcast over managing Disney's ABC broadcasting assets. And he never looked back.

Stagnation was Steve's enemy long before he entered the executive suite at 30 Rock. For the year leading up to Comcast's takeover, NBCU was like a ship moored in the harbor. All they were doing there was trying to look good every day; shining up the place so GE could get the most out of it and Comcast would close the deal. Everyone was showing up for work, but there was no exciting leadership because they all were afraid to make a move. Standing still like that is dangerous.

At the time of Comcast's takeover, NBC was emerging from a very difficult time. Advertising and ratings were slowly rebounding, but the NBC TV Network was still fourth in primetime ratings and losing about $500 million a year. To turn things around, Comcast was going to have to drop the cable mentality and assume a broadcaster's perspective, and that came with a learning curve just at a time when an explosion of interactive technology was changing everything about media.

Comcast had more than a year before taking over NBC to study the landscape and begin devising plans. Steve was prohibited from getting involved during the regulatory review process and was taking notes so he could hit the ground running when the deal closed. The entire NBC TV Network had to be rebooted in a process that required face-to-face meetings once Comcast took over. Burke was rapidly forming opinions about people and testing out what he thought against others' perspectives.

When Steve first reached out to me by phone, I was pleased to hear from him. He asked if I would share my insights and advice from 21 years in the position he was about to assume. Being retired from NBCU for several years gave me a more detached perspective that would benefit any new owner.

"Set your own agenda," I told him at lunch that day. "Draw up a forward-looking business plan, get GE to sign on to it or agree to get out of the way, and then just make it happen." I cautioned him that the CEO of a newly merged company needs to focus on rebooting the organization. The companies might be very different, but the process is essentially the same. It's about huddling with senior executives to identify the most exciting and important goals and objectives, and then establishing a plan to execute on them. Ask the hard questions: If we aren't where we should be, then why not? Where have we been? What do we need? Who's going to do it?

The issue of how to handle legacy costs and practices amid rapidly changing technology was top of mind for Comcast senior executives, just as it is for most companies today. You suddenly become fixed on pay packages, pensions, contracts, and practices that have been in place forever. You must ask yourself if the organizational structure and directives are right for the changing times and then have the courage to change them if need be. Are we anticipating and embracing the right trends? What should our agenda be? There are limitless questions, no easy answers.

There was only one sure thing I could advise Burke: "Make the company your own. Don't be beholden to the past. Take your best stab at the future." I told him to go where he thought these new developments were taking the combined company in deference to its unique position as a content producer and consumer. "It requires new thinking. Put your best people on it and see where they take you," I urged.

Less than 5 years later, Comcast proposed expanding its dominant national cable footprint by buying Time Warner Cable for $45 billion. NBC would become a smaller global entertainment piece of a larger cable systems operator—something Jack Welch and his GE board would never have imagined.

❖ **Steve Burke, executive vice president Comcast, president NBC Universal.** One of the things Bob told me that sticks in my mind: "When you get this job, remember that it's your company. You should surround yourself with people you are comfortable working with, who have the same ideals you do. Don't be afraid to make changes in people and strategy. Have a good time, and realize that it's your course to chart. Don't be too beholden to the past." It was great advice that I continue to follow.

A lot of what Bob said to me during that interim year of regulatory review confirmed what I was thinking. Since Comcast is based in Philadelphia, I would spend 2 or 3 days a week in New York having breakfast, lunch, and dinner with NBC senior executives, or people who had left the company, or people who were in the business who had opinions about NBC. You really get to know somebody after you have had four or five meals with them. After 6 months I started to see patterns and options and visualize things I could change or do differently. It was a great opportunity to be able to tell Bob, "Here's what I'm thinking," and he could say, "That's exactly right" or "Here's how you should be thinking about it." It gave me a lot more confidence that I was on the right track. We would laugh a lot. I would tell him stories about people and he would say, "Yeah, that's going to be a huge problem for you…" And then he'd just grin. They no longer were his problems; they were mine.

I now believe the broadcast television business is a huge opportunity for NBC. The real engine of Comcast NBC Universal will always be the cable channels. But if you look at the next 3 to 5 years, there is a lot of growth in broadcast and in films, and you want to make sure the cable channels continue to grow.

NBC was such a distant fourth when we took over, and as a broadcast network moves from fourth to third in the ratings, that might be worth $500 million. And if the NBC television stations ramped up their performance, that probably would be worth $100 million to $150 million. And if we can be competitive with the other broadcasters in syndicated television programming, so that ties back into the ecosystem of the network that translates into more revenues and earnings. So there is a huge increase just by getting to average performance on the network side. Retransmission consent is real and will continue to generate huge fees for the broadcast networks, stretching to $500 million and even $1 billion, according to estimates. When you put all that together, there are huge possibilities on the broadcast network business. ❖

Comcast's bid to acquire Time Warner Cable collapsed in 2015 in the shadow of plummeting cable subscriptions across all major cable operators even as video became dominant on smartphones, spurred by Netflix and other over-the-top streaming services. It pushed into broadband with investments in social digital media hubs BuzzFeed and Vox Media to recapture young consumers. But the NBCU content assets we built that could play on any media platform with strong, consistent returns turned out to be Comcast's most potent asset.

❖ **Brandon Burgess.** Comcast has a structural advantage of owning cable systems and benefits from so much integrated clout now. It's much harder for them to screw it up with such extraordinarily high growth assets. They are playing against themselves in businesses like broadcast television and film and theme parks they are still learning. The goal isn't just growing profits; it's putting everything together in a way so that 2 plus 2 equals more than 4. ❖

❖ **Steve Burke.** There is a personal aspect to all of this. One of the keys in these large, complicated media companies is having a sense of balance and knowing when to concentrate on the bread and butter of doing things the way they've always been done and have worked. But you also have to carve out enough time and energy for a handful of new things. People are very sensitive to what they perceive as the direction of the company. So it's important to identify a cause or goal that everyone sees as important and part of the DNA of the company. But that's what you do when you have a job like mine: you just sort of try to figure out what bets to make and where to put your chips on the table, realizing that the majority of the money today comes from the bread and butter. The worst thing you can do is abandon all of your current businesses in the pursuit of new ideas. I think it has to be in balance, and that's the art of management.

I think all of this starts with creating a culture where people feel it's OK to take a risk and it's OK to fail as long as you're trying. This will encourage people to come up with new ideas. That's the culture we want to integrate into the company. Cable was broadcasting's first disruptor in decades, but now you see digital affecting music and newspapers, books, and every traditional media and everything in business. Our biggest challenge is to make sense of it and carve a new path; to manage and mine the disruptive chaos. So we are trying to redefine the merged culture of our two companies. We've been trying to create a company that has a culture that matches the environment and fosters success.

It's all about approach and attitude. There is a human side of bringing companies and people together that involves intellect and values and creativity. It's not exclusively about the bottom line. Bob helped to remind me of that. So my plan is to periodically check in with Bob and tell him what I'm doing and ask for his advice. I have a feeling he will always be my reality check.

We sped up the 7-year timetable to buy out GE's minority interest in NBCU in 2 years in 2013 because we really do like the businesses and knew they would do well. I think they're worth maybe twice what we paid for them now, and we wanted to share in 100 percent of that upside. Although NBCU will be yet an even smaller part of our overall company when we complete the acquisition of Time Warner Cable, it will be better supported by owning cable systems in Chicago, Los Angeles, and virtually every large television market where NBCU content can be cross-promoted and shown. We run the two businesses completely separately, so we do whatever we think is right for NBC Universal and, in some ways, the content side operates as a hedge so our cable side pays a lot of retransmission consent, but we get a lot of retransmission consent on the NBC side.

There are so many viewing options now, there's so many new television shows. There's 250 new television shows a year, and that's just a staggering amount of original content. And people are using DVRs a lot more than they were just a few years ago to take advantage of managing what they want to watch from many more outlets. That makes it harder to launch a show and get people to show up for linear programming. That's the big sort of head scratcher, which is why must-see live special events like sports remain so important. We were concerned about the unpredictability and volatility of the content business, but we've been surprised by the responsiveness of these core businesses to rebounding with the right teams in place. ❖

By late 2014, NBCU was poised to become an even smaller part of the whole when Comcast announced plans to pay $45 billion to acquire the second-largest system operator, Time Warner Cable, in an unprecedented consolidation of power. It was an easy move for Comcast, but it brought new problems: maintaining and leveraging costly cable systems and subscribers to launch new streaming businesses. It was more evidence that despite churning technology, there are no new dilemmas or challenges in the business world, only new players to ponder them. The deal was abandoned in April 2015 over regulatory objections.

❖ **Steve Burke.** Bob and I had lunch or dinner every 3 months between signing and closing, and I bounced my ideas off of him along the way, and showed him organizational ideas and businesses I thought were worth investing in, and I talked to him about a lot of what I did. His advice was very valuable, and I've done a lot of the things that he thought were the right things to do. Many of the things he said to me then resonate with me now. He generally felt these are good businesses, you need to be careful, you need to invest appropriately, but these are good businesses and you know, there's room for improvement, and we've made the improvements and they're working.

We're smarter than we otherwise would be before we acquired 100 percent of NBC Universal in 2013 because now we understand things from the distribution *and* the content side. We have more of a 360-degree view of what's going on in the world. As a result, we have developed new initiatives that we otherwise wouldn't have, leveraging what we have using emerging technology. Comcast is now in the electronic sell-through business, so we offer consumers the opportunity to buy and not just rent a Universal movie online when they choose to pay per view. That's a big $50 million business that didn't exist. You'll see us do more of that.

It's a complicated time and there's a tremendous amount of technological change, and that presents opportunities and challenges, but we're the best situated I think of any of the media companies because we have a window on distribution and a window on content, and the ability to do things with both sides of the company that are unique. We're definitely going to have businesses delivered directly to consumers with the Internet in the near term. It will be different from what we already do through Netflix and Hulu and NBC.com. I think we would rather create new brands and packages and tap some of what we have in NBC, USA, SyFy and Bravo—to package differently and deliver directly to consumers. This will be our hedge against the millennials who do not subscribe to cable.

I've thought a lot about what Bob said when he advised me to make NBCU my own. One of my signatures so far has been what we call Synergy Symphony, and it's how we get all parts of the company working together, especially for the really big events like our Olympics telecasts or launching the fall primetime schedule or a big movie, or moving *The Tonight Show* from Los Angeles back to New York. Those changes are risky, and they're scary, and they're difficult, and you don't always get it right. But when you get it right, it's great, and it successfully sets up the company for a long, long time. ❖

Wright to the Point

Steve Burke had a great opportunity in front of him. He just had to avoid being caught up in the minutiae of the day-to-day operations, because that can really slow you down. You have to be tough on that. The car's got to get cleaned. People have got to show up on time. They've got to make their numbers. OK, we've got all that. But the real difference comes in determining the viability and the strength of plans that exist in each part of the organization. If they are not on target, why? And if they are, is the target a good one? That's where you need to be focusing.

Comcast has done a very good job of integrating and expanding sports. Film has done very well. Entertainment on NBC is getting better and is still very good on cable. News has a major problem that needs work. Here is a cornerstone of a network, and its cable channels must be top rated. CNBC is doing very well.

You have to make a determination whether or not the organizational structures—the ones you bring and the ones that are already there—are the best way to deliver those messages and implement them. You can have the best plan in the world, but if the organization isn't geared to responding to it, it's not going to work. You've got to take that organizational concept and make sure that train on the track runs right. You've got to find ways to test that. A good executive constantly is testing the idea flow, the execution, and the people. You always have to be sure the right people are listening.

It's not that difficult to test it out. You get a list of the initiatives you believe are really key and then you see how your organization is dealing with them. Which part of the organization seems to be taking them on more aggressively or better than the others? Where are the weak links and the strong links? In media, for example, advertising is 50 percent of the revenues, so it is critical. Ask yourself who is blocking it and who's championing it. Are the programming people in sync with the advertising and marketing people? Are the advertising agencies in sync with what you're trying to do? Do affiliates understand it? Do the cable operators understand it? To get moving, you have to get the various parts to all be working in synchronization, and it can be pretty tricky to work that out.

That has to be top of mind for any of the senior executives, in any industry. Is my organizational structure and motivation the right one at this point in time? There is no easy way to answer that. You've got to constantly make judgment calls. You don't want people abandoning what you are doing. You want people to be able to access new ideas and new approaches, but you don't want them abandoning things that are already working. It is a constant issue of determining where we should be. You have to have a bit of a map, and the organization needs to participate in that map a bit.

You can't do it from the bottom up, because that takes too long and is too complicated. You have to try it from the top down. When you run into resistance, you have to decide whether the resistance is justified or not. And if it isn't, then you've got to break some glass. If it's justified, then you back off a little bit. Breaking the glass means you would move people out or move them around and reshuffle an organization.

When major issues or trends arise, assign a small crack team to go after them so they don't require your daily attention. When strategies and action become clear, rally the troops around them and execute. Done. Then move on. For Comcast, the issues were cable fees and streaming over-the-top video and how to respond to them. Every company and industry has its hot topics and hotspots.

In some ways the CEO's job hasn't changed much, although the percentages of time spent on certain things has changed. Fifteen years ago, you still had to make creative bets and plot a direction for a news division to give way to a cable channel. A portion of your day would be spent thinking about new technologies and a portion of your day would be dealing with people and a portion of your day would be dealing with finance. These jobs have become so complicated and so diverse, there are lots of experts in one of those things but not all of them.

There is more focus today on new technologies and distribution mechanisms. Before, it was broadcast or cable; it was sort of a binary world. Now you have to get your arms around so many new technologies—and which ones are important and which one to prioritize—that it's almost overwhelming. But these businesses still are fundamentally all about sending news crews to cover events happening in the world and someone coming in with a good film or television idea.

And all of this holds true no matter the industry. The content of the job is the same but the amount of time and resources you have to allocate to a broader range of urgent matters has changed fairly dramatically.

Building a successful business under any circumstances is a lot like a golf swing. It's a lot of movement, but it all has to be coordinated. You can't move your arm without your feet and hips and everything in sync. And that's what good business is about. To get moving effectively, you have to get the various parts synchronized. That includes costly legacy issues and tricky co-ownership issues. And it especially involves people. That's trickier to work out than you think. That's why so many mergers and merged companies fail.

I've tried to pass on some of what I learned to my employees and everyone who works with us at Autism Speaks. I think of it as a personal approach to best practices. And some of them were taking notes. In a handwritten note to me days before Comcast acquired majority ownership interest in NBCU, Steve thanked me for my advice and support, assembling cable assets that at the time were less than a third of NBCU's revenues but more than 60% of its overall earnings. "Those are the businesses that now make the real money and it's not lost on me that they wouldn't be there if it wasn't for you," Steve wrote. Many of the executives who worked with me at NBC now head their own successful companies, abiding by their own principles. A lot of things change because of technology, economics, and politics. But doing the right thing, setting your terms and living by them... that never changes.

20
My Roller-Coaster Ride with Jack Welch

W hen I arrived at GE's facility in Pittsfield, Massachusetts, in 1969, I heard about a young general manager in the plastics business there named Jack Welch. At 33, he was the youngest GM ever. With a doctorate in chemical engineering from the University of Illinois, he was working with miracle plastics in a business division that was on fire. Within a decade, GE was the leading supplier of everything from Apple iPods to NASA moonwalk visors. Pittsfield Plastics is where Jack became famous, and I arrived just as he was being promoted up the GE food chain. It's also the focus of my own professional transformation.

In the early 1970s, under the mentorship of the unit's general counsel Arthur Puccini, I prepared a defense strategy to head off a challenge by Germany's Bayer AG to our multibillion-dollar Lexan patent. That made a solid impression on Jack, who recommended me for lead counsel of the plastics division. But the powers that be considered me too inexperienced for the job, which just made Jack angry; he didn't like being overruled. So, determined to keep me in the fold, he offered me a managerial position that put me on an 18-month fast track through other executive operating positions. I went from strategic development to head of national sales. It was an enormous leap of faith on Jack's part.

If I had gotten the legal appointment Jack wanted, things would have been different. Everything happens for a reason.

So Jack's former office became mine, and I found myself knee-deep in strategic planning, the hottest game at GE. Now I was running a business and managing people, and one thing I quickly learned was the importance of spotting trends. Most businesses aren't prepared to handle the black swans—the unexpected events that can have extreme consequences. All businesses need people who can project trends and create appropriate response strategies.

Jack moved on to Connecticut in 1977 to become a sector executive in charge of consumer products at what was then called GE Credit Corp. Two years later he was named vice chairman of GE, and 2 years after that Jack Welch became GE's youngest chairman CEO. For my part, I decided it was fitting that I inherited Jack's office back in Pittsfield, where he had taught me to get ahead playing by your own rules. I didn't know I would soon follow.

The front lawn of Jack Welch's home
Pittsfield, Massachusetts
June 1977

Who knew an old-fashioned ringer washing machine could weigh so much? But Suzanne and I were determined to drag the most hideous-looking one from a nearby city dump in our station wagon to place it on Jack's front lawn down the street from us on Rockland Drive. We set it up in the middle of the night with a sign congratulating Jack on being "all washed up!" The prank honored Jack's new position overseeing core GE appliances and GE Credit Corp., stepping-stones to his way to the top. It was our last bit of creative mischief.

Jack Welch was my boss, mentor, and friend for more than 3 decades at GE. The ebb and flow of our relationship mirrored the fluctuating connection between General Electric and NBC. If it wasn't for Jack, I wouldn't have been able to transform NBC into a major cable and entertainment player—but it also wouldn't have been as difficult to accomplish. As chairman, Jack relied on divestitures and acquisitions as GE's main growth strategy; I kept NBC focused on organic value creation buoyed by strategic partnerships. Our personalities and agendas were as complicated as the issues. The press never fully comprehended the breadth of our relationship, reducing it to simple equations like father-son, rival brothers, and best pals.

But it was never that black-and-white. Jack and I were both products of an Irish Catholic New England upbringing. We were both only children with strong-willed mothers who instilled in us a strong sense of ambition and self-confidence. We both were self-made businessmen.

Yet for all the places our professional and personal lives intersected, we were fundamentally different. I came to understand how he operated, in the way that good friends do. Knowing how and when to pull each other's strings and press each other's buttons was the key to working well together for so long. But I was never under any illusion. Jack would do what was right for Jack and GE first.

❖ **Donald Trump, billionaire real estate developer, producer/star of the NBC series *The Apprentice*.** Jack Welch was a great businessman and visionary who loved Bob Wright because he saw something in Bob that he just respected. You know I have a way of selling things. Bob used me so brilliantly to get a long-term deal with Rockefeller Center to acquire the floors occupied by NBC and GE. Jack saw Bob's business acumen and he was attracted to that. There's nobody that Jack Welch respected more than Bob Wright at the time. He really relied on Bob, and Bob did great deals for him in cable. ❖

Jack lived life as fully as he could. If he had three open hours, he would play 27 holes of golf. He'd get off a plane and he'd go out and have dinner twice. He drank too much and he ate too much, but he would never sleep enough. He could stay up all night and show up at a meeting the next morning looking like he had slept 8 hours. We all took shifts because no one had the stamina to be with him all the time. He was almost impossible to keep up with, although Suzanne somehow managed.

For several years the plastics division hosted ski weekends at the old Lake Placid Inn for all our big accounts. We would start the evening with a cocktail party, then a big dinner, and then everyone would take to the slopes for ski races. One typical Jack Welch weekend in the winter of 1976, we flung open all the windows because the radiator heat couldn't be properly regulated. It was cold as hell outside, and Jack couldn't wait to get out there and take on everyone. I remember Suzanne shouting out the window that she could beat him even though she'd only taken up skiing 3 months earlier. So she took him on. Everyone was shouting like they were at a baseball game: "What a bum you are; you're a lousy skier!" It was hilarious.

Jack loved customers who wanted to play. He loved people who were competitive. I remember a dinner one night that went on forever, and everybody had too much to drink. Jack stood up and declared it was time to start the hockey game! The hotel had an outdoor hockey rink, so Jack chose up sides and pretty soon a bunch of 40-year-olds were running around, banging each other over the head with their sticks, yelling and laughing in the cold. The next morning Jack was the first person downstairs with a cup of coffee, organizing the day's meetings.

Jack worked hard, partied hard, and played hard. That's the reason he didn't blow up, because he didn't keep things in. Playing and partying were ways for him to shake off stress. That sometimes was awkward for other people, even if they knew it was a release for him. Jack was not a perfect person, but boy, did he have remarkable energy and great ideas! Jack was anxious for success, and he expected everybody around him to work as hard as he did. If you did that, he wanted you on his team.

———————

From 1980 to 1983 I was in Atlanta with Cox Cable—a position Jack made possible. I was happy there and doing very well, but in April 1983, when Jack had been fully in charge as GE chairman CEO for 2 years, I got a phone call. "Listen, Bob, you've done a great job down there. I've been watching. But I need you back here at GE!"

This was Neutron Jack talking. He was already a legend for buying businesses, extracting the excess, and leaving only the buildings intact. Jack invited me to fly from Atlanta to North Palm Beach. "I have a nice story to tell you. I'll pick you up at the airport!" So I met with Jack, Art Puccini, one of GE's lawyers I had originally reported to, and Ralph Hubregsen, GE's human resources vice president. I remember Puccini stretched out on the couch, ailing from a bad back, making a compelling argument for why I belonged at GE. That evening we all went to dinner with our wives, to a restaurant where jackets were required. I still have the white linen jacket I ran out to buy on the way, a memento of good times and warm climes. It was a great dinner with lots of boisterous conversation. Everybody was excited. That's what it was like in those days. It all happened quickly, and I was sucked back into Jack's gravitational pull.

The following month, Jack flew Suzanne and me to his home in New Canaan, Connecticut, to celebrate. He asked me to manage, evaluate, and recommend the potential sale of GE's housewares and audio electronics businesses, which encompassed everything except televisions. Then he added an inducement. "If you get this right, you have a good shot at running GE Capital."

That's the most I ever trusted anyone making an unwritten offer. I thought it was a hell of an opportunity. So we relocated to Southport, Connecticut, near where the housewares division was located. Within 6 months I had traveled the world, assessing and more tightly managing the housewares and audio electronics businesses whose margins had virtually collapsed in a sea of cheap foreign exports. By December 1983, Jack had single-handedly negotiated a sale of GE's small appliances and housewares operations to Black & Decker for $300 million in cash, stock, and notes. My job was to make Black & Decker executives comfortable with that deal before it closed in March.

And Jack kept his word: in 1984 I was promoted to CEO of GE Capital, reporting to Larry Bossidy. From then on, Jack and I worked together buying and selling, growing and redirecting GE's businesses, often through GE Capital. One of the businesses we passed on was CBS. I thought it was a very good opportunity until we found out it wasn't really for sale. Then in 1986 GE turned its sights on RCA and NBC instead, and that changed everything.

❖ **Chuck Dolan.** I remember Bob's office on the 52nd floor of Rockefeller Center. The door was always open. And on the floor right above him was Jack Welch's office, with a staircase that came down right next to Bob's office. When Jack came down to see him it looked a little like God descending. But to Bob, it was just Jack. That's how close they were. It was a wonderful partnership. ❖

I reported directly to Jack Welch for 14 years, from 1986 until his retirement in 2001. Before that I was never more than one report away from him. So I probably was closer to him for a longer period of time than almost anyone else at GE. I am very proud of our relationship. I racked up many successful deals and accomplishments that became part of Jack's overall legacy. And he couldn't help himself from getting more involved than usual in some of those business decisions. Jack could be my best ally or worst adversary as I pursued my contrarian game plan for NBC. He supported me one minute and then scuttled some of our best deals the next.

He couldn't tolerate Ted Turner, so we never pulled the trigger on negotiated deals to acquire Turner Broadcasting and CNN. He trashed the acquisition for the Golf Channel that I negotiated when Suzanne and I were with Johnny and Alexis Carson in Scotland, out of concern that the GE board and investors would too closely align him with the sport. The irony was that NBC eventually did buy that asset, for market price. We could have bought the Golf Channel for an initial $50 million; a decade later Comcast, NBC's new owner, paid more than $1 billion.

Jack had an incredible way of separating personal relationships from business. So while he loved his friends, he really loved business achievement more and he was vicious about it. If he could do business with his friends, it was great. And if he couldn't, it was fine because not many of his friends were high enough achievers. Our friendship was steady, but our work relationship was sacred— and they were always separate.

Jack was a bit of a cowboy—a damn smart cowboy. Many of the aggressive things that he did back then he couldn't do as easily today. When times were good, some board members would say things like, "You may not like the media business, but this guy can sure make money!"

GE's board and senior management had little idea of how NBC worked. They thought it was like gambling at the Beverly Hills Hotel. For years Jack and I defended GE's continued ownership of NBC—only to have him periodically shop NBC around behind my back, particularly when ratings and finances declined, as in 1991 and 1992. They were agonizing times.

While Jack didn't give me a blank check, he did give me leeway to forge ahead, because we both knew broadcasting's free cash flow business would change. I worked really hard to double NBC's value my first 6 years as CEO while expanding the company's cable horizons. Jack really didn't want to sell the company so much as take the pressure off GE stock and appease institutional investors who were more comfortable with tangible assets like jet engines and light bulbs.

❖ **Tom Rogers.** There was no doubt that the most important relationship in Bob Wright's working life was with Jack Welch. Don Ohlmeyer called it "as close a relationship as I have ever seen in business," and any of us who witnessed it firsthand felt the same way. The relationship between Bob and Jack clearly involved a lot of mutual respect, but there always was some degree of tension that most people didn't see. It was obvious to those of us working with them. Bob wanted autonomy to advance NBC's business and had to go through Jack on most things. There were some occasional blowups and screaming matches behind closed doors. What was amazing to me was the way that Jack inserted himself more deeply into NBC's business than he has admitted or was appropriate for somebody in his position. There was really no way to stop it or cut that off. But he never gave any sense—inside

NBC or publicly—that he was undermining Bob. So, while Bob's authority was never questioned, the level of Jack's involvement could rankle him.

Bob felt that Jack could be unpredictable. Sometimes they were unable to get a consistent viewpoint going that was as strategically clear as it should have been. I remember the proposal to acquire the Sky Cable satellite service. It was something that NBC should have made happen and didn't, largely because Jack didn't want it. Had it turned out well, with a small company like Cablevision Systems driving the initial foray into satellites, NBC likely would be the co-owner of DirecTV today. But GE, which was already in the military satellite business, and Jack Welch had other designs.

Because of Bob's GE pedigree, Jack gave him more leeway and sometimes quietly exempted NBC from some of GE's controls. The access they had to each other, and the way they related in and out of work, was integral to the way they got things done. Then, about the same time Jack retired from GE, he and his wife, Jane, divorced. I think Jane and Suzanne were very close. And all of a sudden everything changed. Relationships unraveled and it was never the same. ❖

Jack did a lot of good for GE and its shareholders. But the stock increased an astronomical amount between 1996 and 2000 ($7 to $60 a share, creating a $530 billion in market cap) and got way ahead of itself. Jack began to believe the company was special because of him, and that created an absolute disaster. He got out with his publicity, and everyone else got stuck with the aftermath. The results after 2000 were just awful. The post-retirement exit package he negotiated was inappropriate and selfish (it included unlimited free use of a $50 million plane for the rest of his life!). He brought down all kinds of other people and horrible stuff happened. It all unraveled as he was leaving. He should have retired as

CEO years earlier, but he didn't want to go. If he had left in that 1998 period, maybe GE would have been a hell of a lot better off. GE should have used some of its inflated stock to acquire good businesses from 1998 to 2000.

Jack did such a good job for such a long time, and then in the late 1990s he let things get out of hand and the business got too big. Using GE's overly inflated stock, GE Capital acquired too many diverse and risky businesses. That's just a fact. Everybody knew it, but nobody knew what to do about it. A decade later, on his way out the door, Jack tried to redeem himself with the $42 billion Honeywell acquisition. But he waited too long, and the deal never happened. I believe he panicked. He was never going to fix it. That would have been a smart acquisition 2 years earlier, when GE had a P/E ratio of 40!

❖ **Suzanne Wright.** Over time, Jack started believing his own press. He just became a totally different person, and it hurt so much to see him change. He refused to come to our children's wedding. Instead of just saying he couldn't come for some reason, he said to us, "I don't do weddings anymore!" That was it. It was personal. ❖

Jack Welch was preparing to retire from GE (a year later than expected) when he told me he was moving Andy Lack into my job as operating head of NBC. A year or two later that became a problem. Andy and Jeff Zucker were not getting along. Jeff had the runway to be CEO. I had taken NBC from basic broadcasting to cable and through erratic swings in profits. I was focused on ways to expand NBC's audience and revenue base so it could compete with larger media players like Walt Disney, Viacom, and AOL Time Warner without hurting GE's earnings per share. GE had no reason to be displeased.

I quietly convinced GE's board that NBC's divided house was not in the company's best interest. I resumed as NBC's sole commander in chief in the fall of 2001, with Jeff Zucker waiting in the wings. Jack had already retired, agreeing to personally pay for any of the controversial perks he sought that went beyond the normal exit package for a chief executive. GE was hit with a sever reprimand by the Securities and Exchange Commission. And Andy left to become chairman of Sony Music.

Wright to the Point

I always understood that many people had a love/hate view of Jack. They saw him as the greatest manager of all time or the biggest jerk of all time. There is a positive side to him and a dark side, too. I've seen all sides, and I know I was very fortunate to have worked with him. I got a lot out of our relationship. In the end, our falling-out was disappointing to me. It didn't even have to do directly with the company. It had more to do with the way Jack handled his own personal and business affairs. That's the nature of complex, layered relationships. It was more like divorce in a marriage where both parties still talk to each other and don't hate each other, and wish things had happened differently. It is in part why Jack declined to contribute to this book when I asked. The thing is that Jack is stubborn Irish. Of course I wouldn't know anything about that! So he never admits a mistake, and he's not going to start doing that in his 80s.

21
Suzanne: My Life's Partner

The entire time I was chief executive officer at NBC and at Autism Speaks, my wife, Suzanne, was the chief passion officer. She threw herself into everything with tireless vigor, determination, and humanity. They became her calling cards in redefining the role of corporate wife, launching a global crusade for autism, and finding treatment for our grandson, Christian. Suzanne was never dull or obscure or reticent. That made her my perfect alter ego and confidant. Grounded in shared values and invigorated about achieving our loftiest goals, our 48-year marriage has been a true, enduring partnership.

I think of it this way: We are traveling down a divided highway. I'm in the left-hand lane and she's in the right-hand lane. And you need both lanes to complete the journey and to win. I'm in the lane of crafting the organization structure, getting the fundraising, pulling together the pieces like any good chief executive. But somebody has to be the chief passion officer, and that's the lane she's in. The term sounds so inadequate because Suzanne actually *accomplishes* her passion. A lot of passionate people never see their wonderful ideas become reality. They don't know how or they are just not lucky that way. Or they don't want to risk controversy or criticism for what they believe in. She does.

Whether it was making NBC a family or Autism Speaks a distinctive cause, Suzanne was the emotional, passionate heart and soul of everything she touched.

❖ **Bob Okun, Washington lobbyist Autism Speaks and former VP NBCU.** Intellectual curiosity and passion are essential ingredients in the Wrights' partnership, which was crafted at NBC, tested by autism, and bloomed. Bob's secret weapon is Suzanne; she is an absolute force of nature. When the word got out she was visiting Capitol Hill, most veteran senators and congressman ran for cover. ❖

If I were back in business, I would have said that her chances of accomplishing what she set out to do at Autism Speaks would have been slim to none. She just made it happen! There's an excitement about it, and she keeps coming up with ideas. And I silently keep saying to myself, "You're killing me!" But she's just what we need—what I need. And she never stops or gives up. Suzanne will get on the phone and start calling people endlessly until she gets something going. She taught me that it was worse to not try than to fail. All of my adult life, Suzanne has been the spark and driving spirit behind every success.

One thing I know for sure—you never forget where you came from when the people who champion your values and passions are by your side.

❖ **Brian Kelly, real estate developer, Autism Speaks successor CEO, founding Autism Speaks board member, and parent of autistic child.** The Wrights' impact as a couple cannot be overstated. She made him a more well-rounded CEO; he made her a smarter advocate. I do not think that either of them could have accomplished individually what they have together.

They complement each other's strengths, like the yin and yang. Together, they are the whole package. Shaping a corporate family at NBC for 2 decades was one thing. But committing themselves and their time, emotional energy, and resources to supporting the cause of autism is quite extraordinary. It is easy to write a check, but it's another thing to devote your life to something. ❖

❖ **Suzanne Wright**. When I was 16 years old, I worked part-time in menswear at Abraham & Straus. One of my pals there was a stock boy named Jim Beale. When Jim asked me to his junior prom at Holy Cross, an all-boys' college, I had no way to know it would change my life. At the prom, Jim introduced me to his friend Bob Wright. My mother, on her deathbed, said she couldn't believe she let me take the Greyhound bus to Worchester, Massachusetts, for that prom weekend. I was a junior in high school.

I fell in love with Bob immediately. There was something very different about him. He was so smart, so kind, and had extraordinary integrity. Bob was always the quiet intellect, the classy guy who never blew his own horn. I remember one time I said to my dad, "Oh, my gosh, Dad. Bob's so wonderful." And my dad looked at me and said, "Suzanne, he doesn't have a chance!"

Bob and I dated for about 3 years while he attended the University of Virginia Law School. We became engaged in the basement of my family's home in Queens, New York. I was having a good-bye party in our basement for all of my friends who were returning to college that fall. During the party, my brother, Dennis, came downstairs and handed me a package he said he found out in the street. I wanted to get rid of him because Dennis was 10 years old and I didn't want him bothering me and my friends. But he insisted I open it. And I did, and it was the diamond ring! My father was up at the top of the basement stairs laughing because Bob had just asked him for my hand in marriage. And that was how we became engaged. The next day Bob and I were at the church to set a wedding date.

After we were married on August 26, 1967. We spent the first year of married life in Charlottesville, Virginia, where Bob worked as a waiter while he was studying for the bar exam and I worked as a receptionist. When Bob passed the Virginia bar exam, my mom and dad came down with a U-Haul truck to move us to New York, where Bob studied for the New York bar exam. The Vietnam War was raging and Bob's student deferment ended when he graduated law school. That's when Bob passed the New York bar exam and joined a US Army Reserve unit. He was sent off to Fort Polk, Louisiana, for basic training. Our first child, Katie, was born December 20, 1968. Bob had a very nice job offer from GE and its plant at Pittsfield, Massachusetts, which allowed him to connect with his reserve unit he was assigned to at Utica, New York every month. That's how we started at GE.

When my parents drove us to Pittsfield, we literally took a drawer out of my father's bureau and put it in the backseat of the car, and I put our newborn, Katie, in that drawer, and I sat with her there. We drove up to the house we rented. I remember my parents couldn't wait to get out of there because of the snow that never seemed to stop. And that's how we started our life as a little family together. Bob worked very hard and he took and passed the Massachusetts bar exam in our early days in Pittsfield. ❖

❖ **Katie Wright.** My father grew up with a mom who had very high expectations and demanded the best grades and the best behavior from my dad—which I am sure he found annoying as a child. But it meant he was never threatened by a strong woman, so he wasn't threatened by a woman like my mom, who is very outspoken and expected to be a full partner—not a stereotypical wife of the 50s and 60s. I think he was progressive for his time in choosing a mate who was more of a partner.

They work together as a team. My dad never thought his success was totally due to him. I don't think you see many corporate executives comfortable with their wives being in the spotlight and outshining them. My mom has always been way more outgoing and extroverted, and a lot of men would be intimidated by that.

I think that a lot of people in business thought my dad was just kind of a boring guy because he's still married to his one and only wife. ❖

❖ **Vera Myer, VP research NBC and longtime friend.** I started at NBC in 1967 and retired in 1997 at age 70. I knew all the CEOs, and Suzanne was the only wife of a CEO who really got involved. No one had ever seen anything like her. She remembered birthdays, engagements, and new babies. She knew many people, especially other women, and she made sure they were recognized. The NBC pages were very afraid of her because she wanted them to be very nice to everybody who came in. They used to have a picture of her posted in the pages' room to be sure that everybody paid attention when she was there.

I often went along with Suzanne on her projects. One of her early projects was giving musical instruments to a high school in the Bronx that was in a horrible neighborhood. It was so bad that our NBC driver refused to take us any farther. So Suzanne and I got out of the car and started walking down the street. She's in her high heels with lots of gold jewelry and it didn't bother her in the least. We would go back periodically to hear the students play, until someone stole their instruments. ❖

❖ **Lisa Myers, correspondent NBC News**. Suzanne made it her business to regularly meet with the women of NBC News at her apartment or at a small social gathering, to hear about our projects and concerns and support us where she could. I did a controversial interview with Juanita Broaddrick during the Monica Lewinsky business in Clinton's second term. I talked to this woman off the record for a year before she finally agreed to sit down and do an interview in the middle of the Clinton impeachment proceedings.

It was explosive. People within NBC News were so freaked out they wanted to kill the story without ever looking at the tapes. Friends started wearing "Free Lisa" buttons, and protesters outside the White House carried posters reading "Free Lisa." Fortunately, I had the late Tim Russert on my side. It finally aired when Bob Wright got involved. The next day I got flowers from the Wrights with a handwritten note from Suzanne saying "Good job!" That kind of support and camaraderie meant everything when you were clearly outside the boys' club. ❖

❖ **Suzanne Wright.** After our three children went off to school, I wanted to go to college. And I didn't want anyone at NBC to know about it, so I used my maiden name. I wanted to do it on my own. It took me 7 years at Sarah Lawrence, a liberal arts college in Yonkers, New York, until I was outed when *Vanity Fair* magazine did an article about Bob.

Bob would read my papers and the kids would help me with the research. I loved it, but it was torture to get through. You know, I give Bob a lot of credit; he was as determined as I was that I would finish. When I graduated, Bob gave Sarah Lawrence a very big check and they named the Suzanne Werner Wright Theater after me. Now I have four honorary doctorate degrees. It's hysterical! ❖

I developed a great deal of confidence after I passed four bar exams and was admitted to practice in Virginia, New York, Massachusetts, and New Jersey in 4 years. Only Suzanne would have put up with that disruption. So when Suzanne said she wanted to return to school to earn a college degree, I wanted to do everything I could to support her. Suzanne went through a long and difficult process to get her degree from Sarah Lawrence. I was so proud. I believe it gave her added confidence for everything she did from that day forward. She would be able to take on the world! I experienced that hard-won exhilaration years earlier.

I took my first bar exam shortly after we were married in 1967 as a third-year student at University of Virginia. I took my second bar exam for New York state in the summer of 68 just as I was going into my military service. I took my third bar exam for Massachusetts in the winter of 1969. The written notice that I had passed came with an unexpected request to appear at the bar examiner's office early on the day of my admission ceremony. Suzanne and I drove to Boston with a lot of apprehension. Did I make a mistake filing my papers? Did I screw up some part of the test?

The bar examiner's office was on the second floor of a walk up in a back bay townhouse. Suzanne waited downstairs in the only chair available and I went up to meet the examiner. He asked me what I thought of the exam and how it compared with the Virginia and New York bars. Seeing that I was visibly nervous, the examiner told me I had one of the highest scores ever achieved on the test. I was so excited I could shout for joy! Suzanne and I treated ourselves to a fine Boston lunch before the courthouse for the admissions ceremony. Eighteen months later I took the New Jersey bar exam. That whole experience provided me with a great deal of confidence about my own ability and about the profession. I was ready for anything!

❖ **Donald Trump.** I think that Bob and Suzanne Wright are truly one of the great couples. She is a dynamic, incredible woman who is totally for her husband, which is both new school and old school. And when their grandchild was diagnosed with autism, it turned out to be a blessing in disguise, because they've been able to help so many people. ❖

❖ **Cheryl Gould, VP NBC News.** Suzanne was a real cheerleader for women breaking new ground. She did it in her own personal way, without fighting the GE or NBC stratospheres. She treated the women of NBC News that she came to know and respect as girlfriends. She made us feel like we were part of a corporate family in which there was no sure gender equality.

Suzanne was just so generous with her time, spirit, and money. When someone was in trouble or a family member was ill, she was right there asking what she could do to help and then following through. You didn't have to ask. She truly believes if you can be positive and laugh and love, your life is going to be better.

Suzanne and I first met during a trip to China in the 80s for a week of live broadcasts for *The Today Show* and *Meet the Press*. I saw her with the troops, reaching out to them in her own way while being at Bob's side. Bob is kind of shy; he gets right to the point and talks business. Suzanne is the soft side. They are on parallel tracks, hand in hand. They finish each other's sentences. It's a true love story. They are a great example of how to use your skills and apply what you've learned in the business world in a totally different way to do good. It is a very good model for many of us looking to write the next chapter in our lives. ❖

❖ **Andrea Mitchell, anchor and correspondent NBC News, Washington, DC.** Suzanne always took a strong interest in our welfare, which wasn't easy in an all-boy network. There was a long period when we had extreme budget cuts and we didn't have a Christmas party. Well, Bob and Suzanne would come down and host a holiday party for the Washington bureau.

They always made the news division feel it was important to the company. There were times when we all were deeply affected by our coverage in Iraq and the Middle East, when we lost colleagues and suffered devastating blows. And the Wrights and Tom Brokaw very much held us together. ❖

The Today Show
New York City
February 25, 2005

❖ **Elena Nachmanoff, VP NBC News talent.** The first time Bob and Suzanne went on television to announce the formation of Autism Speaks, Suzanne had not done much public speaking. But I remember the camera went to her and she said, "I'm a mother and I'm a grandmother. For the thousands of people out there whose families are affected by autism, I'm one of you. I'm going to be your champion." And I saw her bloom before my eyes. I already looked up to her because she was such a force at NBC for families and for giving back and for making people's lives better. I saw all the pain and suffering that she felt, for herself and for her family, directed into a single purpose and mission. She marshaled all of her energies and came out of her shell. The public persona of Suzanne Wright was born that day on *The Today Show.* ❖

❖ **Harry Slatkin, entrepreneur and philanthropist, parent of an autistic child.** Mothers are important because they are in the center of things, holding it together, advocating, and that's what it's all about. Suzanne and Bob as a team are inseparable and invincible. You can't refuse the two of them. Suzanne's a real dinger. She'll pound you and hound you until you can't say no to her. She takes a lot of criticism from a lot of other places; some of it is OK and some of it isn't. The beauty of it is when she hits something and it really is right on—you pick it up and do something about it—that's worth all the efforts that didn't work out, and it really makes a difference. That's why I keep doing this. ❖

It's been interesting to watch Suzanne grow as a confident leader. We still discuss many things, and I will offer my recommendations about how to proceed. But she generally goes off and does what she believes is best. She looks more to me for advice rather than to fix the problem. While she doesn't have a formal business background, Suzanne has great instincts and is extremely aggressive about the objective that she is trying to reach. Sometimes she encounters different personalities and people who are tricky, and she likes to take them on. She's just wonderful with this.

There is almost nothing Suzanne won't try to advance the cause. Imagine calling up someone at the United Nations and advocating for a World Autism Day because the condition is so serious and prevalent you want to see global recognition, and you draft Middle Eastern countries as sponsors. Who else does that?!

Lots of people work for us at Autism Speaks, but not one of them has the emotional passion that she does, because it is hard to find. In business, it's dynamite if you have somebody like that working with and for you. That enables you to really do things quickly. This is one of the reasons why we are so successful with Autism Speaks, and it's what has won us support from so many countries, the United Nations, the World Health Organization, and other important NGOs. It's her creation.

❖ **Elena Nachmanoff.** Bob and Suzanne individually could have done anything in their lives and succeeded. But together, they have the same moral compass and huge generosity of spirit that enables others and makes things happen.

They were never drive-by people. They were always in it from the beginning to the end. They wanted to make sure everyone had time with them, had a conversation, and felt involved. I think that is a unique skill. Who didn't look forward to one of her incredible notes with the flamboyant handwriting and heartfelt words in bright felt-tip pen?!

For every event, whether it was just one night or the entire Olympics, the hardest-working people were Bob and Suzanne. She would be up at the crack of dawn, greeting the people at breakfast until the last person would go to sleep. She would go around at every party, meet everyone. She never missed anything. Every year she would bring Make-A-Wish kids onto the ice at Rockefeller Center just as the Christmas tree was lighting up there. When Brandon Tartikoff was in that car accident with his young daughter Calla in January 1991 near Lake Tahoe, Nevada, the Wrights were on the next plane out there. They stayed by Brandon's side and his daughters and wife, Lilly. They just didn't stop in for a day or send flowers and a note.

The same thing with the terrible tragedy of young Teddy Ebersol, who was killed in a plane crash near Telluride, Colorado, in November 2004. His father, Dick Ebersol, the president of NBC Sports, was critically wounded but pulled from the wreckage by his college-aged son, Charlie. The Wrights were on the next plane in 2 seconds flat. There was a problem with the wreckage, and I remember Bob telling Randy Falco to go to GE for whatever they needed for Dick and his family. Suzanne was even looking out for Dick's assistant, Amy, because she knew how devastating it was for her. When you have Suzanne and Bob thinking clearly for you in a tragedy like that, you can just be in your state of shock and raw emotion, and you know they're taking care of everything else. What a gift.

When NBC News Iraq war correspondent David Bloom suddenly passed away in April 2003, Suzanne made sure his family had what they needed—right down to someone making meals, babysitting, and cleaning the house. Suzanne thought of every detail. She didn't miss a thing and followed up on everything. She helped arrange David's funeral at St. Patrick's Cathedral in New York City during Easter week and then a reception at the Metropolitan Club. She organized a group of about 20 of us from NBC and from the Catholic schools and churches to help write the thank-you cards on behalf of the family.

Anyone who knows Suzanne is not surprised all of this morphed into what she does at Autism Speaks. She was like Robin Hood, using Bob's and NBC's platform for good. That is not just being a corporate wife, but being a woman in her own right who found her own voice and her own calling in the most unlikely places. ❖

❖ **Mark Roithmayr, first president Autism Speaks (until 2012).** A community member once told me that because of the Wrights, families with autism no longer see themselves on a deserted island trying to make fire. Maybe that's because they have been there. ❖

❖ **Katie Wright.** My parents were so devastated at first about Christian. I really admire them because so many of my friends' parents mourned and grieved, but they were paralyzed. Most had a terrible time handling it. But my mom and dad just jumped right in to do what they could and what no one else would do. I always felt really lucky. I was really surprised about how quickly my mom brought together the international stuff and got so many other countries involved.

When she first told us about what she wanted to do with a World Autism Day I thought, "OK, Mom, good luck with that!" I didn't honestly think that she'd be able to pull it off. I remember the first time actually going to the UN on World Autism Day and sitting there and thinking, "Wow! We really did it. There's my mom and my dad on the stage at the UN, and I'm looking around a jam-packed room of people who can begin to make good things happen." My parents taught me, "No excuses. Don't blame other people. Don't take the easy way out—only one right way. You have to do the right thing—easy or not." They raised me to believe that anything is possible. ❖

❖ **David Glazer, Google Genomics director of engineering.** The way the Wrights work together is quite an impressive thing to watch. Their hit 'em high, hit 'em low style of dealing with people is just the outward show. There are plenty of little things. After we briefly met at an Autism Speaks charity gala, we got a nice thank-you note from Suzanne. It's just one of those things that feels slightly quaint and antiquated in today's world, and boy, does it matter! It is both a genuine, warm act of affection and an effective tactic. They're both good at it and very real. ❖

❖ **Liz Feld, president Autism Speaks (2012 to present).** Suzanne gave me some great advice: never hire someone for a senior position you haven't had dinner with. You learn a lot about people that way, watching their manners, how they treat other people, how do they treat the waiter. Do they sit up straight? How do they eat their food? If they're going to be a public face for the organization, it's important to see these things.

After Bob offered me the job as President of Autism Speaks, but before it was announced, I attended one of our charity events at the Winged Foot Golf Club in Westchester, New York. During the evening reception, Bob came up to me and very quietly walked me off to the side. "You know, there are three important ingredients that will make you successful," he said. "You need passion, good judgment, and poise. Poise is all about timing, and that's something you get better at the longer you're in leadership." I was not only inspired but grateful for the advice. It was wisdom, pure and simple. I wrote those three things down on a little piece of paper that stays pinned to the blotter in my office. I put the three points in different colors and protected them with a coat of clear Scotch tape, and they have been sitting there ever since. ❖

❖ **Suzanne Wright.** Some things are just meant to be. Bob was diagnosed with Merkel cell cancer in 2000, and the doctors gave him 7 months to live. We were at Sloan Kettering for his surgery, and the doctors told us they thought they had got it all out and would know for sure in about a week. And unbeknownst to me, Cardinal Egan had asked the pope to pray for Bob. So I said to the doctors I was appreciative for everything they had done, but I was going with the cardinal because he reports to the pope, and the pope prayed for Bob.

My mother on her deathbed said she was sure Bob survived that terrible cancer because he would need to be there for autism. At the time, we didn't even know what it was. We always considered Bob's triumph over a near-death experience to be a sign that God meant him to do some other important work, and that turned out to be Autism Speaks. His law practice and GE and NBC experiences and everything about our marriage was leading to this. This is the culmination of the work he needed to do on earth. ❖

I was far from home and my family September 11, 2001, when terrorists flew commercial jets into the Twin Towers in New York City, killing thousands of victims. I watched in horror as the surreal events unfolded on television in my hotel room in

Long Beach, California. The only familiar voice was *Today Show* host Katie Couric, struggling to keep composure and calm when the plane hit the first tower. It was still dark before sunrise as I dressed to host a meeting of 200 GE sales people. And I felt the same despair and hopelessness as so many Americans. My first instinct was to call my family. My son Chris, who was just beginning his career at Goldman Sachs, told me he could see the tower on fire from his office, and I told him to get out of that building as fast as he could and go north. I tried to call my wife Suzanne, who was also in New York, but at that point all cell phone calls to NYC were halted. At that moment I did what so many did that day. I prayed and cried and longed to be with those I love.

I had flown to Long Beach in a GE corporate jet, which was parked at John Wayne airport. I immediately called Jeff Immelt, who was in Seattle at a GE Business meeting. He told me that US airspace for general aviation was shut down and that we were both stranded. He was trying to get GE mobile power generation equipment, and other resources and personnel to New York City. I suggested making a $1 million gift to the city to start a fund for relief assistance. For the next hour my communication with my family in New York was by text message on my BlackBerry. My son sent me a message that he was walking home to his apartment on 68th Street on the west side because there were no cabs or buses or any form of transportation available. At one point he told me that he could see the collapse of the first tower as he was making his way north. Suzanne had left a breakfast in Midtown and immediately walked to Central Park. Her father, a long-time New York cop, had always said the park would be the safest place to be if there was a dangerous situation in the city.

When I was finally cleared to leave Long Beach, I opted to hop a chartered flight with 70 Novartis pharmaceutical employees returning to New York City so that the GE corporate jet I would have flown in could take Australian riggers to New York to install gigantic power generation equipment for GE. I told the pilot to load up on food and beverages for the rugged outdoorsmen, who consumed everything in sight! When I returned to 30 Rock, I went with Jeff Immelt to make our way downtown to see GE mobile power generators operating and our NBC News teams on the job everywhere we turned. These mobile trailers were providing emergency power to hospitals, temporary patient centers, relief and rescue locations. I was never more proud of GE, its people, and its power to mobilize help when it was really needed. It was the beginning of an incredible outflow of generosity from corporations and individuals to form an enormous relief fund for the families and victims of 9/11.

Wright to the Point
The Wright family home
Palm Beach, Florida
April 19, 2015

Suzanne and I call this Paradise. It is the place we come to rest and recharge our batteries, especially in the cold-weather months. Sometimes I think I'd just as soon relax on our sunny veranda in Palm Beach, where the inlet waters lap up to our backyard on their way to the open Atlantic. Breathing deep and slow without anywhere to go is like a holiday for us. But it is not our nature to retire, especially when there still is so much to do. Besides, Suzanne wouldn't hear of it.

Life has been such a whirlwind. Autism Speaks became bigger and more demanding than we originally imagined. But how could we not have done it, considering the good that has come of it? The 10th anniversary of Autism Speaks prompted a lot of reflection. Even though our whole-genome sequencing project with Google will bring us closer to the answers about treatment and cause, there still is much to do in research, with legislation, and capitalizing on our grassroots strength and resources. But we would not have come this far without Suzanne pushing. None of it could have happened without Suzanne.

I've never been much for scandal. I have been married to Suzanne Warner Wright for nearly half a century, and we have three children and six grandchildren. Some of the most important days of my life have been family events tucked in between the scores of business meetings and obligations in my day calendar. I still consider myself a working stiff who has taken his notable accomplishments in stride and been humbled by forces of science, nature, and medicine that I cannot command. I would give up the good-life trappings if it meant finding ways to help people with autism lead fuller, richer lives.

In business everything is measured. You try to get your mission as tight as you can, measured and executed. In the end, the shareholders hold you accountable. You show up, do your best under pressure, take your lumps, and reap your rewards. Through these all-consuming, exhausting crusades, Suzanne has been my north star. She has been by my side through it all, sharing the load, being my reality check, my sounding board, my friend, my love—and the spark that made all the difference.

When I realized that the autism community needed a voice, I used all of my years in business to develop a strategy for how we'd be heard. My tenure as Chairman and CEO of Autism Speaks had direct parallels to my experiences at NBC.

The television industry was ready for change and I knew the Internet would be a big part of it. Bill Gates (right) was an important partner in launching the MSNBC cable news channel and companion dot-com website. The alliance was announced with Gates joining by satellite from China and me in New York before we had a final signed agreement.

Beloved NBC Entertainment chief Brandon Tartikoff (far right) never tired of the old ball game. The passionate baseball fan was joined by (right to left) major league baseball player and former Los Angeles Dodgers manager Tommy Lasorda, his wife Lilly Tartikoff, Suzanne (a Brooklyn diehard), and me.

My executive team at NBC Universal that contributed to our success included (left to right) Sports President Dick Ebersol, Entertainment President Jeff Zucker, NBC Networks President Randy Falco, and stations president Jay Ireland with me.

The success of Jerry Seinfeld (center) drove revenues and ratings which Don Ohlmeyer (left) knew just how to mine to rebuild the network's prime time schedule.

Below, Susan and Randy Falco (left) joined Meredith and Tom Brokaw, Suzanne, and me in feting the veteran NBC News anchorman's lifetime achievements.

NBC's telecast of the Seoul Korea Olympics in 1988 was in place when I took over as NBC president. Led by Dick Ebersol and Randy Falco, my team negotiated an unprecedented rights commitment to televise 7 consecutive Olympics Games from 2000 to 2012.

Lorne Michaels is a dear friend who has been the face of NBC entertainment for 40 years. He made *Saturday Night Live* one of television's jewels and a favorite of mine and Suzanne's.

Donald Trump's demonstrative style made *The Apprentice* a homerun for NBC and sent American politics into a tailspin in the 2016 presidential election. Back then it was easy to be amused.

Late night talk show king Johnny Carson and his wife, Alex, were best travel buddies for years, whether it was at our summer home in Nantucket (above), or on safari on the African Serengeti Plain (below). There was no place that Johnny felt out of his element. He amused anywhere, anytime, in any language.

"Am I really going to do this?" Jack Welch would ask about all of my bold proposals for NBC. My longtime mentor and friend trusted me to take the network into lucrative initiatives from CNBC to the NBC Universal merger.

My appointment on September 1, 1986 as NBC President succeeding Grant Tinker (far left) was orchestrated by GE Chairman Jack Welch (center), who trusted me to rein in the spending and roll the dice on enterprising new business ventures.

The original Wright Stuff. Before there were weddings and grandchildren, there was just the five of us (left to right): Katie, Chris, Maggie, Suzanne and me.

Suzanne had our immediate family pose every summer at our Nantucket home for an informal portrait featured on the front of our annual holiday card. The photos marked how quickly our family had grown and how far we had come. (left to right front row) Maisie (9), Mattias (12), Morgan (11); (second row) Chris, Sandi, Alex (5), Suzanne, Bob, Christian (14), Katie; (third row) Greg, Sloan (3), Maggie and Andreas.

Christian's autism diagnosis was a mixed blessing and special challenge for our family and most especially his younger brother Mattias (leaning left) in a playful moment (top) and (to the right) seated on the sand dunes of Nantucket. Whether protecting or defending, supporting, and loving his brother, Mattias exemplifies the best of who we are for Christian and other autistic persons.

I was elated with the birth and early development of our first grandchild Christian, which began taking a troublesome turn in his second year before he was diagnosed with autism in February 2004.

Suzanne (left), West Palm Beach, Florida Mayor Jeri Muoio (right), and me celebrated our important fundraiser and the emotional re-commitment of autism families at the annual Palm Beach, FL Walk for Autism on March 8, 2015 with a special proclamation.

Suzanne and I were joined that sunny Sunday March 8, 2015 by 7,000 participants raising more than $400,000 for Autism Speaks. Dignitaries included (left to right) Rep. Patrick Murphy, South Florida Ford dealer rep Al Young, Rep. Lois Frankel, and West Palm Beach Mayor Jeri Muoio.

The 8th annual World Focus on Autism September 30, 2015, in New York City convened first spouses and dignitaries from across North America, Asia, Africa, Latin America, Europe, and the Middle East. Participating nations discussed finding 21st Century Answers to autism services and treatments.

The 8th Annual World Focus on Autism festivities September 30, 2015, included presenting Dr. Shekhar Saxena (second from the right) the 3rd Annual Bob and Suzanne Wright Global Achievement for Autism Award. We were joined (left to right) by Dr. Liri Berisha, the second recipient of the award, and Mrs. Ban Soon-taek, spouse of United Nations Secretary-General Ban Ki-moon.

Reauthorizing the Combating Autism Act for 3 more years on September 30, 2011, was the strongest show of support for our families by President Barack Obama. It was an especially joyous occasion for musician-composer Billy Mann whose wife Gena and son Jasper were invited to the signing. (left to right) Rep. Chris Smith, Scott Badesch, president of the Autism Society of America, and George Jesien, executive director Association of University Centers on Disabilities.

Flipping the switch in the lobby of New York's iconic Empire State Building to Light it Up Blue at the start of World Autism Awareness was a very big deal, April 2, 2015. Suzanne and I were joined by our grandchildren Mattias Hildebrand, Morgan and Maisie Wright, and honored guests Deron Williams, his wife Amy Williams (second from the right), and their son DJ.

Even the New York Sanitation Department embraces World Autism Awareness Day, April 2, 2015: (left to right) DSNY Chief Anthony Adolino and wife Dana, son Anthony Luca, and Suzanne and me with our grandon Mattias Hildebrand.

2014 United Nations Panel for World Autism Awareness Day. On my left in the green is US Ambassador Elizabeth Cousens, on Suzanne's right is U.N. Secretary-General's Chef de Cabinet Susana Malcorra.

I have loved Suzanne my whole life; I have loved Christian all of his. Even without eye contact or conventional affection, we've learned how to love each other, just like all families in the autism community do.

ACT THREE. 2004-Now: Nonprofit Transformation

22

1 in 166: The Hidden Epidemic

Creating a global springboard for autism made the process of transforming NBC look like child's play. At NBC, although it took 2 decades of pushing, the warring constituents—affiliates, advertisers, program producers, and NBC and GE executives—were eventually reconciled. Autism is a different story. On autism's broad, disjointed spectrum, there are as many points of view as there are conditions, resulting in many dissonant factions. I'm not sure they can ever be reconciled.

My experience in crusading for change in the two different circles—corporate and philanthropic—reveals uncanny parallels as well as stark differences. Both organizations challenged the status quo and innovated inside of rigid institutions. NBC was a major GE asset governed by the conglomerate's internal processes. Autism Speaks' advocacy hinges on Congress, the medical and scientific communities, and insurance companies, and its interface with all of them can border on the absurd. NBC and Autism Speaks rely on strategic alliances for resources to launch new projects. In both cases, properly motivating and empowering others has been critical. As the new president of NBC in 1986, I inherited a challenged broadcast system and workforce that had to be rebooted for cable and the digital age. Rapidly changing technology and interactivity would inevitably force the transformation. Autism Speaks offers no such assurances; we must fight for every measure of change.

But the beginnings of Autism Speaks presented one challenge that has no parallel at NBC—the question of awareness. I seriously doubt there were a dozen people in the US who were unfamiliar with NBC in 2004, but practically everyone, including extremely intelligent, well-informed people, knew nothing about autism, had never even heard the word. I knew from the very beginning that if we were going to accomplish anything, increasing awareness had to be the first priority, because everything else—raising funds, supporting research, getting better legislation, putting pressure on insurers, everything—flows from it. Awareness is the gateway through which we accomplished everything else, and it still is.

❖ **Suzanne Wright.** We had no idea what was behind the terrifying change in our grandson. Then one night, before we had the official diagnosis, my daughter called me in tears. "Mom," she said, "I know it's autism." And I said, "What the heck is autism?"

Can you imagine that? This was only 11 years earlier, and I had no clue. We had no idea what we were dealing with.

Then, that terrible day when we got the diagnosis, I knew just one thing: I'll do whatever it takes to get help, go anywhere I need to go to get some answers. ❖

With the assurance of $25 million in startup funds from Bernie Marcus and plans to launch Autism Speaks under way, Suzanne and I traveled around the country seeking the support and wisdom of doctors, researchers, and other professionals involved in autism study and care.

Many times it seemed to us that modern mental health was more like medieval medicine. It's people talking about problems to other people but not having drugs or real treatments to deal with it. And until you get drugs or really proven treatments, you can't get into the category of medically treatable. And that category is where you get insurance and it's where you get reimbursement for the cost—a very critical juncture.

That catch-22 existed when we launched Autism Speaks. At the time, legislators, doctors, scientists, and insurance companies would not listen to our plight because they didn't have to—not until our numbers and individual achievements demanded it. That's when I knew our first task was to create a tidal wave of awareness.

Then, in late October 2004, there was a kind of turning point.

Bernie and I had gone to a conference at the Kennedy Krieger Institute, which is affiliated with Johns Hopkins. We were there at the invitation of the center's director, Dr. Gary Goldstein, who had come to our home with Bernie for that very first meeting. At this conference, listening to various physicians and scientists, it hit me just how bizarrely unequal are the resources for autism.

Jose Cordero, an assistant surgeon general assigned to birth defect studies at the Centers for Disease Control, presented a chart tracking the incidence of leading diseases and conditions. On that chart was one alarming statistic: 1 out of every 166 children in America would be diagnosed with autism. I was stunned. Bernie and I looked at each other in dismay. Cordero, however, seemed indifferent. I couldn't keep quiet.

"Jose, I just don't understand that chart you have up there. You talked about autism in the same vein as diabetes and AIDS, cystic fibrosis, and muscular dystrophy. But the numbers on your chart don't add up. None of the conditions you have listed up there are as prevalent as autism, but they all receive far more government funding."

"Yes, that's correct," Cordero agreed.

I was almost shouting. "The number of children being diagnosed with autism is climbing at an alarming rate, and yet pediatricians and other medical professionals we speak to are not aware of the statistics!"

"It is a terrible situation," Cordero replied, trying to calm me down.

"But why don't people know?" I pressed on. "Why don't they have this information?"

"Well, we don't really know a lot about autism and these statistics would be very disconcerting. We wouldn't know what to tell them. They wouldn't know what to do. There's no treatment or cause. We're not ready to explain it," Cordero conceded.

I couldn't believe my ears. Here was our own government completely oblivious to an emerging epidemic. The guy with the numbers doesn't even tell anybody! "All the more reason to raise awareness with parents, doctors, and the scientific community!" I bellowed.

Then, almost as an afterthought, Codero said the CDC had budgeted $2 million for a national informational campaign to begin spreading the word about autism.

"Do you know how much advertising $2 million will buy?" I demanded. "Maybe two days' worth! That's not a national campaign!"

Now I was on solid ground; I understood the world of advertising, and I knew what to do. So Bernie and I huddled briefly, and then after the presentations, we approached Cordero with an offer.

"We'll make you a deal," I began. "We will help you raise autism awareness with a national public campaign that we will pay for. You will use the $2 million to enlighten pediatricians and other medical professionals. You will give them all the statistics the CDC has on the subject." Cordero agreed.

That was the catalyst for the award-winning Autism Awareness campaign that we developed with Andrew Robinson, chief executive of BBDO, one of the world's leading ad agencies, and the Ad Council. Andrew assembled a creative team led by famed producer David Lubars, and the Ad Council donated airtime. The ads they produced became famous for their simple effectiveness. In one memorable spot, a dad plays catch with his young son as the voiceover narrator says, "The chances of your child becoming a major league baseball player are 1 in 40,000. The chances of him being diagnosed with autism are 1 in 166."

That one statistic—1 in 166—became a powerful weapon for us, and Suzanne knew how to use it. She was ferocious.

❖ **Suzanne Wright.** Until this point, autism was winning. It was going into these homes, taking these children into the darkness, and these poor parents couldn't do anything. I was so determined to get some answers, some help.

So Bob and I made up a card: the numbers of leukemia, the numbers of diabetes, and so on. And then the numbers of autism: 1 in 166. I took that card to the NBC news department. "OK," I said, "this is something that has to be covered. There is a hidden epidemic of autism. Tell me why we don't know about this? Why? Nobody is talking about it, therefore we have no awareness, therefore we have no answers." It was a story waiting to be told. Within months, the autism crisis became the focus of a series of compelling NBC News reports, and that prompted government hearings and independent studies.

Then I gave that same little card with all the numbers to all the congressmen and senators. "These are not my numbers," I said, "these are your numbers. From the CDC. These are numbers that you give out and nobody's doing anything about this. How can this be?" That's what I convinced them on, because there's no arguing with the numbers.

Early on I had the idea of involving Toys "R" Us as a supporter. So I went to see the CEO, Jerry Storch, and I just laid it out for him. I said, "Jerry, do you have any idea how bad this is?" He was very honest, and he said no. Then when I gave him the numbers, he said, "How could that possibly be?" And I said, "Yes, Jerry, that's exactly what I said at first. How can this be that nobody's talking about this? How could this be that you are running a toy company, and here I am, the wife of the president of NBC, and we don't know about this? These are the kids that you're selling toys to. You need to do this."

He was shocked at the numbers. As a matter of fact, he didn't really buy it at first. But when he looked into it, he said, "I'm in." Every April, they collect donations at the cash register, then they sponsored our walks nationally, and over all these years we've collected almost $20 million. ❖

❖ **Andrew Robinson, CEO BBDO Worldwide.** One day I got this call from Bob Wright, who at the time was vice chairman of GE, a very important client of ours. "I'm going to ask you something," he said, "and you can say no." That was the only time I've ever heard Bob say that. He told me to expect a telephone call from the Ad Council asking if BBDO would prepare an ad campaign to raise awareness about the rising incidence of autism and the need for early detection. He warned that this pro bono assignment would be a lot of work and I should not feel obliged to accept it. How could I refuse?

We recruited celebrities whose lives had been touched by autism, and the Ad Council donated $250 million in air time. High-profile celebrities, from Billy Mann to Ed Asner to Tommy Hilfiger, who closely identified with the pains and uncertainties of autistic families because of their own personal experiences, volunteered their time. We made 25 public service spots, and won lots of awards, and people still remember them because they were so powerful.

We were only a year or so into the awareness campaign when Suzanne started working her magic by convincing the United Nations to host an annual Autism Awareness Day and getting companies around the world to light up their buildings blue for a day. That took the issue of awareness to a whole new level.

It's all about going big or going home; finding things that are really going to matter and have a huge impact even in a relatively short period of time. ❖

❖ **Laura Slatkin, founding president Candela Group and NEST Fragrances; founder New York Center for Autism and the Developing Brain and NYC Autism Charter School; Autism Speaks board member**. When our son, David, was diagnosed with autism, we got in touch with our very dear friend, Deeda Blair. She sat on the board of the National Institutes of Mental Health foundation and arranged a meeting with NIMH director Tom Insel. This was April 2003. We wanted to tell him about our plans and get his advice on how to best move forward. We thought it would be as simple as identifying the problem and solving it.

But Tom did not give us much to feel happy about. "We do not really know much about autism," he said. "It is a very complex disorder. There are not a lot of great opportunities to fund important research. We just have no idea what causes it, let alone how to cure it. With so little to go on, there is not much immediate hope."

Then, not long after, Bob and Suzanne Wright created Autism Speaks. Bob told me something I've never forgotten: he said if we raised awareness about autism, the money would follow. And he was right. They let the medical community know that money would be invested in autism. When scientists, universities, and hospital administration or the leadership of these hospitals and universities find out that there is a lot of money going behind a disorder, they then begin to devote resources to it.

The sad thing is that even though we spent a lot of money on research, we still do not know what causes autism. We know more than we did 5 years ago, but we do not know what causes autism and how to cure it. We don't know how to treat the new wave of people with autism, 85 percent of who are under age 21 and we do not know how they will be cared for and supported through their adult life. Without a cause and a cure, these are the next most critical issues we face as a society. ❖

❖ **Dr. Gary Goldstein, president and CEO Kennedy Krieger Institute of Johns Hopkins.** I have been head of the Kennedy Krieger Institute in Baltimore, Maryland, for 24 years. Our commitment is to developmental disorders of the brain, and developmental disabilities broadly—both physical and the behavioral. Autism represents about 20 percent of what we do.

But Bernie Marcus and I knew we could never have pulled off what the Wrights have done, which is why we traveled to meet with them at their Connecticut home in July 2004 to solicit their help. Building an infrastructure for autism has to be a national, public effort by people who have enormous leadership skills, resources, and reach. They're raising $60 million a year in mostly small donations and the local walks. It's a grassroots effort.

Bob and Suzanne orchestrated a red-carpet grand opening of Autism Speaks in Hollywood in the fall of 2005, complete with Jerry Seinfeld after a $1,000-per-plate dinner. Then came Light It Up Blue and United Nations Autism Day, and the Wrights were involving the entire world. Nobody else had ever done that. And they began tapping into the families of autistic children and the power of these families to raise funds, share experience, and bring their energy and passion to the cause. It's an amazing force capable of influencing state government and federal government, the medical community, and the research. ❖

That day in 2004, when I first heard the 1 in 166 number, I was flabbergasted. It seemed impossible. But as it turned out, things were worse than I realized. I didn't know it at the time, but even then that statistic was out of date. One in 166 was the CDC prevalence for the year 2000. By 2004, it was 1 in 125.

Today, things are even worse. On March 27, 2014, CDC released new numbers: 1 in 68 American children have autism spectrum disorder. In spite of all our hard work, autism seems to be winning. Some might say that the new statistic is evidence that our push for awareness is succeeding, that more children are being accurately diagnosed. I try to hold on to that, but some days, knowing that more of our children are being diagnosed with this devastating condition is small comfort.

23

Building from Scratch, Block by Block

T he year 2007 was a time of profound professional and personal transition for me. It started with my retirement as chairman CEO of NBC Universal and ended with Autism Speaks emerging as an advocacy group with global scale.

In early February, my attention turned from daily management of NBCU to growing the clout of Autism Speaks by cashing in every last chip I had. Over the years my Rolodex had grown fat with names of smart, influential, caring people. There was very little need for arm twisting. Most of the people I approached unhesitatingly stepped up with time, resources, and money.

That year we also brought into the fold the last of three regional advocacy and research groups, Cure Autism Now (CAN). Earlier we had brought in two others—Autism Coalition for Research & Education (ACRE) and the National Alliance for Autism Research (NAAR). Despite their distinctive, sometimes conflicting focus, we were eventually able to integrate all three under the Autism Speaks umbrella, even though that process took 3 years. In contrast, it took NBC decades to rally its warring interest groups (affiliates, advertisers, program producers, and executive corps) while pushing into new frontiers. The unforeseen prize in both cases was the extraordinary people I learned from and worked with along the way, although even now it seems autism's disparate constituents might never be satisfied.

I pursued legislative support for autism funding as diligently and strategically as I had sought broadcast and cable deregulation and copyright protections decades earlier on Capitol Hill. Our fledgling grassroots parents' network made inroads into autism insurance reform one state at a time.

But it wasn't until Suzanne's trip to Qatar in April to discuss our aggressive awareness campaign that we discovered a fast track to going global. (More on that pivotal trip in Chapter 24.) Our mandate was to leverage all we had to uncover the causes and cures across the autism spectrum. Our biggest challenge was building an enduring, effective organization with a business mentality, philanthropic heart, research mission, and worldwide reach. For every step we took locally, we took a step globally; it was all about the grassroots.

Uniting everyone who was involved—or should be—was nearly impossible.

- Parents and professionals splintered into views and agendas as wildly diverse as the full range of autisms.

- The volunteers who organized and participated in annual walks in dozens of cities, generating about half of our revenues, were generally untapped the remainder of the year.

- Scientists, clinicians, and researchers were mired in a painfully slow process of translating well-intended efforts into practice.

- Autism Speaks' board of directors comprised entrepreneurs, corporate executives, scientists, and medical professionals, many of whom had autistic children and grandchildren. They understood how to create value in a world where people could be managed, operations regimented, and rules mandated. But the autistic world is not like that.

On every front, we struggled to change institutional thinking and behavior and to defiantly redefine purpose and process. I had been there before. After more than 2 decades of upending the media status quo, nothing about this challenge surprised me or scared me—except the possibility that despite all our efforts, we might not make a significant difference in autistic lives.

❖ **Dr. Herbert Pardes, psychiatrist, former director NIMH, former CEO New York Presbyterian Hospital, Autism Speaks director.** You can raise public awareness about autism. You can raise funds for research. You can inspire new legislation. You can raise the bar for extraordinary individual efforts to build schools and centers. Putting an illness like autism on the map, getting the very top levels of government to decide that this is a critical thing that has to be addressed, is an amazing accomplishment.

The Wrights and Autism Speaks have done all that superbly. They have used every bone in their bodies and leveraged every connection they have to build an organization that is extremely effective politically and in so many other ways. At one point the only two illnesses in tight economic times which were recommended for increase in medical research dollars at the federal level were cancer and autism. That was no accident.

But you cannot mandate the ultimate outcome; you cannot command the cause and cure. And in the meantime, the clock keeps ticking and autistic children become adults. That is a source of frustration and pressure. That is the challenge. ❖

Wright to the Point

When you build something worthwhile, you can't just stop. You have to go a step further and build more so that the effort can be sustained and nurtured even without you. You can't go outside and plant a kernel of corn and scream at it and get a bushel. It just doesn't work. Here's what grassroots really means: You have to seed the field, you have to fertilize it, you have to care for it, and you have to pull out the weeds so that the healthy blades of grass will thrive. You have to put the right supports in place: the sunshine and water and food. You have to choose the next generation of leadership to tend the fields. All of that takes a lot of time and a lot of effort.

For Autism Speaks, five building blocks provided the same kind of fertile ground: the global expansion, political heft and legislation, the grassroots network, business principles, and strategic partnerships. In the chapters that immediately follow, each of those efforts is described. I want to stress, however, that even though they appear in sequence, because that's the way it is with the written word, we should not jump to the conclusion that one is more important than another because of its relative position. All are, and will continue to be, equally critical.

24
Building Block #1: Global Expansion

Shafallah Center
Doha, Qatar
April 23–24, 2007

❖ **Andy Shih, senior VP scientific affairs Autism Speaks, Autism Speaks Global Public Health Initiative.** The tiny nation of Qatar on the northeastern coast of the Arabian Peninsula is one of the world's wealthiest countries, and one of the least known to westerners. So when Her Highness Sheikha Mozah bint Nasser Al Missned, the emir's second wife, invited Suzanne Wright to visit, we didn't know quite what to expect.

Sheika Mozah, whose position as wife of the monarch is similar to queen, had led many educational and health initiatives for her country's 1 million people. She has a special passion for improving the lives of children and was a driving force behind the $200 million Shafallah Center in the capital city of Doha, for special needs children, nearly half of them autistic. Our aggressive public service media campaign caught her attention, and she invited Suzanne to speak at a conference there about what we were doing at Autism Speaks. Suzanne also was hoping to enlist her sponsorship of the first United Nations World Autism Awareness Day.

After her presentation, and with just half an hour's notice, Suzanne was invited to Sheika Mozah's office for a private conference. We were told she had cleared 10 minutes in her schedule.

Suzanne already knew what she wanted to say, speaking from the heart, one mother to another, but she felt the need for a visual aid. I had tagged along on the trip to talk up fund-raising. One of the few graphics in our toolbox was a world map—a universal bridge to span language and cultural differences. Suzanne grabbed the map on her way into Sheikha Mozah's office to make the point that Qatar could be the first Arab country to lead the cause. And it worked.

Thirty minutes later, Suzanne emerged, beaming, with a commitment of support from Qatar. She leveraged that endorsement to gain collaborative co-sponsorship from a dozen other countries in the Middle East, Asia, and Europe. Our first overseas alliance jumpstarted a new global health dialogue and movement. ❖

❖ **Dana Marnane, VP communications and awareness Autism Speaks.** I had been at Autism Speaks for less than a year. On June 28, 2007, Suzanne was invited to address the United Nations about autism during a special seminar. The head of the Department of Public Information at the time, Juan Carlos Brandt, was also a parent of a special needs child. He immediately connected with Suzanne. She asked for the first World Autism Awareness Day. As soon as her speech was over, he sent his assistant to draft a petition supporting the creation of an annual World Autism Awareness Day—and got everyone in the room to sign it that same day.

The UN folks warned us that getting full acceptance of the idea was not going to be easy or quick, but Suzanne was not intimidated. She was determined to have the first World Autism Day on the following April 2. And she did! In less than 6 months, which is some kind of a record at the UN, the petition unanimously passed. Until we find a cure, it still stands. When you get enough of the right people behind you, and you are focused, anything is possible. ❖

❖ **Suzanne Wright.** The personal connection to autism that all of us have is what has helped us to grow quickly all over the world. Coming from where we were 10 or 11 years ago, when so many medical professionals were reluctant to even use the "A word," I have seen extraordinary things happen. The movement took off when parents and grandparents from different corners of the world realized we are a global society bound and supported by new technology. Social media and the Internet make it easier for people to reach out and help each other.

In the early days of Autism Speaks, I went to the Ad Council to ask for their help with creative marketing. Throughout my presentation, there was a woman in the back of the room sobbing. As it turned out, she had a child with autism and had never told anybody. Well, she was the head of communications at the Ad Council, and it wasn't long before they agreed to help us. The ad agency BBDO created the PSAs pro bono, and the Ad Council went on to earn us nearly $500 million in donated media. And of course those amazing public service spots won lots of awards, and opened lots of eyes and hearts. Like I said, all of our personal connections to autism are endless.

When we first had to deal with autism in our family, the hardest thing was that we had nowhere to go for information or answers. I couldn't talk to anybody about it. So the first thing we did is create the 100-day kit that translates into any language. And now we have over 50 more toolkits parents can download from our website on specific topics in travel, education, socialization, and more.

Our global expansion helped us to realize that the one thing in the world that is bipartisan is children. Children don't have any ambitions other than to grow up as healthy human beings. That's what we have in common with other countries around the world. When I was in Israel in 2008, I visited some autism centers near the Palestinian border. They do a lot for their kids there. And in one of the rooms I met a Palestinian woman with her autistic child. The mother was crying and I was crying. She was crying out of gratitude for the compassionate care her child was receiving in an Israeli center. I was crying because it was such a moving example of the way the world should be: taking care of our children is more important than politics.

What the world's governments did for AIDS, we need to do for autism. We need to be a global family for all of our children around the world to help us solve the mysteries of autism. ❖

❖ **Kevin Murray, investor, director Autism Speaks, founder Autism Coalition, father of autistic child**. Suzanne told me one day that she had this idea: get lots of buildings, all around the world, to light their exteriors blue, for just one night each year. If they all did it on the same night, it would be a strong visual way to call attention to autism. And especially to drive home the fact that it is most prevalent among young boys. You may know that Suzanne can be pretty persuasive, but I wasn't at all sure. "Well, OK," I said, "but what about the science and what we are doing for people on the ground? How is lighting up a few buildings going to change things?"

Everyone underestimated the impact of Light It Up Blue. Especially me. The pure energy and vision she had executing on that idea, and how that brings in corporate players and opens up a whole new opportunity for discussion, was truly brilliant. ❖

❖ **Suzanne Wright.** I was tired of everybody dancing around autism. We needed the world to know about this! I had the support of the UN secretary general Ban Ki-moon and his wife; they both understood the importance of reaching the largest number of people with messages about early intervention and education. The Light It Up Blue campaign was intended to bring attention to autism in a dramatic way every year. It has contributed to a 50 percent increase in world awareness since we began.

I was at a dinner at Donald Trump's Mar-a-Lago Club near our home in Palm Beach when I found myself sitting next to Lenny Boxer, an attorney who represents the Empire State Building and the group that owns it. He's a big, high-powered real estate attorney in New York City. I told him about our plans to shine a light on autism all over the world, and added, "I'd like to start with the Empire State Building." He looked at me and said, "Not a bad place to start, Suzanne!" He warned me that they received thousands of inquiries each year and that I would need to submit an application along with our proposal. So I did, knowing that Lenny would make sure that it got to the right hands. I figured if we could get the Empire State Building, we could get anyone in the world.

They've said yes every year we have applied. The general manager and head of operations, Joe Bellina, meets us every year down in the lobby for a little press conference. We always ask a celebrity with some connection to autism to come help us flip the switch. Ethan Walmark, a 7-year-old piano prodigy who has autism, joined us one year, along with Yoko Ono.

Many celebrities who have children and siblings with autism step forward to post tweets, tape public service messages, and make other fund-raising appearances to support our research and awareness efforts. Model Jacquelyn Jablonski, Robert De Niro, Holly Robinson Peete, Dan Marino, and Jenny McCarthy, so many of them. Fashion designer Tommy Hilfiger and former model Dee

Ocleppo have a blended family of six children. Each brought a teenage child with autism to their 2008 marriage, and they have since joined the Autism Speaks board.

The blue light has become a universal way of recognizing and communicating compassion about autism. Almost everybody I ask agrees to participate in Light It Up Blue without hesitation. Now we have more than 18,600 structures (including 100 major places of worship) in 142 countries on 7 continents lighting up blue every April 2. In 2015, we only have 53 countries to go and we will have the entire world. That's my goal. ❖

25
Building Block #2: Political Muscle

Breakfast with Democratic presidential candidate
Barack Obama
Home of Billy and Gena Mann
April 20, 2007

❖ **Billy Mann, recording artist, producer, and songwriter, director Autism Speaks, parent of an autistic child.**
When you are struggling to understand what it means when your child is diagnosed with autism, it is utterly terrifying, utterly quiet. The air gets very heavy and there are not a lot of sounds. You lose your footing like you are in a fun house of distorted mirrors. It was like a lightning bolt hit me and my wife, Gena. When you live in New York City, which often thinks of itself as the center of the universe, you assume there are experts all over the place that know exactly what to do for autism. You figure there's got to be protocol and medication in a city with every kind of hospital and technology available. And instead, we found what the Wrights and so many other families sadly discovered: there aren't a lot of answers.

I'm a musician and a creative executive and a songwriter and a record producer. I was in the recording studio working on Jessica Simpson's Christmas album in Los Angeles at the end of 2004 when we got the news that our son, Jasper, was diagnosed as autistic. What happened over the next 8 years was outrageous and terrifying. We struggled with the tough realities of autism like so many other parents.

My search for answers led me to a meeting with the Wrights in February 2007 at a restaurant in Fairfield, Connecticut, near where we both live. Picture it: Bob Wright looking dapper in a straw hat, Suzanne dressed for the back nine at Pebble Beach, and me—6'4", 235 pounds, with long curly black hair. But it could not have been a more commiserate pairing.

The three of us sat and talked about our frustrations in searching for better ways to help our autistic children. Shock and desperation with the scarcity of information and support drove my wife and me to get involved. I wanted to know what we could do. I grew up in inner-city Philadelphia and I'm a pretty scrappy guy. I'm not afraid to take on something tough.

The Wrights are very powerful people, and that, in part, has to do with the strength of who they are as individuals and the integrity in the way that they communicate with people. If Bob asks you how you're doing, it's not a drive-by question. If Suzanne wants to know how your kid is, she really wants to know, because in the back of her mind she's thinking about how her own kids and grandchildren are doing. They really are, for me, the autism godparents for my family.

Because of all the help and support my family has received from the Wrights and Autism Speaks, I wanted to find a way to give back. About the same time, I was talking to people managing Senator Obama's presidential campaign about hosting a fundraiser at my home, and I decided to try to tie it into autism. I remember asking

Bob if I could count on him to be there with his friends. Bob said, "Sure, kid," in the same way you'd say it if a little kid comes to you and asks if Derek Jeter will come to his birthday party.

I wanted to get autism on the radar of people in power, so I asked Senator Obama if he would take time to listen to family members of autistic children and reserve his remarks until the end. Obama brought his campaign to our home bright and early one Saturday morning. He briefly visited with my wife and me, and with the Wrights, and then spent 3 hours in our living room, listening to parents' stories.

After that, I was asked to work on the Obama campaign's policy statement on autism, which got a full page on his website. My family and the Wrights were present in the Oval Office on September 30, 2011, when President Obama signed the Combating Autism Reauthorization Act. Our autistic son, Jasper, who was 9 at the time, received the first pen used by the president signing the bill into law. The moment was captured in an official White House photograph. Although direct eye contact is very difficult for my son, he looked directly up at the president in the photo.

But autism doesn't care much about such auspicious moments. Jasper has trouble staying still and asked me to put him on my shoulders. We tried to maintain protocol as long as we could before I excused myself to the president and said I had to answer to a higher power. I picked up a very agitated Jasper, placed him on my shoulders, and quietly exited.

The Wrights have used their position without hesitation, not just because they are looking to cure their own grandchild but for all autistic children and their families. That makes it impossible to not want to go stand right next to them and do what is necessary when it's game-on time. They really took on autism to say this is not OK for the rich or for the middle class or for the poor. It's not

OK regardless of ethnicity. There still are no answers for autism. And the journey inevitably leads through Washington. ❖

That was the last meaningful rapport we had with presidential candidate Obama and his staff. Suzanne was bitterly disappointed about not getting the Obama administration to agree to lighting up the White House blue for autism awareness in April. First Lady Michelle Obama, like Laura Bush before her, shunned her invitation to join the first ladies of other nations at an annual gathering for autism awareness. We could never get them to support anything we did at the United Nations. It has become such an obvious slight to us even though we have succeeded in securing congressional support for major autism-related legislation. It may have had something to do with that day in the Oval Office when we gathered for the bill signing. While posing for the photos, I may have leaned over to the president and quietly said something like, "You've been a disappointment." OK, so my timing wasn't great.

❖ **Suzanne Wright.** We never had the level of support from the Obama administration we expected after his initial interest as a presidential candidate. We tried to pass on letters and invitations using deputies or people having dinner with the president, to no avail. We tried to get answers from people closest to them, like Valerie Jarrett and Tina Tchen. The standard response was that if the White House did things for us, it would have to do things for everybody. To which I would say, "You know, that's a good idea!" 2016 marks the 7th consecutive year we have asked the Obama administration to join us in lighting up the White House blue for autism.

Every year we host an autism awareness event at the UN for the first ladies and spouses when the presidents and prime ministers of nations around the world come to the General Assembly. They are accomplished women. The former first lady of Albania, Dr. Liri Berisha, is a pediatrician. Sonia Gandhi is president of the Indian National Congress Party and widow of former Prime Minister Rajiv Gandhi, who was assassinated in 1991. Then in 2015, three representatives from China joined our eighth World Focus on Autism with first ladies from around the world for the first time. And now Peng Liyuan, China's first lady, has invited Bob and I to attend the First Autism Conference sponsored by the Central Government of China in spring 2016. Although our global reach widens, Mrs. Obama never attends; neither did Laura Bush, but that doesn't stop me from trying. We have a whole generation of children being born into autism. They don't have time for political games. ❖

So I never apologized for a bare-knuckle approach to fighting resistance to change. You don't get a lot of gold stars for being the maverick or the status quo disruptor. It's a constant battle and many chief executives retreat from the front lines, hoping things will take care of themselves long enough to make it their successor's problem. You often have to hope the grassroots will support your efforts or that some major event will be a catalyst. But sometimes you don't have the luxury of time. The clock is ticking and something has to change.

The most difficult thing we face at Autism Speaks is the constant denial by the medical and science communities, and even the average person, that autism is a serious health epidemic that we can do anything about. It requires a constant flow of funds for new research and treatment that challenges conventional thinking. Every time a new cancer is announced, everyone applauds, the news covers it. Every time we come out with something about autism, the first thing the doctors and scientists say is that it can't be true. It's incredible! No one says that about cancer or multiple sclerosis.

I experienced the same stubborn dissent at NBC when I tried to convince everyone that cable TV and digital interactivity would change everything about the media business. Resistance came from all sides—our own executives, affiliates, and both the broadcast and cable industry. GE simply didn't want to deal with it.

Some of the change I lobbied for at NBC was more subtle and took a while to be revealed on balance sheets. I had tremendous pushback on the elimination of federal rules barring broadcast networks from having financial interest in the syndication of TV programing they financed but did not own. The fin-syn battles were fierce with Congress, Hollywood, and affiliates. They said the TV networks shouldn't own entertainment, and of course now they own everything. But it took 10 years to win the right. It was our Korean War at NBC.

In both cases, the pushback led us to Washington and a fight for new legislation that would support our progressive efforts. Having the law on your side silences all kinds of denial.

❖ **Suzanne Wright.** It was 2004 when Bob and I first went to Washington to try to get some funding support for autism research; at the time, we were still trying to pull together the different autism organizations under one roof. We met with Sen. Chris Dodd and the late Sen. Ted Kennedy, who said to us, "Suzanne and Bob, this is not going to work because you've got the Hatfields and the McCoys. You've got all these groups fighting about what causes autism and what to do about it." So we said, "If we can get these guys together under one roof, under Autism Speaks, we're going to be back here and we're going to need your help." Sure enough, a year later, we were back.

And I handed out those little cards to all the congressmen and senators that showed the incidence of autism at the time, so much higher than other conditions. So we learned to go to Washington with an army of people and the facts. And we posed the question, "How can it be we have no answers to the most serious developmental disability? These are the CDC statistics, your own numbers that nobody's doing anything about."

Probably our biggest fight that year was passage of the Combatting Autism Act. It would double National Instiues of Health funding on autism research, create an early detection program, and authorize $1 billion over 5 years. It had passed the Senate and had 227 cosponsors in the House. But it was being blocked by Rep. Joe Barton of Texas, the chairman of the House Committee on Energy and Commerce. He contended the autism-related matters would be adequately covered in the National Institutes of Health Reform Act.

Barton had openly told a group of his constituents, all of them parents of autistic children, that he was not putting the bill out. So on October 5, right in the middle of his reelection campaign, some of the mothers organized a protest outside Barton's district office in Waco, Texas. His chief of staff came out to confront them and said only five or so families would be allowed inside the office. The rest of the parents angrily demanded to see him, and someone called the cops. The entire confrontation was captured in a YouTube video that has since been taken down off the service and is no longer available.

When the Combatting Autism Act finally came up for a vote in the House, it passed and was soon after signed into law. Not long afterwards we were on Capitol Hill for some occasion when two congressmen who shall go unnamed invited us to step into an office, where they scolded us for playing too rough! ❖

That was just the beginning. We had to rally governors and individual state legislators for research funds and for health insurance reform, and we had to do it one state at a time. We also had to use our lobbying efforts at the federal level, because the armed services make the federal government the country's biggest insurer. The full story of how we tackled the enormous problem of insurance coverage is in the next chapter, on the power of the grassroots (Chapter 26).

On November 12–14, 2013, Autism Speaks held its first-ever national policy and action summit in Washington, DC. We brought together more than 200 leaders from across the country, including top Obama administration officials, members of Congress, governors, prominent scientists and policy experts, key stakeholders, volunteers, and activists. It got Congress and our advocacy team squarely focused on the legislative goals we had for 2014. We ended the summit with 150 Autism Speaks representatives visiting all 535 congressional offices with 155,000 signed petitions in hand calling for a national strategy for autism.

A year later our efforts culminated in two key pieces of legislation passed by the most dysfunctional Congress in this country's history. The Autism Collaboration, Accountability, Research, Education, and Support Act of 2014 (Autism CARES) extended federal funding for autism research, surveillance, and intervention through 2019. The Stephen Beck Jr. Achieving a Better Life Experience Act of 2014 (ABLE Act) allows people with autism and other disabilities to save on a tax-advantaged basis for disability expenses and still remain eligible for Supplemental Security Income (SSI), Medicaid, and other means-tested federal programs.

Shaping federal and state policies has been a slow but steady process. Our single biggest legislative challenge going forward is securing housing, employment, and educational opportunities for autistic adults. It's not clear right now that we have a government standing with us. Compromises are being made left and right. Without government support, we can't make this happen.

❖ **Rep. Mike Doyle, PA-D.** When Chris Smith (NJ-R) and I founded the Autism Caucus nearly 15 years ago, most members of Congress didn't even understand what autism was. And NIH was devoting darn little money to any research. Early on we had trouble signing members up for the caucus. So we met with a lot of these grassroots organizations and said, "You know, the best thing you can do for us initially is call your congressional representatives and ask them to join the Autism Caucus." And our phones started ringing off the wall because groups like Autism Speaks got this word out. That allowed Chris and me to build a coalition that increased NIH funding tenfold and reauthorized the Combatting Autism Act to provide $260 million annually for 5 years of autism research. We were nowhere near those numbers when we first started this endeavor.

Where we're heading now is we have to invest more money in services for these kids that are aging out after their 21st birthday so that they can become contributing members of society. And one of the things we're trying to stress here in Congress is that autism costs taxpayers about $250 billion annually. We know that 10 years down the road that cost can go up to $400 billion. But we also know that we can reduce those costs by 2/3 with early intervention. If we get to these kids early and get them into services and treatment, then they can become productive members of society, especially if they are on the higher functioning end of the spectrum. We can spend $100 million upfront being proactive about these things and save $125 billion down the road. ❖

❖ **Katie Wright.** The Combating Autism Act never would have passed had it not had such huge grassroots support and participation by many parents. I think that's something that scientists forget. There are hundreds of families just showing up on Capitol Hill with their autistic children, saying, "I'm just going to sit here until you can tell me why you're not supporting this bill!" Those are grassroots forces at their best. A lot of naysayers about the bill insisted we couldn't afford it. Then families with autistic children would show up and say, "Let me show you what this is like. See for yourself. Then I want you to tell me that this isn't a priority." My dad taught me early on this isn't a personality contest; this is a mission. ❖

26
Building Block #3:
Grassroots Strength

There are two kinds of grassroots assets: groups of volunteers and professionals working together regionally, and individuals with their own resources and clout to make a difference. Autism Speaks is fortunate to have both, and because of that strength, we have been able to lobby faster and more effectively.

Ideally, we'd assign one of our advocates to each of the 535 voting members of Congress to establish ongoing rapport that will yield favorable legislation. But that actually requires a multi-pronged approach.

For example, 4 years ago we created Autism Votes, a grassroots lobbying initiative. It was a quick way to mobilize local support for legislative action, and it's been extremely effective. State by state, we have what I call a standing army of extremely strong volunteers—lobbyists, if you will. They are determined, persevering, even pushy. They may not be directly involved with our organization, or go on one of our walks, or send us money. But they are aligned with our objectives, and they are passionate about getting involved in the well-being of the citizens of their particular state. It's the ultimate partnership. They had a very strong hand in our push for insurance reform.

Many autism families around the country have been hit with the worst kind of 2-sided problem. Diagnosis is difficult, and treatment, when it is available, is expensive, and in too many cases, their insurance doesn't cover the costs. So we put a heavy focus on insurance reform.

Change has to be won the hard way, state by state, through each state's legislature and insurance commission. In many states we have relied on the provisions of the Americans with Disabilities Act. But state insurance laws don't cover large corporations that are self-insured, so they aren't required by law to provide coverage for autism treatment. (Interestingly, GE was one of the corporations that didn't cover it, but now they do.) So we knew we would have to change the laws, and we would have to do it one state at a time. Through our army of volunteer lobbyists, right now (mid-2015) we have succeeded in 41 states. And many of the largest corporations in America have voluntarily agreed to provide insurance; we acknowledge them on our website.

Our next challenge is the federal government. Because of the military, the federal government is the largest employer in the country, at 8 million people. Using our capable army of volunteers, we're now encouraging them to resolve this coverage gap with legislation mandating autism health insurance.

All this is being done at the grassroots level. It's now up to the people we have helped empower to get these kinds of things done on their own home turf. We've created the awareness. We created the contacts. We've created political strength for them to leverage and do things. They have all they need to accomplish anything—the clout and savvy that build on determination and passion from within.

❖ **Liz Feld.** The most extraordinary thing we achieved at the grassroots level has been state insurance reform. All across the country we have fought for changes in state laws governing medical insurance coverage for autism treatment. With out-of-pocket costs often exceeding $60,000, this coverage saves families a huge portion of their endless expenses related to autism care. A decade ago, insurance companies rarely provided reimbursement for anything involving autism diagnosis, therapy, treatment, or care. It was discrimination of the worst kind. Today coverage is mandated by 44 states and we continue to fight the battle in the remaining states. ❖

❖ **Shelley Hendrix, grassroots coordinator Autism Speaks and parent of an autistic child.** I grew up in a family where lobbying for what you believe in was second nature. My mother was a teacher frustrated with rules about how my gifted dyslexic brother could be educated at home since the schools were failing him. That's where I first learned that a petition drive can lead to awareness; you're signing up people who may not have known about the problem but can support you with time or resources.

So I literally started my own little nonprofit organization and I boarded a plane and I started doing major grassroots work and organizing rallies on Capitol Hill. It's mostly trying to teach parents how to get involved in political advocacy, how to make a compelling argument and negotiate with political officials.

You may not get everything you want, because it's a compromise and they have to represent their entire constituency, which includes your opposition. We don't all get the magical pony with the rainbow sparkles, but settling for a donkey at least means you're not walking!

We are working with consultants to construct an infrastructure that will provide a more systematic way of training and managing these volatile, amazing volunteers. My mother taught me about missed opportunities. And so I'm reaching for the 78 percent of people participating in our local walks who are not already in our Autism Speaks database. Depending on the city and the walk, that could translate into 37,500 new advocates or donors who can be involved year-round. Multiply that by 90 annual walks and you have the possibility of major expansion. ❖

❖ **Liz Feld**. Bob's big word is leverage. He can turn an acorn into an oak tree better than anyone I've ever met. I look at what we've done as more than leverage—we have built power. With our partners, and the support of small and large donors, we have given the 3½ million people in this country—and 70 million people worldwide—a real voice. And that goes well beyond just raising awareness. We've given them a voice, and we've given them tools and access to resources, and helped them learn how to use their collective power to advocate. Nothing is more grassroots than what happens in your own backyard. It's where families can have the most impact and the most control. It is where the parents of autistic children shine the most.

To make it easier on parents to communicate with legislators, we invented the Champions initiative which is a technology platform that empowers and enables parents everywhere to send a message to be heard, or seek action by pushing a button on their smartphone or tablet. They can communicate with their congressman from their kitchen table about a proposed bill that would make a difference in their lives. Their messages have been heard loud and clear.

With this incredible level of grassroots power in 2014 we were able to advance critically important legislation with bipartisan leadership and support—and with that dysfunctional Congress, it wasn't easy. Under pressure from families, Congress passed the ABLE Act, which is going to help the larger disability community with these tax-free medical savings accounts, and reauthorizes the Autism Act, Autism CARES. And for the first time ever that updated bill requires a strategic plan to address the needs of the adult population. That was a big win for the autism community.

Today we have over 90 walks around the country and 400,000 people who walk for us. We have members of Congress who supported us, we have the support of local legislators in most states. We have many partners, from the major sports leagues to large corporations that help drive our agenda. We've been able to attract Google as a partner for a pioneering genome project, and you can't do something like that unless you have the credibility and vision to get you through their grueling vetting process. But we are far from where we need to be. The unmet needs are staggering and our Autism Response Team receives over 40,000 emails and phone calls a year from families, many of them in crisis.

We also need a comprehensive national strategy for autism that addresses the needs of the individual across the lifespan that mirrors what Congress and the White House committed to Alzheimer's. And that starts with the 2016 presidential candidates. If the president says autism matters, the drug companies pay attention, the schools pay attention, the employers pay attention. Ultimately our work should be the ideal public/private partnership. ❖

27
Building Block #4:
Business Principles

The world of philanthropy is not very business oriented. I don't mean to say that nonprofits should be more commercial, but I do mean that they'd see more success at their mission, whatever it may be, if they approached it the way business leaders do.

There are things that business people do routinely, especially when they're growing a business. You have to know the market you are serving, inside and out. What kind of people are they, and what's the best way to communicate with them? You have to really understand the customer base and how your product or service is going to relate to them. You have to find out how to make that interrelationship happen. You must think hard about how you build a business—even if it is a nonprofit. Or maybe especially if it is.

❖ **Harry Slatkin, founding CEO Slatkin & Co, a home fragrance giant; parent of an autistic child.** All of us are entrepreneurs. Brian Kelly, Jim Simons, and I all started our own businesses and foundations, and we approached Autism Speaks the same way. When you're an entrepreneur, you need to figure out how to get where you want to go. It doesn't come easily, so you have to create a road map and then you can carve out your own path. And when someone says no to us, it makes us want to do what we need to even more. We want to actually prove that it can be done.

It's the business side of our world that gets us to where we are and allows us to be successful, and I think that's why we are treating autism like a business. It's not just a malfunctioning child. It's not just a scientific issue. It's a business, and in business there are formulas for devising solutions for problems. You analyze and weigh the options, decide on one, and execute it to the best of your ability. That's exactly what we're all doing with autism.

We all have our own style of doing it. I built my business from the ground up. Bob has a different style from his days at large corporations. But our different styles allow us to create all of the approaches and solutions in the autism world, which, hopefully, will lead us to a cure. We all would love not to ever have had autism enter our world, that's for sure, but it has. When you're a businessperson confronted by such drastic, overwhelming issues, you have two choices. You can either tackle it or whine about it. And whining adversely impacts your business. You're going to lose a lot of money if you don't figure it out. And so for all our children, we have to figure this out. Our goal is that someday my normal child will not have to fear having a child with autism. ❖

What's happened with cancer in this country may be instructive. Richard Nixon declared the war on cancer in 1972, more than 40 years ago. Today we've got sharper knives and more knives, but still no firm answers about cause and cure. But what we have done is to make cancer treatment local. Most people don't care about the cancer research, they just care about their own treatment, and there are so many good places that provide it locally. And yet the NIH still has to spend $6 billion on research because they don't know what causes it. While autism will continue to be in a costly research mode, we need more and better local treatment options since it is not a contagious condition but needs constant attention.

People don't realize what it takes to make the National Institutes of Health take an active interest in a condition as prevalent as autism. We have to create our own bill in Congress to drive money to the NIH, which receives $30 billion annually in federal funding, with $260 million earmarked for autism research. To date, we have helped raise $3 billion in NIH funding for research, and even then we don't have real control over how they spend that money and are never told the final results. It's an imperfect system. That would be unacceptable in the business world.

We will never have enough money or resources, so we have to be very efficient with what we have. That requires the kind of discipline and processes businesses use to succeed.

❖ **Andy Shih.** Bob is known for his management prowess and business acumen, while Suzanne has a reputation as a fierce and passionate advocate. They brought rigorous business processes and practices to the advocacy world. The Wrights brought a laser focus on the stakeholders and return on investment in autism advocacy. Working at Autism Speaks has opened my eyes—as well as provided me a strong sense of purpose—to the importance of always keeping the families at the heart of everything I do. It's how we accomplished so much so fast. ❖

❖ **Brian Kelly.** There are no easy roads on autism. Every aspect of what you need to do to advocate for your child is real work. It requires a lifelong family commitment. And if you layer financial hardship on top of that commitment, it is a devastating combination. That is the part for me that is really destroying the fabric of the family. When the fabric of the family is destroyed, who serves? Our challenge has become the human beings and executing the strategy that can improve the quality of their lives. I have found that putting on a businessman's perspective is very helpful. It keeps you focused, keeps you from drifting into unproductive thinking, helps you see the next right thing.

I really think that it is about being decisive, and to do that, you have to do your homework on whatever initiatives you are going to undertake. Be decisive about tackling the initiative and applying the best human beings and resources to do it. Many of these challenges and decisions are time sensitive. Even though we have a formal board process for approving expenditures and making decisions, there are many subcommittee discussions that are ongoing all the time. We try to move and take action quickly. That's where the business perspective is critical. ❖

Jim Simons is America's best-known mathematician, and he has become one of the wealthiest people in the country. He's in his 70s. When I first met Jim, 7 years ago, he was spending about $3 million a year on genetic research involving autism. I wanted him to come with us, and he wanted to, but only if he could have absolute control over the science program. Which I could not do.

So I made a good decision, a business decision. "Jim," I said, "You go and do your thing. We will be at your disposal. We will help you in any way you want. We will invest with you if you think that that's appropriate, if you want us to. We're going to be your partners, but you can operate on your own." He formed the Simons Foundation and hired some top-notch people, and they now spend about $50 million a year for autism. And it's deep science, it's genetic research. Jim Simons is the real deal. I admire him a lot. He is the second largest source of research money for autism behind the NIH. We're third, having raised nearly $600 million in 10 years.

❖ **Dr. Herbert Pardes.** Harry and Laura Slatkin came to me in 2000 when I was CEO of New York-Presbyterian Hospital, asking for support to establish an autism program and center. They hosted a fundraising dinner where I listened to their heartfelt descriptions about what it was like to have an autistic child. This youngster was virtually dysfunctional in communication. Children like this have trouble telling their parents or doctor the pain they are feeling, especially when they are agitated. They were dealing with a child who needed almost literally constant attention.

The Slatkins were determined to raise money and secured donors, including the Wrights. They also did the bulk of the work to build the Center for Autism and the Developing Brain in White Plains, New York. It provides comprehensive care in a single setting for individuals living with autism spectrum disorders (ASD) and other developmental disorders of the brain. It is a collaborative program between New York-Presbyterian, Weill Cornell Medical College, and Columbia University College of Physicians and Surgeons, in partnership with New York Collaborates for Autism.

The Autism Center at New York-Presbyterian's Westchester campus opened last year, working on diagnosis evaluation treatment, and it will continue to evolve with more programs related to autism under an executive director, Catherine Lord. The Slatkins got that done and the Wrights gained attention for the disorder. They rapidly and aggressively raised money for grants and started to work the politics of it. They go after anybody and everybody. Another remarkable couple, Jim and Marilyn Simons (he is a successful hedge fund manager) have their own foundation which focuses heavily on autism. And they've convened a very substantial scientific and administrative group working on research.

So you've got this network of people who are putting their resources and passions to work on autism. What I bring to the Autism Speaks board and efforts—as one who has been very heavily involved with getting attention to mental illness and a former head of the National Institute of Mental Health—are the lessons I have learned. It's a rare privilege to work with smart, dedicated people to get tough, impossible things done. We're all exhaustive workaholics who are committed to doing something about this darn disease.

Then the challenge becomes how to sustain all this. The story is good for about an hour and a half, right? That's where the Wrights come in. Bob is trying to bring a certain set of sensibilities and principles that are inherent to the corporate world. In that way he's like John Mack, chairman of Morgan Stanley, who built the Morgan Stanley Children's Hospital, and Herbert Irving of Sysco, a major supporter of the Herbert Irving Comprehensive Cancer Center. They are businesspeople with a set of strong contacts and widespread influence. They know how to handle big issues. They are big thinkers with the confidence and know-how to get things done.

The Wrights, and others like them, have a very sharp sense of how to use your time, all your assets, your money, your people, your contacts, all directed to solve this problem. That's what business leaders do. And Autism Speaks, like any other organization that wants to be successful, is a business. So you have to bring in the right financial people, the legal people, and the public relations people. And most important, it is unacceptable to spend an enormous amount of time, money, and resources on something without moving it forward. ❖

28
Building Block #5:
Strategic Alliances

O ur whole-genome sequencing partnership with Google and Toronto's Hospital for Sick Children is the most significant alliance Autism Speaks has had in a decade. This amazing project, now called MSSNG (the absent vowels remind us the autism puzzle still has missing pieces) is especially noteworthy because of the distinctive good it will provide the most people in the shortest time. It's not overstating the matter to say that it represents a major turning point for us. Such great alliances are rare but increasingly necessary as technology speeds things along and heightens the urgency for solutions to big problems. Other new partnerships will continue to shape our mission and outcomes.

❖ **Laura Slatkin.** I gave birth to twins in 1999, David and Alexandra. When David was diagnosed with autism in 2000, like any other parent, we went on a search for schools, support, treatment, and medical attention. In the process we realized that New York City—the most important city in the world—was surprisingly weak when it came to the quality of services it offered people with autism. My husband and I, as business professionals, philanthropists, and just good New Yorkers, were shocked at this. The best schools for autistic people were in New Jersey.

That's when we embarked on this plan to establish the first charter school for autistic children in the state of New York, the New York Center for Autism. We worked closely with Joel Klein, the chancellor of schools, and Mayor Michael Bloomberg to make it part of the New York City public schools and be a model for the public school system. The goal was to raise the bar in autism education within the public arena, to make it accessible to all autistic children and their families who do not have the financial means or connections for private education.

We know that if you get to a child early enough, there is a way of reconnecting the brain so half of the children can actually go up into some sort of functional life because the brain is still malleable. So if you get to the training and you go through the proper autism education, a school system can help. By the time this became reality, we knew our son would never attend it because a charter school is a lottery system. The chances of him being selected were slim. So we did not pursue this change for David. We did it for the autism community, because it needed to be done.

We have since changed the name to New York Collaborates for Autism because it is truly a broad education partnership so that we can have a greater positive impact on the overall population. We realized there were not enough qualified educators, so we built a training institute in conjunction with Hunter College. We gave them seed money and continue to help fund the program, and they took off with it. Today they train more teachers in New York City than any other university.

Another problem we identified was that none of the hospitals or universities in Manhattan had a first-class, state-of-the-art center for autism. So we began plans to build one. After a lot of research, we zeroed in on Columbia, near Presbyterian Hospital—Columbia and Cornell—as the correct institutions to collaborate with. Real estate is expensive in New York, and New York-Presbyterian had these beautiful rolling green hills in Westchester. That property was available. When we saw this property for the very first time, we said, "This place can serve people with autism across their lifespan, from birth to death. It can encompass employment, vocational training, residential housing, and a facility that someone could take their child to in an emergency, like an inpatient emergency care unit."

We began to raise the funds to build this center, which is now called the Center for Autism and the Developing Brain, with our partners Columbia and Cornell. One of our key points was that we needed to be able to accept everyone despite their ability to pay. It needed to be covered by Medicaid and Medicare, and it needed to address early intervention. We solicited funding and raised about $12 million through partners and donors. Autism Speaks gave us a $1 million grant and the Simons Foundation gave us $5 million to start the institute. Nothing would have been done in the autism space as quickly and completely as it did the past decade without partnerships. ❖

Vatican Summit on Autism
The Vatican, Rome
November 20, 2014

❖ **Andy Shih.** Something happened during my trip with Bob and Suzanne to the Vatican for the Summit on Autism that surprised me and will forever guide me. I'm not religious. My family is Buddhist and I don't practice a religion. But I understood how important this visit was to Bob and Suzanne personally, as devout Catholics, and to their goal of engaging The Catholic Church to help awareness and acceptance of our families. The standing ovation Suzanne and Bob received from the cardinals and bishops and everyone in attendance that day was a way of saying they respected their broad and deep influence for good. I knew that an alliance with The Catholic Church would pave the way for partnerships with other world faiths, in much the way Autism Speaks partners with the government of so many countries. It is another way to reach families and the people who can help them.

We all worked diligently, preparing for their remarks, stressing not only our accomplishments but a vision going forward. But Bob, being Bob, paid careful attention all during the first 2 days of the summit and asked lots of questions. Then, right before he is scheduled to address the group of Vatican representatives and experts, he tells me he is going to throw his prepared remarks out the window. Instead, he wants to respond to what he had heard in the other presentations. The speechwriter who was traveling with us was about to jump out the window.

Some of the other speakers refused to acknowledge that there is a major challenge with autism; in their country, they said, they had the problem under control. But one researcher from Nigeria talked about how important it is to decentralize expertise so that at the primary care level, all the needs of families and communities can be met. They don't want to create a system where people have to travel to a medical center or an urban center to get care. They believe we should be able to support a family where they live, no matter where they are in the country, and that means providing capacity at the local grassroots level.

That resonated with Bob: the idea that you can actually break down complex intervention into components that can be taught and delivered with fidelity by non-specialists like parents and community health workers. Low-income countries like Nigeria have to find ways to help people when there are no experts around.

This task shifting is a relatively new concept gaining momentum, and Bob discussed it with me to make sure he had understood it correctly. So part of his remarks were improvised, and he talked about why task shifting is important, why that is the way to help as many families as possible in the world. In the US, we have other problems. We have lots of need and lots of experts, and yet what you often hear is that there is a long waiting list, 3 months or more, to even see a specialist for a diagnosis. That's because we still don't have enough people to meet the demand. So we also need to decentralize expertise and get capacity into the community level as much as possible. Then the outcome for our community as a whole will be so much better.

Part of the problem is that we have this perception that cognitive behavioral therapy or behavior intervention is so complicated it requires years and years of schooling to become proficient. Recent research has shown that's not the case. As an example, we have an intervention protocol called Pivotal Response Treatment, PRT, here in the US. It helps build social skills and traditionally has been delivered in a clinic or a health center. Some researchers have started to teach elementary school teachers and parents this technique so they can apply it. If we can train more primary care physicians, or even nonprofessionals, to deliver services, from identification to intervention, then we can do a much better job of helping families in minority and rural communities.

Our Global Autism Public Health (GAPH) program is working with 66 partner nations to develop and deliver culturally appropriate services in underserved, rural communities.

We are making sure more children than ever are getting the proper education from a very young age to reach their optimum potential. But we are troubled to find that kids with developmental disabilities are systematically excluded from these programs. There is a systematic bias against our children and families. So we're addressing the whole issue very brilliantly, effectively, and remarkably quickly on one level, only to have it totally unravel at another level.

Part of our global strategy is partnering for the most long-term impact. We leverage the right connections with the decision makers to expedite or accelerate development processes. Identifying the right sustainable leaders in every country is the challenge, even though we navigate these political waters with the help of local stakeholders, middle management, and career bureaucrats. They're the ones with the knowledge and the institutional memory, so we throw our support behind them. So, as an example, the Catholics offer a unique opportunity: a strong leader of over a billion believers can encourage compassion and understanding by the clergy as well as members of their congregations. This will have the most impact in Africa and Latin America.

Strong relationships with the business community and investors make it possible to scale up in a major way. When that happens, you can go deeper and stay longer in a community to make sure that the interventions that you're using are actually successful and fully integrated. Bob's been able to move mountains to make that happen.

This engagement can be in the form of resources or logistics. And creative thinking helps. Here's an example. A lot of medicines that are being used require refrigeration, which is a big problem in some developing countries. But even where there is no reliable refrigeration, there are Coca-Cola machines! So piggybacking on Coke, it's an easy thing for the corporation to do, and it would reach millions of people through a public-private partnership. It is a very big impact at very little cost. ❖

❖ **Dr. James Perrin, president American Academy of Pediatrics.** We need a stronger partnership with primary doctors as a point of entry, as a clearinghouse, as a practical matter. We need to do something to make this work so the general pediatrician in the community can provide the bulk of care. And I think we probably have three or four steps to get there. One is we need to pay them better. We need to get insurance reform so that doctors and nurses can spend enough time with families. Right now there are strict limitations on the amount of time that doctors can spend with patients to meet productivity expectations. But autistic children take more time. So we need to change the payment arrangements.

We also need to provide better backup to primary care and general pediatricians. I'd love to see statewide telephone exchanges so primary care doctors could speak with a medical expert within a half hour of a patient presenting with something in their office. Another idea is for mini-training for local doctors in community practices, giving them above-average familiarity with autism. This might take the form of tele-medicine in parts of the country where a family must drive a day away from home to see a specialist. There also needs to be a payment coalition set up between doctors, parents, health provider groups, and the business community to revamp the payment structure so it is fair for everyone. Autism Speaks and the Autism [Treatment] Network are laying the groundwork to explore these alternatives instead of waiting for someone else to do it. ❖

In many ways, the audience Suzanne and I had with Pope Francis during the Vatican's first Autism Summit in November 2014 was the culmination and the beginning of so many things for us. He had a special calling to help the poor and people with disabilities. As a proud Roman Catholic and Christian, our visit to the Vatican on behalf of all autistic families honored their compassion and commitment to improve their loved one's quality of life. The recognition and support there of Autism Speaks' tireless efforts provided impetus for intensifying our work with other world faiths and people. So we set out to expand all of our global initiatives in 2016 with new strategic international partners.

29
The Future for Autism Families

C *hange will come to autism. It's no longer a question of if but when. And it will be spurred by 3 catalysts initiated on my watch.*

The first is MSSNG, our genomics project with Google that is upending the insular world of scientists and researchers. Together with Toronto's Hospital for Sick Children we are sequencing 10,000 whole genomes from autistic persons and their families in an open science portal. For now, access is free to qualified scientists and researchers encouraged to share their findings. This will unleash new forms of collaboration and discovery to crack the mysteries of autism and other medical conditions. It is a first. And it all came together in less than 2 years. (The full story of this trailblazing project is presented in Chapter 31.) We can say that the future of autism will be dictated by science and biology far more than in the past. With Google bringing order and productivity to a deluge of genomic data, we will reap the benefit of more affordable, more manageable technology.

The second catalyst for change is relying on Google to reorganize and manage our organization's digital resources into a

one-stop portal for autism. Autism Speaks powered by Google will provide WebMD functionality. It is vital for any not-for-profit organization to have timely, accessible information for its online users. This is especially important as Autism Speaks evolves from an advocacy group into an all-around facilitator of proactive resources for families, educators, doctors, and scientists, and big pharma and small business. The process of gathering and disseminating vast amounts of digital information on many topics would require Autism Speaks to make prohibitively expensive software investments every single year. So Google's assessment of Autism Speaks' online resources and plan for powering its website are critical. My hope is the project will be completed in 2016. It will be a natural evolution for us and a godsend for anyone autistic.

The third change agent is strengthening Autism Speaks to excel in family services. It requires refocusing the vast field organization responsible for nearly 100 successful annual awareness and fundraising walks on increasing community-based services for autistic people and their families. Making service a cornerstone of our local efforts requires that our volunteers and paid staff work effectively with local, county and state government agencies, education, fire, police, and juvenile and adult services.

These three initiatives comprise my simple bucket list for Autism Speaks.

My goal now is to make sure *Autism Speaks is positioned under a new leadership regime to accomplish these 3 major challenges: creating a scientific research portal with Google called MSSNG, becoming more of a comprehensive interactive resource for autism (Autism Speaks powered by Google), and leveraging our grassroots resources to increase services for autistic persons and their families.*

The MSSNG genome project in particular came into being just as I was contemplating the next phase in my own life and my tenure as founding CEO of Autism Speaks. Even under the best of circumstances, succession is never an easy thing. But I've learned it's better to shepherd the process as best you can to assure your intentions are preserved. The person I selected to succeed me as CEO of Autism Speaks is Brian Kelly, a decisive, successful real estate developer and father of six whose oldest son is autistic. He is driven by the same passion, sense of responsibility, and visionary control I prized in my own life.

"I don't know how you and Suzanne do it," Brian said when we first talked about him taking over. About a year later he told me that after much thought, he was ready for the job. Brian and his family live most of the year in Santa Barbara, where their oldest son, Patrick, attends an autism school. They come home to Massachusetts for the summer. In 2013, Brian and his wife, Patricia, established a postsecondary scholarship fund to support individuals with autism in college, vocational, and other transitional programs in the US. Brian is a hard worker with a Midas touch in business. He is a low-key leader who prefers to keep the spotlight on autistic persons and their families. He has everything needed for this expensive, demanding job. He's only 53; I am 72. I thought to myself, this is a gift, and I'm going to take it.

Once I transferred the reins of power on May 1, 2015, I discussed my 3 missions with Brian Kelly and others, and the agenda that I had set out for 2015 and beyond. Brian moved quickly to leverage the gains we have made to take Autism Speaks into a new phase that didn't always feel aligned with my vision. Although the situation was of my own making, it can sometimes be difficult to let go. Brian immediately began reducing the organization's size and programs. Things became tense when our board and management team failed to rally behind some of Autism Speaks' highest profile projects including the research science portfolio we had worked so hard to forge. Brian reinitiated discussions with the

Simons Foundation about collaborating in our genome sequencing efforts. In October 2015, I raised another $4 million from the Dolan Foundation earmarked to sequence the last of the 10,000 whole genomes and complete the initial phase of MSSNG.

Remaining on the board and executive committee will ensure my continued involvement in MSSNG and Suzanne's extensive international awareness activities. I picked the guy. I picked my timing. I'm thrilled to be giving up administrative responsibilities. But by no means am I or Suzanne disappearing.

I have a challenge of my own: to make sure that this new generation is passionate about taking risks. I don't want them falling asleep on me. I certainly hope MSSNG and the open science it represents will remain part of Autism Speaks for a long time. It all remains to be seen. But the fundamental mission remains the same: moving forward to do everything we can for autistic children and their families.

I am concerned that Suzanne and I have raised so much money for this organization—roughly $100 million—that it will be difficult for them to match that going forward. Angela Geiger's charge as the new chief executive of Autism Speaks, succeeding Liz Feld, is to help raise special funding and gifts. And if they aren't able to raise those kinds of funds then there will have to be changes in the Autism Speaks mission statement and plans, which I hope are not too dramatic. Some of that is inevitable. But hopefully they can maintain and support the breadth of our successful activities.

Even though I am no longer in direct control of these three missions I certainly remain supportive of them. So I hope the new leadership of Autism Speaks will look to the past for ways to succeed in the future. *We demonstrated how dramatic change is possible by effectively working with individuals, corporations, foundations, and local and national government.*

- We raised $3.2 billion cumulatively over the last 8 years for research primarily utilized by the NIH.

- We instituted insurance reform in 44 states covering the vast number of employees who are not covered by self-insured companies.

- We achieved critical legislative support including passage of the ABLE Act in 2014 which creates tax-free savings accounts for people with significant disabilities of all types.

- We launched global health initiatives with countries around the world to transfer knowledge we gained in our US efforts with the assistance of UN-based organizations, especially the World Health Organization.

- We supercharged our awareness efforts with Light It Up Blue, a campaign driven by Suzanne Wright involving more than 19,000 structures in nearly every country on the UN-sponsored World Autism Day every year.

- We forged a substantial family services organization encompassing tool kits, workshops, grants, peer support and other resources.

Now MSSNG is thriving under the brilliant direction of Dr. Stephen Scherer at the Hospital of Sick Children in Toronto—in coordination with the province of Toronto, the Canadian government and Autism Speaks Canada, David Glazer and his Google team, and our departing science chief Rob Ring. Others will continue to build on what we have done.

Still, I have been reminded during the transition of power at Autism Speaks that despite your best efforts and intentions, you can't control other people and events. Your legacy is what you make it. You do the best that you can for an organization, and the future will take its own course.

❖ **Brian Kelly.** The best way to honor the founders, Bob and Suzanne Wright, is to continue to move the organization forward in a way that it deserves. They will continue to be part of a team of people who do our bidding and deliver our message. That process has already begun—we brought the best strategic minds around a table with a whiteboard and Sharpies to hammer out a new strategic plan. We will continue to build on the strength in awareness and advocacy that we developed in the first decade. We've earned a great degree of credibility that allows us to be the convener of various partners we can work with to move our cause forward. So it's really leveraging everything that we have done in the past decade.

Our ability to convene and create partnerships with private companies, public companies, governmental agencies, and individuals will be key. We're seeing the power of these partnerships with Google and MSSNG to get researchers and scientists to make autism a primary focus. It's leveraging what Google and Autism Speaks each brings to the table that is more valuable than money; it is human talent and expertise. It's a way to lead without directly paying for everything yourself, and that can be really powerful.

These are the areas where we're going to get the most leverage and return on our mission—the core pillars of which remain family services and science, awareness and advocacy. While our community continues to be underserved, we will be looking for new ways to provide even more resources for families from the time of early intervention and diagnosis through adulthood, because autism is a whole-life commitment for most of us. We'll be looking to do fewer things better and limit our initiatives to what we do best and most need in our community. We'll be pushing more of our efforts to the local level. We will move swiftly and decisively as things change. This is not about us at Autism Speaks; it's about the people we serve.

Bob has had a very different way of looking at autism than the rest of us, and that guided the way he approached it and his game plan to attack it. He constantly reminds us that we cannot rest on our laurels because our real, true success will be determined by whether we can provide all families of autistic children the support and attention they deserve. He will not rest until that happens.

It is easy to write a check, but it is another thing to devote your life to a cause. Bob and Suzanne spend the majority of their time on Autism Speaks—often at their own expense. That is a very big, lifelong commitment. That is extraordinary. I think that people lose sight of that sometimes, that this is a very public commitment. There is a lot of pain that we as families are going through with our loved one, and to be public about those struggles is not easy. It defines who you are for that period in your life.

We are trying to be every bit as proactive about this as the Wrights are for the same reasons, starting with commitment and passion. That is how things get done. I do not know what they talked about when they made the decision to completely devote themselves to this cause. But my wife, Tricia, and I know that when you embark on something like this, you are making a decision to take on a really significant challenge and commitment that will dominate your lives and family. It is very hard what we are doing. There are just no easy roads on autism. ❖

❖ **Liz Feld.** We have demonstrated the most meaningful role Autism Speaks can play is Change Agent. We have changed public perception and public policy; we have compelled change in insurance practices; we have changed the autism research landscape and succeeded in increasing federal research for autism and more.

Now it is time for us to partner beyond the autism community to help the autism community. Many of the challenges we face are not unique to autism: access to care, supports and services, employment, housing, caregiver shortages, safety across the lifespan, too few treatments.

Autism Speaks is uniquely positioned to lead on these issues. We know how to convene, organize and advocate. We have credibility and we can leverage it to drive partnerships between the public and private sectors to find solutions.

Moving forward, the biggest risk for Autism Speaks is trying to do too much. With such vast unmet need, and too few public resources, there is an urge and tendency to cover the entire landscape of challenge and opportunity. The threat of being "all things to all people" looms large. For any business, this is one of the biggest dangers. Local groups should drive local supports and work on areas of local need.

Driving policy change—in health care, education, employment and housing—will help the most people, and Autism Speaks should focus on that. The weight of a massive footprint can keep resources from other places. It happens in business all the time. You end up having to raise money to feed the beast.

"Advocating for better services" and being a "service organization" are two different things. They require different levels of resources and focus. The autism community needs both. As Autism Speaks charts its course for the next decade, choices will need to be made about which path to take. ❖

The drugs commonly used in autism are off label from some other disease or condition. We're getting closer to encouraging drug companies to develop drugs that can positively reduce the presentation of autism. That's the goal. They've gone through animal testing with a lot of success, and now they're doing it in human testing. It could possibly restore speech or stop the waving and hand movements and allow somebody to be more typical. That would be huge. That would be a real start.

The biggest breakthrough we've had is authenticating Applied Behavioral Analysis (ABA). It's a relatively rigorous form of therapy, designed to teach an autistic child how to mimic the way a typical child would act in a given situation. So it's trying to get a child to be more comfortable in a social environment but less comfortable with himself. But it's a major breakthrough that enabled insurance bill passage, because ABA is a way to treat autism.

I would like to think we could create an autism treatment network of some 40 sites around the country, all heavily financed with a deep community connection. It's taken 40 years to begin breaking down the different kinds of cancer. There is a trail there we can follow and a process we can learn from. Breaking autism down into hundreds of subtypes is the endgame because the treatment and cure can be much more precise and effective.

Several of our established programs could come into play. The Interactive Autism Network, established in 2006 by Kennedy Krieger Institute and operated out of Johns Hopkins, is an online research exchange among parents of autistic children and assisting professionals overseen by Dr. Paul Lipkin, director. The Autism Treatment Network headed by Dr. James Perrin is a collaboration of some of the best hospitals, medical professionals, and researchers in North America specializing in medical care for autistic children, developing protocols and standards of care. Global Autism Public Health Initiative (GAPH) seeks to improve the quality and reach of autism services in underserved communities worldwide.

In the years to come, the findings from the MSSNG genome project will give us so much more to act on. It will profile diverse forms of autism to identify specific causes, treatments and cures. But until then we must continue to push hard for the same level of resources and attention the government devotes to breast cancer, AIDS, diabetes, and even obesity. In testimony I gave before the House Committee on Oversight & Government Reform on November 29, 2012, I laid out the case for a national autism strategy to accelerate scientific efforts, early diagnosis, development of effective medicines and treatments, support and services for autistic adults, and putting autism on equal footing with other behavioral health treatments for minority groups and our military.

Since then, we worked hard to close some of those gaps while the prevalence of autism worsened. Today, it affects 1 in 68 children and 1 in 42 boys—a 100 percent increase in the past decade. During that same time the cost of autism to society has more than tripled to $137 billion. The lifetime cost for caring for an autistic individual in the US ranges from $1.4 million to $2.3 million, depending on the severity of intellectual disability. A new National Health interview survey in mid-November 2015—the first to include more recent data from 2011 to 2014—estimated that 1 in 45 children in the US has an autism spectrum disorder—an alarming increase from the CDC numbers which would not be revised until later in 2016!

And that's why I say nothing moves fast enough.

◆ **Liz Feld.** Our success with the passage of the ABLE Act and Autism CARES was the product of building power—or leverage—and knowing how to use it. Now we are fighting for Senate passage of 21st Century Cures Act, already passed by the House. Among other things, it will improve the regulatory environment by bringing in the Federal Drug Administration's review process in line with advances in medicine and technology. For more people affected by autism these reforms are essential. As MSSNG yields results in our understanding of autism, we will need to translate that knowledge to personalized treatments. 21st Century Cures encourages innovation. It would streamline clinical trials and call for enhancements in patient representation for the autism community and millions of others living with a medical condition. ❖

❖ **Dr. Gary Goldstein.** Over the next 5 years there will be at least two new courses of action for autism. One is the science: new genes, new pathways, and new potential drug targets being identified. It takes a long time to go from that to some meaningful change for a patient and a drug that really works. But there's a lot of activity in that realm. And then there's this recognition that, short of a cure, early intervention in the first 2 years of life makes all the difference.

The second primary focus needs to be on major life transitions as autistic children grow into adults. The first big hurdle will be how the educational and school systems prepare autistic children for transition to independent life. The next big hurdle will be what that is and who will pay for it. ❖

Our biggest, most pressing concern is how to accommodate and support the growing number of autistic adults. Much like the insurance reform we successfully achieved after a decade, self-directed local Autism Speaks chapters and grassroots volunteers need to lobby for local housing and employment in their own backyard. We have empowered them to take on critical matters like this. They don't always realize how much leverage we have created for them. This is the hardest sell of all, and I believe the way to do this is to get the walks to focus almost entirely now on increasing services in their local communities.

A good model for this is the Coleman Foundation, a private, independent grant-making organization that is a fundraising and support catalyst for its Chicago-area entrepreneurship education, cancer care, and developmental disabilities services.

They raise money and take 25 percent off the top for the umbrella organization, and the rest of it stays local. But the grassroots organization is responsible for all their fundraising, so it's not a gift. Autism Speaks pays all of our fundraising costs of the walks. So we're taking 55 percent back but we're paying all the bills. The Coleman people know every single public and private service that's available in their communities for women with breast cancer and people with developmental disabilities. They know what the county does, they know where the doctors are, and they're tight with the American Medical Association. I'd love to see Autism Speaks duplicate this. ❖

❖ **Brian Kelly.** We can't be sure of the future, where we will be or how we will feel. We moved from our Boston home to give our autistic son, Patrick, a chance at life in Santa Barbara in a program between UCSB's Koegel Autism Center and the local public school. They specialize in Pivotal Response Treatment (PRT), a comprehensive intervention method for autism. It has worked out very well for Patrick. That's why we've stayed during the school years the last 10 years. Patrick's progress has been everything that we hoped for, short of a cure. And so now Patrick's 18 and we are working on transitioning to semi-independent living. The difference between us and 99.9 percent of America is that we have the resources and the time to figure out ways to support Patrick. That is very rare. It is part of the reason why I spend my time giving back.

Trying to provide opportunities for families who don't have those resources is what I am focused on the most. Many of them are struggling and it's very complex. Autism is different for every person and every family. Some people will require constant coverage 365 days a year by a qualified, trained caregiver. The cost is prohibitive. So we will continue to spend time coming up with ways where the state and federal government can help. The requirements can be the same as for people with dementia, those who need a roof overhead and lots of human services.

We can take our successful model of mandatory insurance reimbursement for therapies and replicate it in areas of need such as adult housing and services. We can point to best practices. We can pursue private-public partnerships. We know we have to convene these various stakeholders and develop a broader coalition to come up with areas where we can work together. Bob has provided a pretty good template that we can replicate. But we'll always benefit from his strategic thinking. ◈

◈ **Suzanne Wright.** It is different for every autistic person and their parents. Whether it's the actor Robert De Niro or businesspeople like Harry and Laura Slatkin, or Michelle and Robert Smigel from Saturday Night Live, or Autism Speaks' communications manager Michael Rosen—every parent of an autistic child pieces things together in their own way. One has his son in a small private home in New York City that cares for a half dozen boys; another founded the New York Center for Autism Charter School and the Center for Autism and the Developing Brain in Westchester, New York State. Bob and I supported the growth of The McCarton School in New York City, where Christian attends. Dr. Cecelia McCarton is an expert in diagnosing and treating children with developmental disorders.

So many parents are afraid to let go for fear that their autistic children will not be as well cared for somewhere else. But transitioning out of the home and into a residential school gives them a running start into adulthood. They are being trained to cope and succeed as an adult with what they have, with dignity and a job. Parents have no idea how much better their children could be. ◈

Timing is critical. One headmaster of a residential school told us that autistic children often come to him too late, at age 16 or 17; he thinks age 13 is ideal. The professionals who run these schools with love and affection are trying to teach life skills the young people will need as adults, to hopefully operate on their own to some degree. I think they are trying to do more under the Affordable Care Act, which provides that mental health now falls under the essential health benefits. The transition process requires at-home and community services and support, most of which do not yet exist. Parents who are by then financially dilapidated and communities that are overstressed have limited means to help.

Providing autistic adults with meaningful work and routines will require support from private companies and individuals, as well as technological solutions. The combination of intensive repetitive work, a consistent daily experience, and supportive technology play to many of their strengths, as companies like PepsiCo, Best Buy, Walgreens, and OfficeMax have already discovered. So we must push for more workplace inclusion.

In mid-2015, Autism Speaks launched the House to Home Prize project aimed at generating ideas for and examples of breakthroughs in housing and residential supports for adults with autism. It backed the effort with $150,000 in prizes. Local town hall meetings and our adult transition tool kit were provided as a base for other new community catalysts.

❖ **Harry Slatkin.** Many of us with autistic children have learned to empower each other. Today, my wife and I are still on the board of the charter school. We still have New York Center for Autism Care, which we started, and we're on the board of Autism Speaks, and we have built The Center for Autism and the Developing Brain in Westchester, New York. We decided to do that project because in all these years we started realizing how many crossovers there are in the brain disorder area. And if we can unlock schizophrenia, if we can unlock bipolar, then maybe we can unlock autism, because they all really react to each other in the brain. That might move us to the third chapter—housing for children with autism and the adult population.

That's the tsunami that's about to happen when these children age. Where are we putting them? How can we help them have somewhat functional lives going into the community? Can we help them find useful work? We have to leverage everything we have achieved the past 10 years to deal with all that. ❖

❖ **Andy Shih.** We're conducting the first-ever US adult prevalence study over 3 or 4 years to determine how many adults in the US are affected by autism, to better understand their needs because very little is known about it.

We can be more effective as advocates and we can create programs that are more targeted to this population. There hasn't been a lot of emphasis on independence and job training for individual autism. We're belatedly starting to recognize that it's a real issue. Other places in the world are better at it. For example, Lima, Peru, where a community is educated about autism and prepares for how they can best train and place autistic adults in jobs where they can be excellent employees. It's not about charity. They look at people on the autistic spectrum for their strengths at a very early age so that those who can will function as productive, satisfied, independent adults. They invest in training upfront instead of maintenance in perpetuity. Everyone wins.

Here in the US, there's a lot of resistance to that kind of planning. It's politics, it's money, and even resources. Right now the money goes to multiple institutes: Mental Health, Child Health and Human Development, Communication and Hearing Disorders, and the Environment of Health and Sciences. Those are the main institutes that give autism money right now. Now imagine having an institute that is focused on autism. What would that mean to autism? And if we are able to understand the different types of autism, we can have more effective treatment and training. It paves the way for more self-determination and self-advocacy.

For years, Autism Speaks has thrown money at academics and scientists and waited for them to move their research into new areas to get more out of it. So now with the MSSNG project, we're just going to jump forward with Google as a partner. Autism Speaks has always had a high risk profile. We want to take educated gambles when the potential payoff is immense or even transformational. The implications of what we find out from the research that comes from all this genomic data can change the course of everything, including adult autism.

We are trying to help as many families around the world as much as possible with feasible, sustainable solutions and a policy program level. For me, this is personal. I have told people it's always been a fantasy of mine that someday—even in the most remote areas of the world—if a parent suspects his or her child is having problems, there would be an easy, sure response. It would be a finger prick, a drop of blood to do an analysis on a portable machine. The data will feedback from the cloud somewhere, render a diagnosis, and then provide a plan of community-based solutions by professionals that can begin right away. The technology is already here. The handheld laboratories, the smartphones and tablet-sized computers, the chips, the social media networks are already in the field. ❖

❖ **Harry Slatkin.** There are great scientists out there who will eventually find this all out. That's not really the issue. We do need more government funding; we need to press the government to take it more seriously. But my wife and I, and so many parents, feel we need to help these children now. We have children with autism now. How do we make their lives better for our David and the Wrights' grandson Christian, both severely autistic? Other parents, like Marilyn and Jim Simons, have a child who is high functioning, but we're all worried about the future.

I'm worried about the pharmacological side and the pills my son is taking. He's been on the same heavy psychotic drug now for 8 years—that's an adult drug being used on a child with autism. There is really nothing out there yet that can be used for David. That has to be something we have to fix in the future.

These children are getting older. Where are they going to be housed? How are they going to be taken care of? Will we always be fighting the insurance companies to make sure there is enough insurance reimbursement so that families can take care of their children when they are diagnosed without losing everything? It is a devastating issue for many, many families. Most cannot afford caregivers, and if they can, they can be hard to find. Two family incomes are reduced to one when one of the parents has to stay home to care for an autistic child, because it is a full-time job and a huge expense. What happens to these kids when the parents are no longer around to take care of them? These questions need answers in the future. These circumstances need to be changed. ❖

❖ **Brian Kelly.** We are in the infancy of working on this issue of adult transition. It is a huge issue because not only is there a housing component but there is a human services component and just very few options out there for families. Right now, Autism Speaks is doing a survey of everything that is out there in America so we can start a database of all those in a position to help us. It is a very tall order. ❖

In so many ways, NBC GE was a dry run for what we have done at Autism Speaks. We learned supreme organization and management of events and people. We learned how to interface with politicians and businesses. At Autism Speaks we have had to construct and adapt a framework that conforms to and transforms the philanthropic world. We have been beholden to many rigid institutions: science, medicine, academics, government. I have been in a race against time, trying to figure out what I could do to make things better sooner. Had I invested all the money I had, I could not have forced a cause or cure or treatment. I've learned that science is on its own course, but I still believe it can be accelerated. MSSNG will do that.

Wright to the Point

After a year of preparation and 10 years of development, Autism Speaks is moving to another level of growth. That required a significant examination of everything we do, all our staffing, and all our objectives. It was not easy, and there was fallout, but if your goals remain intact, then you constantly have to figure out ways to achieve them. It's like rock climbing: the first few steps are relatively easy, but pretty soon you're looking at a rock face that seems almost vertical. You have to stop and rethink your next moves. Where is the next foothold? So much of what you do in life is like that. You often cannot build on your progress without making some changes in your approach. You assume responsibility, you channel your passion, you take control, and you still might fall short of your goal.

I'm hopeful that there is going to be a huge breakthrough in autism. We have already accomplished one important transformation in the way science is conducted with our MSSNG project. If that open science experiment continues to gain speed and results in any kind of treatment or cure for my grandson Christian in my lifetime,

I will feel like we have accomplished something very important.

If we can come to grips with what caused it, we may find that Christian is probably one gene off and one pathway off normal, maybe two. We ought to be able to figure out how to reengineer one or two genes. It's a question of isolating them. And if we could, that could mean giving him a voice or getting some control over his own body. Maybe where science takes us in the future is an earlier diagnosis that would show that a system breakdown is taking place earlier than we think. If we know it's coming, perhaps we could limit or manage the damage. That's the challenge. That's the future.

30

Vaccines and Other Controversies: A House Divided

The Wright family home
Fairfield, Connecticut
June 18, 2007

Of all the internal and external controversies that plagued Autism Speaks, the most divisive, toxic debate involved routine early childhood vaccines and their possible connection to autism. It remains a complex challenge.

The vaccine controversy is real and a big part of the story of autism. Those in opposition believe that vaccines, and specifically the synthetic mercury preservative in some, played a role in their child's autism. Today scientific evidence has not validated that position. Our daughter Katie, Christian's mother, was among the most vocal opponents. The discourse about vaccines—created in the absence of definitive answers about autism cause, cure, and treatment—tore at our family's heart and soul.

Suzanne and I became lightning rods for some of this strife—despite our good intentions. A front page story in the *New York Times* June 18, 2007, painfully chronicled the internecine feud that strained my leadership of Autism Speaks for a decade. Our hearts sank when we opened the paper at home that morning to see our personal struggles so prominently displayed. Under the headline "Autism Debate Strains a Family and Its Charity," our private differences had become very public.

Months earlier, it played out on national television when Katie declared to talk show host Oprah Winfrey that she believed measles-mumps-rubella (MMR) and another 37 routinely administered pediatric vaccines played havoc with Christian's already compromised immune system. She forcefully condemned the scientific community's failure to understand autism as an environmental neurological condition complicated by other disorders, rather than as a genetic mental illness.

The contentious rift widened shortly after Katie's appearance on *Oprah* when Alison Singer, Autism Speaks' first communications director, posted an unauthorized statement from Suzanne and me on the Autism Speaks website apologizing to our "valued volunteers" for Katie's remarks and clarifying that she did not espouse our views and was not an Autism Speaks spokesperson. Katie felt betrayed and rejected—and so did we. While we did not retract the statement, we sought to soften the blow by hastily adding to the online post our love for Katie and our appreciation for her angst. Alison was a cunning former CNBC news producer with a daughter and brother on the spectrum. She openly continued to be at odds with Katie, primarily over the vaccine issue—and, in hindsight, was not always completely upfront with Suzanne and me. Alison abruptly resigned to launch her rival Autism Science Foundation in 2010 with $1 million in donor funding and several Autism Speaks staffers in tow.

It wasn't until 2013 that Geri Dawson, Autism Speaks' then chief science officer and a career academic, went on the record stating there were no proven links between vaccines and autism, and encouraging parents to consult with their pediatricians. A year later, her successor, Rob Ring, a neuroscientist hired from Pfizer, stated definitively on the Autism Speaks website: "Over the last two decades, extensive research has asked whether there is any link between childhood vaccinations and autism. The results of this research are clear: vaccines do not cause autism. We urge that all children be fully vaccinated."

Katie immediately took to her blog and Twitter, urging a boycott of Autism Speaks and questioning the qualifications of our chief science officer. That set off a flurry of calls from Autism Speaks' corporate sponsors and donors. Privately, we asked Katie to refrain from the nastiness; publicly we thought engaging her and others would only make things worse.

Clearly, more work was needed in the undeveloped area of vaccines and environmental research, which will *always* cause reactions in some segment of the general population. The annual federal government vaccine court awards some $100 million in damages. It is a testament to the need for improved vaccine safety. While mercury preservatives were still being used in flu vaccines, questions lingered about thimerosal and other mercury derivatives as earlier preservatives.

It was something I didn't want to be tied to because it was bigger than me, bigger than Autism Speaks, even bigger than autism. ***What made vaccines so controversial was the unknown: the inability to more accurately anticipate a child's response based on their genetics. We were on the verge of realizing that there were many autisms, each a patchwork of many different conditions.*** Every autistic person would have a different filter for experiences. And so there could be no definitive right or wrong in the way an autistic child presented or a parent's response. That is what made me angry about the emotional wrangling of parents attacking Autism Speaks or any of us as parents and grandparents for presenting autism as we knew it, however different that was from their own. Higher-functioning autistic children and adults are entitled to their own truth. The rest of us have as much right to our autism experiences and struggles, even if they are more dramatic and gut-wrenching, as the detractors have to theirs. Yet the detractors were quick to call it hostile and inhuman.

This flurry of finger-pointing is painful, but the core controversy very familiar.

The endless controversy made it difficult for our nonprofit to get things done in Washington, DC, that benefited everyone on the autism spectrum. Many Washington lawmakers were hardened against helping the community for fear that they were going to be pilloried by an anti-vaccine backlash. The CDC's lack of integrity on the matter and big pharma's lobbying record—both stretching back to the 1990s—didn't help.

When I went to Congress seeking funds for autism research and services in the original Combatting Autism Act in 2005, I ran headlong into resistance from Senate majority leader Bill Frist, a Tennessee Republican, doctor, and cofounder of the for-profit Hospital Corporation of America. Frist said he had been "professionally humiliated" by the false claims and was not interested in helping us. I argued that the CDC methodology for identifying and addressing vaccine problems was ineffective—and an administrative nightmare. Significantly improving vaccine safety would improve reporting procedures, compliance, and public trust. Through a lot of determined effort, I eventually won Senator Frist's support and friendship to get the act passed and funded. It was just one of many close calls and battles we waged on Capitol Hill on behalf of all autistic children and their families.

The Combating Autism Act plus two extensions have appropriated $3.2 billion to NIH and HHS for autism research and services. And to this day, you still can't have a legitimate discussion with the CDC about vaccine safety. ***RCW proposes new vaccine safety measures to HHS but gets turned down by White House! My biggest loss!***

So I spent 18 months investigating the vaccine question myself on behalf of Autism Speaks. I put together a stellar team: Andy Shih, our Autism Speaks senior vice president of scientific affairs; Dr. Louis Z. Cooper, professor emeritus of pediatrics at Columbia University and a former president of the American Academy of Pediatrics; and Dr. Samuel L. Katz, the Wilburt Cornell Davison professor and chair emeritus of the department of pediatrics at Duke University School of Medicine and a former chair of the Advisory Committee on Immunization Practice at the CDC. Their 18-month study was published in 2008 in *Pediatrics*. ***We couldn't determine any direct connection between vaccines and autism. But we also recognized that using the same vaccines with very different children would yield some very different results. Resolving those differences would require detailed reforms including developing new vaccines, improving informed decision making by the public, peer review of the vaccine safety program, a less aggressive vaccine schedule, and annually executing on new research priorities.***

In the spring of 2008 we presented to Health and Human Services as the Bush administration was winding down. I thought that Bush as a lame-duck President would easily move on our Vaccine Safety proposal. I was wrong! We were looking for a recommendation from the White House for peer review of vaccine safety. It is unusual to make a presentation to the entire HHS staff. We made our presentation to former Utah Gov. Mike Leavitt. The audience was very receptive. The Governor told me he supported us, but he had to clear it with the White House. Two weeks later he called back and said the White House was afraid of press reaction. And I lost that battle. We made the same pitch to the Health and Human Services Secretary Kathleen Sebelius, the former Governor of Kansas serving under Barack Obama. She and her staff were very supportive but the White House staff turned us down! Valerie Jarrett!

This was an unbiased recommendation from people who had worked in the vaccine business for years. To this day there is no peer review of the vaccine safety program. They'd rather pay $100 million a year in damages. The community that Katie is in needs to understand all the work I did and how establishing peer review of vaccine safety would do a lot to alleviate the pressures on vaccines going forward. Sadly, we were not able to do that.

The Centers for Disease Control supported our recommendations but not the notion of spending more money on studying vaccines. On its website, the CDC simply stated in bold letters, "Vaccines do not cause autism... There is no link between vaccines and autism... Vaccine ingredients do not cause autism." A deeper look indicated some of the supporting studies were under scrutiny by their authoring scientists. The whistle-blowing was compounded by a dearth of checks and balances, and politics run amok at clashing regulatory and scientific agencies. Then came the disqualifying language: "Autism Spectrum Disorder (ASD) is a developmental disability caused by differences in brain function. People with ASD may communicate, interact, behave, and learn in different ways."

The only aspect of this I could get my arms and head around was the inadequate nature of vaccine education and assessment methodology to assure safety. In my 2009 testimony before the US Health and Human Services Department, I recommended new response mechanisms for the Centers for Disease Control at the first sign of any vaccine problems. Although the CDC said the proposal had merit, it was rejected by both the Bush and Obama White House for fear of acknowledging that vaccine safety could and should be improved. The destructive rancor over vaccines, which extended well beyond autism, could have been blunted. It was all so political.

These hot button issues tore through our organization and even the second nationally televised debate of leading Republican presidential candidates in mid-September 2015 when Donald Trump reasserted a connection between vaccines and autism, and Drs. Ben Carson and Rand Paul waffled on the matter. Autism Speaks responded to the exchange by lobbying for more government support for autism-related matters adding, "Over the last 2 decades, extensive research has asked whether there is any link between childhood vaccinations and autism. The results of this research are clear: Vaccines do not cause autism."

I fired off a disappointed email reply to Autism Speaks leaders, board members and key donors. "This point of view is unnecessarily argumentative. Trump said it a lot better. We support vaccines, but if parents have concerns, spread out the shots. Even Dr. Carson said there are too many shots. We want to reach a broad community. Mimicking the CDC's non-peer reviewed vaccine safety program is not a step in the direction of authenticity."

Soon afterward, Autism Speaks removed its statement and reposted one of my earlier responses to the continuing vaccine controversy. "Over the last 2 decades extensive research has asked whether there is any link between childhood vaccines and autism. Scientific research has not directly connected autism to vaccines. Vaccines are very important. Parents must make the decision whether to vaccinate their children. Efforts must be continually made to educate parents about vaccine safety. If parents decide not to vaccinate they must be aware of the consequences in their community and their local schools."

The most important thing for me is a recognition that the CDC vaccine safety program needs to be augmented with new math and science tools to quickly evaluate adverse vaccine occurrences. The vaccine safety program needs to be peer reviewed! As a businessman I quickly realized that the world heavily relies on the CDC and FDA's pronouncements that a vaccine is safe. There is huge potential liability for us if we are wrong about any approved vaccines. The cost to meet better standards for vaccine safety is very small.

❖ **Kevin Murray.** The vaccine question comes up still to this day as a big issue. Even our board is not always on the same page about everything. One of the things I'd say that's unique is that we all understand that you don't have to believe everything as long as collectively that you believe in the same tenets, because we're more powerful together than we are apart. And rowing in the same direction is valuable. We created Autism Speaks by integrating three regional groups that represented the conflicting ideologies of the community at large. No controversy will ever deter us from accomplishing things for the greater good. ❖

So much of what divides us stems from the wide-ranging symptoms (generally involving social impairment, communications difficulties, and repetitive stereotyped behaviors) and levels of impairment that loosely define the autism spectrum disorder. They might be reconciled if more of them could be classified into similar autisms that could then be catered to and treated differently. That would include deciphering similar vaccine reactions. This is the promise of MSSNG, Autism Speaks' whole-genome sequencing project with Google. The industry was already leaning in this direction a year earlier with the reclassification of Asperger's syndrome and PDD-NOS as high-functioning on the autistic spectrum in the updated *Diagnostic and Statistical Manual of Mental Disorders* (*DSM-5*) used globally by doctors.

The battle over vaccines wasn't our only controversy. Autism Speaks also came under harsh attack from high-functioning autistic adults who demanded more representation, services, and respect. They don't want to be associated with the autism spectrum; they want to be viewed as "normal variation from typical." Many are satisfied being who they are. It is completely understandable; theirs is a condition that deserves life-enhancing support rather than a disease requiring a cure. And with that, many autistic persons go on to make important contributions to society.

It wasn't that Autism Speaks had ignored them, but rather that we focused more keenly on the needs of autistic children in keeping with our original mission statement to seek "causes, treatments, and cures." Michael John Carley, a highly regarded spokesperson for high-functioning autistic adults, advised us on expanding and modifying Autism Speaks' agenda to be more inclusive. They don't have a lot of services available to them for jobs and training anywhere in the country. We recognize the needs of autistic adults, and we will have a broader legislative agenda from housing to employment.

Katie was quick to remind everyone that high-functioning individuals, while being the best-case scenario, were hardly the norm. After an episode of Katie Couric's talk show featured gifted, articulate Asperger's children and adults, she wrote a response that presented the dilemma plainly and from the heart. "I couldn't help but be reminded of the huge disparity that makes up the autism spectrum. My son lives on the other side, the severely affected side of the spectrum. I am so proud of my 11-year-old son, Christian—no one works harder... [he] is not a savant, not a professor, not an artist, but just a typical kid struggling with severe autism. He was toilet trained at age 9 and needs 24-hour-a-day supervision because he has no awareness of danger. Christian cannot be interviewed on talk shows because he cannot speak.

"This wide spectrum of autism really can become a tricky issue. I want the public to see the many gifts of people with autism and how much they contribute to our world. It is also essential that families with more severely affected children with autism not feel isolated," Katie continued. "Living with severe autism asks everything you have to give: all your money, all your time, all your energy, all your spirit, and sometimes even your career and marriage. I want us all to acknowledge the hard work of those parents and kids."

Even when Katie had valid, reasonable points, her message could be lost in her bludgeoning style and militant attitude. In her *Age of Autism* blog posts, her Twitter feed, and in person she would lash out at Autism Speaks board members and executives. She gets on her computer in the middle of the night and says anything to anyone that she would never say in the light of day. This is what autism is about for many people.

The fact is, Katie represents a group of parents who need to be heard and who deserve answers on vaccines, environmental damage, and the best way to manage their children's care as autistic adults, which is the next major autism crisis. Like other parents of severely autistic adolescents, Katie and her husband, Andreas Hildebrand, now wrestle with the gut-wrenching decision of how best to care for Christian as an autistic adult who is tall, strong, nonverbal, and at times unwieldy.

Throughout the past decade, Katie has worked hard to put forth her ideas and the concerns of many mothers dealing with autism. They are unhappy there aren't better treatments or work being done to propagate better diet and attention to environment.

She doesn't agree with a lot of the things we have done at Autism Speaks, including our science efforts, but she has done a great deal of work in her community writing and traveling to attend meetings around what she believes in. I wish that Autism Speaks had gone to many more meetings that were related to Katie's concerns and the many parents she deals with. I have respect for all that she has done. The whole aspect of the environment contributing as much as 50 percent to the prevalence of autism is not getting addressed very well. Katie and the people she works with have been trying to open the doors to these new ideas with scientists, doctors, and care providers. The problem is that established standard-bearers in North America and Europe are stuck on evidence-based medicine that requires peer review before they will prescribe or perform treatments. That time-consuming, laborious system revolves around roughly 700 million people in the world. But another 5 billion people on the planet, who are not as tightly governed by all that convention, benefit from extraordinarily long-standing far east and other old world practices and beliefs that have withstood the test of time.

It is unfortunate that we are unable to intellectually and positively grab those treatments and understandings and bring them into our homes and lives and insurance. I think it is because we don't have enough documented history of medical practices and procedures that were handed down from generation to generation and shown to be effective, like there is in places like Asia and the Middle East and India. We hold our noses to holistic medicine and everything going on in parts of the world where the outlook and outcomes for patients generally is better than it is here. Trying to change things in this country is frustrating when you are stuck with a long, arbitrary, awkward peer-review process. We run into evidence-based medicine autism rules every day! It is staggering.

The American Medical Association is no help either. The AMA is a huge lobby for doctors; sort of the national union for docs. No help at all for our autism families.

Friends have told us they marveled at how we maintained close family ties despite the strained dynamic. The ground rules were simple, although not always easily enforceable: when we're together, call a cease-fire on sensitive issues and things we don't agree on. We unconditionally love our children and grandchildren and will do anything for them.

Suzanne and I continue to gather our family for holidays, birthdays, vacations, and autism-related fundraising events. Some times are better than others. Our annual family vacation in March 2015 was to the Galapagos Islands. When family members weren't fighting, they took turns being sick; it took us two days to get there and to get back through a third world nation. I don't know what I was thinking. But there have been many wonderful moments when our son, Chris, and his wife, Sandi, and our younger daughter, Maggie, and her husband, Greg Tomlinson, and their children have shown great love, support, and acceptance. Katie will not be happy until someone ties a link between vaccines and/or environmental harms to Christian's autism. We've accepted this.

❖ **Katie Wright**. It's been hugely painful for our family like it is for other families with children on the extreme end of the spectrum. I don't think many give a second thought about what this costs the parents and families emotionally. It's so hard for Christian most of all. His whole life is public and I was fine with that because I thought we really didn't have a choice on an ethical level about what to do. I think the fact that the medical and scientific communities have ignored so many of his issues is disrespectful to my family and not fair to him. My parents respect the medical profession and really thought that they would come through and be able to fix things. I really admire how hard my father fought to win insurance coverage of autism state by state. But I have been troubled by how cautious and even terrified people are of crossing the CDC, or how worried they are about what other people think.

Autism is not for people who want to be liked or who care about what other people think. People like that usually don't have kids on the spectrum. I just want to see progress, and I don't understand for the life of me why people are satisfied with less than what we owe to children with autism and their families. I'm thinking about this 24 hours a day. My expectations are unfairly high, but I think it is a privilege to work in this field with these children and families.

Doing the right thing can come at a personal cost and you might be disliked for it, but my father taught me early on that being liked is overrated. ❖

As the years wore on, Autism Speaks was chided for a focus on "fixing" autism rather than adapting to its reality. That meant eventually taking dead aim at scientific research, the medical and academic establishment, and big pharma. As the era of personalized medicine and translational science emerged in 2014, MSSNG plans to deliver a path to that new template. Until then, vaccine research is a no-win proposition. No one wants to do it for fear their funding will dry up because it is such a political hot potato.

❖ **Katie Wright.** Vaccine research is so political and such a career ender. The people who have the strength of character to continue with this research, because they know they have to or they feel compelled, pay a price you can't even imagine. The

French researcher Luc Montagnier, who was awarded the Nobel Prize in 2008 for co-discovering the HIV (AIDS) virus, came forward at great personal cost to discuss the role of vaccines and the immune system. He addressed an autism conference I attended, where he said he was able to do this at the end of his career but that it was otherwise terrifying to a scientist. That's what we're up against. ❖

Cracking open the autism dialogue and debate and trying to unify voices in order to accomplish some good sparked a firestorm that often took direct aim at Suzanne and me. Even after I stepped down as chief executive officer of Autism Speaks on May 1, 2015, and passed the mantle to Brian Kelly, Suzanne and I remained moving targets, despite all the good we continued to do.

Some opponents claimed we had crossed the line between raising awareness of autism and promoting our own organization with blowout global events such as Light It Up Blue. Others charged that increased awareness gave the illusion that something was being done to halt the escalating autism rate and that instead we should be turning attention to action for appropriate care, education, and medical services. In fact, we initiated that transition as early as 2012. We were taken to task for not having more autistic persons on our board and committees, not doing more for high-functioning and adult autistics, and accepting autism as a natural part of "neurodiversity"—not an epidemic. In late August 2015, Autism Speaks president Liz Feld tried to halt the counterproductive attacks with "A Call for Unity." Her online essay reminded everyone that the diverse ideas, voices, and conditions within the autism spectrum were all valid and deserved equal respect.

Liz learned to effectively deal with dissidents inside and outside an organization as mayor of Larchmont, New York, and a White House operative in the Reagan administration who went on to head information for ABC News. There always was plenty of opportunity to do the same at Autism Speaks. The fact is, none of the good we were able to achieve for autism over a decade would have been possible without our initial efforts to raise awareness and to focus on early diagnosis and treatment in children that would improve their odds for attending public school with full services. It was grounded in defining research conducted by our first chief science officer, Dr. Geri Dawson, which we also used to build our state-by-state insurance reforms. Autism Speaks focused on children because we knew we had to help them. They are the freshman class. Our efforts have been focused on awareness, early diagnosis, and treatment—to significantly improve the children's condition and prepare them for public school with lots of help.

❖ **Jamitha Fields, vice president community affairs, Autism Speaks.** There always has been a struggle with the idea of "fixing" autism—solving the problem. That was one of the debates behind closed doors around here and everywhere. Do you accept it and manage it like other medical conditions, or do you try to find out the cause to cure it? America is still trying to figure out what this autism thing is, with all its different faces. They're not sure what it's about or how it affects their world. I sometimes compare it to AIDS—people don't need to be affected personally by AIDS to understand the impact that it has. We've had a tough job figuring out how to tap into the autism community because these families are so devastated financially and emotionally. Autism really just sucks the life out of you. So it's never a matter of being behind on the mission—it's a matter of embracing the impossible. ❖

There was backlash even to some of our most well-intended efforts. A *Time* magazine story from November 6, 2009, said it all: "Few medical conditions rival autism as a magnet for controversy. Practically everything about the disorder—its cause, its treatment, the way it is diagnosed, how it is studied—is subject to bitter dispute." The story was about the public service announcement *I Am Autism* created by songwriter Billy Mann, a member of the Autism Speaks board, and Academy Award–winning director Alfonso Cuarón— both parents of autistic children. The nearly 4-minute video featured images of autistic children accompanied by a sonorous voiceover: "I am Autism… I know where you live… I live there too… I work faster than pediatric AIDS, cancer, and diabetes combined… And if you are happily married, I will make sure that your marriage fails." The film ended on an upbeat note, reinforcing the powerful notion that families, friends, and professionals dedicated to autistic children would not be defeated. Still, some advocates were outraged over what they called the film's tone of pity and fear.

❖ **Andy Shih.** The most important controversy is over self-determination and self-advocacy. Some countries like Sweden don't care as much about Autism Awareness Day or the color blue. Their autism community sits down at the table with the government to develop a social support plan. For decades they have gradually moved away from labeling autism a disease and calling it a condition. But few places in the world are like Sweden, where everything is based on individual human rights, and so we must press for self-advocacy.

That is what I have been doing with autistic people and families all over the world—trying to develop grassroots solutions. We get traction by presenting it as a health education issue that everyone—autistic adults and children, parents and grandparents, doctors and scientists—can rally around. Then it becomes a shared priority even though everyone has their own individual autism experience and their own filter.

In this way, I think it is really important—and very much underestimated—to have autistic people advocate for themselves. To the extent they are capable, they should be participants, because they aren't just someone to be treated, but to be connected to the universe and function as well as possible.

In low-resource countries there are not a lot of self-advocates and there is an oversimplification of the issues. In places like the United States there should be more opportunities for self-advocacy; with new science and new technology, this will surely be possible. Until then, autistic people need to be part of the process so that they—and not the critics and detractors—can shape the narrative. ❖

In the dawning age of Precision Medicine, engaging parents as equal partners in children's diagnosis and care was one way to quell the storm. Andy Shih and his team, working with the World Health Organization and other partners, successfully rolled out Parenting Skills Training in 16 countries as far flung as China, Iran, Russia, Iran, and Egypt. It was designed to close the 6-month-plus wait time for diagnosis and treatment, and create a patient-centric standard of care. It gave caregivers on the frontlines more power to effectively cope and shape outcomes. In 2016, at Brian's urging, Shih turned his attention to intensifying such public health initiatives at home in the United States, where the need for such grassroots reforms were as great and unheeded.

❖ **Dana Marnane.** There is definitely still division within the community. There are some autistic people who are very capable, have graduated from college, can live independently, can self-advocate. They don't use the word cure, and some are offended by it because they accept where they are and just want to focus on improving the quality of their lives with supportive services. Their attitude is, I am who I am. But Autism Speaks is about science. We know that there are many families and children out there who want a cure, and they are right to ask for it. And a cure could mean something different for every person.

Autism Speaks can't be all things to everybody. But it can continue to provide a lot of hope and a lot of support with tools, resources, and services to a lot of people in the autism community. The "fix" Bob talks about is really his business shorthand for discovering the causes and therefore identifying treatments and cures. Who would ever argue with that? ❖

❖ **Dr. Herbert Pardes.** Bob and Suzanne launched a personal attack on autism. And they used every bone in their body, every connection and leverage they have, to build an extremely effective organization in just 10 years. The organization is so effective politically it has an impact on the NIH budget and an increase in medical research dollars for autism in tight economic times. They got autism on everyone's agenda. They have been tenacious and passionate. They were driven to answer the question, "How does a child vanish in plain sight?!" That is what autism looks like to many people, but not everyone.

The Wrights have run headlong into the many dissenting viewpoints and have endured a lot of backlash for what hasn't worked right or hasn't been solved. But because they are doers, they have wanted to fix what they can in the autism world for everyone, and everyone—even their critics—have benefited from what has been achieved. ❖

Wright to the Point

Resistance and conflict are nothing new to me. I have wrestled with them throughout my corporate career and now for 12 years with autism. At NBC I could handpick my team and have them execute against a corporate timetable governed by quarterly profit reports. Autism Speaks was built on the goodwill labor of volunteers and passionate professionals more interested in science and solutions. Opportunity to discover and succeed was not as easily—or ever—mandated. As it turned out, the politics of autism and medical science were far more complicated and stinging. But somehow we have found ways to make progress and productive change. I have used every personal chip I had to make Autism Speaks a going concern.

It will never be enough for anyone on the spectrum—or for me. But I will not be deterred.

31
MSSNG: From Beijing to Google

I took a hard look at Autism Speaks in its tenth year and realized two things. First, although we had made great strides in state insurance reform, federal legislation and services, and global awareness, we still had no sure way to crack open the genetic secrets to cause and cure. It also was clear that our extensive field organization needed to do a better job of capitalizing on existing local services and leveraging the national awareness and political support we had developed. Instead, our boots on the ground were stuck in a reoccurring cycle of relying on nearly 100 annual volunteer-supported walks. Too few of Autism Speaks' grassroots members have effectively used the power they have to demand and receive local services for autistic people and their families. They don't leverage what we have built nationally to achieve what they should locally.

That's when Google—one of the most influential companies on the planet—swooped in to save the day on both fronts.

We had always known that if we were ever to understand the mystery of autism, unlocking the genetic code was key. Over the years, Autism Speaks and the Autism Genetics Research Exchange database had stockpiled more than 10,000 whole genomes of autistic people and their family members. The next step—and it's a big one—was to analyze all that data. Whole-genomic sequencing would be the Holy Grail. But identifying the complete DNA makeup of whole genomes was a new science, time-consuming and expensive.

We had tried once before. In 2011 we worked briefly with the Beijing Genomics Institute to classify and evaluate parts of the whole genomes we were collecting, but the effort failed when their technical and financial capabilities fell short. Then, in one brilliant flash of timing and luck, Google and Dr. Stephen Scherer of the Hospital for Sick Children in Toronto stepped in. Together we set out to develop the largest bank of decoded genetic data from the DNA of people with autism spectrum disorder, using the same boundless cloud platform that supports Gmail and YouTube. Google's unparalleled algorithms would be used to analyze, categorize, and cross-match billions of data points.

The collaboration originally began on a somewhat smaller scale. It started with several casual conversations between us and Google about tracking autistic children who wander and creating resource networks for autistic families but quickly evolved into much more. When Google offered its vast storage and algorithmic capabilities to analyze the DNA data, everything changed.

Google cofounders Sergey Brin and Larry Page instilled in their organization a passion for scientific advancement that served us well. In less than a year, Google's genomics scientists and data engineers developed and launched a searchable online data platform accessible for free to qualified researchers anywhere in the world. The ultimate goal was to identify various forms of autism in a way that could translate into individualized autism spectrum disorder treatment and therapies. It would be a shortcut to answers that had eluded our best efforts for a decade.

Google agreed to power the genome project and was interested in doing the same for Autism Speaks' operating infrastructure. By managing our operations and resources, Google could help us create real-time data and video networks. It meant we could make it easy for our diverse community to find and share information on critical matters like housing, medical care, socialization, and education. It's putting social media and search capabilities to work in very specific ways, and in that arena, Google had a huge head start.

❖ **Liz Feld.** When Rob Ring, our science officer, met Adrienne Biddings, Google's policy counselor, in mid-2013, it was the beginning of a new world order. The revolution grew out of their initial discussions. The lightbulbs went on everywhere. That's when our relations with Google took off like a rocket. They both were focused on using technology for social good. Google was attracted to the power of our brand and our global footprint and wanted a partner who shared their vision, took risks, and did big things. Rob came into our organization determined to put science to work for our families. Adrienne was personally committed to aiding and supporting people with disabilities and made a cold call to Rob after seeing one of our autism awareness announcements. She is a lawyer who understands technology and was motivated by Google's practice of requiring employees to devote 20 percent of their work time on personal initiatives that further its corporate mission. That's what it takes to give good people the chance to do great things. ❖

All my life I had been a fixer and problem solver. At NBC and GE, I initiated action and achieved goals by leveraging emerging technology and strategic partnerships. But at this point in the development of Autism Speaks, I felt paralyzed by forces beyond my control. I was crushed by an inability to do more for Christian and others as they slipped from childhood into young adulthood. Getting to the core of autism would blunt the looming challenges of an exploding autistic population aging out of inadequate health care and social services. The collaboration with Google promised to provide significant research and actionable data for a generation.

Rob Ring, Autism Speaks' chief science officer since 2013, was instrumental in securing Google's interest and participation. Rob was a neuroscientist with the sensibilities of a venture capitalist and the heart of a researcher. He had previously led the first pharmaceutical industry group at Pfizer dedicated to the discovery and development of neurodevelopment disorder meds. As president of our venture philanthropy arm, Delivering Scientific Innovation for Autism (DELSIA), he worked with Dr. Dan Smith, president of DELSIA and vice president of Innovative Technologies, to convert scientific breakthroughs into products and services to fill the autistic community's unmet needs. This was Google's wheelhouse. We were shaking things up and it felt good.

Google Genomics director David Glazer shared my resolve to swiftly tackle this uncharted territory. Within 6 months of our initial discussions we hammered out an unconventional agreement and soon uploaded ¼ of our whole-genome sequences online, hoping to change the face of autism with open science. We had relatively few takers at first. The concept of open collaboration was unnerving and unnatural in most science, medical, academic, political, and philanthropic spheres. Everyone wanted to protect their own turf and agenda. Our Google alliance caught many by surprise, leapfrogging the institutions and protracted research processes that had been our only recourse. I eagerly announced our alliance with Google on June 10, 2013, without all the fine points nailed down. By late summer 2013, *Fortune* ran a provocative story about Google Ventures working with Flatiron Health to find a cure for cancer. Google was still free to date anyone it wanted.

It simply managed a database owned by Autism Speaks. So it was imperative to keep Google engaged.

The Metropolitan Club of New York
1 E. 60th Street
September 26, 2013

Sharing ideas during our first formal meeting at dinner, we all knew we were on to something big. My experience at NBC taught me that the intersection of Silicon Valley, Main Street, and Wall Street could have surprising, explosive results. Google's data-mining scientists, Dr. Scherer's team, and Autism Speaks' impassioned advocates shared the same goals and sense of urgency to know more in order to do more about autism. I spoke about how the genome project would change the world. There was an immediate connection with Pablo Chavez, Google's then US policy director and father to a child with cerebral palsy. He invited us to Google headquarters to connect with engineers led by David Glazer, who later told us he considered this the biggest data challenge and "sexiest" project the company faced at that time. The autism community would be liberated—rather than limited—by data.

❖ **Adrienne Biddings, lead policy counselor Google.** I'm in the middle of the cool and awesome things that happen inside Google every day and you kind of get numb to them. But having someone you've looked up to reaching out to you to work together to make a difference can really get you going! I was a former television producer who went on to law school before coming to work at Google, so I was a little thunderstruck meeting Bob Wright for the first time. There I was, a young lawyer from a small town in the South sitting in the Metropolitan Club of New York with Bob Wright, a TV icon.

Bob is a mellow guy but I could see the passion and the fire he had for what he called the new frontier in medicine and science with the genome project. I was personally driven to finding ways for Google to help persons with disabilities. For Google, it was a practical matter. Ten percent of the population has a disability, so we are not connecting with or assisting a potentially huge user base. It was a new level of thinking for many Googlers jazzed to take adoption to a whole other level. They are on the top of the mountain when they can build something to fix or solve a problem. ❖

❖ **Dr. Stephen Scherer, director The Centre for Applied Genomics, Toronto's Hospital for Sick Children.** That Autism Speaks scientific advisory board meeting at New York's Metropolitan Club was fascinating. It was a mix of Google analysts, JPMorgan financiers, and parents of autistic children who were independent businesspeople and understood the importance of breaking conventions.

Bob gave us a little sermon to essentially kick our asses into high gear. He said everyone was moving too slowly. "It's great you're doing all this basic research," he said, "but we've got a lot of parents who need answers and help *now*." And it was the intensity of how he delivered that message that inspired most everyone there. It was just exactly what I needed. Scientists get stuck in the details, and that's important, but we need to have people who have the vision to get the ball rolling. When I looked around me to check the reaction in the room, what I saw on many faces was, "Oh shit! This is how the business world works!" This CEO wanted results yesterday. It was blunt-force honesty. ❖

Google headquarters
Google X conference room

Mountain View, California
July 17, 2014

By mid-July 2014, Rob Ring was in Mountain View, California, meeting with Google's genomics group and Dr. Stephen Scherer, director for the Centre for Applied Genomics at Toronto's Hospital for Sick Children. Dr. Scherer had agreed to oversee the project, which by then had a name: MSSNG. The advertising agency BBDO, which had earlier developed the memorable public service spots for autism, created the label without vowels to remind us that the autism puzzle still has missing pieces.

Dr. Scherer, a geneticist, was a trailblazer in whole-genome sequencing for autism and was pivotal in procuring some of the funding from Canadian federal and provincial government agencies and private donors like philanthropist Steven Wise. Autism Speaks pledged to raise the other 2/3 of the initial $50 million in project funding through private donations, eventually led in the US by the Dolan Foundation, the Gordon and Llura Gund Foundation, Mel Karmazin Foundation, Hearst Foundation and Bloomberg Philanthropies. More creative financing involved the sale of eclectic DNA time-lapse crystallization posters. At a cost of $1,300 per genome, we committed to sequencing all 10,000 whole genomes by the first quarter of 2016. There would be an ongoing cost for keeping Google.

At that meeting in Mountain View, the core MSSNG team wasted no time confronting the thorniest issues: how to protect the privacy of genome donors, the legal liabilities of handling personal data, who owned what, and generating future revenues. Google handled the mechanics and would work with BioTeam, a Massachusetts-based scientific computing firm, to build the cloud platform. Together they compiled a master to-do list.

The next day, Rob Ring sent an e-mail to me, Suzanne, and Liz Feld. "Great first day of face-to-face meetings yesterday out here. Among everyone in the room is a very palpable and invigorating sense that we are making history."

❖ **Dr. Stephen Scherer.** When Dave Glazer, Rob Ring, and I initially met to work out the MSSNG details, we were like kids in a candy shop. Rob and I were excited to be at Google because everyone wants to go see how this place works. We were in a meeting room in Mountain View at their main site, where geeky people ride around on their bikes and get free food. Google Genomics and Google X were the two divisions working with us. We were surrounded by innovation! David had his interactive note-taking device and everything he said was coming up on a big screen in the room. You got an instant sense that this is how science should be done—openly, collaboratively with other smart people from different places, with a chemistry and energy that made things happen.

The three of us were working together to set up a Henry Ford–style assembly line, getting the whole genome samples sequenced and into the database. Our job was to get that database in a form that would feed the genome-sequencing information back to the families, the physicians, the scientists, the pharma companies… and then see where it takes us. Anything we accomplished would fill a void. At the very least, a breakdown of data and analysis of genomes families contributed would help them to better manage their child's condition and influence their lives. The portal wrapped around this database enhanced interaction between families and specialists. That was our science project.

David Glazer pushed for aggressive timelines. It was Google-time and Google-speak. David didn't have a background in genomics or in autism. But we knew he could put the genome data into a form that scientists like me could use; we knew Autism Speaks could raise the money to maintain that system. We learned so much from each other. It was big data brought down to human terms. Until we could translate the information into real action, it was all about managing expectations.

Bob pushed us to reinvent how we do science as open science. He told us that if you're going to pay to generate this dense data, it's your social responsibility to put it into a form that others can use. And what happens in autism will happen in cancer and other conditions and diseases. This is a time for precision medicine and venture philanthropy; that's what we're doing here. Many people are looking to see what business model evolves. We all believe in 50 years people will look back on this time in awe. ❖

❖ **David Glazer.** I've been a software guy my whole career. I was ready for my next 7-year itch change at Google and a project where I could apply 15 years of experience in data science to the world of life science. So I started a genomics team that would take the data science Google is already good at and find meaning and value in information that can be used to help people in the life sciences.

It is a pioneering effort because MSSNG is encouraging the science and medical communities to contribute and collaborate in the best possible way to advance understanding. Google works best on a grand scale to solve problems for millions of people. Google's original mission statement is to organize the world's information, make it universally accessible and useful. We are now just starting to include the world's genomic information and the world's health information and make it universally accessible and useful in the orbit of that mission.

The natural cycle in scientific research is peer review, then journal submission, then acceptance and publication. That cycle gives way to waves of adoption and it can take decades to accomplish. Bob's vision was to use technology and meld different disciplines to speed up how we collect and use a rich level of data that we can mine for more discovery and collaboration. Then people will start to replicate MSSNG's pattern, and in the long run, that will lead to an even bigger impact transforming the science of genomics. This will be a lightning spark that accelerates two trends in a powerful way: precision medicine and the democratization of access to health and medical information. So that we come to treat individuals and their specific kinds of autism and cancer or other conditions. That's Bob's vision: using technology as a springboard for change. ❖

❖ **Dr. Stephen Scherer.** To think that as a student 20 years ago we conducted half-baked experiments in order to gain a little piece of information. Now you're given the telescope that allows you to see Pluto and everything in between. So you have the technology that gives you the best vision of the question or problem you are trying to address. Technology will be the great leveler.

In our hospital and center in Canada, we have a lot of big computers that can analyze 5 genomes a day. Google will fully analyze more than 10,000 whole genomes in a year. This science will be part of regular diagnosis within several years. The difference will be scanning a million different sites on a gene chip versus up to 3 billion in whole-genome sequencing. I've staked my reputation on cracking this thing, and I know the difference will give us some answers to the three biggest challenges in autism that make us human: cognition, speech and language, and social interaction. It's actually hundreds of different conditions that present in the same kind of clinical endpoints—things like social interaction challenges, communication issues, and anxiety issues.

Once decoded, MSSNG's massive repository will enable autism medications, treatments, and insights. The database is a means to that end; it's an engine of discovery. So it's like building the Internet or building a railroad system in North America in 1890. If you don't have it, you can't get there! So this began as a partnership of a couple of people who got fire in their belly and worked well together. Every Tuesday, David Glazer, Rob Ring, me, and our teams meet for a couple hours and it's magical. It's science in action. I was a graduate student when my PhD mentor, Dr. Francis Collins, a former head of the NIH, was in a lab that identified the cystic fibrosis gene. I remember those days as magical science. So much was happening every day, you didn't want to go home, and that's what's happening here. ❖

On January 26, 2015, MSSNG released its first 1,000 whole-genome analyses. The project was up and running with the legalities, ethics, and mechanics in place within just 6 months!

In true capitalist fashion, Google wasted no time approaching hospitals and universities about storing their genomes and raw DNA data needed for genetic research, an average 100 gigabytes, for $25 a year. Google created a Tree of Life plan for applying the same whole-genome sequencing template for other diseases and disorders. First "branches" included the National Cancer Institute's Cancer Genome Atlas and the Veteran's Administration's Million Veteran Program, which identified genomic variations in different cancers and other conditions. A goal was to use big data to build health participating in the US Presidential Precision Medicine Initiative; an approach to personal disease treatment and prevention that takes into account individual variability in genes, environment, and lifestyle.

This was going to be really big, but we were first in line.

For starters we paid Google a discounted $200,000 for storage in the Google Cloud. The plan is to keep the database accessible to qualified researchers, scientists, and medical clinicians as well as to autistic families donating their DNA. We were hoping to spur collaboration as a shortcut to discovery. But open science does not mean free science. Those who can afford to will pay, and the funds will be used to run the analysis. Prospective new services and products could be developed through DELSIA, or our other venture capital groups. MSSNG also was an effective demonstration of how Google could help solve other industries' big data dilemmas. Google would replicate our template to profitably do the same for other industries, causes, and conditions.

A major obstacle to getting MSSNG off the ground in the spring of 2015 was convincing potential users in the scientific and medical research communities that it was *not* a medical research project. In fact, it was unlike any research project ever seen in that we had built an open online portal and scientific library giving the world free access to information that had never been widely available to spark real-time collaboration. Google would facilitate a new age of accelerated discovery, although the concept raised new questions and concerns about protecting the privacy of DNA donors as well as control and ownership of the data.

Think of the Hudson River separating New Jersey from New York, and assume that there is a lot of interest in making your way across the water in something other than a tiny boat. Then along came the great big George Washington Bridge, allowing travel back and forth with ease. That's what MSSNG did. We're connecting this foreign land of whole genomes in autism to scientists who can come across a portal and make the most of the connection. We're like the Port Authority, and people are starting to build bigger vehicles to go over there for their own purposes. The George Washington Bridge and MSSNG demonstrated there was a better way to get to the destination we all wanted.

To make the most of funds and efforts, we wanted to work and align with other genome sequencing efforts at places like Stanford and the Simons Foundation. We tried to reengage the NIH to become a major investor and supporter in a unified scientific—not political—process. When things get political, everybody freezes and doors get locked.

The real work begins when researchers go into the portal, start going through material, and come up with hypotheses and comparisons. And Google is in the background trying to make sure that the library books are available to them; they're clean, they're fresh, and they're in the right storage area. And these people can now go in and see material they've never seen, and they can drill down into it and manipulate it and write papers about it. We were validating their work and giving them a place to do it. Google was not looking for economic gain or to restrict what could be done with the data. We both wanted to see a hundred published scientific papers come flying out of there.

The money to fund this exploration could come from the NIH and universities—if they would just stop seeing us and MSSNG as a competitive threat. NIH hadn't approved whole-genome sequencing because it was very expensive. So the NIH researchers haven't had access to use whole-genome sequencing with NIH money. But a genetic profile doesn't tell you anything unless you have the bioinformatics. So you need the context of a person's complete phenotyping—entire physical, biochemical, and physiological composite. This is the vicious circle we're trying to break. I raised the more than $10 million of the nearly $18 million we needed for our initial whole genome sequencing project with Google. Most of that came from the Gund and Dolan family foundations. At least another $10 million came from Canadian sources including businessman Steven Wise, Autism Speaks Canada, and Dr. Stephen Scherer's *Centre for*

Applied Genomics in Toronto, which is supported by federal and regional government funding.

Making the most of what's out there to move forward is a complicated process. It's about matching up and building on the research someone has done on gastrointestinal or muscular or nonverbal or other characteristic areas of autism in one place, with the work that's being done in another. And then look at the genetic research for treatment being conducted by drug companies, and the translational medicine going on at great clinics like Mayo, and the whole-genome sequence breakdown to find the common elements that could really change things.

Until we achieve that, we need more scientific intelligence. Physicians are stuck with the science they have available to them. The NIH feels all the overlapping scientific efforts are often wasted because they're all based on the *DSM-5* presentation and diagnosis, which propagates sameness and a lack of breakthrough. Former NIMH director Tom Insel, who is now with Google Life Sciences, believed all participants should be working together to do extensive brain research, which will produce information useful to all of those different conditions—and maybe determine that many of those conditions have the same roots.

This is why we are trying to stretch and push science as opposed to being beat up by it. We want to get ahead of the curve, move from the back of the class to the front of the class. I think we have a shot at doing something here that in 2 years can move us 20 years forward. And the politics and history of academic research have been the biggest obstacles.

It reminds me of the days when we were arguing with the affiliates about MSNBC and CNBC. I was looking around, watching USA grow, watching ESPN grow, watching everything else, and I said, "Wait a second, wake up—pay attention! This world's changed, we need more science, faster."

❖ **Gordon Gund, philanthropist, sports team owner, founder Foundation Fighting Blindness, and major autism donor.** I progressively lost my eyesight from retinitis pigmentosa, an inherited retinal degenerative disease for which there was little research and no cure back in 1970. The Foundation Fighting Blindness that my wife, Llura, and I began 44 years ago is changing all of that. It was an early model for what the Wrights have done with Autism Speaks. With an autistic grandchild of our own, we wanted to help with the MSSNG project because we appreciate firsthand what gene discovery and collaboration can mean.

After spending more than half a billion dollars on research, we have made breakthroughs with normal gene replacement therapy for retinal degenerative disease. We understand the process of de-risking therapies in the preclinical stage to translate research from the lab to the clinic. Taking a venture capital kind of risk with the entrepreneurs brings them along to where pharma and biotech step up. ❖

❖ **Rob Ring.** In 2015, Bob and the Autism Speaks board made the bold strategic decision to place most of our bets on MSSNG, which meant not attending as many conferences or awarding foundation grants. We understood the value that would be created by leveraging the whole sequencing of these genomes, and of keeping Google engaged and this story narrative and scale alive. Once we moved from talking about it to actually planting the flag in the ground and showing what it can do, it would gain momentum and create new possibilities.

The difference in our organizational cultures was most notable when we negotiated a formal agreement to work together. Bob was eager to speak publically about our work with Google because it would raise our profile and be something we could monetize through fundraising and other support. That created a lot of tension with Google, who preferred to stay very low-key about the program until it was tangible.

Another source of tension stemmed from negotiating an agreement with BioTeam, the company Google recommended to build our user portal for MSSNG. Since we were hiring them and MSSNG was our asset, Autism Speaks would own the code they were writing. That was the deal. But since Google and Steve Scherer's genomics group at Toronto's Hospital for Sick Children would be providing a lot of intellectual input to shaping what they built, they had a vested interest. Steve and his team especially had done extensive work discovering numerous disease susceptibility genes and defining genetic factors underlying autism. One of the early issues that came up revealed some fundamental differences between how we and Google think about the world around us. It focused around BioTeam's desire to have an exclusive license to the code that they were developing for us. It didn't take long for them to recognize that what they were building for us was a solution for much more.

It was surreal to go from that chaos to the state of denial researchers and scientists were in when the MSSNG database began to emerge. After the shock, they began diving in—which was, of course, the whole idea. "You're actually doing it? There is no way!" And then they would plow forward—which suggested we were doing the right thing! ❖

❖ **David Glazer.** We've been waiting more than a decade, since mapping the human genome was complete, for someone to come in and act on it, and it didn't happen. It's not that the world was static so much as the medical and science establishment was stuck. So now we're doing it ourselves. The difference with technology today is that the rest of us no longer have to wait. What Bob has been doing is surfing on the very forward edge of the wave of the next generation of science. And as soon as he saw the possibility—that it was now practical for the first time to do this—he said the future is now. That's when autism went from being a disorder to being an opportunity to change lives for the better. We lucked out because we were standing there at the right time with some tools that will be very helpful. ❖

During the summer dog days of August 2015, Google announced the creation of a new corporate umbrella called Alphabet to encompass its progressive business ventures: life science research, space exploration, YouTube virtual reality, driverless cars, Google Glass, health management wearables, and the genomics that include MSSNG—changing old business paradigms. Google's restructuring provided context for Autism Speaks' transformation from an advocacy group into a proactive, real-time resource and support network for families, educators, doctors, and scientists and big pharma. Once again in my life, technology was the catalyst.

❖ **Ned Sahin, founding CEO Brain Power.** I first met the Wrights at a United Nations World Focus on Autism event hosted by Google for first ladies from two dozen countries in New York in April 2013. Everyone was excited to try on the Google Glasses specially programmed for autistic children. And they immediately got it. Soon afterward Google pulled the glasses from commercial sales, but for the autistic community, the wearable interactive devices were a harbinger of the astounding things to come using new technology. While other people are debating diagnosis and exploring cause, the Brain Power software allowed us to help autistic children develop practical life skills from challenges in social engagement, language, and other communication, controlling of personal behaviors, and learning abstract categories. We are decoding autism.

When I was more of an academic, writing and publishing papers on neuroscience at Harvard, I felt like something was missing. I wasn't able to immediately help people who came to me in a more proactive way. I entered a contest in which Google awarded Google Glasses to people with worthy ideas on how to use them. It was clear they could be used as a vehicle for offering autistic children a way to have self-sufficiency, dignity, and a very enjoyable and productive life. The special software developed for Google Glass provided autistic children their first opportunity to connect with the world around them and communicate with their families. The interactive set of tools help the wearer understand what others intend or feel while recording and transmitting data about the wearer—things like facial expressions and sounds. Recorded data can be analyzed and used to tailor instruction and care in real time. ❖

There are likely to be hundreds of different autisms out there that are explained biologically, and genetics is one of the more obvious lenses through which we can begin to see the differences. Separating autism into more clearly defined subtypes creates value for the future treatment of these individuals. It holds the promise of personalized medicine. Our hope is that MSSNG will not only reduce clinical complexities surrounding autism but also clarify genetic risks. Since whole-genome sequencing involves literally pinpointing where in someone's DNA autism factors may exist, MSSNG is an important part of the precision medicine conversation. There is no question this open science format will be replicated and adopted by others in medical research and science.

❖ **Dr. Stephen Scherer.** This project has started to introduce a culture change in the way researchers think about whole genomics and working together in an open science platform. By the end of 2016, we will be looking at a lot of aggregate data from 10,000 genomes in MSSNG that will have an immediate impact on research and families. We will change the culture and outlook for autism and genetic disorders. I have been surprised about how quickly things already are happening. We're working with people researching epilepsy, Alzheimer's, cancer, and other conditions [which] puts us all on a fast track. Some of the families donating their DNA are already participating in clinical trials based on our early research. We took a little gamble moving forward on this in 2013.

But by the end of 2016, I will have underestimated the timetable and everything we thought we would accomplish. We've accomplished so much and so much faster than we thought we could. We already are discovering new target genes we could never have predicted and a new set of genes involved in regulating series of brain function. It may take 10 years for this to translate into the first autism-specific drugs, but that's half the time it used to take. Maybe we find some are accessible to existing medicines. More than 20 percent of institutions signing on to MSSNG are pharmaceutical and drug companies; other interested parties included Yale, Stanford, Johns Hopkins, Mayo Clinic, and IBM Watson. Now everyone is scrambling to get on. Bob stood up to the NIH. We needed someone like him to say, "This is such an obvious thing to do—we're doing it!" ❖

❖ **Katie Wright.** I fully appreciate the phenomenal science involved in MSSNG. I know it takes genomics 25 years into the future—changing the whole field. Autism Speaks was the first organization to see that and take the risk. What MSSNG needs is a multivariate plan. I am very worried that autism spectrum disorder can never be phenotyped effectively using genomics. Scherer and Ring have poor understandings of autism—primarily as a heritable brain disorder characterized by social problems and rigidity that represents about 10 percent of the spectrum. MSSNG desperately needs an immunologist and an environmental scientist on the same level as Ring and Scherer since ASD is not a single-gene disease which can be neatly characterized like cystic fibrosis or tuberous sclerosis. And many of us believe autism is idiopathic and environmentally triggered: it's like someone's genetic predisposition to lung cancer being triggered by smoking. Pairing the genetics with individual immune chemistry would yield so much actionable information. I am sure we will find those with a family history of autoimmune disease are much more susceptible to ASD—hence the need to reduce risk in that population via separating vaccines. I think doing that alone would reduce ASD by 25 percent. Cross-matching genetic with gastrointestinal data would yield a total goldmine. I am concerned that no parents like myself are involved with MSSNG, nor people really knowledgeable about this intersection. I am very, very worried MSSNG will not live up to any of the hype and tarnish my dad's legacy. ❖

❖ **Rob Ring.** Autism Speaks has been empowered by the MSSNG project to function more boldly if it chooses. We began pursuing this course when we formed DELSIA, a venture capital arm designed to invest in entrepreneurs and small businesses who needed partners to move their ideas forward. It was an unusual move for a nonprofit. But it is one of the most important ways Autism Speaks can make a difference in the future: connect technology and science to move along our understanding and treatment of autism.

It's going from a raw diamond in the rock and making some of those initial cuts where the value is created. You might have a unique opportunity to participate in the commercial success of the entities that you're funding. For instance, the groundbreaking therapeutic game Akili that Interactive Labs developed is being prescribed like medication would be, as a different treatment modality. That creates a pathway many others can take. This stretches us to think beyond drugs to new behavioral interventions and raises some very profound questions about our nonprofit mission and what we're doing. Deploying capital into parts of the value chain to make things happen more quickly and making bets on where things are going. So we're not just raising funds; we're raising expectations. ❖

By the end of 2015, 7,000 of the whole genomes had been sequenced. In less than a year the MSSNG data bank had attracted support from 86 users and 34 institutions in 7 countries including China, Australia and England. We were ahead of schedule reaching all of the milestones we set on the 3-year project. Half of the $20 million cost of MSSNG came from federal, regional, and local Canadian sources. The Canadian government awarded another $18 million in grants for Dr. Scherer to take over all of the whole-genome sequencing in-house and then transfer the data to Google's cloud platform. That further reduced the time and expense of sequencing a single whole genome to 2 days and $1,100.

By the time he published his second scientific paper about MSSNG in early 2016, Dr. Scherer had made some stunning early findings. He had developed new approaches to looking for permanent DNA mutations in the 99 percent of each genome that until now had been unexamined. He was able to identify new classes of genes and genetic changes that support the notion of a spectrum of many different autisms. Suddenly he could focus on what is happening outside of the genes in response to external factors such as food, water, toxins, and even older parents waiting to have their children later in a knowledge-based economy.

There was even an opportunity to set up experiments to measure epigenetics (changes in gene expression rather than gene code) and how environmental factors like stress, environmental toxins and nutrition can alter DNA, the production of proteins and cell behavior. Epigenetic change in the building blocks of DNA could be reversible and could have profound developmental impact. It was just the beginning of where MSSNG would lead. We would start to see steady returns on initial MSSNG investments as third parties reached deep into the data and made break-through connections to create a new ecosystem.

Even before the data from sequencing the initial 10,000 whole genomes was loaded onto the Google Cloud platform in early 2016, big pharma such as AstraZeneca, Janssen Pharmaceutica and Pizer and several foundations were considering funding the program into its next phase. It would involve sequencing of another 7,500 whole genomes from autistic persons and developing improved analytic tools. We will roll out a community portal which would give families contributing DNA to the project opportunity to tap into, understand and share findings to improve their treatment plans aided by partners like Quest Diagnostics. A specially devised mobile app will support data collection and sharing to provide an anecdotal dimension to better understanding genetic subtypes of autism. The program we have created is flexible and open enough that anyone can interface with and support it. It is delivering results on time. It is the catalyst for an entire new science information business for Google that is challenging us to open the door to new partnerships and relationships.

We call it "Googling" the human genome to find clues about personalized autism treatment—from setting new research targets to recruiting specific individuals with a known genome type to participate in more targeted clinical trials.

It's merging the power of genetics with the power of big data, which is at the heart of understanding the human genome. While genome sequencing once took years and billions of dollars, today it can be done in a day for $1,000. The big problem now is storing and manipulating the 100 gigabytes of data for the 3 billion data points generated by one decoded human genome. The bigger problem is making it easier for scientists and researchers of all kinds to dip into the well and make medical magic.

❖ **Dr. Stephen Scherer.** As the MSSNG database continues to grow and be analyzed, one of our most interesting new findings has been the presence of genetic alterations linked to autism in some people who are never diagnosed. Whole-genome sequencing allows us to zero in on why some parents and non-ASD siblings carry genetic alterations that by all estimates should trigger autism as it does in their child—but they are resilient to it. Studying the complete genes of these family members would help us to create new pathways to treatments. Until now we were limited to studying a mere 1.5 percent of a typical gene. Using this genomic framework we can test environmental and other factors exerting changes in DNA composition that would result in autism. We are running a year ahead on new models and new targets for genetic research across autism and many other medical conditions. At that rate, our biggest challenge may turn out to be balancing growth with managing expectations. ❖

Wright to the Point

This is the most difficult challenge that I've ever undertaken because there are two unmanageable things going on. One is that the number of children being diagnosed with autism is increasing dramatically, like nobody's business—1 in 68 in the US. I believe that will settle in shortly at approximately 1 in 50, or 2 percent of all children and 3 percent of all boys. And the other is that the services that are available to people are essentially the same services that have been available to them for a long time, and most people cannot afford the best of them.

The first time I felt in my bones that we stand a chance of cracking this thing in my lifetime came in early October 2015 when Suzanne, Rob Ring, and I visited the Googleplex city campus in Mountain View, California. David Glazer and his team of scientists were elated about sequencing the first 5,000 of our more than 10,000 whole genes from autistic donors. In 2 to 4 years, they were sure that scientists and researchers from around the world would be working on this new cloud platform exploring and comparing whole genome data from autism, various cancers, Alzheimer's, Parkinson's disease, and other conditions. They expected to find astounding numbers of commonalities. They expected new insights to causes, treatments, and cures.

The only new wrinkle in all of this Glazer and his brilliant team found was the archaic conditions governing the use of available and donated DNA that even included samples from our early Beijing genome project. So many of the authorizations had been written a generation earlier, before the prevalence of digital sharing.

Many of those authorization agreements for the MSSNG genomes are having to be renegotiated for today's digital realities that reach beyond country and company boundaries. The science of our MSSNG project was blowing through the politics and privacy barriers of an earlier generation.

The irony: these days people regularly provide enormous amounts of their personal information—credit card numbers, social security numbers, phone numbers, addresses, birthdates, and the like—on the internet just to buy a $10 pen!

Autism is such a broad spectrum, unlike schizophrenia or Alzheimer's or Parkinson's or so many other conditions. There have been very few substantial scientific developments over the last 20 years, which is really surprising and shocking to a lot of people. For all the money that we spend at the National Institute of Mental Health—$35 billion every year—we still cannot claim any advancement in the science of medicine on behalf of persons with autism. In Google we have a new strong, committed partner who is motivating everyone to think outside the box.

❖ **Dr. Stephen Scherer.** My dream is that one day there will be a pill developed that can help alleviate at least a few of the core deficits in autism in some individuals and maybe all of the deficits in others. Individuals with autism spectrum disorder might have their own unique genetic form of autism, so this might complicate coming up with a "magic bullet." We are however finding that autism risk genes all seem to work together in the same biochemical pathways, so there may be common targets universal drugs can make an impression on. If we can put a man on the moon and learn how to sequence our own genomes, we can surely figure out autism. ❖

EPILOGUE:
Christian at Fourteen

The Wright family home
Nantucket, Massachusetts
August 15, 2015

It was a perfect Saturday afternoon for the birthday barbecue. Family and friends had gathered to celebrate the birthdays of our two oldest grandsons: Christian was turning 14 and Mattias 12. The children were playing in the pool under the watchful eye of a lifeguard while guests enjoyed grilled hot dogs, hamburgers, and roasted vegetables outside our cabana. Suzanne used an electronic megaphone to lead the singing of "Happy Birthday" over a double-layer sheet cake decorated with the logo and team colors of the Detroit Tigers—Mattias's favorite team. Christian was oblivious to the bustle of activity around him, fixed mostly on the pure joy of jumping into the pool, with me and an aide by his side. That was birthday gift enough. Like most autistic children, he is attracted to water. Pool time gives us both freedom to connect and share smiles in ways that are otherwise difficult for Christian.

That morning, our entire family joined in the 9th annual Autism Speaks Walk on Nantucket's Jetties Beach, raising awareness and nearly $440,000. Our children—Katie, Chris, and Maggie—their spouses, and our six young grandchildren are tirelessly supportive of our efforts. Honored guests and supporters included philanthropist Gordon Gund and three-time championship NCAA basketball coach Jim Calhoun. Local real estate investor Bruce Percelay donated Good Humor bars—served from his original Good Humor truck—which were handed out halfway through the nearly 2-mile walk. A Nantucket Fire Department truck flew the Autism Speaks flag from the top of its extended ladder. There were balloons and pinwheels, music and movement. It is the quintessential hometown event. In so many ways, Nantucket is home; we have been entwined with the community for nearly 4 decades.

You see the full gamut of autism at these annual walks: children and adults from all parts of the spectrum and families of every means gathered for the same reasons: support, unity, and a sense of hope. Some of the autistic children wear helmets in cycle chairs pushed by parents and siblings. Others walk as far as they can. They know it is a special day.

My grandson's story is very sad. Christian is one of the severely autistic people who will never be able to be higher functioning without some kind of intervention—scientific or medical or even divine. We have tried them all. He has slipped from an infant to a toddler to a young boy to an adolescent. Next thing you know, he's going to be an adult. He's a big boy, and because of that size, he'll become much more difficult to handle in the coming years. Our hope is that Christian will attend a well-regarded residential school where full-time services can help him to realize his full potential as an adult who will never live independently.

All parents of autistic children have this fear hanging over them as their children get older. Many of them now receive benefits under Medicaid, and the children get a lot of care until they're 19 or 20. States have the ability to move it up a year or so, but it doesn't go beyond age 21. After that, you're on your own. It's heartbreaking and scary.

The issue of adult care for autism is a huge, open-ended problem that has no immediate solution. Long-term, most states don't have any effective legislation to aid this situation, even though some do really well. Mostly, it's parents getting together to fund special care facilities. But that takes money, and without it, it's unlikely they're going to find much.

We created a section on our Autism Speaks website for autistic adults. We have pulled together a whole group of different organizations around the country devoted to caring for autistic adults. We've tried to position them into a much stronger force. Generally what that means is they try to exchange information with each other on their state guidelines, on governmental help and support, on medical support, and on social security and Medicaid benefits. We have had some success as an organized lobby for autism families. Our committee on adult care is the largest we have, and we are constantly putting together new materials and projects, because we can't move fast enough in this area. We produced an excellent toolkit for parents focused on adult care and options. This will be a primary focus for Autism Speaks in the years ahead.

Although Autism Speaks provides more than $1 million in annual funding to existing resources and external organizations for autistic children who come of age, there is no legal framework to govern their care or needs. Unlike youth autism, there are no mandated individual educational plans for autistic adults. So, just as it has been with insurance reform, we will have to go state by state in pursuit of change. The burden essentially falls on each individual family, including ours, to figure things out for themselves.

For our Christian there are finite options. He has limited intellectual or emotional connection with anyone at this point. It is profoundly difficult to communicate. I'm not at all certain we have any clear path for him as he gets older. And I know all the other families face the same heartache. There are literally thousands of autistic children moving into adulthood—they estimate half a million by 2020. I just wish we could do more for Christian and others like him. I always will regret that we could not do more.

❖ **Suzanne Wright.** It's hard to believe that Christian is a teenager now. He's as tall as me. But he is pretty disabled. I would say he's on the very serious side of autism. I don't know what the future is for him right now other than all the therapy he has, and all the love he has. I wish I could see the future for him, but then again, maybe I don't want to see it.

It's very difficult to communicate with Christian because he doesn't speak. When he wants to eat or do something, he points to pictures on a touch screen tablet. It's pretty hard to give him kisses and hugs, but I do, and when he sees me he knows who I am. Every once in a while he'll come over and just tap me on the shoulder or rub my back or squeeze or pinch me. It's his way of letting me know that he knows who I am and why we're together. Those little signs of affection tell me that he really knows that I'm his grandmother and that I love him very much. So there can be very sweet moments. He is such a wonderful boy, and I marvel at how he shares love in so many different ways.

I think that he understands, on some level, what we've been doing with Autism Speaks. I always tell him how much I love him and how he is changing the world and making a difference in autism, and he sometimes smiles. And that makes me think that he does understand what we're doing.

At the same time, he also can have a meltdown, and that makes me feel sad and helpless. He will be screaming and hitting himself, and I won't know how to help him. That is the worst. I cannot believe my poor daughter and how she tries to calm him down and help him. It's just a nightmare to see that. It is really shocking and horrible to see a big boy, a teenager, screaming and hitting himself. Katie holds his hands, but she is smaller than Christian. Because he is getting big physically, his daddy, Andreas, has to sit on his lap to hold him down. It's extremely hard to watch. Andreas is always by his side, anticipating and meeting his needs and giving him support and love.

Even though we work with autistic children and families all the time, it's heart-wrenching to watch your own grandson go through those motions now as a young man. Most teenagers scream and yell because they don't like what their rules are. Now we have a teenager who maybe does not like something but can't express to us what that is or what he wants or how to make him happy. We all live for the moments when Christian seems happy. My daughter Katie will say, "He's happy. I'm exhausted, but he's happy."

One thing we always have to remember is the other children in these families. It can be very hard on siblings. That is why we worked for 7 years with our partners at the Sesame Street Workshop to create Julia, representing all those with autism, for all members of a young family struggling to understand and accept. Making her debut in late 2015, Julia is only 1 of 5 Muppets with disabilities in Sesame Street's 45-year history. These siblings are rock stars in their own right. Christian's younger brother, Mattias, is like an only child. He is always there to support and love his brother. But he is pretty much on his own path. If it's handled right, it certainly can be positive. Most of the parents of autistic children I have met are so proud of their non-autistic children because they really have a full range of compassion, something most kids really don't have, especially at a young age. Mattias always thinks of Christian first. It's heartwarming to see how fully he understands as he gets older that his brother needs to be protected.

By the same token, the siblings need to be protected. I asked my daughter, Katie, if I could create a special place for only Mattias and his friends when they come over, since the entire house is otherwise dedicated to Christian's therapy and care. We redecorated Mattias' bedroom—an autism-free zone—with a soccer theme. We didn't make a big deal out of it, but it is a safe place where Mattias can celebrate who he is. Now Mattias has a place in the family home where only he and his friends can visit. And he is so happy to have that.

I hope to God that when we get an adult transition plan, Christian will be able to have dignity and have a job someday doing something fulfilling. But it's very hard for me to put that telescope out there and look into the future, because the future for me with him is now.

All of our special loved ones with autism remind me of a quote from one of my favorite movies, *The Imitation Game*. "Sometimes it's the very people who no one imagines anything of—who do the things no one can imagine." ◈

October 29, 2015 was the worst day of my life. **My love, Suzanne, was diagnosed with pancreatic cancer.** She is the healthiest member of our family. She has no family history of cancer, much less pancreatic cancer. We all are doing everything we can to treat her condition and make every day enjoyable. Suzanne and I have been together for 50 years! The Lord is our Shepherd.

This tragic revelation came out of nowhere after weeks of Suzanne suffering through what we thought was a stomach infection. The first few days were devastating; we were overwhelmed with grief. Within 2 weeks we had a chemotherapy treatment plan in place at Sloan-Kettering.

Drawing on the amazing inner strength and faith she had used to lead our family through many crises, Suzanne courageously moved forward. She was buoyed by the outpouring of well wishes and love from family, friends, and so many people she had touched but didn't know personally. The handwritten cards especially made her smile. We shared times of tearful desperation, and other times of side-splitting laughter—remembering all the good times we had been blessed to know right down to when our dog swallowed the children's goldfish and the cat had its litter in my closet inside my shoes!

Our family always included pets, so it was not surprising when Suzanne almost immediately decided the time was right for us to get a dog that our grandchildren would look forward to playing with when they visited, and that would be good company for us through our ordeal. She named the teddy bear poodle Happy. Our children and grandchildren picked up Happy from the breeder to bring him home the first weekend in December when we hosted our annual family get-together at the River Café in Brooklyn with the magnificent Manhattan skyline as a backdrop. We had done this for years to kick off the holiday season with our children, grandchildren, and extended family. This was home; this was tradition, and Suzanne was not about to depart from it for any reason before we would head south for the winter, like snow birds, for our little piece of paradise in Palm Beach, Florida.

❖ **Michael Rosen.** There have been tears and disbelief among the Autism Speaks staff about Suzanne's illness, and because of who she is, there is hope that if anyone can beat pancreatic cancer—she can. People would not know autism were it not for Suzanne Wright. It's not a cliché to say she has changed the world when you think of World Autism Awareness Day, World Focus on Autism, the unanimous vote at the United Nations and Light It Up Blue. Even as the organization the Wrights built is undergoing major change with new leadership, their partnership remains triumphant. Not bad for a cop's kid from the Bronx who made her husband a better man and better businessman, and through the sheer force of will changed the world for 70 million people. ❖

❖ **Liz Feld.** I was at the Wright's New York apartment November 18th in the late afternoon. Suzanne and I sat at the dining room table and talked about a whole lot of things—personal and work. I had sat with her at her recent chemo treatment and she looked good. Then she brought out a birthday cake for me—imagine that. We sat in the living room with Bob, and I have never seen them laugh harder. They were finishing each other's sentences, telling stories about everything from midnight parties at NBC to life with kids and goldfish.

It was wonderful to see. There is a tenderness to their relationship that doesn't always come across in more public formal settings. I think they are more reserved that way. Their love is so strong and soft at the same time. And what comes with that love is a deep respect.

They are like one unit. It's the two of them facing the world and facing everything together. Their faith is obviously at the root of all they do, and the root of their love. They don't take anything for granted in the relationship. She will talk about him every day like there is a new discovery in how smart he is, or how thoughtful, and it is authentic. They marvel at each other. When Suzanne stands at a podium to speak, Bob is so proud of her and the way she can capture people's attention, passion, and imagination and harness it. And she's the same way about him. No matter how many times she hears him give a speech, she mouths the words in agreement and smiles. She's so loyal, not just defending Bob but promoting him. She wants to be sure people see the best of him.

We all have a race to run. Suzanne's race has been a sprint, and their race with Autism Speaks has been a sprint. And now there's no more sprint. I think the most unnatural thing for them now is how everything just stopped at once—Bob's leadership transition from chairman and then Suzanne's cancer diagnosis. For two people who have given so much of themselves to others to now be facing a clock is bittersweet. When I joined Autism Speaks in January 2012, Bob had already been talking about stepping back.

Then he realized instead he would have to reengage in the business. Suzanne, on the other hand, wasn't slowing down at all. In fact, she was in high gear expanding Light It Up Blue and being a driving force behind MSSNG. Few on the Autism Speaks board seemed to appreciate Bob's vision for the project, but Suzanne gave him so much energy and reinforcement to see it through. She didn't feel their work was done yet.

Now, Suzanne recognizes her mortality. She cannot save and control everything that goes on, and external forces have required her to let go. Her faith has allowed her to handle that. The Autism Speaks they built is not what Autism Speaks will be going forward. And that's what happens in business, especially with founders. Bob knows that and he warned that the second ten years would be harder than the first ten years. He knows leadership transition is tough, no matter who, or what, the circumstances.

But the Wrights' legacy is set. Someone once told me, "while the whole world was asleep, Suzanne put autism on the map." Nobody going forward will have the same impact, but others will do big things. Bob wants to pass the baton believing that. Bob and Suzanne are believers. They started Autism Speaks because they believe positive change can happen. And they were right. ❖

Plans were made by Autism Speaks for a tribute dinner on February 5 at the opulent Flagler Museum in Palm Beach to present Suzanne with a Lifetime Achievement Award along with a leather-bound case filled with notes and letters from friends and supporters. With a $1 million gift from our old friend Bernie Marcus, the Forever Blue campaign was launched memorializing Suzanne's leadership and Autism Speaks' enduring commitment to global awareness. Suzanne was already steeped in cards and tokens from well-wishers spread out over our kitchen table. She continuously worked on hand-written responses in the bold round cursive that was her signature.

Most dear to us were the times our three children, their spouses, and our six grandchildren huddled to be as close to each other as possible. The 14 of us spent 8 days between Christmas and New Year's in Palm Beach sharing meals, swimming in our pool, taking golf and tennis lessons, and playing with our new puppy, Happy—the star of the show and Suzanne's best buddy. We have six family birthdays in December including Suzanne, Katie, and Chris, so it has always been a magical time of year for us. We dressed up in our best clothes for a Christmas Party at a nearby club. The grandchildren entertained us with talk of their school, friends, and sports participation, and showcasing their talents: from playing guitar to reciting their own poetry. When Christian inevitably had a difficult moment, even the youngest of our family knew to show him compassion and support.

As difficult as it has been, autism and cancer have brought our family to a higher level of love and acceptance than we otherwise would have known. Suzanne was involved every day in as many of the family activities as she had the strength to do and loved it. There were gifts going in all directions—some humorous and others more thoughtful—but not as much as in years past. This was all about being with Suzanne, and Suzanne being with her family.

When the children and grandchildren left, Suzanne and I spent as much time as we could together around the ebb and flow and exhaustion from her treatments. Even with nurses flying by me every day, I doted on her every need. Suzanne was pretty remarkable with it, but her response to the strong chemo was unpredictable; she would be in fine spirits and within minutes it would turn on her. Pancreatic cancer was like autism when we first confronted it; no significant funding or research. No one knows how to deal with it. Professionals are overwhelmed by it because it is just too difficult. It has a 93.5% mortality rate.

There is nothing I can do and she knows that. So we cling tight and just do the best we can. We never completely move past the shock and disbelief, but we resolve to live every day to its fullest. We would try to get out of the house every day for lunch. We lingered a little longer over every glance and conversation and simple task. When the weather was nice and Suzanne was up to it, we would take the boat out in the late afternoon to find a moment of peace and watch the sunset.

It was something we both looked forward to.

APPENDIX A: NBCU

Vintage Wright: What Next?

O ne thing I've learned: paying attention to what's going on can give you and your organization an edge.

The last week in July 2015 was a time of rare events. A blue moon—the second full moon in a month—was a reminder of the natural course to all things. So it seemed appropriate that in that same week Facebook surpassed General Electric's market cap at $275 billion, with Netflix not far behind. Amazon topped Walmart, the world's largest retailer, at $250 billion when its stock rose 20 percent on a rare quarterly profit report. Google Auto LLC was established to manage Google's driverless cars when partnerships with any of the leading manufacturers failed to materialize—perpetuating the notion of a Google Nation. The New World Order was taking over, led by the Big Four—Facebook, Amazon, Netflix, and Google—or what CNBC's Jim Cramer called FANG. They had tipped the world on its axis, toppled and transformed the old guard, and forged new business paradigms. The bar was set high and, for some companies, out of reach.

What complicated things for media—in the broadest sense of the word—was its integration into all things digital. The entertainment, information, and communications that bind our lives were imbedded in the emerging Internet of Things: a constant churn of data-driven connected devices and objects that reshaped all aspects of personal and work life. Our favorite TV shows, movies, and music lined up with our e-commerce, photos, and messages, all suspended in the ethereal cloud. Security, propriety, and other laws of limits buckled under the weight of voracious use.

In that bubbling cauldron of change, media companies and consumers were redefining the value of their entertainment, communications, and information. The only way to stay in the game is to study and respond to the trends. Connecting the dots and taking risks were never more important. In media, your crystal ball is your gut. It is paying attention to what's going on around you, constantly reading, listening, and analyzing. It is accepting change as a necessary constant and opportunity. And it is a willingness to think the unthinkable. In this book I have done my best to honestly recount what happened when I proactively responded to events and trends. It's just the way I am wired. I have openly shared my perspective on the past and remain eager to use my filter to predict what the future holds.

On the domination of Apple:

It is entirely possible that Samsung, LG Electronics, or someone else will come out with a much better phone than Apple's iPhone and has the ability to market it. And it is entirely possible that Apple gets tripped up. Maybe it holds on like Nokia did. And it's not impossible to think that Apple becomes Nokia. Apple's entire business today is based upon iPhones. They only debuted in 2007, after succeeding with music and the iPod, which gave Apple a base to build on. But its most recent business is less than half as old, so it's not impossible for somebody else—some black swan—to do the same thing, only better. My iPhone could use dramatic improvement. Siri (the voice command service) doesn't work half the time. There is a lot of stuff that doesn't work that great. But the ecosystems they are part of carry them along.

On microdata:

There is so much information and data floating around and relatively few reliable filters. Credibility is going to become more of an issue; it is going to get a lot worse—almost medieval. People are forming opinions and acting on information that may not be credible. Everyone is a newscaster these days because of Twitter and social media.

Even major news organizations like Fox are breaking down news and information into microbits and slamming it around the world, just putting it out there in bits and pieces without context or examination or investigation. It is going to become very hard for people to digest all that on their own. So they will resort to any kind of service that only gives them the stuff they want and screens out all other news and information. The danger there is that people will only know what they think they want or need to know. Other people will pick up the wrong stuff or make too much out of it. This all requires a lot of serious sorting out that no one wants to take the time to do. So it's really about coming up with better filters.

The terrorist group ISIS is a perfect example of what I'm talking about. Everybody, even its most ardent supporters, will admit this stuff is a supreme misreading of the Koran. But they know how to manipulate social media. They know how to send out a marketing message. They've got the money to organize and buy resources. They can move faster than anybody can think about it, so they're already off and running even though they're based on total travesty of information.

Donald Trump's initial 2016 presidential bid came at this from another angle. He knows there are a lot of people out there who really want to hear it straight from the gut. And he knows that he's not really a politician so he doesn't have to worry about his base that he's established over 50 years. He just goes out there and says outrageous things, and the press is quick to pick up on it and spread it around. He doesn't have to rely on anyone to raise money to stay in the political spotlight. CNN, Google, Facebook—they're all doing it for him.

On the unbundling of content and services:

Netflix founding CEO Reed Hastings put media on the track to consumers selecting and only paying for what they want, when and wherever they want it. In just a few years, that one company changed everything because of subscribers' swift adoption rate. Consumers were hungry for choice. Hastings was successful because he did not hesitate to jump from one risky business model to another. And he did it ahead of the competition. I don't think many of us believed that he could do that so well. Now he's overcoming territorial content licensing agreements to ramp global expansion with a new Netflix Everywhere service. Like Facebook, Netflix had enormously sharp technical support, and the shift Netflix made is analogous to what Facebook has done in mobile. Both have been guided by the power of the single selection, which is all about microdata and micro-billing.

On the other hand, Twitter has just not been able to monetize itself, and there are all kinds of reasons why. A lot of this is the way they've designed it—they're not flexible. They don't seem to be able to easily undo what they started out with, including 140 characters per tweet. So Netflix and Facebook hit homeruns because they had great engineering and far-seeing executives; Twitter didn't have either. Twitter got trapped in its engineering underwear!

We have been gradually moving from selling things in bulk that you can access with an app to being charged 50 cents or whatever if people just want to buy one selection. And there's still plenty of room for commerce when you consider that the National Basketball Association believes it can get $6.95 per game from someone who wants to access that one bit of content by streaming. It looks like a leap of faith now, but a year from now it may look brilliant.

If you break things down into this small format, that's where the margins get really high. That's going to make you a lot of money. Hulu and others have done well with their payment programs, but micro is where you get right down to just one selection at a time for a premium price. And that's going to have long-term impact.

On live sports being digital's last great audience draw:

The pricing for live sports, unlike any other content, will continue to rise because it captures an engaged audience in an otherwise fragmented digital world. Advertisers would still rather go where they know they will be seen. Live sports consistently offers the only really big mass audience on television, which provided the perfect display with big, beautiful smart screens.

With Magna Global and other ad agencies predicting that the digital revenues are going to equal the television revenues in 2016, advertisers clearly are learning to spend their money on digital advertising with a completely different set of metrics and objectives. They all expect to get something special out of digital. They also expect to pay almost nothing for digital, like they have been doing, which will never again be the case. It's like going into a tapas bar instead of a full-plate restaurant, and some advertisers just want to gorge themselves. It remains to be seen how satisfactory that meal is going to be.

On the transforming effect of the sharing economy and big data:

Two trends are catching everybody's attention. One is the sharing economy that is represented by Uber and Airbnb. The other one is big data, or analyzing and harnessing vast sets of information in novel ways to produce valuable insights. How will those two trends impact media? Big data will break down the walls that right now slow down technical and scientific development. Big data is like a supertanker of information versus the smaller fishing boats.

An example in media: Fox News is going after the so-called 28 percent—the people who continually voted for George Bush. That's a big audience in the United States, and they don't mince words about the fact that they feed that audience and they honor that audience's interests. They keep at it. No one else has done it as well. There's an audience out there for that kind of material, and they've always been able to pull that audience in.

On a going-forward basis, everything is going to be available in a micro form, and that includes news and information of all kinds that will blur together. The downside of that is it gives you soundbites instead of education. And you leave the door open to ISIS and militant groups with a singularly destructive message. At some point people are going to have to start to recognize real credibility and judge it in some kind of a context.

You're going to have silos of people who really believe certain things and they only want to hear about that. That is exactly what the Internet does best—gives you slices of what you want and allows you to skip over what maybe you need—and that's a dangerous thing. We're almost going back to the Middle Ages.

On the future of local television:

Traditional print newspapers have to go away at some point, which means that digital news will take over. And that means an informed public becomes even more selective about what they know and don't know. They don't just happen on stories about things they never expected to read or advertisements they never expected to see the way you do thumbing through a newspaper. The local town crier has been relegated to Facebook or Twitter.

That's why local television has a much brighter future in news than it understands. And if I was there 5 or 6 years ago, or yesterday or tomorrow, I would be screaming this. *Local television news programming is too superficial.* A house burns down; they show pictures of the police and firemen and everybody says, "Oh, my Lord!" And then a politician comes on and says, "We have to really understand whether the codes we have are any good." But local news never gives us any of the pertinent follow-up details: Who owns the house? Have they been cited for violations before? Here's a picture of him: where he works, where he frequents, what else he owns. And the reason that's valuable is because that's where people are going with social media.

Somebody in local news has got to wake up!

Traditional broadcast television is losing viewers; they don't need more motivation than that. News is one area they control, and they can turn it into a thriving business if they can start being smarter about it by following up on things and not just offering pictures of events with no rational explanation. The fact is that nearly any television news story could be more thoroughly investigated, and it doesn't require a team of people.

People know what it is today to get on the Internet or social media and flush out information, so they expect more from the arbiters of news. They expect you to get in there and make the story come alive with deep facts and insight. But that rarely occurs. A perfect example is when a child goes missing. News organizations are in a position to build a pervasive social media campaign, to flush out more helpful information, to be proactive with the community. You can get third parties involved. When you start doing that, people are going to be much more interested in the newscasts.

So what's the answer? Restructuring the time, the newscast, the dynamics. You've got to have a mindset that says, OK, that's what we're going to do. We're going to take 20 minutes out of a

30-minute block and do just a couple of stories like that. You have plenty of time. Twenty years ago, Roger Ogden turned KNBC (Denver) into all news for 20 hours a day and won the local ratings. You'll dig down deeper because, heck, they can get the headlines anywhere. Then you'll figure out what the limitations are and work around them. Right now, broadcast television doesn't have a mindset for that.

You've got all this great emerging technology to use in developing this approach to micronews. It could be a really big business if you don't leave it all to social media.

On Google and Facebook as advertising and marketing destinations:

Google and Facebook have become major marketing and sales destinations now. It's incredible. They are like the three networks were in the 60s and the 70s. Marketing is getting awareness out to your brand and your products in general, and selling is selling a product. And they are able to do both. Google can show brand and product, and Facebook pages are full of brand, of marketing trying to get you to understand the brand. What's even more remarkable is that they have become marketing and sales destinations for corporations and businesses. They are now staples, and it took them only 3 to 4 years to get there. It took newspapers and television and radio forever to do that. So that's a huge achievement in terms of changing the media landscape.

The question is how broad a platform will Facebook become— how much content, communications, and commerce? And what will that mean to existing platforms?

On television as a device:

Television is going to be incredibly successful going forward, but it's more about engineering than creative content. It's a piece of equipment. It's this big, beautiful screen in all different sizes for your home, your office, whatever. And it's a conduit for everything. That's the television I'm talking about—a big, smart, beautiful screen that automatically connects to all other devices. That's why the NFL ads are so expensive, because people are seeing that new Mercedes on a 70-inch screen, and it looks gorgeous. And then they go to Facebook or Google or some other place to follow up on it and they do it on that same screen.

So the television set is now a primary screen for all kinds of interactive content and communications with unbelievable reception and video quality. These are smart devices designed to plug and play faster and cheaper, making the television a unique wireless smart screen and alternative to your smartphone, laptop, and tablet. With that as a new baseline, people will be watching more "television" than ever without distinguishing between cable and broadcast, streaming Netflix, or YouTube.

That means content producers will have to be smart about making their programs stand out. And they'll probably have to use every means possible to make them available. All the barriers to entry are coming down. The licensing and regulation that governed broadcast and cable television and satellite will become more irrelevant.

With universal access assured, the biggest concern will be how content and service providers are compensated for their costs. There are more ways to charge but no acceptable template for how much and when. So you need to have very good businesspeople making the decisions about how to compensate for every kind of access and exposure and use possible. There's no single answer. Success will be about business skill as much as creativity.

On wearable technology:

Where the television screen pulls together everything big, wearable technology takes you inside everything small. It's all about what you are thinking and feeling and buying and doing—all the minute information about your health and preferences, with incredible accuracy. It's a small screen with deep tentacles and endless opportunities, and it will happen faster as the device manufacturers perfect it. And we are going to be the big beneficiaries.

I gave up my beloved BlackBerry in 2008 and went to the iPhone. I was one of the reluctant ones. BlackBerry killed itself because it wouldn't change. I could see that video was taking off. Now it's all about microdata, and for the longest time BlackBerry would have none of it. It had a loyal and large consumer base willing to wait. That mistake will never happen again.

This is the black swan phenomenon: your greatest opportunity is going to occur in response to your greatest problem, and you never know when that will be. But you do have to be ready to respond to it quickly and effectively. Wearable technology will be like that for a lot of companies.

Smaller wearable technology and the giant television screens will be completely compatible as they connect to everything in the future. There will be plenty of people making product and slicing up product for that, and the more micro they think, the more successful they will be. Old-fashioned marketers are into wearable technology. Heinz Ketchup's bottle now has "wear ads" for other companies' products. More ads than Heinz info! Newman's will soon be "wearing" ads for others as well!

On continued media mergers and acquisitions:

Mergers and acquisitions in media, entertainment, and information will center on generating and the use of data and cloud streaming to forge new business models. That means some of the companies that rule this space today are more relics of the past than pioneers. Their content and services will need to be converted. And the next generation of leadership will have to take them there, although not necessarily by merging with or acquiring social media or tech companies. The cultures, economics, and expectations are too different.

So some of the traditional media giants might not all make it into the future in their current state; that means Viacom and CBS, Time Warner, even News Corp. When older owners pass on, like Sumner Redstone especially, their companies will go through a period of sorting out assets, even in court, so there may be a period of more selling than buying. Like CBS and Viacom, Fox stock is controlled by a family estate, which means these companies could be tied up in litigation after their chairmen leave the stage. It's not clear who is in charge and how they will survive. At least one of the major media companies will be busted up in some way.

The NBC Universal I built translated very well to the Internet compared to some of the cable-only properties, some of which are now being dashed on the rocks by streaming content and services. It takes some time for these things to shake out, and you have to be paying attention and making alternative plans every step of the way. NBCU has a wonderful array of content it creates and distributes wherever it can. Its library of material is vast. So it is going to feed on the Internet situation one way or the other.

Disney is another company that's got it. Bob Iger has done a great job! Disney is one of the few companies that doesn't have to do much differently and it will continue to succeed. They are too big for anyone to buy and they will continue to acquire select assets. Disney has been very good at that. But Disney is clearly the exception. The future is as uncertain as it is promising for most of its media peers.

One company that I think will continue to expand is Discovery Communications. David Zaslav is one of the media CEOs that we have to pay attention to. Discovery is more likely to be an acquirer than it is to be acquired, in my opinion, because of its size, its capability, and its economic ability. There aren't many media companies big enough to acquire Discovery, which might choose instead to expand by merging with a company like Scripps or any one of half a dozen other companies inside and outside the US. Zaslav's also been very smart about putting his hand to the ground in Europe by purchasing the European television rights to the Olympic Games. That was a big step for him. David may take on strategic partners like John Malone, who remains very involved in those kinds of deals.

John Malone is going to be around for a while, engineering more strategic deals and continuing to be a force. He has people working with him who will continue his legacy of investing. Holding companies like his Liberty Media don't usually survive as easily as single-product companies. Without John Malone there, I don't know what Liberty would do. It has huge assets and it can easily sell some down.

On the generational leadership change in big media:

Every media company faces a different fate based on what the old guard has done—or not. Viacom has not had much influence in the business of media for at least 5 years, and its chairman, Sumner Redstone, has been out of the daily operations. The real strength lies in CBS and the MTV crowd. The Viacom and CBS pieces likely will be acquired but not before they become entangled in some Herculean situation that Redstone has created. It will be left up to his estate.

Comcast founder Ralph Roberts just died at age 93. The company lost a huge opportunity by not being able to close its acquisition of Time Warner Cable, which would have given it valuable digital Internet Wi-Fi connection for data and video. That's hurtful for them. They are probably the most advanced company technically of all the media operators, although Cablevision Systems is a close second. What happens there will be up to Jimmy Dolan, Chuck's son.

John Malone could have his eye on Cablevision, but he has to be increasing his risk against Verizon just trying to hold on to that cable connection. If I were John Malone, I'd be saying, "Why not? I mean, I want all that digital, and Cablevision has a very good distribution of data."

Rupert Murdoch has turned over operating management of News Corp. to his son, James. It happens that Lachlan, Rupert's other son, will not be part of the decision making regarding what happens to the company and its parts.

The real question is whether conventional media and entertainment companies under the next generation of leaders will take a leap of faith and cross the line by reinventing themselves through mergers and acquisitions with completely different companies. Technology will be the driver, allowing them to do things with content and services they never have before. But how quickly will these players adapt? Staying in their comfort zones will become as risky as experimenting.

Nothing happens in isolation anymore. Information and entertainment are integrated with communication, education, and every form of discovery. This will lead to new forms of productivity and enlightenment. That will lead to new companies, new industries, and new opportunities for existing companies. This is unlike any time in my lifetime. The early days of the Internet were disastrous for many companies because either the marketplace wasn't ready or technology wasn't advanced or affordable enough and legacy companies were not receptive. NBC experienced that with Snap.com and NBCi. All of that has now changed.

On messaging:

There's no question Facebook and Google have changed everything. One of the most meaningful future trends will be how companies and individuals learn to use messaging in more productive ways. Messaging and sharing represent the future both in technology and in products. Because messaging is now a globally accepted technology, the idea of short-verse messaging or texting like Twitter could become a communications backbone. But there are pros and cons to that.

It's going to have an enormous economic impact on the cost because it's cheaper and quicker to message than it is to do other forms of communication. E-mail will not be a thing of the past, but it will become yesterday's communications tool with the universal growth of smartphones. It will be looked at the same as the PC and Outlook, which is the Ice Age. It's just a matter of how easily or cheaply it can be done. That kind of change used to be a generational or institutional issue, but new uses of technology are being adapted so much faster now everywhere in the world—sometimes out of necessity.

Sharing is another huge opportunity. It is a way to break down and make use of large amounts of data. Sharing plans allow you to selectively send data and other material so that we are not being overwhelmed by everything out there. It helps people to focus on what is relevant or important in their lives. And it can be done automatically by Google if I can write my own personal merger to do that. That technology will be perfected to simplify things and make more efficient use of our time and resources, to uncomplicated things, because right now we are all treading a tidal wave of photos and information of our own making.

If I could advise a younger person who wanted to get into the business, I would tell them to get involved in the lower end of the scale and even fish around the bottom of sharing and messaging for opportunities, because those two areas are going to explode. Google and Facebook have a huge head start, but there are always black swans, and by their very nature, you can't predict them, but they are powerful forces for change. It can be a call for help, a crusade, a way to rally people and incite action, start a movement or a war.

Consider that social messaging is the core of ISIS and the way people respond to spontaneous events through Twitter.

On net neutrality and the onset of streaming video:

Net neutrality is a terrible term because it has no natural meaning, but it will continue to be evoked by anyone who thinks all things are equal on the web or that they can put the Internet back into Pandora's Box. The reality is that there should be no regulation of the web as it relates to speed and function. The notion that Internet service providers should enable access to all content and applications regardless of source, without favoring or blocking particular products or websites, is unreasonable. Not everything on the web is created equal. But net neutrality is not something we should be engaged in whatsoever.

Broadband isn't really a utility, but if it was a utility, people would be pricing based on usage—which is what net neutrality advocates don't want. Pricing based on usage—and covering the cost to provide service—is the only reasonable and fair thing to do. And if you want faster service or more storage space, you pay for it. The services that are hogging bandwidth have to pay for it. Many of the new services and uses require extraordinary amounts of broadband, and whatever consumers or companies want, they will pay for. Somebody has to pay.

This is what makes net neutrality extremely awkward. Pricing is embedded in tying the Internet to Title II, which is the regulation of a utility. What's confusing is that the system that they have now allows the content seller to negotiate with the carrier to get preferred treatment, which filters into the subscription fee passed on to the consumer.

Netflix hogs a lot of bandwidth, so video is the killer. But changes in the law would keep that from happening, in which case the distributors will find new ways to charge the users when they order content and services that require more bandwidth. If the consumers want Netflix, under the Federal Communications Commission's proposed rule change, they will now have to upgrade. This is a very traditional model—which wouldn't be any big step forward.

The whole issue of antitrust violation also has to be worked out over time. You regulate companies after a period where you've seen a number of violations, and then you make a decision. It's premature in my opinion to be doing what the FCC is trying to do here, which is to create a template of circumstances and practices. That's not going to be helpful to anybody, because technology is changing and moving the bar, and consumers and companies keep adapting in new ways. This, of course, falls right into the net neutrality game.

Apple is still a walled garden, right? It thinks it can continue to manage everything like it has. ESPN has been a commanding franchisee, and it suddenly faces the prospect of being minimized by consumers slicing and dicing what they want. Over-the-top economics are changing everything, even for institutions like ESPN that have thrived.

On how mobile digital technology and social media will change advertising:

Another force on the horizon that represents the next generation of media is Facebook. It's also in the communications business with Messenger, and they are a major distributor of advertising like you wouldn't believe. Facebook has become a landing spot for all kinds of advertisers. To a lesser extent, there is Twitter. Twitter's management doesn't seem to be anywhere near as capable as Facebook's. The real story is how Twitter can have so much promise worldwide and be such a unique service yet have limited prospects because of poor management and a poor board of directors. Twitter's problems are technical in nature. They just have to come up with a game plan and then execute on it. When Facebook went public, they made a statement. They were going to make a big effort to get into mobile advertising, and a lot of people were skeptical that they could do that—and I was one of them. And I didn't buy the stock on that basis.

Mobile advertising is very complex and it requires a lot of tech. So when Mark Zuckerberg declared that the next big thing for Facebook would be mobile advertising more than 3 years ago, he faced a lot of skeptics. There was no reason to think they could do it, but they have absolutely done it! They hired the right people, they bought the right business, and they merged it in. They've developed stuff that I don't think anyone else can do the same way because of the Facebook platform. The stock has shot up so high because the people on Wall Street who follow them really respect what they've done. And Facebook flew right by GE's market cap in mid-2015. That's the difference a driven vision makes. The same with Netflix. Reed Hastings didn't hesitate to change course at the first inkling that his mail-in, download movie business was being compromised by streaming.

There is a lot of pressure for advertisers to feel that they're getting a lot more productivity out of every viewing of an advertisement for their product or service. They want the full benefit of digital distribution and viewing at a time when there was never more immediate accountability and response, whether it is the consumer posting something or pressing the "buy" button or clicking on to something they have seen. But that no longer is a mass response; it is all about the individual and the most finite demographic. So while the connection is stronger and more specific, the penetration may not be as great overall. That is a big change for mass-market advertisers.

Media's historical groupings of demographics, whether they are old or young, were always designed around relatively large groups of viewers. The advertising focus on digital is really targeting thousands. That kind of tighter targeting means dealing with smaller, more desirable groups. Then it becomes a question of whether you can make it limiting yourself or whether your product has more width than just one demo.

So it's going to be a struggle. There's no question that there's going to be a lot of pressure on traditional TV and revenues. There's going to be a lot of growth in video data files (VDF) and digital media. But there's also going to be a lot of sorting out as to what real productivity can be achieved, how expensive it is, and whether enough people are seeing your product and learning about it. That's one of the benefits of linear television, and it's one of the difficulties of digital. A lot of exposure in linear, and very tight exposure in digital, and they're both important.

On the digital opportunities advertisers are missing:

We are moving into a world of wireless video communication. And essentially what that means, without trying to be simplistic, is that we will be using Wi-Fi in the future for our video communications. And it will not be cellular. Cellular may stick, because Wi-Fi cannot handle audio as well, but right now, it is comparatively more expensive because of the use of relay towers. We should be able to use all our other electronic devices without having to go through a phone. So smartphones will use a Wi-Fi signal, make calls, and watch video. So there will be a natural integration of cellular and Wi-Fi.

The winners of this are still going to be the same people: the cable operators who have all of the data and all of the Internet connections. Verizon has been trying for FiOS in order to get an Internet connection into the house. The hope here for a cable company today is much less in cable television, where the growth has been historically. Future economics favor the data connection and the embedded Internet capability that comes with the video. And so does telephone. We used to call it the triple play.

That dynamic has already prompted major changes in content companies. HBO in the early days, 10 to 15 years ago, was the largest purchaser of film licenses. Not anymore. Today they produce a lot of their own content and do a lot of other things and basically said to the film companies, "You know, we'll take your stuff, but it's not worth that much to us. Our viewers really are interested in our special shows that we produce." Like Netflix, HBO has been very successful making that shift with its 30 million household base. They both know how to produce original programs for this era of new consumption: edgy and tailored to specific tastes. Netflix has been going around paying a lot of money for the rights to television programs all over the country. And if the television program's a hit, they pay a lot of money to put it on Netflix. And now others like Amazon are following suit.

All content producers have to be careful about defining what the lifespan of their programs is designed to be. Where do we get our money back and where do we get our profitability from— streaming or video on demand (VOD)? It's really a question for large and smaller companies alike. How many content producers are selling instead, from the outset, to Amazon Prime or to Netflix? And then there is the afterlife of some shows on the Internet just like it used to be in television syndication. At this stage, you really have to do a lot of experimentation to find out the answers.

Because of the streaming options that let consumers select specific content when they want it, the general cable program channels like TBS or TNT are not as powerful as they once were. That is why Time Warner will continue downsizing and spinning off its assets. CEO Jeff Bewkes has done a great job in breaking up the company and selling it piece by piece. Time Warner today is three different companies. They are mature businesses running at, maybe, a collective 20-times multiple. One is the old Turner Cable properties that are seen on TBS and TNT; another is HBO, which has all kinds of issues if they are trying to turn it into Netflix; and the third is Warner Brothers Studios for television and film.

On the hacking and compromise of media and entertainment companies:

Hacking is the one thing I see that I think could stop the whole boat or really slow it down. It has the potential to wreak havoc and disrupt everything. And because everything is connected, taking down an information platform or a power grid will have a lot of ugly implications. It's not that difficult to do, and there's not that much stopping hackers now. It is a huge risk globally.

From a media standpoint, it is a scare tactic that will obviously impact how companies cover the news and go about their business. It was devastating for Sony Entertainment to have its e-mails hacked and *The Interview* film premiere plans spoiled. But things will likely get a lot worse in ways we can't even imagine.

None of the leading news organizations was willing to show the defiant front page of the satirical French publication *Charlie Hebdo* with an image of Mohammed following the murderous attacks on its Paris staff in early 2015. But it sold 3 million copies worldwide. That is worse than intimidation or manipulation. That represents a new standard of response in a new world. This is not a new phenomenon for media, which has always been under attack and has had to be concerned about reprisals.

The nature of the Internet and social media makes freedom of speech and terrorism different issues from what they were in the past.

In general, people seem to be getting numb about hacking and cyber security and the lack of protection. All it would take is a major breakdown of power and light utilities that would cause shock waves. And that would create lots of governmental regulations on the internet. And it probably would be overdone. It will take a widespread utility breech to rattle people's cages. Because when the lights go out it will be different.

On retooling Twitter, Yahoo, and Viacom:

The retooling of media companies everywhere on the spectrum is underway. And it's going to get ugly.

It is unrealistic for a board to hire a CEO for a $20 bill company like Twitter when that same person, Jack Dorsey, already is the CEO of another company, Square, which is seeking an IPO. Twitter needs so much engineering and marketing help, the last thing it needs is a part-time CEO. A lot of potential already has been lost and Twitter stock is selling 45 percent below its IPO level. I just don't think it sends the right signal to the market.

Yahoo has been a tracking stock for Alibaba during the term of its CEO Marissa Mayer, and she's made millions and millions of dollars as a result. She spent millions of dollars on things that haven't panned out or had any value. If the Alibaba stake had been spun off as originally planned, it probably would have been time for her to leave. Either way, Yahoo faces the prospect of being sold to private equity or merged with another strategic company.

It would be a great opportunity to put someone like Tim Armstrong and his team in charge. He has been a market builder from his days at Google and now AOL, although I'm not sure that would be possible with its $4.4 billion acquisition by Verizon. But that's the kind of bottom-up, operating and sales leadership Yahoo needs. That's the heavy toll years of failed leadership will take on a company.

Viacom suffers from too many very low-rated channels that probably receive too much money from cable operators and other carriers. These negotiated payments might well exceed the values of the programs, which in some cases are being pushed off of systems. They got caught in the gears of competitive and economic change.

A company like Viacom has milked the cow too many times. They took too much money out paying top executives on the basis of a P/E under pressure. Now, companies like Viacom have to work very hard to reestablish their value in the sales and carriage industry. Otherwise I see that as a fast breakup after the passing of Viacom's ailing Chairman CEO Sumner Redstone.

On Comcast streaming:

Comcast and other traditional linear media companies are going to cover as much streaming video ground as they can with cable ratings declining 10 percent every month and Netflix accounting for 37 percent of primetime broadband usage. Don't count them out. They are producing tremendous amounts of content, most of which has value somewhere. Their program libraries can be endlessly monetized. They will learn to play both the linear and digital fields, and my sense is they will be just fine. That includes ESPN, which has shocked the world with its new vulnerability. In fact its costly rights contracts, talent, and production just need to be realigned for the realities of a streaming world. It's still one of the most valuable brands around.

On the Rentrak-ComScore merger and user measurement:

This is a hold-on game.

Nielsen has the history and companies continue to rely on its measurement reports—archaic as they seem—to charge exorbitant prices for their consumer connections and attention.

The smaller companies like Rentrak Corp. with good new measurement ideas don't have much capital to execute. It's been that way for 30 years. So consolidation among players in this space is inevitable.

The fundamental difficulty in the nature of getting better measurements is intrusion and most people don't like it. This is even in an age in which our interactive devices are intuitive and unobtrusive about collecting, processing, and utilizing our personal information about choice and preference. The measurement companies still have to get you to wear something or say something or do something to get better results. That effort has been tried and hasn't panned out.

It's not the technology as much as the implementation of the technology that requires a lot of human cooperation. Those kinds of privacy issues don't sit well with people. In the 1980s, TV viewers in a 13-channel universe completed handwritten diaries to record their media use. Today, Google knows everything about you with every keystroke. The same people object to being involved with more interactive measurement devise give away all their personal information buying things on the web.

Today's streaming media may seem automatic and always-on, but it poses the same interface issues. The user must be engaged. The end game is who's watching.

Some Deal Hits, Some Misses

I orchestrated a record number of mergers and acquisitions during my 21-year tenure at NBC. But for every successful deal my executive team and I negotiated, deals that helped transform the network, there were as many failed efforts. They would have further reshaped NBC but died due to complications from circumstance and ego.

One case in point: In 1999 I met with Edgar Bronfman Jr., whose family business, the Seagram Company, then owned Universal, and together we hammered out a plan to merge NBC with Universal. We even had the support of the contentious Barry Diller, who became a director of the Seagram board after assuming controlling interest in their shared USA Networks Inc. In the end, family patriarch Edgar Bronfman Sr. decided not to relinquish control.

It turned out that 1999 was an active year for aborted big deals. That spring, NBC came close to merging with Sony Pictures Entertainment, but in the end accounting issues and negative tax consequences got in the way.

Chancellor Media Corp., a Dallas-based radio and outdoor advertising concern, aborted its $900 million acquisition of LIN Television Corp., in which NBC was minority partner with the

Dallas buyout firm Hicks, Muse, Tate & Furst. It would have been a way to recover hundreds of millions NBC invested in various television and radio station partnerships with Hurst, which was a 12 percent owner of Chancellor.

You can't always anticipate such opportunities; you simply have to be ready to act. You also have to recognize that you might not be able to do anything with those opportunities, and you can't just shoot yourself. In business, you can calculate probabilities about the value you hope to create. But you really don't know when you are buying something if it is going to be worth three times more in 4 years or one time less. It's always an educated risk.

Hits

- Negotiated a 65-year lease extension on a dozen floors of the 30 Rock building at Rockefeller Center, crowned by NBC's iconic peacock logo. New York City dispensation for low-interest financing and tax breaks to renovate its midtown Manhattan facilities secured the NBC/GE deal and rendered the Big Apple's first street-side TV studio.

- Launched CNBC (Consumer News and Business Channel) in 1988. Chuck Dolan's Cablevision Systems became a short-lived 50 percent equity partner in April 1989. NBC acquired the resources and affiliates of bankrupt Financial News Network for $154 million in 1991 to fortify CNBC on the Tempo TV cable platform it bought for $21 million from John Malone's Tele-Communications Inc.

- Acquired a 50 percent equity stake in Rainbow Programming Services in 1989 from Chuck Dolan and Cablevision Systems (including regional sports channels, AMC, and Bravo). (Assisted by Tom Rogers.)

- Bought WTVJ, Channel 6 in Miami, for $270 million from Wometco Broadcasting Co. in 1989. The first broadcast network purchase of a rival's affiliated station.

- Acquired 76 percent of SuperChannel as an international platform for CNBC in 1993. (Assisted by Tom Rogers.)

- Sold 49 percent stake in Court TV in 1994–95.

- Acquired TV stations in San Diego, Birmingham, Dallas, and Denver from Ronald Perlman in 1996. (Assisted by Warren Jenson.)

- Acquired 25 percent of AMC for $13 million.

- Acquired Outlet Communications TV stations in Hartford (CT), Providence (RI), Columbus (OH), and Charlotte and Raleigh (NC) for $311 million in 1996. (Assisted by Warren Jenson.)

- Launched MSNBC cable and online in 50/50 venture with Microsoft Corp. in 1998. (Assisted by Tom Rogers, David Zaslav and Andy Lack.) NBCU bought out Microsoft's interests in two phases for about $1 billion.

- Acquired 32 percent stake in Paxson Communications for $415 million in 1999 and full control of the 60-station broadcaster in 2006, rebranding it the ION Network. (Assisted by Brandon Burgess.)

- Acquired 76 percent ownership of WXAS Dallas and KNSD San Diego in joint venture with LIN Broadcasting 1999. (Assisted by Warren Jensen.)

- Acquired KNTV from Granite Broadcasting for $250 million, converting it to NBC's San Francisco area–owned affiliate in 2001. It replaced powerhouse KRON-TV over a compensation dispute with Young Broadcasting. The upset changed network-affiliate station economics. (Assisted by Randy Falco.)

- Acquired Telemundo for $2.7 billion equity and debt in 2001 in a deal I negotiated myself. Acquired Bravo from Cablevision Systems for $1.25 billion in a tax-efficient cash-out of NBC's 25 percent interest in their Rainbow Partnership with Chuck Dolan's Cablevision in 2002 in another deal I negotiated myself.

- Acquired 80 percent of Universal from Vivendi in 2004 for $14 billion. Acquired Vivendi's minority stake in 2005. (GE/ NBC sold 51 percent of the company to Comcast in 2011 for $13.8 billion. Assets included Universal Studios, theme parks, USA, and SyFy cable channels, and Universal TV.) (Assisted by Brandon Burgess.)

- Created NBCU Internet, Inc. (NBCi) in 1999 as a publicly traded umbrella portfolio for NBC's online acquisitions and ventures. Its value fluctuated from $2.8 billion to $0 when the Internet bubble burst. It was disbanded by 2001.

- Acquired iVillage for $600 million in 2006.

- Launched Hulu partnership with News Corp. in 2007 to stream network programs.

Misses (the ones that got away)

- Declined initial stream of early offers in 1986–1987 as GE digested RCA and NBC. NBC refused a 20 percent stake in Discovery Communications and buying the satellite programming assets of Warner Amex Satellite Entertainment (including MTV, Nickelodeon, and Showtime) for roughly $500 million. The joint venture between Warner Communications and American Express eventually went to Viacom. NBC also could have acquired Viacom from

CEO Terry Elkes, who eventually sold out to Sumner Redstone.

- Offered $400 million cash for 25 percent of Turner Broadcasting System and its CNN service in 1987, which was rejected by the major cable operators, who assumed majority control after rescuing the company from debt after spending $1.4 billion to acquire MGM in 1986.

- Announced but never launched the $1 billion SkyCable satellite programming equity partnership of NBC, Cablevision Systems, News Corp., and John Malone (contributing program channels and funds) and General Motors' Hughes Communications satellite (contributing satellites and debt financing). After outlining the 108-channel service to areas without cable at New York's St. Regis Hotel February 21, 1990, overleveraged media companies pulled out in response to financial pressures from 1991 recession and bank covenants.

- Jack Welch spent a fair amount of time as GE chairman entertaining many would-be suitors for NBC, including Marty Davis of Gulf and Western in 1992; comedian Bill Cosby and former CBS-TV/TBS executive Robert Wussler in 1993; Walt Disney's Michael Eisner in 1994; and investors Marvin Davis (who bought and flipped Twentieth Century Fox to Rupert Murdoch in 1985). Ted Turner made several runs at NBC.

- Failed to acquire an interest in DirecTV with Cablevision System and John Malone in 1993. Tom Rogers considered this his biggest deal disappointment. It would have been about a $40 million investment in what has morphed into a $40 billion business.

- In the early 1990s, NBC considered acquiring Paramount and making a joint bid with Chuck Dolan's Cablevision

Systems for Madison Square Garden and Radio City Music Hall. Jack Welch nixed the deals, fearing they would further highlight GE's already controversial media involvement.

- Jack Welch unraveled NBC's signed and sealed acquisition of the Golf Channel in 1996 for $150 million while I was in Scotland on holiday with Johnny Carson. Jack was concerned that his critics already thought he spent too much time negotiating deals on the links, would further associate him with golf. A decade later Comcast paid close to $1 billion for the Golf Channel, which it brought into the fold when it acquired NBC Universal in 2011.

- Prolonged negotiations with Hicks, Muse, Tate & Furst for broadcast joint venture collapsed in 1999 over concerns about the management, emerging Internet and NBC's fluctuating fortunes.

- Declined an offer from Thomas Middelhoff to acquire Bertlesmann's music and publishing businesses, which were scooped up instead by Sony.

- Proposed $3 billion buyout of Turner Broadcasting System and its CNN service was squashed by Jack Welch after a testy meeting in Atlanta with Ted Turner in 1995. NBC's offer ($22 a share) fell short of Turner's asking price ($30 a share), and Welch feared Turner's chaotic presence on the GE board.

- Could have acquired USA Network and Sci-Fi channel from Paramount/Time Inc. in 1999.

- Could have merged NBC with Sony Pictures Entertainment in 1999 were it not for thorny accounting and tax issues.

- Could have merged NBC with Seagram-owned Universal in 1999.

- Failed to attract Dow Jones as partner in CNBC, which put the publishing company on track to be sold to Rupert Murdoch's News Corp.

- Considered acquiring MGM in 2000 but reluctant to own a movie studio, especially one with a tired film library and low television production involvement.

- Tried unsuccessfully to acquire the remainder of Court TV from its equity partners, John Malone's Liberty Media and Time Warner 1998.

- Considered acquiring a stake in or all of AOL Time Warner in 2002 but GE didn't want to finance an unwanted takeover.

- In 2003 bid $12 a share (below the $20 a share asking price) for Time Warner, which wanted to avoid paying hefty retransmission fees to networks. Deal fell apart over price and not knowing how to value AOL.

- Failed to swap investments that would have resulted in an ownership stake in National Geographic Channel in 2006.

- Failed to acquire DreamWorks in 2006. GE chairman Jeff Immelt likewise sabotaged the deal shortly after the NBC Universal merger, having already heavily waded into media. DreamWorks SKG live action studio eventually sold to Viacom.

- Considered Universal theme parks spinoff with backing from The Blackstone Group, a major private equity investor.

Where Are They Now?

Many of the people who played a role in realizing my vision for NBC now head their own major media enterprises, where they embrace and leverage my core leadership principles.

Al Barber Was: *first president CNBC 1990–1994; CFO NBC 1987–1990 following 27 years at GE; COO and later president CEO of e-media streaming services firm;* Now: *president, COO Catholic Charities in Fairfield, CT 2004–present.*

Mark Begor Was: *executive VP and CFO of business development NBCU 1998–2002 following 18 years at GE;* Now: *CEO GE Energy Management 2011–present.*

Bill Bolster Was: *chairman CEO CNBC International 2001–2004; president CNBC 1996–2001; president GM WNBC-TV NYC 1991–1996;* Now: *retired.*

Tom Brokaw Was: *anchor and managing editor* NBC Nightly News *2004–1983;* Now: *author and special correspondent NBC News 2004–present.*

Don Browne Was: *president Telemundo Communications Group, Hispanic TV 2005–2011; joined Telemundo (American Spanish-language network) in 2003; bureau chief, president and general manager of WTVJ 2003–1979; VP NBC News in 1991;* Now: *retired.*

Brandon Burgess Was: *executive VP NBC/NBCU Global Strategy and Digital Media 2002–2005; NBC CFO 1999–2001; VP NBC*

Business Development 1989–1999; Now: *chairman CEO Ion Media Networks 2005–present. Ion is an American broadcast, cable, satellite, and digital TV network rebranded from Paxson Communications in 2007.*

Lynn Calpeter Was: *CFO NBC Television Stations 1999–2001;* Now: *VP and CFO GE Power & Water 2012–present.*

Rick Cotton Was: *executive VP and general counsellor NBC/NBCU 1989–2013; president and managing director CNBC Europe 2001–2004;* Now: *senior counsel IP Protection at NBCU Inc. 2013–present.*

Dick Ebersol Was: *president and then chairman NBC Sports 1989–2012;* Now: *senior advisor for NBCU Sports and Olympics.*

John Eck Was: *president Media Works and NBC Television Network at NBCU 2005–2011; CIO NBC 2005; senior VP, CQO, and CFO for NBC International and Business Development, structured MSNBC partnership after joining NBC in 1993 as VP Financial Planning and Analysis;* Now: *executive VP and COO Univision Communications 2011–present.*

Randy Falco Was: *president NBC Broadcast and Network Operations 1993–1998; group president NBC Television Network 1998–2003; president NBC Television Network 2003–2004; president NBC Universal Television Networks 2004–2006; ran NBC Olympics operations 1992–2006; negotiated first reverse affiliate compensation deal with Granite Broadcasting; chairman CEO AOL Inc. 2006–2009;* Now: *president CEO Univision 2011–present (Univision is a leading Spanish-language media company with 16 broadcast, cable, and digital networks, 61 TV stations, and 67 radio stations).*

Jay Ireland Was: *president NBC TV Stations and Network Operations (including NBC's 10 stations and Telemundo's 16 Spanish-speaking stations until 2007 after beginning at GE in 1980);* Now: *president CEO GE Africa in Nairobi, Kenya, 2011–present.*

Warren Jenson Was: *CFO NBC 1992–1998; CFO Delta 1998–1999, CFO Amazon 1999–2002, Electronic Arts 2002–2008; CFO Silver*

Spring Networks, smart grid tech startup, 2008–2011; president Jenson & Co. Consulting 2011; Now: *CFO and head of technical operations Acxiom 2012–present (Acxiom is an enterprise data, analytics, and software service company).*

Andy Lack Was: *president NBC News 1993–2001 after 7 years as executive producer CBS Reports; president COO NBCU 2004; CEO Sony Music Entertainment 2004–2006; CEO Bloomberg Media Group 2008–2013;* Now: *chairman NBC News and MSNBC 2015–present.*

Warren Littlefield Was: *president NBC Entertainment 1998–1991 (protégé Brandon Tartikoff);* Now: *president The Littlefield Co. 1998–present.*

Vince Manze Was: *president creative director NBCU Agency 1991–2007; president NBCU Creative Services 2009–2010;* Now: *CEO creative director Invincible Marketing 2010–present.*

Pierson Mapes Was: *president NBC Television Network 1982–1994; director Pico Productions 1994;* Now: *retired.*

John Miller Was: *executive VP NBC Advertising and Promotion 1993–1999; chairman NBC Agency (first full-service in-house agency) 1999–2010; chief marketing officer NBCU Television Group 2004–2011; chairman NBC Universal Marketing Council (across all divisions);* Now: *chief marketing officer NBC Sports Group 2011–present.*

Lorne Michaels Was and Now: *producer, creator* Saturday Night Live *1975–present.*

Conan O'Brien Was: *late-night talk show host NBC 1993–2009 (after comedy writing and producing for* Saturday Night Live *and* The Simpsons*); host NBC* The Tonight Show *2009–2010;* Now: *host of* Conan *on* TBS *2010–present while doing live comedy tours and TV specials.*

Roger Ogden Was: *president and managing director NBC Europe 1995–1997; general manager and news director KUSA-TV in Denver* *from 1997–2005; senior VP Gannett Broadcasting 1997 after a 17-year career with NBC; president and CEO Gannett Broadcasting 2005–2007; senior VP of Design Innovation and Strategy of Gannett Co. Inc. June 2006–July 2007 (Gannett is an international news and information company);* Now: *retired.*

Don Ohlmeyer Was: *president NBC, West Coast Division 1993–1999;* Now: *professor of television communications Pepperdine University.*

Bob Okun Was: *VP government relations NBC/NBCU Washington 1995–2011;* Now: *CEO The O Team (independent lobbyist group in Washington, DC) 2011–present; also represents Autism Speaks Washington lobbying efforts.*

Bob O'Leary Was: *VP finance Cox Cable Communications 1982-1999; executive VP and CFO Cox Enterprises until 2007;* Now: *retired.*

Kevin Reilly Was: *president NBC Entertainment 2004–2007; chief creative officer Fox Broadcasting Co. 2007–2014;* Now: *president TBS and TNT; chief creative officer Turner Entertainment 2014–present.*

Tom Rogers Was: *first president and chief strategist NBC Cable 1987–1999, launching CNBC and MSNBC after helping to draft the Cable Act of 1984 as a senior counsel to the House Telecommunications, Consumer Protection and Finance Subcommittee and to the US House of Representatives; chairman CEO Primedia (a targeted magazine publisher);* Now: *non-executive chairman, TiVo; president CEO TiVo 2005–February 2016 (TiVo is an advanced television entertainment tech company).*

Josh Sapan Was: *president and CEO Rainbow Holdings;* Now: *president CEO AMC Networks (where he shaped the creativity of AMC, the Independent Film Channel (IFC), Sundance TV, and WE TV) 1995–present.*

Neal Shapiro Was: *executive producer Dateline 1993–2001; president NBC News 2001–September 2008;* Now: *president CEO PBS WNET NYC 2008–present.*

Lawrence Tu Was: *executive VP and general counsel NBC Universal Media (negotiated Universal deal) 2002–2005; senior VP and general counsel Dell 2005–2013;* Now: *senior executive VP and chief legal officer CBS Corp. 2013–present.*

Ed Scanlon Was: *senior VP NBC after a career at RCA;* Now: *retired.*

Tom Wheeler Was: *president National Cable Television Assn. and Cellular Telecommunications & Internet Assn.;* Now: *chairman Federal Communications Commission.*

David Zaslav Was: *president NBC Universal Media, LLC 2006; executive VP NBC Cable 1999–2006; president NBC Cable Distribution 1996–1999 after joining NBC in 1989;* Now: *CEO and president Discovery Communications 2007–present.*

APPENDIX B: AUTISM

What We've Learned About Autism

1. Autism's prevalence has skyrocketed.

Ten years ago, autism's estimated prevalence was 1 in 166. Today it's 1 in 68—an increase of more than 100 percent in 1 decade.

2. Direct screening suggests that autism's prevalence may be even higher.

In a landmark study funded by Autism Speaks, screeners went into schools in South Korea and found 1 in 38 children affected by autism, most of them previously undiagnosed. Autism Speaks is now working with the CDC to conduct a similar direct-screening study in the United States.

3. Autism can be reliably diagnosed by age 2.

Because earlier intervention improves outcomes, Autism Speaks is redoubling our efforts to increase early screening, especially in underserved communities.

4. High-quality early intervention does more than develop skills.

Early intervention can change underlying brain development and activity. It's also cost effective, as it reduces the need for educational and behavioral support in grade school and beyond.

5. Behavioral therapy for autism can transform lives.
Though children with autism vary in how far they progress with behavioral therapy, we now have solid evidence of its benefits. This has enabled Autism Speaks to successfully advocate for health coverage of behavioral health treatment, now the law in 38 states and counting. Now many families are getting desperately needed therapy that was once denied.

6. One-third of children and adults with autism are nonverbal.
Autism Speaks continues to support research on the best uses of assistive communication devices and has donated thousands of the devices to individuals and families who could not otherwise afford them.

7. Assistive communication devices encourage speech in some nonverbal children.
An Autism Speaks–funded study dispelled the belief that nonverbal children with autism who don't speak by age 5 will remain nonverbal for life.

8. Autism-related GI disorders are real.
Research by the Autism Speaks Autism Treatment Network revealed that half of children with autism have GI disorders and the pain can worsen behavioral symptoms. The ATN has developed effective treatment guidelines for pediatricians and toolkits for parents.

9. Autism-related sleep disturbance is common and treatable.
Thanks to research funded by Autism Speaks, we now have evidence-based medical guidelines and toolkits to help parents improve the sleep of those with autism.

10. As many as 1/3 of people with autism have epilepsy.
The potentially dangerous seizures are not always obvious without specialized testing.

11. Autism can affect the whole body.
Seizures, disturbed sleep, and painful GI disorders are just some of the medical conditions commonly associated with autism. The Autism Speaks Autism Treatment Network is dedicated to advancing a "whole person" approach to autism health care.

12. Autism's genetic causes are so personal that we need whole-genome sequencing to guide the development of individualized treatments.
Early findings from the Autism Speaks MSSNG project reveal that autism's genetic causes even differ between affected siblings. Such complexity is why we need MSSNG to change the future of autism through the genome sequencing of thousands of affected families. Already, this data—available to researchers worldwide on a portal on the Google Cloud Platform—is identifying targets for the development of new medicines.

13. Environmental factors can play a significant role.
Experts once believed that autism was almost entirely hereditary. Then research with families participating in the Autism Speaks Autism Genetic Resource Exchange showed that no inherited influences on early brain development account for nearly half of a child's risk for developing autism.

14. We've begun to identify autism's environmental risk factors.
These factors include maternal infection and high exposure to air pollution during pregnancy. And we now know that prenatal vitamins with folic acid can reduce the risk of autism if taken before conception and through pregnancy.

15. Nearly half of those with autism wander or bolt.
Autism Speaks has taken the lead in promoting wandering preven-

tion and recovery through the funding of programs that increase awareness, train first responders, and teach water safety.

16. Nearly 2/3 of children with autism have been bullied.
Autism Speaks has partnered with the National Center for Learning Disabilities and others to raise awareness and combat bullying of special needs individuals.

17. Most adults with autism (84 percent) remain living with their parents.
Autism Speaks is advocating for federal and state policies that will increase community living options for adults with autism.

18. Nearly half of 25-year-olds with autism have never held a paying job.
Autism Speaks is working to increase vocational and postsecondary educational support for young adults with autism and is working with employers to expand job opportunities.

19. Each year, an estimated 50,000 teens with autism age out of school-based autism services.
Autism Speaks continues to work with public and private partners to provide the support that individuals with autism need to successfully transition into adulthood and become valued and valuable members of their communities.

20. The cost of autism across a lifetime averages $1.4 million to $2.4 million.
These costs, which increase with intellectual disability, place a tremendous burden on families and society but can be dramatically reduced with high-quality interventions and adult transition support.

05
Autism Speaks
Suzanne and Bob Wright, the grandparents of a child with autism start Autism Speaks. Their longtime friend Bernie Marcus donates $25 million to help launch the organization.

06
"The Odds" Campaign
Autism Speaks partners with the Ad Council to launch "The Odds" PSA campaign. It is the first in a series of award-winning PSA campaigns created pro-bono by BBDO.

06
Global Research on High-Risk Infants and Toddlers
Unsurpassed research by Baby Siblings Research Consortium and Toddler Treatment Network identifies early risk factors and interventions for improved outcomes.

05
Walk Now for Autism Speaks
Initiates "Walk Now for Autism Speaks" signature fundraising event. To date raised nearly $250 million through walks in more than 100 cities nationwide.

05-06
Historic Mergers
Building on the great achievements of the Autism Coalition for Research and Education, National Alliance for Autism Research and Cure Autism Now, Autism Speaks merges with the organizations, becoming one of the world's largest autism foundations.

06 -14
Combating Autism
National autism advocacy strategy results in more than $3 billion in fede funding, including passage of the 200 "Combating Autism Act," the 2014 "A tism Cares Act" and the "ABLE Act."

05
Autism Cares
An ongoing assistance program is initiated for families facing unplanned hardships. More than $700,000 has been donated. When Hurricane Sandy hit the East Coast in 2012, more than $100,000 in emergency funds was sent to 280 autism families to help them rebuild.

07
Community Grants
Funds first community grant. To date, more than $5.4 million has been awarded to local organizations such as Meeting Street, a service provider for children with disabilities in Rhode Island.

YEAR HIGHLIGHTS

07

Genetic Resource Exchange

New funding helps expand Autism Speaks Autism Genetic Resource Exchange, the largest private collection of DNA samples from families affected by autism.

07

World Autism Awareness Day

In an unprecendented global effort, the United Nations designates April 2, "World Autism Awareness Day," to be celebrated in perpetuity.

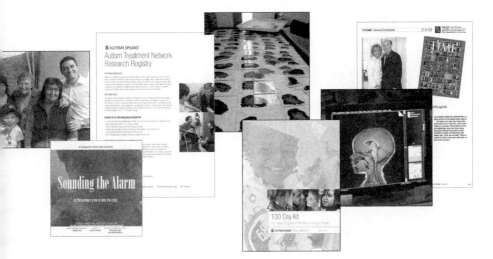

07

Resources Within Reach

Establishes the largest resource guide of its kind with online access to more than 75,000 services, products and resources nationwide.

07

Autism Speaks Responds

The Autism Response Team (ART) is established to support individuals with autism, their families, caregivers and healthcare professionals. To date, specially trained professionals have responded to more than 100,000 calls and online inquiries.

08

100 Day Tool Kit

A Tool Kit is created to guide and support families through first 100 days. Translated into seven languages and downloaded more than 140,000 times, the kit has helped parents like Christy Kraus navigate the early stages of her son's journey with autism.

08

100 Most Influential People in the World

Autism Speaks co-founders Suzanne and Bob Wright named among the "100 Most Influential People in the World," by Time Magazine.

09

Housing and Employment Services for Adults

$3.7 million donated to date, through grants including the Brian and Patricia Kelly Postsecondary Scholarship Fund that enables programs such as the nonPareil Institute in Plano, TX, to provide scholarships to students with autism.

08

Autism Treatment Network

The federal government provides funding for the Autism Speaks Autism Treatment Network (ATN) to serve as the nation's Autism Intervention Research Network on Physical Health. ATN centers across the US and Canada provide the highest standard of coordinated medical care for children and teens with autism.

08 - 09

New Ad Council PSAs

A new round of "The Odds" PSAs are launched featuring Toni Braxton, mother of a son with autism. The Braxton television spot garnered more than 10 million impressions on the first day it launched. PSAs also feature Pro Golfer Ernie Els. They compare the odds of winning the US Open twice to the odds of having a child diagnosed with autism.

10

Light It Up Blue

Introduces a global autism initiative to light the world blue on April 2. To date, more than 136 countries in 7 continents participate.

11

Help With Community Living

Launches the first online housing and residential support portal for adults with autism.

10

"Closer to Home"

Autism Speaks and the Ad Council launch PSAs called "Closer to Home." Directed by Oscar-nominated director Lasse Halström, the PSAs depict a real family affected by rising autism prevalence through the years.

11

"Learn the Signs"

New Ad Council PSAs feature fashion icon and Autism Speaks Board Member Tommy Hilfiger and NASCAR driver Jamie McMurray. The PSAs chart their rise to stardom against the odds of having a child diagnosed with autism and encourage parents to learn the early signs.

09 - 14

Affordable Care Act

Leads the fight for autism insurance reform, expanding coverage to more than 80% of the population covering two-thirds of the U.S.

12

Early Access to Care

Research funded by Autism Speaks substantiates the benefits of early intervention in improving learning, social and communication skills.

14

MSSNG Project

Groundbreaking collaboration between Google and Autism Speaks creates the world's largest open access genomic database on autism in Google Cloud.

13

First Annual Autism Investment Conference

Develop innovative think tank for investors and entrepreneurs in the creation of products and services for the autism community.

14

Vatican Shines a Light on Autism

Bob and Suzanne Wright address the first ever Global Vatican conference on autism. Pope Francis calls for an end to the stigma and isolation of those with autism.

13

"Maybe" Launches

New PSAs entitled "Maybe" depict parents observing unusual behavior in their children in ordinary situations. Since 2006, Autism Speaks' PSA campaign has been one of the most successful in the Ad Council's history, earning more than $478.6 million in donated media space. The campaign has raised awareness of autism prevalence among parents of young children by nearly 50 percent.

13

Advancing World Health

Co-sponsored the World Health Organization's first international conference on autism for worldwide coordination of autism research and services. To date, Autism Speaks has partnerships in more than 60 countries through its Global Autism Public Health Initiative.

Acknowledgements

This book is made possible by my family. My wife Suzanne, my daughters Katie and Maggie, and my son Chris. All of them have participated and have been enormously supportive of me in my business career and my not-for-profit career culminating with Autism Speaks. I thank my grandchildren Christian, Mattias, Morgan, Maisie, Alex, and Sloan. They have been a cornerstone of my life for the last 15 years.

Diane Mermigas has been a journalist friend of mine for 30 years and the researcher, co-writer, and coach of this book. Diane has been tireless in her efforts to wade through 40 years of my business and personal life. There would be no book without Diane.

Maggie Stuckey has been our angel editor, cutting, pasting, and bringing life to every paragraph. And to Bob Thompson of Columbia Business Press, for introducing us to her.

I am grateful to Donna Lombardo, my trusted executive assistant who brings order and productivity to my diverse business endeavors. And to personal assistants Marika Diczhazi and Connie Tunley who aided Suzanne and me with photos for the book.

My thanks to Arthur Klebanoff, Peter Clark, and the Rosetta Books team who designed the covers and interior of *The Wright*

Stuff and guided me through the publishing process; and to Sandi Mendelson for effectively getting out the word about it.

I am grateful to **the people who have helped advance Autism Speaks** over the past decade, most notably: Phil Geier and Mel Karmazin, who have been with me from the beginning of this journey. And to others contributing to this book: Adrienne Biddings, Congressman Dan Burton, Dr. Dan Coury, Dr. Geri Dawson, Congressman Mike Doyle, Liz Feld, Jamitha Fields, Thomas Flynn, Senator Al Franken, David Glazer, Dr. Gary Goldstein, Matthew Goodwin, Gordon Gund, Shelley Hendrix, Dr. Thomas Insel, Brian Kelly, Billy Mann, Bernie Marcus, Dana Marnane, Cecelia McCarton, Kevin Murray, Duncan Niederauer, Dr. Herbert Pardes, Dr. James Perrin, Rob Ring, Andrew Robertson, Mark Roithmayr, Michael Rosen, Ned Sahin, Dr. Stephen Scherer, Harry Slatkin, Laura Slatkin, Michelle Smigel, and Congressman Chris Van Hollen.

I appreciate **the people important to my work at NBC and General Electric**, many of whom were interviewed for this project. The abundance of wonderful material would have filled volumes. Especially near and dear:

Al Barber—Good friend and early draft from GE who excelled as CNBC president.

Kathy Bayer—A very special person who knew me and my schedule better than I did.

Mark Begor—Top flight GE executive and NBC CFO.

Bill Bolster—Bigger than life good friend, dynamic guy, and president of WNBC and CNBC.

Tom Brokaw—The best broadcaster of his time! Always helpful; the flag of NBC News.

Don Browne—Superior person who came from CBS and ran

NBC News, Miami TV and Telemundo.

Brandon Burgess—Very focused business guy, fabulous business development manager; created real value with ION.

Steve Burke—A straight talker in my old job; big-time player with Comcast.

Rick Cotton—My general counsel for many years, excellent lawyer, advisor and counselor; no problem he couldn't tackle.

Chuck Dolan—My pal and partner for 30 years! A cable GREAT; created HBO.

Jimmy Dolan—Chuck's son, who has control of Cablevision; hard worker, carrying a big load.

Arthur Dwyer—Excellent marketing man, with me for many years; big help during Cox Cable years.

Dick Ebersol—Superior executive and producer, put NBC Sports on top, Olympics MAVEN!

John Eck—Key finance and operating guy for me at NBC/NBCU, strong and dedicated.

Randy Falco—Long-time NBC executive with finance and operating history; President of the Network, AOL then Univision!

Jean René Fourtou—CEO of Vivendi, very bright, thoughtful, and a superior executive; my partner at Universal.

Ralph Del Deo—My boss in private law practice in New Jersey with wide-ranging interests and skills from real estate patents to bird hunting and dog judging.

Marianne Gambelli—Always one of the highest ranked commercial executives at NBC; a problem-solver with great personal skills.

Victor Garvey—Number-one man with events—long association; always had my back.

Cheryl Gould—NBC News career executive; very smart;

good friend of Suzanne and me.

Herb Granath—Drove all cable activity of ABC; guided ESPN from scratch.

Gus Hauser—My competitor in the early cable days, very sophisticated, thoughtful leader and entrepreneur.

Eddy Hartenstein—There would be no DTV without Eddy! From Aerospace to TV, very special.

Sue Herera—A founding journalist/anchor of the Financial News Network, star of CNBC and distinctive interviewer who makes business people feel comfortable sharing their insights.

Bob Iger—The most successful entertainment executive of the past 20 years!

Warren Jenson—From GE investor relations to NBC, special CFO with real deal skills; a builder and problem solver!

Jeffry Katzenberg—Did a great job at Disney and drove creation and operations of DreamWorks. No one works harder!

Ann McLaughlin Korologos—A friend and mentor. Straight shooter who made corporate boards better or she left! An under-recognized woman executive and leader.

Andy Lack—Great Job with NBC News; polished, aggressive, tireless.

Warren Littlefield—Behind so many successful NBC hit shows. Even-tempered and hard-working.

Greg Maffei—Drove Microsoft team in creation of MSNBC. Smart, down-to-earth, and now running Liberty Media with John Malone.

John Malone—The brains behind cable business success. Invested cash flow as a key measure of cable stocks and never saw a tax he liked! Incredible deal maker.

Vince Manze—Father of Must-See TV! That says it all! Extraordinary promotions guy.

Pierson Mapes—Bigger than life NBC Network President, loved Madison Avenue and NBC.

Bernie Marcus—Brought cash and history to Autism. Remains our biggest contributor.

Vera Mayer—NBC's first female vice president; smarter than all the boys with an incredible work ethic; a good friend to Suzanne and me.

Ron Meyer—A very special guy. Helped me understand film, and guided Universal Studios for many years. Unflappable great judgment, and patient when necessary.

Lorne Michaels—The flagship of NBC entertainment for more than 40 years; has no equal. A friend, advisor, and incredible creative producer.

John Miller—From Chicago to NBC Entertainment; drove on-air promotion and marketing for many years. John and Vince were brothers on Must-See TV.

Andrea Mitchell—NBC News's best Washington reporter for more than 35 years; highest White House and congressional correspondent roles; host of MSNBC's Andrea Mitchell Reports.

Lisa Myers—NBC News' outstanding investigative reporter always on the hunt for good stories.

Elena Nachmanoff—Long-time NBC News talent agent; scout, appraiser, negotiator and counsel to many senior executives.

Conan O'Brien—Harvard funnyman, took over Jay Leno's late-night spot before jumping to TBS; excellent writer and performer. A friend.

Roger Ogden—Superior producer, his NBC stature in Denver was 20-hour local and national news, highest rated in Colorado! Highest caliber person.

Don Ohlmeyer—Major sports and nonfiction producer, and bigger-than-life president of west coast NBC Entertainment.

Bob Okun—Friend and right-hand-man in DC for many years. Smart, capable and alert for new information.

Bob O'Leary—From GE to Cox, superior CFO of cable and parent Cox Enterprises. My friend for 40 years!

Arthur Puccini—My boss at GE law and my mentor when I crossed over to business. Lawyer, pharmacist, mentor and 40-year friend.

Kevin Reilly—Wonderful programmer for NBC and Fox. More longevity than some networks. A pleasure to be with.

Brian Roberts—Smart, able, and focused. True long-term player!

Tom Rogers—A half lawyer, half business development expert; tech titan and grey wolf who will prevail in pursuit of his ideas. He was my cable partner point man for many years.

Josh Sapan—Superior program executive and CEO; was with me and Rainbow for many years. He has taken AMC Networks to new highs.

Herbert Schlosser—Investment broker, friend and former NBC president; wonderful mentor for many years.

Neal Shapiro—Topflight producer of Dateline, former president of NBC news and overall outstanding person who has done a great job leading WNET, Channel 13 in New York.

Dr. Gary Tjaden—Father of INDAX, Cox Cable's early interactive TV service; a Bell labs star who brought superior engineering to cable.

Lawrence Tu—An excellent, high-energy counsel who managed Universal before moving on to a big career at Dell.

Ted Turner—Mouth of the South and Class 3 hurricane for 20 years forging cable with The Super Station, CNN, TNT, TBS and The Cartoon Network; environmentalist and nuclear shepherd.

Cyril Vetter—My friend and man for all seasons; song writer, radio and TV station owner, LSU sports encyclopedia, film producer, book writer and publisher... wow!

Steve Volk—Outstanding lawyer and wise man who managed Sherman & Sterling, Credit Suisse, and Citibank's venture capital unit.

Paul Waring—Followed me from GE to Cox, brought strategic planning to cable; the hardest worker ever.

Tom Wheeler—Gave the National Cable Television Association national stature; consummate consensus leader, highly skilled DC mover, and Federal Communications Commission chairman.

Jack Welch—Hard-charging charismatic GE leader and my boss for many years.

Ed Scanlon—The best human resources executive I ever worked with; skilled negotiator with his ear to the ground; my buffer with GE top executives.

Suzanne Wright—The inspiration for this book. My love, wife, and business partner for 48 years!

David Zaslav—Created value with every move as NBC Cable distribution czar and went on to do the same as chairman CEO of Discovery Communications; a national media figure.

INDEX

A

The A-Team (TV series), 137
A&E (Arts and Entertainment), 80, 81, 85, 96, 178
ABA (applied behavioral analysis), 347
ABC, 70, 79, 82, 84, 85, 144, 171, 173, 177, 197
ABC Sports, 71, 81, 120, 124
ABC Television, 85
ABC Westinghouse, 72
ABLE Act, 317, 325, 343, 348
ACRE (Autism Coalition for Research & Education), 300
Activision unit (Vivendi), 32
Ad Council, 295, 296, 306
advertisers, and reaching fragmented audiences, 229
advertising base, 26, 27, 60
affiliate reform, 225–226, 228
affiliate-network relations, 111, 190–191, 220–233
Affordable Care Act, 352
Age of Autism blog posts, 367
Ailes, Roger, 110, 186, 187, 195, 200
Akili (game), 397
Alighieri, Dante, 202, 210
Altice, 100
AMC Networks, 98
American Express, 68
American Family, 123
American Medical Association (AMA), 368
American Movie Classics (AMC), 90, 96, 97
Americans with Disabilities Act, 321
America's Talking, 183, 186, 187, 188, 192, 195, 196, 197
Anthony, Garner, 65, 90
AOL Entertainment Asylum, 139
AOL Time Warner, 27, 165, 201, 270
Apple, 77, 207
applied behavioral analysis (ABA), 347
The Apprentice (TV show), 146, 147
Arledge, Roone, 71, 120, 173, 179–180
Arts and Entertainment (A&E), 80, 81, 85, 96, 178
The Arts, 84

ASDs (autism spectrum disorders), 329, 348, 363, 366, 396
Asner, Ed, 296
Asperger's syndrome, 365, 366
AT&T, 123
Atari, 70
autism
  applied behavioral analysis (ABA), 347
  author's grandson's diagnosis of, 23, 38, 39–40. *See also* Christian (grandson)
  denial by medical and science communities that autism is serious health epidemic, 314
  drugs for, 346, 355
  funding for, 301, 317, 328–329
  future for families with children with, 339–357
  as hidden epidemic, 291–299
  high-functioning autistic adults, 366
  idea of institute focused on, 354
  idea of national strategy for, 348
  inequality of resources for, 293
  insurance issues, 148, 321
  lack of awareness about, 292, 293
  lifetime cost for caring for autistic individual, 349
  need for housing and employment for individuals with, 350, 352, 354
  need for research on, 298
  Obama campaign's policy statement on, 312
  percent of children in US diagnosed with, 293, 295, 299, 315–316, 348, 399
  pursuit of legislative support for funding of, 301
  US adult prevalence study, 353
  vaccines and, 358–371
Autism Awareness campaign, 295, 296–297
Autism Caucus, 318
Autism Center (New York-Presbyterian's Westchester campus), 329
Autism Coalition for Research & Education (ACRE), 300
Autism Collaboration, Accountability, Research, Education, and Support Act of 2014 (Autism CARES), 317, 323, 348

Autism Response Team, 325
Autism Science Foundation, 359
Autism Speaks
  announcing formation of, 280
  on autism and vaccines, 364
  building blocks of, 303. *See also* business
    principles; global expansion; grassroots
    network/grassroots strength; political
    heft and legislation/political muscle;
    strategic partnerships/alliances
  building of as using author's business
    experience, 52, 74, 102, 149, 168, 182,
    233, 243, 246, 260
  as a business, 330
  CEOs of, 342–343, 371
  contribution to MSSNG, 343, 383
  controversies, 366, 373
  database, 323
  evolution of from advocacy group to all-
    around grand facilitator, 339
  first national policy and action summit
    (2013), 317
  future ideas for, 342–348
  grand opening of, 298
  grant to Center for Autism and the
    Developing Brain, 333
  House-to-Home Project, 352
  as integrating advocacy and research
    groups, 300–301
  launching of, 62
  partnership with Google, 102, 233, 288,
    325, 331, 339, 340, 344, 354, 365,
    377–401
  startup funds for, 292
  strategic alliances of, 291
  Suzanne's accomplishments with, 273
  tenth anniversary of, 288
  walks sponsored by, 99, 325, 343, 351
  World Autism Awareness Day. *See* World
    Autism Awareness Day
Autism Speaks Canada, 389
autism spectrum disorders (ASDs), 329, 348,
  363, 366, 396
Autism Treatment Network, 337, 347
Autism Votes, 320

B

Barber, Al, 110
Barton, Joe, 316
Barton, Peter, 84
BBC, 80

BBDO, 295, 296, 306, 383
Beale, Jim, 274
Beijing Genomics Institute, 378, 400
Bell, Jim, 178
Bellina, Joe, 308
Berisha, Liri, 314
Bernstein Research, 36, 249
Best Buy, 352
Biddings, Adrienne, 379
  quote by, 381–382
Biography Channel, 81
BioTeam, 392
Black & Decker, GE's partnership with, 266
Blair, Deeda, 297
Blank, Arthur, 42
Bloom, David, 283
Bloomberg, 109
Bloomberg, Michael, 332
Bloomberg Philanthropies, 383
board members, role of, 212, 214
Bolster, Bill, 110, 226
Bossidy, Larry, 106, 266
Boxer, Lenny, 308
Brain Power software, 393
brands, importance of knowledge of, 87
Brandt, Juan Carlos, 305
Bravo, 27, 29, 90, 96, 97, 98, 175, 208, 226,
  257
Brin, Sergey, 378
Brokaw, Tom, 120, 175, 185, 187, 189, 198
Bronfman, Edgar, Jr., 30, 31
Bronfman family, 30
Burgess, Brandon, 24, 25, 26, 27, 28, 36, 37
  quotes by, 32, 33–34, 98, 208–209, 225,
    235, 238–239, 253
Burke, Dan, 249
Burke, Steve, 36, 237, 248–255
  quotes by, 205, 251–255, 256–257
Bush, Laura, 313, 314
business principles, as building block for
  Autism Speaks, 303, 325–330
BuzzFeed, 253

C

cable
    author's attraction to, 66
    author's belief in future of, 77
    on cusp of becoming mainstream, 57
    as destabilizing broadcast TV, 222
    emergence of first major channels in
      US, 64

impact of mainstream acceptance of, 73
importance of embracing, 60
as television's content core, 37
as turning broadcasting on its head, 221
cable cowboys, 79
Cable News Network (CNN), 107. *See also*
CNN
Cablevision Systems, 31, 70, 80, 89–98, 101,
180, 269
"A Call for Unity" (Feld), 371
Campbell, Bruce, 36
CAN (Cure Autism Now), 300
Cancer Genome Atlas (National Cancer
Institute), 387
Cannell, Stephen J., 137
Capital Cities Broadcasting, 85, 249
Carley, Michael John, 366
Carson, Alexis (Alex), 150, 151, 152, 153,
155, 156, 267
Carson, Ben, 364
Carson, Johnny, 124, 126, 127, 150–158, 267
cash flow investing, 67, 68
CBS, 85, 129, 144
CBS News, 197
The Celebrity Apprentice (TV show), 146
Center for Autism and the Developing
Brain, 329, 333, 352
Centers for Disease Control and Prevention
(CDC), 293, 294, 295, 299, 316, 361, 363,
365, 370
Centre for Applied Genomics (Toronto),
389–390
change. *See also* transformative change
author as crusading for in both
corporate and philanthropic circles,
291
author as demonstrating value of, 126
author as fighting resistance to, 236
author's confidential internal memos
detailing, 60
and choice, 73
corporations/institutions as under
constant pressure to, 49
Dateline as catalyst for, 117
as dependent on assembling, managing,
and empowering the right teams of
people, 61
effect of being open to, 231
establishing an agenda for at NBC, 111,
137, 225
as inevitable, 181, 232

looking past the horizon for, 199
NBC as leading change on many fronts,
124
need to push through resistance to, 58,
314
as the norm, 168
story of NBC as story of anticipating
change and being prepared for it, 87
taking responsibility for creation of, 56
technology as forcing, 232
Chase, Chevy, 123
Chavez, Pablo, 381
Cheers (TV series), 136, 137, 141
Christian (grandson), 23, 37–38, 39, 43, 45,
51, 169, 272, 283, 292, 352, 357, 358, 359,
366–367, 369, 379
CNBC, 29, 66, 92, 93, 94, 96, 103–114, 128,
142, 175, 177, 183, 187, 192, 197, 198,
205, 221, 226, 258
CNBC Asia, 128
CNBC Europe, 128
CNN, 61, 71, 72, 104, 110, 160, 163, 165,
166, 167, 183, 184, 190, 192, 196, 197, 267
Coca-Cola, 336
Coleman Foundation, 349–350
Collins, Francis, 387
Columbia University College of Physicians
and Surgeons, 329, 333
Combating Autism Reauthorization Act,
312
Combatting Autism Act, 316, 318–319, 361,
362
Comcast
bid to acquire Time Warner Cable, 251,
253, 255–256
ownership control of NBCU (2011), 96
potential benefit of NBC's Olympics
franchise to, 180
sale of NBC Universal to (2011), 201–
202, 204–209, 248, 249, 250
Conaty, Bill, 243
consolidation, in industry, 25
consumer habits, shift toward subscription-
based cable, 26
Consumer News and Business Channel
(CNBC), 104, 105. *See also* CNBC
control, as principle for success, 47, 56, 232
Cooper, Louis Z., 362
Cordero, Jose, 293–294
corporate failure, as management's fault, 48
corporate success, as shared by management

and workers, 48
Cosby, Bill, 136
The Cosby Show (TV series), 133, 136, 137
Cosell, Howard, 81
Cotton, Rick, 36
Couric, Katie, 286, 366
Court TV, 128
Cox, Anna, 90
Cox, Barbara, 90
Cox Broadcasting, 72
Cox Cable, 56, 57, 64–74, 90, 135, 247, 265
Cox Enterprises, 67
Cox family, 67, 68, 73, 90
Cox organization, 64
Creative Artists Agency, 137
creativity
   as imperfect process, 132
   importance of, 49, 62, 87, 131, 132
   not letting environment dictate yours,
      231
Cuarón, Alfonso, 373
Cure Autism Now (CAN), 300

D

Dateline (TV news magazine)
   changes to, 128, 130
   "Waiting to Explode" fiasco, 115–118,
      124
David, Larry, 145
Davis, Marvin, 31
Dawn of the Dead (film), 25
Dawson, Geri, 359, 372
Daytime, 80
De Niro, Robert, 308, 352
Delivering Scientific Innovation for Autism
   (DELSIA), 380, 388, 396
DeMetz, Robert, 29, 30
deregulation
   of fin-syn (financial interest and
      syndication), 144. *See also* fin-syn
      (financial interest and syndication)
   impact of, 228
   of networks' financial interest in
      ongoing revenues of series, 148
*Diagnostic and Statistical Manual of Mental
   Disorders* (*DSM-5*), 366, 390
Diller, Barry, 31, 32
DirecTV, 96, 269
Disney, 129
Disney/ABC, 71, 85, 250
The Divine Comedy (Dante), 202

Dodd, Chris, 315
Dolan, Chuck, 31, 70, 80, 88–100, 180, 237,
   342
   quotes by, 88, 266–267
Dolan, Helen, 99, 100, 237
Dolan family foundations, 389
Doyle, Mike, quote by, 318
DreamWorks, 238, 239–240, 246
DSM-5 (*Diagnostic and Statistical Manual of
   Mental Disorders*), 366, 390
DVDs, 228
DVRs, 255
Dwyer, Art, 67
   quotes by, 70, 72, 73, 245
Dyer, John, 67

E

earnings per share (EPS), 82, 83, 270
Ebersol, Charlie, 282
Ebersol, Dick, 58, 118, 119, 121, 124, 125,
   126, 127, 129, 130, 131, 170, 173, 174,
   179, 282, 283
   quotes by, 112, 171–172, 175, 177
Ebersol, Teddy, 282
Eck, John, 36
   quote by, 240
Eisner, Michael, 129
empowerment, importance of, 232
Enron, 203
Entertainment Asylum (AOL), 139
The Entertainment Channel, 85
entrepreneurial potential, importance of
   unleashing of, 48
EPS (earnings per share), 82, 83, 270
equity partnership, 83. *See also* private
   equity
ER (TV series), 126, 127, 128, 141, 142, 223
ESPN, 70, 71, 72, 79, 81, 85, 95, 109, 118,
   167, 177
ESPN2, 81
establishment, bucking of, as element of
   success, 49

F

Faber, David, 109
failure, corporate, as management's fault, 48
Falco, Randy, 36, 126, 170, 171, 172, 173,
   174, 177, 178, 189, 191, 192, 223, 237,
   238, 283
   quotes by, 175–176, 224–225, 229–230,
      236

Family Ties (TV series), 133, 136
Farrakhan, Louis, 185
Feld, Liz, 371
  quotes by, 284–285, 322, 323–324, 345–
    346, 348–349, 379
Feldman, Marty, 69–70
Fields, Jamitha, quote by, 372
Financial News Network (FNN), 92, 93, 94,
  105, 106, 107–108, 109
fin-syn (financial interest and syndication),
  143, 144–145, 227, 315
First Autism Conference (China 2016), 314
Food and Drug Administration, 348, 365
Foundation Fighting Blindness, 391
Fourtou, Jean-René, 30, 31, 34, 36
  quote by, 35
Fox network, 36, 118, 144, 171, 187
Fox News, 193, 195, 196, 197, 198
Frank, Alan, 230
Frasier (TV series), 25, 126, 141
free cash flow business, 206, 268
Friday Night Videos (TV show), 121
Friends (TV series), 25, 126, 128, 141, 223
Frist, Bill, 361

G

Gambelli, Marianne, quote by, 244–245
Gandhi, Sonia, 314
Gannett, 84
GAPH (Global Autism Public Health)
  program, 335, 347
Gartner, Michael, 117
Gates, Bill, 183, 185, 186, 187, 188, 189,
  190, 193–195, 200
GE Capital, 28, 57, 202, 204, 208, 211, 218,
  236
GE Imaging, 395
Geffen, David, 239
General Electric (GE). *See also* Welch, Jack
  as afraid of digital TV, 206
  author's career at, 56
  author's first day at, 55
  author's recommendation to invest
    resources of in cable channels and
    websites, 26
  buttoned-down industrial framework
    culture of, 24
  cost controls demanded by, 128
  cycle of value creation and destruction,
    201, 211, 218
  dismissal of opportunity to buy into

  Apple (1996), 207
  failure of deal to merge Cox with, 65
  financial hell of, 202–203
  focus of on earnings per share (EPS), 82
  impact of Universal deal on, 28
  leadership transition (2006), 237–238
  main growth strategy of, 263
  partnership with Black & Decker, 266
  Peltz and Trian Partners' stake in, 219
  process of establishing strategic
    objectives, 86
  proposed role of in NBC Universal, 27
  purchase of RCA, 57, 58, 60, 133, 204,
    247
  purchase of WMC Mortgage Corp.,
    203–204
  responses by to external threats/
    challenges, 209
  rigid process of, 35
General Motors (GM), 95–96, 115, 116
genome sequencing, 233, 288, 324, 331,
  339, 342, 343, 347, 365, 378, 383, 384,
  386, 387, 389, 394, 397, 398
Genworth Financial, 203
Getty Oil, 70
Gifford, Frank, 81
Glazer, David, 380, 381, 385, 387, 399, 400
  quotes by, 284, 385–386, 392–393
Global Autism Public Health (GAPH)
  program, 335, 347
global expansion, as building block for
  Autism Speaks, 303, 304–309
Golden Girls (TV series), 137
Goldenson, Leonard, 79, 80
Goldstein, Gary, 43, 293
  quotes by, 298–299, 349
Golf Channel, 267
Google, partnership with Autism Speaks,
  102, 233, 288, 324, 331, 339, 340, 344,
  354, 365, 377–401
Google Glasses, 393, 394
Gordon and Llura Gund Foundation, 383,
  389
Gould, Cheryl, quote by, 279
Granath, Herbert (Herb), 70, 84
  quote by, 79–82
Granite Broadcasting, 223, 224
grassroots, meaning of term, 303
grassroots network/grassroots strength, as
  building block for Autism Speaks, 303,
  320–324

Griffeth, Bill, 108
Gund, Gordon, quote by, 391
Gund, Llura, 391

H
Hack, Bruce, 29
Hanna-Barbera, 165
Hauser, Gus, 68
HBO, 79, 91, 118, 132, 165
Health and Human Services (HHS), 362, 363
Hearst, 71, 85
Hendrix, Shelley, quote by, 322–323
Herera, Sue, 108
high-functioning autistic adults, 366
Hildebrand, Andreas, 367
Hilfiger, Tommy, 296, 309
History Channel, 81, 96
Hoffman, Mark, 110
Home Box Office, 90. *See also* HBO
Home Depot, 41, 42
Honeywell, 209, 216, 270
Hospital for Sick Children (Toronto), 331, 339, 378, 392
House-to-Home Project, 352
Hubregsen, Ralph, 265
Hughes Electronic, 96
Hulu, 257
Hunter College, 332

I
I Am Autism (PSA), 373
IBM Watson, 395
Iger, Bob, 129
Immelt, Jeff, 27, 28, 34, 202, 214, 215, 216, 217, 218, 235, 236, 237, 239, 240, 243, 244, 245
Insana, Ron, 108
Insel, Thomas (Tom), 297, 390
Interactive Autism Network, 347
Interactive Labs, 397
International Olympic Committee (IOC), 170, 171, 172, 173, 174, 175, 179, 181
International Radio and Television Society, 75
Internet
    convergence of with television, 199
    emerging role of, 185, 186
    as example of constant rollout of new technology, 83
    idea for NBC to develop, 230–231
    impact of on CNBC, 109
    lack of strategic clarity between cable TV and, 197
    MSNBC and, 184
    MSNBC experience as giving NBC confidence in using Internet productively, 197
    as new platform, 26
    Welch's opinion of, 195
iPad, 77
iPod, 77
Irving, Herbert, 330

J
Jablonski, Jacquelyn, 308
Jaffe, Robert, 24
Jarrett, Valerie, 313
Jenson, Warren, 160
    quotes by, 124–125, 162–163, 190
Jobs, Steve, 207
Johns Hopkins, 293, 347, 395
Johnson, Don, 143

K
Katz, Samuel L., 362
Katzenberg, Jeffrey, 239
Kelly, Brian, 325, 344–345
    quotes by, 273–274, 327–328, 350–351, 355
Kelly, Patricia (Tricia), 341, 345
Kelly, Patrick, 351
Kennedy, Ted, 315
Kennedy Krieger Institute, 43, 293, 298, 347
Kernen, Joe, 108
Ki-moon, Ban, 308
Klein, Joel, 332
KNTV, 208, 222, 223, 224, 225
Koegel Autism Center (UCSB), 350
Korologos, Ann McLaughlin, quote by, 213–214
KRON-TV, 222, 223, 224, 233
The Kung Fu Channel, 90

L
LA Law (TV series), 137
Lack, Andy, 58, 118, 119, 120–121, 124, 125, 128, 129, 131, 184, 185, 186–187, 193, 196, 270
    quotes by, 130–131, 195
Last Call (TV talk show), 139
The Last Great Ride (Tartikoff), 138–139

Index

Late Night with Conan O'Brien (TV show), 126, 228

Law & Order (TV series), 25

Leavitt, Mike, 362

Lee, Tom, 238

Leno, Jay, 124, 126

Letterman, David, 124, 126, 127

leverage, as author's word, 323

Levin, Gerald (Jerry), 164, 165, 192

Lévy, Jean-Bernard, 29, 30, 33, 36

Liberty Media, 28, 31

Lifetime, 80, 81

Light It Up Blue, 298, 307, 308, 309, 313, 343, 371

Lipkin, Paul, 347

Littlefield, Warren, 122, 126, 127, 136, 138, 141 Lord, Catherine, 329

Lubars, David, 295

Lustgarten, Marc, 94

M

Macdonald, Norman, 123

Maceda, Jim, 152

Mack, John, 330

Maffei, Greg, 188

Malone, John, 31, 66, 67–68, 80, 82, 97, 103–104, 105, 107, 108, 164, 178
quotes by, 28, 83–84, 193

management, role of, 56

Mann, Billy, 296, 373
quote by, 310–312

Mann, Jasper, 311, 312

Manze, Vince, 126, 137

Mapes, Pier, quotes by, 59, 110–111, 118, 166–167

Marcus, Bernie, 40, 41–46, 51, 292, 293, 298
quotes by, 42–43, 44, 243

Marcus Autism Center, 41, 42

Marcus Institute, 42

Marino, Dan, 309

Marnane, Dana, quotes by, 305–306, 374–375

Martin, Steve, 123

Mayo Clinic, 395

McCarthy, Jenny, 309

McCarton, Cecelia, 352

The McCarton School (NYC), 352

MCNBC TV, 184

McNerney, Jim, 215, 216, 217

measles-mumps-rubella (MMR) vaccine, 359

media consolidation, 163

Meet the Fockers (film), 25

Mel Karmazin Foundation, 383

mercury preservatives (in vaccines), 358, 360

Meredith, Don, 81

Mermigas, Diane, 57

Messier, Jean-Louis, 24, 31

MGM, 31, 83, 161, 166

Miami Vice (TV series), 133, 136, 143, 144

Michaels, Lorne, 123–124, 125
quotes by, 121–122, 126–127

Microsoft, NBC's partnership with, 85, 98, 101, 183–200

Miller, John, 126, 137

Million Man March (1995), 185

Million Veteran Program (VA), 387

Miss Universe pageant, 146

Mitchell, Andrea, quote by, 280

MMR (measles-mumps-rubella) vaccine, 359

Monday Night Football, 81, 129

Montagnier, Luc, 370

Moonves, Les, 129

Mozah bint Nasser Al Missned (Sheikha), 304–305

MSNBC, 29, 85, 96, 98, 110, 112, 113, 128, 175, 177, 183–200, 205, 221, 226, 228

MSNBC.com, 188, 197, 198

MSSNG, 331, 339, 340, 342, 344, 347, 354, 357, 365, 370, 377–401

MTV, 70

Murdoch, Rupert, 28, 96, 97, 118, 124, 129, 171, 193, 195

Murphy, Tom, 249

Murray, Bill, 123

Murray, Kevin, quotes by, 307, 365

must-carry, 81

Must-See TV, 126, 130, 133–149

Myer, Vera, quote by, 276

Myers, Lisa, quote by, 277

N

Nachmanoff, Elena, quotes by, 280, 282

Nardelli, Bob, 203, 215

National Alliance for Autism Research (NAAR), 300

National Association of Broadcast Employees and Technicians (NABET), 61, 113, 135

National Cancer Institute, 387

National Health interview survey, 348

National Institute of Mental Health
(NIMH), 297, 390, 400
National Institutes of Health (NIH), 316,
318, 327, 329, 343, 362, 375, 389, 390, 395
National Institutes of Health Reform Act,
316
NBC
    acquisition of Bravo (2002), 98, 208
    acquisition of KNTV, 208, 224
    acquisition of Telemundo, 208, 224
    acquisition of Universal, 247
    animosity toward RCA, 135
    author's focus as NBC president, 263
    author's taking of helm at, 57, 59, 62
    bringing of into the cable age, 57–58
    Cablevision as most influential drive of
        NBC's entry into cable, 95
    characterized as industrial media
        company, 60
    cost efficiencies achieved over multiple
        Olympics productions, 175
    as fortunes rose, GE's fortunes fell, 205
    goal of under author's leadership of, 58
    interest in purchasing TBS, 159, 161,
        163, 164
    investment in The Entertainment
        Channel, 85
    as keeping news, sports, cable, etc.
        together, 86
    as maintaining wall between broadcast
        network and cable news organizations,
        191–192
    market value (1986), 204
    market value (2011), 204
    merger with Vivendi Universal, 23–36,
        37, 85
    as partner with Silicon Valley on major
        Internet venue, 199
    partnership in A&E, 85
    partnership with Cablevision Systems,
        89–98, 101
    partnership with Microsoft, 85, 98, 101,
        183–200
    programming overhaul sparked by
        Dateline fiasco, 117
    rebranding of, 126
    record annual profits, 127
    reuse of program libraries, 79
    transformation of into cable player, 75
    transformational decade of, 202
    transition from broadcast network to

        diversified media company, 87
    Triplecast disaster, 180
    value of cable holdings (1997), 112
NBC Cable, 184, 192
NBC Entertainment, 118
NBC News, 29, 61, 104, 115, 116, 118, 124,
    126, 128, 131, 183, 186, 188, 195, 197
NBC Sports, 118, 121, 128, 170, 174
NBC Television Network Group, 238
NBC TV Network, 27, 28, 29, 97, 111, 128,
    205, 225, 229, 250
NBC Universal (NBCU)
    annual revenue (2006), 235
    cable assets as contributing lion's share of
        NBC's profit, 92, 197
    as casualty, 218
    creation of, 28, 35, 38
    current free cash flow of, 206
    GE's decision to unload (2009), 236
    GE's value of (2006), 234
    as not that attractive to or completely
        understood by GE board, 218
    proposed role of GE as managing owner
        of, 27
    sale of to Comcast (2011), 96, 201–202,
        205, 207, 208, 249, 250
    value of (2013), 36
NBC West Coast Entertainment, 123, 126
NBC.com, 257
NCAA football, 81
negotiation, as fine art, 147–148
Netflix, 253, 257
network-affiliate relations, 111, 190–191,
    220
Neupert, Peter, 188
New Line Cinema, 165
New World Entertainment, 139
New York Autism Charter School, 352
New York Center for Autism, 332, 352
New York Collaborates for Autism, 329, 332
New York Post, 122
New York Times, 358–359
New York-Presbyterian, 329, 333
News Corp., 28, 96
Nightly News (TV show), 120, 121, 128, 175,
    192, 198, 223
NIH (National Institutes of Health). *See*
    National Institutes of Health (NIH)
NIMH (National Institute of Mental
    Health), 297, 390, 400
9/11/01

effects of, 201, 202, 203, 211, 228, 236
  personal experiences on, 286–287
Nunn, Sam, 43

O

Obama, Barack, 311–313, 363
Obama, Michelle, 313, 314
O'Brien, Conan, 127
Ocleppo, Dee, 309
OfficeMax, 352
Ogden, Roger, quote by, 108–109
Ohlmeyer, Don, 58, 118, 119, 120, 121, 123, 124, 125, 127, 128, 129, 130, 131, 141, 268–269
  quote by, 126
Okun, Bob, quote by, 273
O'Leary, Bob, quote by, 66–67
Olympic Games telecasts, 128, 164, 170–182, 222, 226, 257
Olympics Triplecast (1992), 95, 180
100-day kit (Autism Speaks), 306
Ono, Yoko, 308
Ovitz, Michael (Mike), 145
Ovitz, Mike, 127, 137

P

Page, Larry, 378
Paley, William, 142
Paramount, 70, 137, 138
Pardes, Herbert, quotes by, 302–303, 329–330, 375
Parenting Skills Training, 374
partnerships. *See also* Autism Speaks, partnership with Google; General Electric (GE), partnership with Black & Decker; NBC, partnership in A&E; NBC, partnership with Cablevision Systems; NBC, partnership with Microsoft; strategic partnerships/alliances
  author's right partnerships, 100, 102, 272–288
  equity partnership, 83. *See also* private equity
  importance of, 232
  Malone on successful partnerships, 84
  reason for forming, 100–101
passion
  as principle for success, 47–48, 56, 232
  of Suzanne for Autism Speaks, 272–273, 281
Paul, Rand, 364

Pauley, Jane, 116
PBS, 80
PCBs (polychlorinated biphenyls), GE's cleanup of in Hudson River, 204
PDD-NOS, 39, 365
P/E (price-earnings ratio), 209–210, 213, 270
Pediatrics, 362
Peete, Holly Robinson, 308–309
Peltz, Nelson, 219
Peng, Liyuan, 314
people
  as building value at NBCU, 206
  importance of assembling, managing, and empowering right teams of, 61, 131
PepsiCo, 352
Perrin, James, 347
  quote by, 337
Phillips, Stone, 116
Pierce, Fred, 70
Pivotal Response Treatment (PRT), 335, 350
The Playboy Channel, 90
political heft and legislation/political muscle, as building block for Autism Speaks, 303, 310–319
politically left-of-center programming, on MSNBC, 196
polychlorinated biphenyls (PCBs), GE's cleanup of in Hudson River, 204
Pound, Dick, 173
Precision Medicine Initiative, 387
price-earnings ratio (P/E), 209–210, 213, 270
private equity, 212, 234, 235, 245, 246
Project Vineyard, 30
PRT (Pivotal Response Treatment), 335, 350
Puccini, Arthur (Art), 262, 265
  quote by, 58–59

Q

Qatar, as first Arab country to lead cause of autism awareness, 305
QUBE, 68

R

radio, performance of, 60
Rainbow Media, 27, 90, 92
Rainbow Programming Services, 89, 97, 98

RCA, 57, 58, 60, 133, 135, 204, 247
Read, Robert, 115
Redstone, Sumner, 129
rerun syndication, 25
responsibility, as principle for success, 47, 56, 232
retransmission consent rules/law, 78, 192, 193, 196, 253, 255
retransmission fees, 196, 225, 227
return on equity (ROE), 209
return on investment (ROI), 209, 211
reverse cable fees, 80
reverse compensation, 222, 225
Rice, John, 203
Ring, Rob, 360, 379, 380, 383, 384, 387, 395–396, 399
    quotes by, 391–392, 396–397
risk taking, importance of, 49, 87, 131
Robbins, Tim, 139
Roberts, Brian, 82, 237, 249
Roberts, Ralph, 80, 249
Roberts family, 248
Robinson, Andrew, 295
    quote by, 296–297
Rockefeller Group, 85
ROE (return on equity), 209
Rogers, Tom, 106, 184, 185, 191, 193
    quotes by, 78, 93–95, 96–97, 105, 107–108, 110, 186, 194–195, 196–197, 198, 268–269
ROI (return on investment), 209, 211
Roithmayr, Mark, quote by, 283
Rosen, Michael, 351
Ross, Steve, 70
Rowan and Martin's Laugh-In (TV show), 123
Rubenstein, David, 234, 236

S
Sahin, Ned, quote by, 393–394
Samaranch, Don Juan Antonio, 170, 171, 173, 174, 179
Sapan, Josh, quote by, 92
Sarbanes-Oxley, 210, 212
Satellite News Television, 71
Saturday Night Live (*SNL*) (TV show), 121–123, 127, 139, 351
Scanlon, Ed, 113
Scherer, Stephen (Steve), 378, 381, 383, 392, 395–396, 397
    quotes by, 382, 384–385, 386–387, 394–

395, 398–399, 400–401
Schlosser, Herb, quotes by, 37, 84–85, 140
Schwartz, Bill, 72
Sci-Fi Channel (SyFy), 29, 31, 32, 175, 205, 257
Seagram, 30
Sebelius, Kathleen, 363
Securities and Exchange Commission, 271
Seinfeld (TV series), 126, 128, 141, 145, 146
Seinfeld, Jerry, 145–146, 298
self-advocacy, 373–374
Shafallah Center, 304
Shapiro, George, 145
Sheinberg, Sid, 143–144
Sherlock, Mike, 188
Shih, Andy, 244, 362, 374
    quotes by, 304–305, 327, 333–336, 353–354, 373–374
Silverman, Fred, 133, 135
Simons, Jim, 325, 328, 329, 355
Simons, Marilyn, 329, 355
Simons Foundation, 328, 333, 344, 389
Singer, Alison, 359
The Site (newscast), 198
Six Sigma, 25, 160
60 Minutes (TV show), 120
SkyCable, 95, 96, 269
Slatkin, Alexandra, 331
Slatkin, David, 297, 331, 355
Slatkin, Harry, 329
    quotes by, 281, 325–326, 352–353, 354–355
Slatkin, Laura, 329, 352–353
    quotes by, 297–298, 331–333
Smigel, Michelle, 351
Smigel, Robert, 351
Smith, Chris, 318
Smith, Dan, 380
Sopranos (HBO program), 132
Spielberg, Steven, 31, 239
Spindler, Michael, 207
state insurance reform (for autism), 322
Stephen Beck Jr. Achieving a Better Life Experience Act of 2014 (ABLE Act), 317, 323, 343, 348
The Steve Banks Show, 139
Storch, Jerry, 296
strategic acquisitions, 205
strategic partnerships/alliances
    as building block for Autism Speaks, 303, 331–338

with competitor, 101
importance of, 48–49, 50, 379
NBC and Autism Speaks as relying on, 291
value creation at NBC as buoyed by, 263
streaming services, 177, 228, 253
stretching, importance of encouraging people to, 49
success
corporate success as shared by management and workers, 48
importance of accepting responsibility for own success, 56
principles for, 47–48, 52
Suddenly Susan (TV series), 128
Swanson, Dennis, 172
Swiss Reinsurance Co., 203
SyFy, 29, 31, 32, 175, 205, 257
Synergy Symphony, 257

T

Tartikoff, Brandon, 126, 133–140, 142, 148, 150, 282
quote by, 138–139
Tartikoff, Calla, 138, 139, 282
Tartikoff, Lilly, 138, 282
TBS (Turner Broadcasting System). *See* Turner Broadcasting System (TBS)
Tchen, Tina, 313
technology
as catalyst, 393
impact of constant rollout of new technology, 83
Olympics as making NBC a showcase for developing technology, 177
putting it to work for autism cause, 233
response to as determining our fate, 232
Tele-Communications Inc. (TCI), 28, 67, 80, 84, 90, 103–104, 107, 164, 222
Telemundo, 27, 29, 208, 224
television
program development of as inexact science, 136
viewers' love affair with as expanding, 77
Television Stations Division (NBC), 224
Tempo Television, 104
Thomas, Philip Michael, 143
Thomas H. Lee Partners, 238
Time Inc., 91
Time magazine, 372–373
Time Warner, 90, 91, 162, 163, 164, 165,

192, 222, 249
Time Warner Cable, Comcast's bid to acquire, 251, 253, 255–256
Tinker, Grant, 134–135, 140
Tjaden, Gary, 67
TNT, 118, 167
The Today Show (TV show), 124, 126, 128, 130, 131, 175, 176, 192, 223, 228, 280, 286
Tomlinson, Greg, 369
The Tonight Show (TV show), 124, 127, 136, 175, 176, 223, 257
top down, versus bottom up, 259
Toys "R" Us, 296
transformative change, 48, 50–51
Trian Partners, 219
Tribune, 79
Trump, Donald, 146–147, 364
quotes by, 263–264, 279
Trump, Melania, 147
Turner, Ted, 71–72, 83–84, 107, 108, 159–168, 267
quotes by, 163–164, 165, 167
Turner Broadcasting System (TBS), 71, 79, 108, 118, 159, 160, 162, 164, 165, 166, 167, 192, 196, 267
21st Century Cures Act, 348
24-hour cable news, 168, 195
tzedakah, 42

U

union-related matters, 113
United Nations
Autism Speaks advocacy to, 281, 297
support for Autism Speaks, 282
World Autism Awareness Day, 281, 284, 297, 298, 305–306, 313, 343, 373
Universal. *See* NBC Universal (NBCU); Vivendi Universal
USA Network, 31, 32, 79, 118, 167, 175, 205, 226, 257
USA Studios, 32

V

vaccine safety program (CDC), 365
Vaccine Safety proposal, 362
vaccines, and autism, 358–371
Vatican Summit on Autism (2014), 333–334, 337–338
Veterans Administration, 387
Vetter, Cyril, quotes by, 191, 226–227, 228–229

VHS, 228
Viacom, 31, 80, 240, 270
virtual streaming connection, 83
vision, 62
Vivendi Universal
    Activision unit, 32
    merger with NBC, 23–36, 37, 85
Vox Media, 253

W

"Waiting to Explode" (*Dateline* report), 115
Walgreens, 353
Wall Street, as not interested in NBC, 60
Walmark, Ethan, 308
Walt Disney Co., 28, 249, 270
Waring, Paul, 67
Warner Amex Satellite Company, 68
Warner Bros., 36, 142, 165
Warner Communications, 68, 70
Weill Cornell Medical College, 329, 333
Welch, Jack
    author's description of, 264–265
    author's partnership with, 100
    author's roller-coaster ride with,
        261–271
    bonus to Tartikoff, 133–134
    call to author asking him to come back
        to GE, 73
    distraction of with selecting successor,
        214–217
    focus of GE during the Welch period, 82
    friction with Gates, 194, 195
    missions of, 209
    negotiations with Seinfeld, 145–146
    post-retirement exit package, 269
    on pursuing Olympic Games telecasts,
        170–171, 174, 177
    retirement of, 202, 215–216
    stranglehold of on GE board of
        directors, 214
    and Ted Turner, 159–162
Welch, Jane, 269
West 57th Street (TV series), 120
West Coast Entertainment, 123, 126
WGN, 79
Wheeler, Tom, quote by, 77–78
Whipple, Lawrence A., 56
whole-genome sequencing, 288, 331, 339,
    340, 365, 378, 383, 386, 387, 389, 394,
    397, 398
Will & Grace (TV series), 126

Winfrey, Oprah, 359
winning "to do" list, 49–50
Wise, Steven (Steve), 383, 389
WMC Mortgage Corp., 203
Wolf, Dick, 25
World Autism Awareness Day, 281, 284, 297,
    298, 305–306, 313, 343, 373
World Health Organization, 343, 374
World of Warcraft (online game), 32–33
Wright, Bob
    bar examinations, 275, 278
    break with Welch, 216
    cancer diagnosis (2000), 285
    as CEO of Autism Speaks, 341–342
    as CEO of GE Capital, 266
    consideration of retirement as GE vice
        chairman, 235, 237
    consideration of retirement as NBCU
        chairman CEO, 235, 237
    and diversifying content for all
        platforms, 78family as insulating factor
        for, 113
    family of, 288, 369
    involvement of in shaping GE's post-
        Welch fate, 218
    marriage of, 275
    as president of Cox Cable, 56, 64–74,
        265
    as president of NBC, 55, 59, 75, 220, 291
    professional transformation of, 261
    retirement from GE (2008), 236, 240,
        241
    retirement from NBC (2007), 240,
        241–242
    right partnerships of, 100, 102, 272–288
    as senior advisor at Thomas H. Lee
        Partners, 238
    travels with Johnny and Alex Carson,
        151–158
    as vice chairman of GE, 216
Wright, Chris, 286, 369
Wright, Katie, 122, 123, 358, 360, 363,
    366–368, 369–371
    quotes by, 275–276, 283–284, 318–319,
        395–396
Wright, Maggie, 369
Wright, Sandi, 369
Wright, Suzanne, 43, 52, 99, 100, 102, 148,
    272–288, 304
    quotes by, 39–40, 44–46, 270, 274–275,
        277, 285–286, 292, 295–296, 306–307,

308–309, 313–314, 315–316, 351

Y

Young, Vincent, 223, 224
Young Broadcasting, 223

Z

Zaslav, David, 29, 36, 179, 191, 192, 197,
    237, 238, 239
  quotes by, 78, 91–92, 104–105, 119, 178,
    198–199
Zucker, Jeff, 36, 142, 237, 238, 239, 270, 271